Education, Culture and Values

Volume II

The six volumes that comprise the *Education, Culture and Values* series bring together contributions from experts around the world to form, for the first time, a comprehensive treatment of the current concern with values in education. The series seeks to address this concern in the context of cultural and values diversity.

The first three volumes provide a wide-ranging consideration of the diversity of values in education at all levels, and thus represent a framework for the second three volumes which focus more specifically on values education (moral, religious, spiritual and political) *per se*. The six volumes, therefore, bring the fundamental domain of values together with the important issue of pluralism to generate new, fruitful and progressive reflection and exemplars of good practice.

The series will be of huge benefit and interest to educators, policy makers, parents, academics, researchers and student teachers. The six volumes contain:

- diverse and challenging opinions about current educational concerns and reforms in values education
- chapters from more than 120 contributors of international repute from 23 different countries
- conceptual clarification and theoretical analysis
- empirical studies, reports of practical projects and guidance for good practice.

Volumes I–III: Values Diversity in Education

Volume I – Systems of Education: Theories, Policies and Implicit Values is concerned with the theoretical and conceptual framework for reflecting about values, culture and education and thus provides an introduction to the series as a whole. It is concerned with state and policy level analysis across the world.

Volume II – Institutional Issues: Pupils, Schools and Teacher Education considers values and culture at the institutional level. What constitutes a good 'whole school' approach in a particular area? There are discussions of key issues and reports of whole-school initiatives from around the world. Several chapters focus on the vital issue of teacher education.

Volume III – Classroom Issues: Practice, Pedagogy and Curriculum focuses on the classroom: pedagogy, curriculum and pupil experience. Areas of curriculum development include the relatively neglected domains of mathematics and technology, as well as the more familiar literature and drama. There is a useful section on aesthetic education.

Volumes IV–VI: Values Education in Diversity

Volume IV – Moral Education and Pluralism is focused on moral education and development in the context of cultural pluralism. There are highly theoretical discussions of difficult philosophical issues about moral relativism as well as practical ideas about good practice.

Volume V – Spiritual and Religious Education distinguishes religious and spiritual education and takes a multifaith approach to pedagogic, curricular and resource issues. The important issue of collective worship is also addressed.

Volume VI – Politics, Education and Citizenship is concerned with political education and citizenship. Again chapters from several countries lend an international perspective to currently influential concerns and developments, including democratic education, human rights, national identity and education for citizenship.

Education, Culture and Values

Volume II

Institutional Issues: Pupils, Schools and Teacher Education

Edited by
Mal Leicester, Celia Modgil
and Sohan Modgil

London and New York

First published 2000 by Falmer Press
11 New Fetter Lane, London EC4P 4EE

Simultaneously published in the USA and Canada
by Falmer Press, 19 Union Square West, New York, NY 10003

Falmer Press is an imprint of the Taylor & Francis Group

Typeset in Galliard by RefineCatch Limited, Bungay, Suffolk
Printed and bound in Great Britain by
TJ International Ltd, Padstow, Cornwall

British Library Cataloguing in Publication Data
A catalogue record for this book is available from the British
Library

Library of Congress Cataloging in Publication Data
Institutional issues: pupils, schools, and teacher education/
edited by Mal Leicester, Celia Modgil, Sohan Modgil.
    p.   cm. — (Education, culture, and values; v. 2)
  1. Educational sociology. 2. Values—Study and teaching.
3. Multiculturalism. 4. Teachers—Training of. I. Leicester,
Mal. II. Modgil, Celia. III. Modgil, Sohan. IV. Series.
LC191.J485 1999
306.43—dc21   99–36824
                                                 CIP

ISBN 0–7507–1018–7 (6-volume set)
        0–7507–1002–0 (volume I)
        0–7507–1003–9 (volume II)
        0–7507–1004–7 (volume III)
        0–7507–1005–5 (volume IV)
        0–7507–1006–3 (volume V)
        0–7507–1007–1 (volume VI)

Contents

Contributors

David N. Aspin Professor of Philosophy of Education, Faculty of Education, Monash University, Australia

Maria Paz Avery Senior Project Director, Education Development Centre, Massachusetts, USA

Jean M. Bigger Former Deputy Head Teacher, now a Lecturer at Swindon College, UK

Karen Caple Coordinator, Schools Values Project, Association of Independent Schools of Western Australia, Australia

Rhett Diessner Professor of Psychology and Education at Lewis-Clark State College, Lewiston, Idaho, USA

Yuval Dror Senior Lecturer in Education, School of Education, Tel Aviv University (and Oranim Teachers College), Israel

Philip Garner Professor of Education, The Nottingham Trent University, UK

Katherine Hanson Senior Project Director, Education Development Centre, Massachusetts, USA

Graham Haydon Lecturer in Education, Institute of Education, University of London, UK

Brian V. Hill Professor of Education, School of Education, Murdoch University, Western Australia

Peter Lang Senior Lecturer in Education, Institute of Education, University of Warwick, UK

Mal Leicester Professor of Adult Learning and Teaching, University of Nottingham, UK

Terence J. Lovat Professor of Education, Dean of the Faculty of Education, University of Newcastle, Australia

Michael Marland Head Teacher, North Westminster Community School, London, UK

Jane Martin Research Fellow, School of Education, University of Birmingham, UK

Celia Modgil Senior Lecturer in Education, Goldsmiths College, London University, UK

Sohan Modgil Reader in Educational Research and Development, University of Brighton, UK

Fernand Ouellet Professor, Faculty of Theology, Ethics and Philosophy, University of Sherbrooke, Canada

Jane Pearce Lecturer in Education, School of Education, Murdoch University, Western Australia

Ismael Abu Saad Lecturer in Education, Ben-Gurion University of the Negev, Israel

Cyril Simmons Senior Lecturer, Department of Education, Loughborough University, UK

Joan Stephenson International Office, De Montfort University, UK, Former Head of Department of Education.

Keith Sullivan Senior Lecturer and Associate Dean of Postgraduate Students in Education, Victoria University of Wellington, New Zealand

Monica J. Taylor Principal Research Fellow, Editor of Journal of Moral Education, National Foundation for Educational Research in England and Wales, UK

Bobbie Turniansky Lecturer in Education, Ben-Gurion University of the Negev, Israel

Heather Fiona Wainman Head of Religious Education, The Hayfield School, Doncaster, UK

Editors' Foreword

This is one volume in a series of six, each concerned with education, culture and values. Educators have long recognized that 'education' is necessarily value laden and, therefore, that value issues are inescapable and fundamental, both in our conceptions of education and in our practice of it. These issues are particularly complex in the context of cultural pluralism. In a sense the collection is a recognition, writ large, of this complexity and of our belief that since values are necessarily part of education, we should be explicit about what they are, and about why we choose those we do and who the 'we' is in relation to the particular conception and practices in question.

The first three volumes in the series deal with values diversity in education – the broader issues of what values ought to inform education in and for a plural society. The second three focus more narrowly on values education as such – what is the nature and scope of moral education, of religious and political education and of political and citizenship education in and for such a society? Thus collectively they consider both **values diversity in education** and **values education in diversity**. Individually they each have a particular level. Thus volumes 1–3 cover the levels of system, institution and classroom. Volumes 4–6 focus respectively on moral education, religious and spiritual education, politics and citizenship education. This structure is intended to ensure that the six volumes in the series are individually discrete but complementary.

Given the complexity of the value domain and the sheer diversity of values in culturally plural societies it becomes clear why 120 chapters from 23 countries merely begin to address the wealth of issues relating to 'Education, Culture and Values'.

Mal Leicester, Celia Modgil
and Sohan Modgil

Part One

Pupils and Teachers

1 Understanding the Diversity of Diversity

GRAHAM HAYDON

Many people working in education are trying to see how best they can respond to diversity of values; everybody working in education, whether they think about this consciously or not, is actually working in a context of diversity of values. So understanding this diversity seems a precondition of successful education, and failing to understand it will make educational aims more difficult to achieve. This means not just that academics, writing in books such as this, should seek to understand the diversity of values, but that education is likely to be more successful if everyone working in it has some understanding of diversity of values. If that is too Utopian an aspiration – since it would include administrators, secretaries, caterers, cleaners, etc., etc. – then at least we should recognize the importance of all *teachers* having this understanding. At present, most courses of initial training for teachers include very little, if any, systematic attempt to address teachers' understanding of the issues. Of course, some attention will often be given to issues of multi-culturalism and anti-racism, but, as I shall show, these issues by no means exhaust the field across which diversity needs to be understood.

My speaking of 'understanding diversity of values' may suggest to the reader that I consider there is one correct understanding to be had. I do not mean to imply that. Perhaps it will be that different teachers will come to have rather different understandings of diversity of values – it is, after all, a thoroughly familiar fact that any complex phenomenon is open to a variety of interpretations, and that the task of trying to establish that one interpretation is correct is never straightforward; indeed this point will run as a theme through this chapter. I think it better, of course, that teachers' interpretations of diversity of values should be well-grounded rather than arbitrary, but I am not particularly interested in seeking one correct interpretation. The more important question is whether the teacher is aware of the complexity of the issues, has given thought to the issues, and has come to some working understanding that at least assists her in making sense of the day-to-day variety she faces.

In making sense of variety in any field, one cannot avoid some kind of classificatory scheme. Classificatory schemes always run risks of arbitrariness and of inappropriate pigeon-holing and indeed stereotyping, but we cannot avoid them. To say 'there is simply an indefinite variety of values that people may hold in an indefinite variety of ways' would do nothing to help any teacher to recognize what is in front of her, and so would be hardly better than failing to acknowledge diversity at all.

What I want to do in this paper is to produce something like a guide to the understanding of diversity, by drawing attention, in a fairly systematic way, to some important distinctions. In doing this I shall, broadly speaking, be proceeding in a philosophical rather than sociological manner. I mean by this that I shall not be drawing my data from any rigorous research into the diversity of values actually found in Britain or any other society. That is only partly because any rigorous research has to get its own classificatory scheme from somewhere. It is also because I want to avoid the dangers of stereotyping that could come from the attempt to claim correlations between membership of a particular group and the holding of certain values. There are no doubt some valid generalizations of the form 'Muslims tend to hold such-and-such values' or 'working class white boys tend to value X', but to the teacher in the classroom the most immediate question concerns the values, or ways of thinking about values, which belong to the individuals in the room. Generalizations drawn from the wider society may be a heuristic aid to establishing this, but they can also, of course, mislead. So what the teacher needs to be equipped with, I suggest, is not a set of correlations that may hold for the society in general, but a classificatory scheme which helps her to recognize and make sense of what she actually finds.

That, at any rate, is one argument for not attempting a sociological approach here. Another good reason is that I am not a sociologist. My own understanding of diversity, such as it is, has been formed above all by reading philosophical reflections on values and by encouraging such reflections in my students. The way in which I shall proceed is not entirely *a priori* – I am certainly drawing in an informal way on my own and other people's experience of life in late twentieth-century Britain. But rather than claiming to back up my analysis by systematic evidence, I shall in effect be saying to each reader 'Here is a way of thinking about diversity of values which seems to me to make good sense; see if it resonates with your experience and helps you, too, to make sense of the complex world you are working in'. Something like this, in turn, is what educationalists could be saying to teachers; and teachers will have to say something not unlike this to their students, when those students are going to be living in a plural society.

One of the ways in which people differ from one another – but only one of the ways – is that they may differ in the values they hold. People may also be uncertain about how much the difference in values actually matters. But that line of thought can lead into complexities that perhaps are better left to the end. I shall start with the more prosaic business of sorting out some of the variety of ways in which values are diverse.

In one sense, all that is needed if we are to speak correctly of a diversity or plurality of values is for there to be more than one value, or 'more than one kind of thing that matters'. If anything in this whole area is indisputable it is that there is not just one value. We can see this, first, because we can speak of different kinds of values; we may, for instance, distinguish moral values from economic ones or aesthetic, political or prudential values. In this kind of classification, 'moral', 'aesthetic' and the like are adjectives; but it may be more helpful to treat these distinguishing terms as adverbs, as qualifying the way in which we value things. It is not only that there are different kinds of things that we can value – works of art, human action, bodily and mental

states, forms of social organization – but that we can value things, even the same thing, in different ways. To see a work of art as beautiful, to see it as an expression of something important about human nature, or to see it as a valuable investment, are different ways of valuing it.

Thinking about the different ways in which we can value things helps us to see that we cannot necessarily pick out a certain set of values and say 'these are moral values'. Some people would not classify 'happiness' as a moral value – they might say that one is fortunate if one is happy, but one has no moral obligation to further one's own or other people's happiness. But it is clearly possible to think that happiness matters morally; that, other things being equal, it is morally better that people are happy than that they are not. Indeed, this idea is central to a whole strand of philosophizing about morality (utilitarianism). Or to take another example, truth figures as a consideration in contexts that have no direct moral import. Logicians can talk of the truth-value of any statement; scientists who see themselves as aiming at a true account of a natural phenomenon do not necessarily see any moral importance in what they are doing; and anyone may sometimes think that telling the truth is a sensible policy. But thinking that one must, morally, tell the truth is different from all of these.

There is some tendency in educational debate and writing to use the term 'values' to refer to *moral* beliefs and opinions. This can be harmless if it is recognized simply as a useful shorthand in a particular context, but it will be misleading if it leads to the neglect of values of other kinds – which will also be important in education – or indeed if it leads to the neglect of any careful consideration of what kinds of distinction may be drawn between moral and other values. After that caveat, I shall concentrate in the rest of this chapter on moral values, but it is worth remembering that some of the values that may matter to us morally – such as respect for other people's points of view – require us to pay attention to whatever values, moral or not, matter to other people.

If it is true that moral values do not exhaust the field of values, it is also true that within the field of moral values there are various things that matter. Anyone can have the experience of being pulled in different ways by different considerations when there is a decision to be made that matters morally. I can think, for instance, that being truthful matters, and that being kind matters, and then, wondering whether to tell someone an unpleasant truth, can find that honesty and kindness conflict. Or I can find that a strict sense of fairness would suggest one course of action, where a concern to avoid hurting people would suggest another. At this experiential level, it is a familiar experience that there is more than one kind of consideration that has, morally, to be taken into account; and this is one truth that can be expressed by saying that there is a plurality of values, even when we confine our thinking to moral values.

If this is a fact of experience, then, like other facts of experience, it is open to a variety of interpretations. There are, for instance, philosophical interpretations which would have it that the experience of a variety of values is, in a sense, illusory; that at bottom there is really only one thing that matters (utilitarianism attempts to do this by arguing that everything that matters, matters ultimately because of what it contributes to the positive quality of experience). But even without going into philosophical interpretations, the plurality of values – at least at the experiential level – means that there is room for one person to differ from another in the way they balance one value against another, and in the values they emphasize. If that is true of individuals, it is also true of social groups. Whole societies may tend to weight and balance various values in distinctive ways. This is one of the ways in which one culture differs from another. So at this admittedly rather abstract level, we can see a way in which people who speak of universal human values, and people who stress cultural differences in values, can both be right. Since there are some common factors in the nature of the human species and in human needs and vulnerabilities – such as the need to eat, and vulnerability to physical injury – it would be surprising if some common values had not come to be recognized. But equally, the world of possible values – the whole range of things that can matter to human beings – is so large and complex that it would be surprising if different cultures, stressing and weighting values in different ways, had not developed. And this is without yet mentioning the different ways of interpreting the nature of moral values – to which I shall come below – where again one kind of interpretation may be predominant in one culture, another in another.

In attempting to understand diversity we need constantly to move back and forth between recognizing commonalities and recognizing the scope for the diversity that these commonalities actually create. Thus, within all the diversity of kinds of values, most if not all cultures will make something like the distinction between moral values and other kinds of values that I have sketched. But they will not all draw the lines in the same places – Western liberal secular cultures, for instance, have gone further than most in drawing lines between morality and religion, between morality and law, between morality and politics. So anyone who has their own way of drawing the lines – even if to them it seems obvious – needs sensitivity to others who do not draw them in the same way. Related to this is the fact that, even where people are in the habit of thinking of morality as a relatively distinct area, there is room for different interpretations of what makes a consideration a moral one.

That is, in fact, the reason why I cannot proceed in this chapter by first defining my terms. Any definition I give of a 'moral value' would only correspond to one way of classifying and interpreting the field.

I can write about moral values here in the belief that each reader will have some sense of what moral values are; but if my overall approach is right, not all readers will share the same sense of what a moral value is. Consider the following ideas. Moral values are ideals about how every person should live his or her life; they are aspirations for every individual, regardless of whether others are or are not living up to these same ideals, but by the same token we should not worry too much if we do not live up to them. Or, moral values are constraints on what each of us in society is allowed to do, and their point is that we should not unduly interfere with each other; these minimal constraints – not killing or injuring each other, not breaking contracts, and so on – are not too difficult to live up to, and provided we respect them, we are each of us free to live in whatever way we like. Or, moral values are whatever values anyone takes to be most central and most important in his or her own life – hence my moral values may be quite different from yours, but we should each of us strive to live according to our own moral values. Or, moral values are universal truths about what is required if human life is to go well. Or, moral values correspond to the commands of an all-powerful deity, and it is not for mere mortals to ask the reason for them.

In a society like Britain at the turn of the twenty-first century, none of these ideas is original or outrageous, and probably none of them are unfamiliar to the reader. Never mind that they may not form a coherent picture of the kind of values that moral values are. It is difficult enough for one person to get a clear and coherent view of what moral values are; perhaps it is too much to expect that a whole society will have a single clear and coherent view. That is one reason why, surprisingly perhaps, I think it is not the business of education to promote one single clear and coherent view, though it certainly is the business of education to promote understanding of the diversity.

Possibly the most striking difference in people's interpretations of moral values, and one that is very important educationally, is that for some moral ideas are intimately tied up with religious ones, and for others they are not. The most obvious difference this makes is that people who have no religious belief cannot attach any religious significance to their moral values. They may still see certain values as invested with a special kind of importance – which will be part of what makes these *moral* values in their view – but they are likely to have more difficulty than religious believers in saying much about this importance. Whereas for religious believers almost invariably their moral values will have religious significance. There is still room, even given some religious connection, for different kinds of significance – the idea that moral demands simply are commands of God is only one kind of account, and (to many Christians at any rate) would not be the most plausible – yet in one way or another it remains true that in the thought and experience of a believer it is possible for an offence against moral value to be at the same time an offence against religion, whereas for the non-believer this, obviously, is not possible.

This means that we have to recognize at least two different kinds of reason that can back up moral values. For religious believers, the fact (if there are such facts) that something is against the divine order of things (or against what is experienced or believed to be the divine order) may be sufficient to make it morally wrong. For non-believers, it may be that the only kind of reason that can make something morally wrong is that it is in some way bad for other people (or animals) – for instance, that it hurts other people (or animals) or shows disrespect. Both these kinds of reason have in common that they appeal to something outside of the individual's own interests and preferences. But their differences are important too; the differences underlie a lot of disagreement about values in a pluralistic society, where for many liberal and secular thinkers the only

question of moral relevance about anything is 'does it do any harm?', whereas some religious thinkers feel that question largely misses the point.

So far I have said little in any detail about the *content* of moral values. This is deliberate, because I think it is important to show that differences in the content of the moral beliefs that people hold, or the moral judgements they make, are not the only kind of moral diversity, and may not even be the most important. There is a tendency, perhaps, to think that differences in values between person A and person B will fit the schema 'A thinks X is wrong, whereas B thinks it is not'. In some cases this is appropriate; for instance, if abortion or homosexuality is substituted for X, this schema will pick out important differences between certain people. But if we concentrate only on differences of this kind we are liable to miss the diversity of interpretation that there may be even among people who will agree that X (lying, say, or theft) is wrong. For instance, some when they say that 'X is wrong' will mean that it is always and without exception wrong; others will mean that on the whole it is best avoided but will also think that there may well be circumstances in which, all things considered, it is justified.

Consider another kind of difference. In a well-known study, Carol Gilligan (1982) turned on its head some of the work that Lawrence Kohlberg had done on the development of people's moral thinking. Kohlberg (1981) had studied people's moral thinking by asking his subjects to think about hypothetical dilemmas, presented in outline only, without all the concrete detail of real-life cases. To some people it seemed quite right that all the concrete detail should be left out, since they felt that this is not what a moral decision turns on. There are broad matters of principle at stake; on abortion, for instance, the issue is about an unborn child's right to life; if the child does have a right to life, then killing it is wrong, and the details of the case cannot alter this. But Gilligan studied the real-life decisions of pregnant women who had contacted an abortion clinic but had not yet decided whether to have an abortion or not. These women tended *not* to decide the issue by taking and applying some broad principle; even if they did think that the unborn child had a right to life, this still only came into their decision as one factor among many others which they were trying somehow to hold together and reconcile. These women were trying to find the best solution they could in the concrete circumstances, maintain ongoing relationships where they could be maintained, thinking of everyone affected – including themselves – and trying to do as little hurt as possible.

Gilligan and others since have distinguished two different 'orientations' or 'perspectives' in moral thinking. Such terminology seems appropriate, because the differences are not in the content of people's moral values, as they would be if some people said 'human life matters' and others denied this, or if some advocated 'individual rights' and others denied it. The different perspectives do not so much give different answers to the same question, as display an interest in asking different questions. Faced with a given problem, some people tend to approach it by working at the level of general principles, asking whose rights are at issue, and what justice demands. For these people, the general form of any reasoning about a moral issue is to start from principles expressed in a very general form and seen as universal – in the case of abortion it will be the right to life or a woman's right to choose – and to draw from the general principles a conclusion for the specific case. Others tend to approach the specific problem without working from the general level first; they will ask in the specific case what is at stake in the relations between the persons involved; who might be hurt and how can hurt best be avoided?

In fact, once we think of different orientations in moral thinking, a dichotomy between two perspectives will certainly turn out to be too simple. Anthropologists and social psychologists have distinguished cultures where moral thinking revolves round the idea of shame and those where it revolves around the idea of guilt. The latter picks out the orientation of the individual who asks – without necessarily worrying about what others will actually think – whether some action would be violating any moral duty or obligation; this perhaps fits with the tendency to think in terms of general principles of justice or rights that must not be violated. But an orientation towards avoiding shame and upholding honour asks not 'Are any rights or obligations being fulfilled here?', nor again 'Is anyone likely to be hurt and can that be avoided?', but 'Is my honour and that of my family and religion being upheld?'[1]

I have been concerned to warn against simplistic conceptions of the diversity of values. If it is simplistic to think that the diversity consists in different people giving different answers to questions of the form 'Is X right or wrong?', it is also simplistic to think that differences in values line up in any neat way with the divisions we make between cultures. It is simplistic to assume that someone else has a different set of values because they are, superficially at least, of a different culture, and it is simplistic to assume that someone else shares the same values because they apparently share the same cultural background.

It would also be simplistic, though, to think that because of the complexity of the diversity, there is no possibility of common ground in values across even the most diverse societies. If anything, to recognize that much of the diversity consists in different orientations and interpretations, different selections and balancings out of the whole human repertoire of things that matter, is to open the way to the possibility that at a certain level, in terms at least of the verbal labels that we attach to certain values, there still can be considerable convergence. This was found, for instance, in the deliberations of the Forum on Values in Education and the Community set up by the School Curriculum and Assessment Authority (for England and Wales) in 1996. It did prove possible to arrive at a consensus on a list of values (albeit with a certain amount of negotiation and fudging over just how some of the values were expressed), but the Forum had to point out that consensus on the list of values did not imply consensus either on the sources of the values (whether, for instance, they were derived from a religious or from a wholly secular background) or on their application to particular circumstances.

In broad terms, this kind of move – to reach consensus at the level at which it can be reached without despairing of the lack of agreement at other levels – seems an appropriate practical way to respond to diversity of values. Because people who have different values – or who put different weights on various values, or interpret their values differently, and so on – do not live in separate compartments but constantly interact with and affect each other, some kind of common language of values is necessary. A list of values on which there is a broad consensus – even if, to achieve the consensus, it has been necessary to express the values in very broad terms that are still open to multiple interpretations – can at least provide a reference point. If two people acknowledge, for instance, that at some level they both subscribe to a value of respect for life, then they can at least ask each other whether their respective opinions on, say, abortion, are consistent with what they understand by respect for life; and so there is less chance that they will be completely talking across each other.

This may seem like a pretty minimal kind of 'common language', but it is not yet clear how much further we can go. Moral philosophy is full of attempts to set out a theory that will cut across all the actual diversity of people's values and deliver answers that will have universal validity. Both utilitarianism, already mentioned, and Kant's (1948) deontological ethics can be read in this way, while recent attempts include Hare's (1981) teasing out of the principle of universalizability from the nature of moral language and Habermas's (1990) communicative ethics. Such theories can be read as attempts to find a common point of reference by which disagreements can be resolved, but to find this, not by the empirical method of seeking an actual consensus, but by rational argument which starts only from premises that are not themselves part of any particular moral position (the theories differ in part in whether they seek these initial premises in non-moral experience or pure rationality). But such theories run the risk that others will see them as failing, after all, to stand outside a particular moral perspective, so that in effect they are seeking to impose something like the values of modern European secular liberalism.

Is there, then, a future for any such attempts? This is too large a question to explore in the present chapter, but any answer would depend in part on the position we take on yet another dimension of our interpretation of diversity. These attempts at finding not just a contingent common ground, but a common way of thinking, may in turn be read in two ways: either as seeking to recognize some deep truth about the way that human nature or human rationality works; or as making pragmatic accommodations at a quite superficial level to deep underlying differences. One of the difficulties in clarifying how educators can best respond to diversity is that interpretations of diversity are themselves diverse and tend to instability; we may see diversity now as superficial, now as deep, and correspondingly we may see attempts to find common ground either as reflections of deep commonality, or as a superficial veneer over deep divisions.

There is a way of thinking, with roots both in religious and in scientific thought, which says that the differences between people do not matter very much. What people have in common is much more important than the differences between them. We are all created equal (for Christians, because we are created in God's image); if we are scratched, we all bleed (Shakespeare's Shylock in *The Merchant of Venice*); we are all capable of rational thought (Enlightenment thinking, above all in Kant); and we share with each other (and with chimpanzees too) all but a tiny fraction of our DNA (modern evolutionary biology). With all this in common, the ways in which we differ from each other must be only superficial. If we were cakes, we would all be made of the same ingredients to the same recipe; only the icing on the top would come in different patterns.

But there is another way of thinking which effectively turns this upside down. It is true that there are commonalities in a biological sense, and that what differs are only our interpretations of our living and the values we put on things; but this does not mean that the differences are trivial. To the contrary, it is in our interpretations that we live our lives. The commonalities across human lives are, precisely, the features of biological life which we share with other animals, and in that way they are not, from a human perspective, what is important. What matters to us is the world of human meaning, and that does not come all of a piece; it always, necessarily, comes in some particular form – we speak a particular language, are born in a particular part of the world, and so on. Of course the basic facts of biology are significant to us, but the point is that the significance is not a biological given. It is always an interpretation, and interpretations differ. Other animals are born and eat and copulate and die, and so do we; but other animals just do these things without (so far as we know) interpreting them; whereas we weave complex structures of meaning and interpretation around the events of our lives. As in our life as we experience it, nothing is deeper than these interpretations (since it is within these structures of interpretation that we sometimes find thoughts and experiences 'deep' or 'profound'), so we have to say that the differences in these interpretations are deep differences. To maintain the cake analogy, all the cakes are basically made of flour; but there are so many other varying ingredients, and so many different recipes, that the fact that they are all made of flour seems merely trivial.

Another way of putting it is that what matters to us – to each of us individually – is our identity, and that our identity is constituted by things that we may have in common with certain others, but rarely by what we have in common with everyone. It may be part of my identity that I was born in England, am male, am an academic, and so on, but that I am human or that I need to eat to survive, is hardly part of my identity. From a scientific perspective my being human – or indeed being mammalian, or being vertebrate – must be the foundation of all the rest, but so far as my identity is concerned, it is likely to be part of the background that is simply taken for granted.

Similar points apply to values that are shared and values that differentiate people. It is not surprising, for instance, that for all human beings being killed is generally something to be avoided, and hence it is not surprising that the idea that 'killing is wrong' is a very generally shared moral value. But the belief that killing is wrong is unlikely to be experienced as a part of someone's identity, unless it plays a particularly prominent role in someone's beliefs – if, for instance, he or she is a pacifist. Being a pacifist is something that sets a person apart from many others, and may create a common bond with certain others who share the position; so it is quite intelligible that being a pacifist might come to be counted – by oneself or by others – as part of a person's identity.

Again, while we do not find that some cultures are distinguished from others by their belief that killing is wrong,[2] we do find that different cultures contain different ways in which the positive value of life and the negative value of death are woven into wider interpretations. For instance, in the context of religious beliefs about service to God and the attainment of happiness in an afterlife, death can take on a very positive significance. There is a profundity here in meanings that are not shared by everyone; the mere biological fact of mortality, which we share not only with each other but with all animals, may seem trivial by comparison. On the other hand, for much of secular, post-Enlightenment thinking, there is nothing more profound than suffering and the fact of death; and structures of values such as equality and the right to life are built on just these common factors.

So the different ways of looking at diversity, seeing it either as superficial or deep, apply to differences in values as much as to any other differences. According to one view, differences in the values people hold are superficial variations on the surface of a deeper truth, which is that there are universal and rational values applying to all. Politically, this view fits with an emphasis on human rights, universal and equal for all, as a bedrock. On the other view, values go deep into people's psyches – we all

see the world through our values, but these are not the same values for all – and so, by inversion, the 'universal' values, such as equality and human rights, are at best a pragmatic fiction that we can attempt to maintain for the sake of an uneasy coexistence. On this second view, the politics of equal rights does not constitute a sufficient recognition of the value of every person precisely because it does not recognize the importance of the differences that go deep into people's identity; we need in addition a 'politics of difference' (Young 1990) or 'politics of recognition' (Gutmann 1992).

So, there are conflicting interpretations of the undeniable phenomena both of perceived commonality and of perceived difference. Faced with two such different interpretations as these, we may wish to ask which is right. But the question may itself be mistaken. There need not even be any disagreement on 'the facts' between one who sees the commonalities as deep and one who sees the differences as deep; they can both agree on what is common and what is different. They are looking at the same facts from different perspectives.

Yet it may be thought that in the context of education we have to decide between these interpretations, because they appear to have different practical implications. On the first view, it would be the task of education to enable everyone to see the deep truth about the universality of certain facts about the human condition, and hence of certain values that are important for human life; in the face of these, actual variations in beliefs and values will seem trivial, and it would be wrong to put too much weight on them. On the second view, it will be the task of education to be sure that the differences that run deep in people's lives are recognized and respected; to promote one particular set of values would be to ride insensitively over the beliefs of many while seeking to impose the values of a few.

However, further reflection may suggest that this contrast is overdrawn. The first view, even as it seeks to promote common values, cannot neglect the fact that differences exist, because among the common values that it is necessary to promote will be understanding and tolerance and respect for the differences. And the second view does not mean that nothing that is common should be taught, because even if we do not think there are deep truths in common, we still need, if only for pragmatic reasons, to promote some common language, some common way of living together.

And so it appears after all that the difference, for

practical purposes, may not be so great.[3] The same tasks face education either way. Not that this makes matters easy for the teacher. Teachers have to be able to move in and out of interpretations: they need sometimes to take the view that the commonalities are what matter, and the differences are trivial; and at other times they need to take the view that the differences are vital – what this person sees, what this person feels, how this person experiences the world are the things that matter, not the putative common ground. And to be able to make these moves, teachers need in turn to have an understanding, both of the diversity of values in all its complexity, and of the kinds of attempts that have been made to find some common ground. Unfortunately, in the educational climate of late twentieth-century Britain, teacher training has barely recognized this educational task.[4]

Notes

1 On honour see Berger (1983); on shame Tombs (1995). Some of the wording in the previous two paragraphs is borrowed from Haydon (1997).

2 Once we insert the X in 'killing X is wrong' then there are some notable variations. Consider Jains at one end of the spectrum, and at the other the headhunters described by von Furer-Haimendorf (1967).

3 While this may be true for the conduct of education, it may not be true for its organization. Interpretations of the significance of differences in values may underlie some of the arguments for and against separate schooling for different cultural or religious groups. On this see Haydon (1994) and Haydon (1997), Ch. 10.

4 Some of the aspects of diversity mentioned here have been treated in more detail in Haydon (1997). My thinking on deep and shallow interpretations of diversity owes much to Steve Bramall and other members of the Philosophy of Education Research Seminar at the Institute of Education.

References

Berger, P. (1983) On the obsolescence of the concept of honour. In S. Hauerwas & A. MacIntyre (eds) *Revisions: Changing Perspectives in Moral Philosophy*. Notre Dame, Ind.: University of Notre Dame Press.

Gilligan, C. (1982) *In a Different Voice: Psychological Theory and Women's Development*. Cambridge, Mass.: Harvard University Press.

Gutmann, A. (ed.) (1992) *Multiculturalism and the 'Politics of Recognition'*. Princeton, NJ: Princeton University Press.

Habermas, J. (1990) *Moral Consciousness and Communicative Action*. Cambridge: Polity Press.

Hare, R. M. (1981) *Moral Thinking*. Oxford: Oxford University Press.

Haydon, G. (1994) Conceptions of the secular in society, polity and schools. *Journal of Philosophy of Education* **28** (1): 65–75.

Haydon, G. (1997) *Teaching about Values: A New Approach*. London: Cassell.

Kant, I. (1948) *Groundwork of the Metaphysic of Morals* (first published 1785). Translated in H. J. Paton (1948) *The Moral Law*. London: Hutchinson.

Kohlberg, L. (1981) *The Philosophy of Moral Development*. San Francisco: Harper & Row.

Tombs, D. (1995) 'Shame' as a neglected value in schooling. *Journal of Philosophy of Education* **29** (1): 23–32.

von Furer-Haimendorf, C. (1967) *Morals and Merit: A Study of Values and Social Controls in South Asian Societies*. London: Weidenfeld & Nicolson.

Young, I. M. (1990) *Justice and the Politics of Difference*. Princeton, NJ: Princeton University Press.

2 Shock, Self-doubt and Rising to the Challenge: Non-Aboriginal Teachers Learn about Aboriginal Values

JANE PEARCE

'How shall we educate Aboriginal people?'

This has been a challenging question for governments since the invasion of Australia. Although at first there were no policies to educate members of Australia's Indigenous communities by the colonizing authorities, successive governments (both Federal and State) since the mid-nineteenth century have attempted various interventionist solutions to the 'problem' of Aboriginal education. This chapter will explore how a group of thirty-six teachers and student teachers working in Australia in 1996, and who provided the initial inspiration for this chapter, rose to the challenges posed by the question.

They were students at Murdoch University's School of Education studying a unit entitled 'Aborigines and Education'. This was devised jointly by Jan Currie and John Hall of Murdoch and Curtin Universities in Western Australia, and offered as an elective for teachers studying for post-initial qualifications, or for students nearing the end of their first degree in education or another related field. I was their tutor. Of the thirty-six who completed the unit, twenty-four were currently teaching Aboriginal students in state schools; eight were either yet to qualify as teachers, or were teaching but had at the time no experience of teaching Aboriginal students; and four were students in fields related to Education but not intending to become teachers. Some students' teaching contracts had taken them into country towns or remote areas of the state where typically they were living and working closely with Aboriginal people for the first time in their lives. All were enthusiastic; hungry for information, ideas, insights, solutions.

As work on the unit progressed, I followed with increasing interest the changes in students' attitudes, understandings and perspectives. What was particularly interesting was a growing recognition that the difficulties of their situations as teachers lay not simply in their lack of knowledge and experience. Central to the problems they faced in the classroom were values issues. These were not only those associated with the lack of congruence between Aboriginal and non-Aboriginal values, but also those associated with their position as teachers; authority figures representing the dominant culture and therefore working within a framework of values that, perhaps, predetermined their Aboriginal students to 'fail'. This chapter will consider the students' responses to the unit they studied, and show how in many cases their studies led them to attempt to first question and then relocate their practice as teachers. The discussion will also consider some of the implications arising for teacher education, in particular the importance of theory and the relevance of values issues. First of all it will be necessary to identify some key aspects of the history of educational provision for Aboriginal people.

Different policies, unchanged values

At the time of the earliest colonizers, officials noted the 'attachment' of the 'adult black . . . to his miserable mode of life' and despaired of ever seeing Australian Indigenous people attaining 'the advantages of civilisation' (from minutes of the Select Committee on Aborigines, 1845, cited in Lippman 1994: 133). This notion, coupled with the view that, as the Aboriginal race was dying out, the only intervention necessary was to 'soothe the dying pillow', not only enabled colonizers to save money (for why bother educating the uneducable?) but also enabled the exercise of total power across the continent by the invading race (Lippman, op. cit. 133). Successive policies were clear attempts to impose white values on Aboriginal peoples, and the dominant culture continues to exercise power through the education system. A brief look at these policies will contextualize the present situation, and in particular help to clarify the current tensions that teachers face in their work with Aboriginal children.

Even the name 'Protectionism', the policy that was operated in various forms throughout Australia from about 1860 to the 1940s, reveals a disturbingly unselfconscious attempt by the white community to maintain its own interests and impose its own values while purporting to protect the interests of others. Set up to 'protect' Aboriginal people, the policy involved the removal of Aboriginal children from their families to be educated in large institutions run by government agencies. The so-called Aboriginal Protection Boards became the legal guardians of children thus abducted. Public opposition to the presence of Aboriginal children in white schools, and a suspicion of attempts to provide comparable education for children destined merely to work as servants and farm hands for white settlers, ensured that the education these children received was extremely basic, provided by unqualified teachers, and clearly inferior to that provided for white pupils. Removal of children was pursued particularly vigorously when the children concerned were thought to have some white ancestry.

This exercise of power by the white authorities betrays the same fallacious thinking that is present in many discourses about cultural differences; that because 'they' are different from 'us' in one respect, they must be different in every respect. Since Aboriginal people seemed not to possess the trappings that would have identified them as 'civilized' to the white society, it was assumed that they were lacking 'civilization' in every respect, including parenting and the ability to educate the children, and concluded that to forcibly remove children from their families would not bring harm. The fact that this policy struck at the heart of what is central to the maintenance of Aboriginal culture, the family, is particularly revealing. Not only did it attempt to ensure the continuing control by white authorities over the kind of education possible for Aboriginal children in white terms, it also ensured that families were no longer able to pass on their own culture to their children. The consequences of this policy proved to be far-reaching and devastating. There

are still today hundreds of Aboriginal adults who have 'lost' their real families, and examples now abound in published writing of the impact on children which these measures had (see Nannup 1992, Pilkington 1996).

The ultimate success of protectionism would have been the obliteration of Aboriginal culture, and the fact that this didn't happen is a measure of the strength and vitality of that culture. It is also interesting to speculate about the nature of the alternative cultural messages that Aboriginal children would have been receiving in government institutions – messages which many Aboriginal people are still hearing from dominant groups in the society, for example about the exercise of power according to race, the stratification of society, the need for their compliance – and to contrast these with the cultural messages that children would have received in their own community, such as understanding of and care for the land, the importance of affiliation, the importance of attending to the interests of the group before those of the individual. It seems that much of the resistance to non-Aboriginal intervention now evident in Aboriginal communities has its roots in the anger generated by protectionism.

The 1940s saw a shift in thinking which was generated in part by an Aboriginal man, William Ferguson, who made a plea for equal opportunities for Aboriginal children. The policy of assimilation, which later evolved into integration, rested on the notion that if Aboriginal children received the same education as white children they were bound to achieve similar educational success. Although this did signal a major shift in thinking, since no consideration was given either to the appropriateness of the education on offer, or to the acceptability of this provision to the Aboriginal peoples themselves (requiring as it did the abandonment of a separate identity), this new direction proved less than successful. Once again, hidden values were working to undermine Aboriginal values, cultural identity, learning traditions. Success was only possible if children recognized and accepted the need to comply with the values of the dominant culture, and were prepared to think and behave like a non-Aboriginal person and thus deny their Aboriginality. Even if children were prepared to do these things, and were rewarded with success in educational terms, embedded racism in the society ensured that they continued to be discriminated against when they attempted to engage with white society. Furthermore, as it was not until 1967 that it became illegal to exclude Aboriginal children from educational institutions, many children continued to be educated outside the general school system.

During the 1960s, deficit theories in education and the concept of compensatory education made it possible for the continuing failure of Aboriginal children to succeed in the school system to be seen as the 'fault' of the children themselves. This convenient myth, that when a member of a minority group fails in a system defined, operated and monitored by the majority group it is not the fault of the system but the fault of the person, can be detected in the thinking of many well-meaning and sympathetic educators even today. In fact, while a glance at the various policies implemented over the last century and a half demonstrates changes in language, little seems to have changed ideologically. Deficit theory seems to have brought us back full circle to the 1845 Select Committee quoted earlier in the chapter.

In the 1990s, figures detail the continuing 'failure' of Aboriginal students in the non-Aboriginal education system, evidenced for example by low retention rates, low examinations scores, low levels of literacy, high levels of truancy and absenteeism. Education in Australia is a state affair and hence provision differs between states. As one illustration of current official thinking (chosen for its relevance to Western Australian students) it is interesting to read the document produced in 1991 by the government of Western Australian (WA Ministry of Education 1991) which sets out its policy and guidelines for the education of Aboriginal and Torres Strait Islander students. This is one of a number of documents produced with the intention of promoting social justice in education. While this document is well-meaning and clearly signals, at least on paper, the government's serious intention to improve education provision for Aboriginal children, an examination of the language used in the document betrays a continuing unwillingness to even seriously analyse, much less address, the real issues for Aboriginal students and their teachers. For example, while emphasizing that teachers 'must recognise' the 'diversity' of Aboriginal students, nevertheless the document itself, by implication, groups all students together by making general statements such as

Objective 1 (continuing improvement in the outcomes of Aboriginal students) will be achieved to

the extent that . . . Aboriginal people have an increased understanding of the benefits that can be gained from educational achievement. (WA Ministry of Education 1991: 8)

Similarly, the document expresses concern at a possible lack of 'confidence' and 'self esteem' in Aboriginal children, promoting for example 'the acquisition of literacy and cognitive skills' as a means of enabling Aboriginal people to 'participate *with confidence* in the wider Australian society' (my emphasis) (page 8). *Is* it the case that no Aboriginal people presently participate with confidence in the wider Australian society? There are a number of problems here. First of all, statements like these label all Aboriginal people as failing to appreciate the benefits of educational achievement and lacking in confidence, and hence establish particular negative expectations about their pupils in the minds of teachers. Secondly, by interpreting others' needs and behaviours in terms of their own cultural position, the ethnocentricity of the authors is evident. Once again, the ideology is little changed, and Aboriginal people are seen as failures in terms of the values system of the dominant culture. Furthermore, implicit is the notion that educating Aboriginal people is a problem because Aboriginal people are lacking in certain attitudes and aptitudes. The deficit model seems to be alive and well.

The flaws in this thinking are exposed by a number of researchers. Groome (1995) for example, describes his conversations with Aboriginal students who 'resented the pressure in schools to stereotype them as being difficult or different'. Furthermore, '[w]hile they did not deny their identity, they believed that the things they had in common with other students were also of importance.' He quotes other research, by Black and Gutman and by Day, which demonstrates that 'contrary to the stereotypes held by many teachers, many Aboriginal students want to achieve'. Groome also warns of the dangers of 'culturalism', identified by Rizvi and Crowley, which is 'the practice of describing or excusing all behaviours of Aboriginal students on the basis of imagined or cultural characteristics'. It would seem that the 'Social Justice in Education Policy' document is not only an example of 'culturalist' thinking but also, by sanctioning this attitude, makes it easy for schools to continue to stereotype Aboriginal pupils as difficult, failing or problematic. The document also fails to consider the existence of conscious resistance to the authority of white teachers on the part of many Aboriginal students, which can be manifested in such action as ' "cheeky behaviour", sullen withdrawal, inattention and absenteeism. For many students, absenteeism . . . is a legitimate and effective oppositional behaviour' (Keefe 1988: 72). The complex responses that Aboriginal people have to education are given scant consideration.

It should be said that the document does not suggest that schools and teachers should bear no responsibility for providing a more appropriate education for their Aboriginal students. There are guidelines throughout relating to the role of teachers and schools in this. For example, the importance of the 'learning environment' is clear; this should be 'supportive', 'positive', 'welcoming', 'free of cultural bias', 'racially tolerant'. Similarly, teachers should be 'appropriately trained', 'sensitive and informed', have 'understanding' of a number of things (including the 'aspirations' of their students), and 'must recognise' their students' 'diversity', 'values', 'bilingualism' (WA Ministry of Education 1991: passim). As well as being well-meaning but unhelpfully vague about how schools and teachers might become all these things – and is it solely for the benefit of Aboriginal students that schools should be welcoming and teachers sensitive and informed? – the document betrays a worrying lack of awareness of the nature of schools as organizations existing in a particular social reality. The role which schools have in managing and modifying pupils' work, social interactions, behaviour is unquestioned, (for example students 'need to learn the school culture', WA Ministry of Education 1991: 13), as is the assumption that schools can become free of racism in a racist society. Additionally, the document is silent on the need for teachers to know about Aboriginal history from an Aboriginal perspective; a particularly worrying entry is on page 8, when the 'past experience of some Aboriginal parents' is cited as a reason why they are not supportive of education for their children. It is what is left unsaid about that past experience which is, arguably, the key to the 'problem'.

The document has a curious schizophrenic quality, as if it has been written by two individuals (or working parties), one of which is trying hard to make value-neutral, libertarian statements about policies and strategies while the other represents the true colonial voice. On the one hand, 'racism is a denial of basic human rights and it has no place in an education system committed to the attainment of equity in education' (page 12), while on the other 'If *we* value an Aboriginal child's skill in language, *we* are also valuing that child and her/his cultural heritage' (my emphasis) (page 7). The message is clear; *we* are the people with the power to validate the 'other's' culture. Clearly the educational outcomes intended by the WA Ministry are those which contain no challenge to the educational *status quo*.

While sending out many worthwhile, humanitarian signals to the educational establishment, this document fails at a fundamental level to address the real issues. By dealing with surface, strategic issues, and by ignoring the history that defines the present reality for Aboriginal people, the document takes education for Aboriginal people little further. The fact remains: as long as educational provision is still envisaged in terms of white values, it can never fully meet the needs of Aboriginal people or truly serve their interests.[1]

Dilemmas for teacher-educators

This is the context in which the thirty-six students who are a particular focus of this chapter came to study 'Aborigines and Education'. While the particular nature of this unit, and of the students' responses to it, will be discussed later, some general issues need to be aired first. For example, how should teachers be prepared to teach Aboriginal students, given that there is a particular policy framework within which (in Western Australia) they will be working? As a teacher-educator, should you aim to maintain the *status quo*, and provide some answers to practical problems, or also attempt to change the way your students think? Do you begin with the policy which has to be implemented, given the urgency (for teachers) of matters of practice? Is it a question of understanding the policy, planning and implementing it, then reviewing? Most of the students of this unit are practising teachers, whose work often entails finding immediate strategies for practical problems. At what point is it then possible for them to reflect in an informed and critical way on the policy of the day? The extent to which classroom teachers are able to influence policy is debatable, but presumably they are the obvious people to look to for insights about the teaching of Aboriginal students, and for ideas about changing practice – if not in the larger arena of state policy then at least in their own schools and classrooms. Yet teachers are notoriously atheoretical (see for example Garrigan and Pearce 1996). Can teachers or student teachers explore the limitations of mainstream government policy without first confronting their own acculturation in that mainstream society? How can this be done without first accessing social theory, reassessing history, exploring their own values?

There is another, more problematic, question about the role of a non-Aboriginal teacher educator, in particular in relation to the selection of materials, given the historical, political and social contexts in which Aboriginal students and their non-Aboriginal teachers are situated. Can people who are not themselves Aboriginal educate others about Aboriginal issues? The question is more than one about effectiveness (if you are not Aboriginal yourself, how do you *really* know what the issues are?); it is an ethical one. Do you have the right to speak about a group of people's culture and values if you don't belong to that group? Can you ensure that by becoming a representative of others (and hence denying them their own voice) you are not continuing the marginalization that you actually hope to put an end to? The problem goes beyond that of ethnicity, social status and power, since as an academic you are a member of a culture that values particular kinds of scholarship, rationality and mental rigour, none of which, as you begin to understand as you do your reading on the subject, seem particularly important or valuable to Aboriginal society. You are caught between university traditions and students' expectations about tertiary education, and the need to signal that Aboriginal people ought (ethically) to have a share in a unit of study that is about them. Yet the 'scholarly' (i.e. 'acceptable') evidence that is available about Aboriginal learning styles, values, aspirations and needs is largely written by non-Aboriginal researchers. Aboriginal participation in tertiary education and beyond is extremely low, and there are few Aboriginal people who would define themselves as 'scholars' in the non-Aboriginal sense. Aboriginal people tend not to define their experiences by writing journal articles or chapters in scholarly publications; it seems that the only way for teachers to really learn about Aboriginal life would be by total immersion, but this is difficult to organize in a ten-week semester, with budget cuts and assessment deadlines. I should not be flippant. The problems are real, and serious.

In a sense, one of the things that 'Aborigines and Education' does is to attempt just this: to immerse students in Aboriginal life, albeit at some considerable distance. As far as possible, writing by Aboriginal people has been included in the unit materials, such as Ruby Langford's autobiography *Don't Take Your Love to Town*. This is the subject of the first assignment of the unit and works powerfully to engage students' sympathies for and understanding of Aboriginality. Also, there are examples of classroom-based action research undertaken collaboratively by Aboriginal and non-Aboriginal researchers. There are materials dealing with contact history from the Aboriginal perspective; there is writing about Aboriginal resistance; there is much about Aboriginal values by both Aboriginal and non-Aboriginal writers. While much of the unit attempts to provide for students' practical needs by including materials that describe and analyse teaching strategies, nevertheless a significant part is devoted to what might be called sensitizing, awareness raising and issues exploration. The need for teachers to develop more than a hazy understanding of the social, political, historical, philosophical and ideological contexts in which they are working is acknowledged by the prominence given to these issues in the unit materials. Out of ten key topics within the unit, only three are directly related to classroom practice (management issues, language and literacy and mathematics teaching). Four are topics designed to help students locate their practice in a particular social, historical and cultural context (contact history; Aboriginal identity; Aboriginal values; language and culture) and two look at general issues in Aboriginal education. In particular they refer to independent Aboriginal schools and Local Government policies relating to Aboriginal education. The final topic is anti-racist teaching.

The unit assignments also encourage students to challenge their own judgements and values by requiring them to respond in a variety of ways to the unit materials, both critically and personally, both in writing and orally. The mere regurgitation of material is explicitly discouraged, instead students are expected to 'bring in original ideas from your own experience', 'explore your feelings', 'think creatively' and examine ideas in terms of 'your emerging intelligence about the education of Aboriginal people' (Currie 1995). The emphasis overall is on developing both students' theoretical understandings and their empathy, which will in turn inform and transform their practice. No easy solutions are presented; instead what is encouraged is an informed alertness that will enable students to debate critically the various policies and strategies that they will encounter in their working lives.

Students' responses

As well as recording students' ideas, reactions, questions and concerns while they worked on the unit, I also surveyed their views about their work with Aboriginal pupils once the unit had ended.

All were external students, studying independently, off-campus, using a set of unit materials and a study guide. Most students were spread throughout Western Australia, with a few living in the Northern Territory and New South Wales. Western Australia is a vast state. Away from the conurbation of Perth, the population of 0.6 million people is thinly spread. The fact that students were living in extremely diverse communities, from urban areas close to the university itself, to small country towns in the wheatbelt, to extremely remote areas where the airstrip is closed on and off for three months every year during 'the wet', reflects in turn the diversity of the Aboriginal students they were teaching. Students who were teaching in urban or suburban schools had, typically, very few Aboriginal children in their classes; children who might be well-integrated into non-Aboriginal culture but nevertheless retained significant aspects of Aboriginality. Others, particularly in remote regions in the north of the state, were living and working in Aboriginal communities where the proportion of children speaking an Aboriginal language was high. The Education students' main forms of communication with me were their written assignments or brief telephone conversations, yet in spite of there being minimal opportunities for in-depth communication I soon became aware that, collectively, these people had unusually high levels of concern and commitment in relation to the issues they were studying. While this was partly due to a need to deal with the daily realities of their classrooms, they also shared an awareness that social justice was not necessarily being done for Aboriginal students, and hence felt the need to make a commitment to try to make things better for them. As work on the unit progressed, the extent to which students developed new insights and critical perspectives, and increased their capacity for self-analysis, was striking. Each

topic and assignment within the unit had a clear impact on students' thoughts and feelings. One example is the early assignment which asks students to describe the personal impact which Ruby Langford's autobiography (1988) had on them. The writer describes life as an Aboriginal woman born in the 1930s, whose experiences of rural and urban life, family tragedy, personal aspirations and struggles to deal with the reality of being black in a divided society are moving and memorable. For each student the impact was profound. Expressions of shock and self-doubt were common. Students typically described themselves as being 'staggered', 'angry and ashamed', 'frustrated', 'sad', 'haunted', 'ignorant and outraged', 'humbled'. The autobiography provided a view of Aboriginal experiences that was a powerful antidote to much of what had already been absorbed by the students from mainstream sources such as school text books and the mass media. Even people who had already taught Aboriginal students found the book a revelation. The highly emotional response to Ruby Langford's book led to an unusually high (for university students) level of *personal* engagement in the rest of the unit. It seemed that once students' empathy levels had been aroused at the outset, their commitment to other relevant issues deepened.

This was particularly evident in their responses to the topics dealing with Aboriginal values. This was without doubt the most revelatory topic for students, and their responses to it were particularly revealing of the development of their awareness and critical alertness. Research over the last twenty years (undertaken largely by non-Aboriginal researchers) into ways in which Aboriginal values differ from those embedded in mainstream education in Australia (such as Davies and McGlade 1982, Eckermann 1988, Harris 1990, Malin 1990) has provided clear evidence of the significance of these differences for children in schools. For example, Davies and McGlade signal the 'all-pervasive effect' (1982: 95) of kinship relations and affiliation on the schooling of Aboriginal children. Affiliation implies the primacy of the group over the individual, and children having near equal status with adults. Not only does this conflict directly with the individually competitive culture found in the mainstream school, but also can be misinterpreted by uninformed teachers as challenging to their authority when students defer to their peers rather than to their teacher (Malin 1990: 320). Davies and McGlade (1982) also detect differences between the reward and punishment systems familiar to Aboriginal children and those belonging to the culture of the mainstream school, and different communication styles (both verbal and non-verbal). The conclusions drawn by these researchers are clear. All children arrive at school already socialized and with certain behaviours embedded. Those whose socialization matches most closely with the expectations of the school culture have the easiest time. Those whose behaviours are in conflict set up negative responses from teachers and risk long-term marginalization in the classroom; Malin's article (1990) is a clear message about the damaging effect of this kind of marginalization for Aboriginal children. In spite of the acknowledged diversity within the Aboriginal population, and even though much Aboriginal culture outside the traditional communities has been heavily influenced by the mainstream Australian culture, the notion that at school, 'Aborigines encounter problems not faced by the majority of Australians', and that these problems can be attributed to 'real and significant differences in values between Aborigines and other Australian students' (Davies and McGlade 1982: 95) has been accepted by educationists for over twenty years.

While there is much available research on the key issues of values, it appears not to be widely known. The shocked surprise characterizing the Education students' response to this discovery was unexpected, particularly since many had already taught Aboriginal children. That many of the 'failures' or 'problems' that they had identified in children they had taught could be traced to conflicts between Aboriginal and non-Aboriginal values was both a consolation ('the problem's due to more than just my inadequacy') and a cause for deep concern. While many students came to understand that it was inappropriate to ascribe failure to their Aboriginal students, and instead were able to ascribe failure to the educational system ('I now understand that it is the system which is failing the students, not the students who are failing the system'), since it is beyond their power to have much influence on the 'system' this discovery came with some degree of frustration and negativity. There were also expressions of regret that their lack of knowledge might have led to inadvertent injustices:

I have never before thought on a conscious level about the notion that Aboriginal children, due to their independence training and because of the more equal status they share with adults are less likely to be in tune with what the teacher is doing. Now that I have read about this it feels as if I already knew and yet if I had I would not have given A . . . such a hard time last year for not being where I wanted him. (Baker 1996)

Other comments revealed how this discovery about difference led to increased empathy ('It's no wonder K . . . was so unhappy'), to a closer sense of identification with students and families, and ideas about transforming practice ('Now I know to do X next time this problem emerges'). The extent to which this understanding also led to a desire for action was evident in students' accounts of their determination to have more input into school policy changes, and in reports of conversations with other teachers in staff rooms and at staff meetings. When for a later assignment students had to present and tape-record a 'tutorial' given to a small group of friends, relatives, colleagues, and lead a follow-up discussion, from a range of possible topics, the majority chose 'Aboriginal Values'. The conviction that the tutorial was an opportunity to inform others and raise awareness about something important was shared by many.

The extent of these students' surprise at the need to consider their pupils' values is extremely revealing of the culture of the educational establishment as a whole, and of schools in particular. Teachers are unlikely to be teachers unless they are themselves successful products of the mainstream education culture, sharing its values. Not only would they have probably been readily assimilated into the school culture as pupils, they are as teachers representative of that culture (and in so far as schools reflect the wider society, representatives of that as well) and obliged to maintain it and transmit it to pupils. Malin (1990) described a teacher who was doing this quite unconsciously; the existence of the 'hidden' curriculum in schools ensures the maintenance of the values and culture of the dominant group. It is difficult to challenge the culture of which you have membership for many reasons: by implication you are challenging your own values, you risk your present status and future prospects, and when your values and judgements are formed by a particular culture it is difficult (some would say impossible) to engage in objective analysis of it. Hence few members of the mainstream education culture are able (or willing) to question the social reality of school; for many it is the only reality conceivable. There are other interesting features of the students' thinking which betray at a deeper level certain culturally embedded ways of thinking. For example, the notion of opposites (bi-polarity) pervaded much of the students' early work; if Aboriginal people value affiliation to the group, then non-Aboriginal people must value and promote the individual (in spite of the persistence of the family unit in non-Aboriginal society, and children's reluctance to stand out in a crowd). Or if Aboriginal children shy away from competitiveness, and resist pressure to answer questions until certain that they know the answer, then non-Aboriginal children must (as opposites) enjoy competitiveness and fall over themselves to answer teachers' questions even if they might get them wrong. Not only does this tendency to polarize not match up with the perceived social or classroom reality, it also puts at risk attempts to find commonalities between cultures. Indeed, much research about Aboriginal children in school reminded me of many children I encountered during twenty years of working in schools in Northern English cities: with close-knit extended families and associated family responsibilities (such as looking after younger children if parents were ill or elsewhere); speaking non-standard English; possessing values and attitudes that often conflicted with those of the school and which ensured that teachers felt it essential to 'socialize' children before attending to other kinds of learning. Many children find schools difficult places to be in, yet rarely is it assumed that it is the school which is the problem.

As their studies progressed, it became clear that the Education students were becoming increasingly aware of particular dilemmas facing them both in their classroom practice and in their theorizing. First, the historical, social and political contexts in which they were working, or intending to work, as teachers were seen as creating enormous tensions. Whose interests should they serve if the stated interests of their employers or colleagues conflict with those of their pupils and their families? How can teachers demonstrate their good will and good intentions towards their pupils if they are white and hence members of an oppressive culture? Second, to live in a racist society as members of the dominant culture puts teachers in extremely problematic situations. Can they, as members of an oppressive culture, act in the interests of the oppressed (Aboriginal) community, or even adopt positions of neutrality? To what extent can they not just understand but also value the values of 'the other' when they

are demonstrably very different from their own? Should they be gaining knowledge about how their pupils differ from them, or should they instead be looking for commonalities? 'What shall we do?', the question which led students to study the unit in the first place, was no longer simply a demand for strategies. It was turning into a question about how to achieve social justice in an unequal society.

Six months later: daily realities

Having sensed the considerable impact that 'Aborigines and Education' had on these students' thinking at the time, I was interested to trace further developments in their feelings, thinking and practice, and find out whether any new issues were emerging as daily realities for them. Six months after their studies had ended, I asked them to complete a questionnaire. This focused first on their thinking about Aboriginal values, and then went on to ask about other significant issues in their teaching.

The results show that while the students see values and associated issues as extremely significant in determining the outcomes of schooling for Aboriginal children, these are only some elements in a complex picture. For example, while there was complete unanimity that 'It is extremely important for a teacher of Aboriginal students to be well-informed about Aboriginal values', there was considerable variation in the level of knowledge which students felt they had. Fifty per cent of students surveyed rated themselves as only 'somewhat' well-informed. Only one student out of the thirty-six felt able to describe themselves as 'extremely' well-informed. Since for all those surveyed, the values conflicts between Aboriginal and non-Aboriginal culture were either 'very' or 'extremely' important in determining an Aboriginal students' educational success, this lack of knowledge is clearly an issue worthy of attention by teacher educators and ministers of education. The next question, about sources of information about Aboriginal values, showed that pre-service teacher education and Aboriginal pupils were equally influential in providing insights into values issues: each source was rated either 'very' or 'extremely' influential by two-thirds of those surveyed. Aboriginal parents, on the other hand, did not play a major role in influencing teachers, nor did non-Aboriginal colleagues. Sixty-seven per cent of respondents found parents either 'not at all' or 'somewhat' influential, while non-Aboriginal colleagues featured even less prominently: 78 per cent found them 'not at all' or 'somewhat' influential. The least influential element was in-service education, with 60 per cent of people rating this as 'not at all' influential. The role of Aboriginal colleagues was significant for some people, 44 per cent finding them 'very' or 'extremely' influential; 56 per cent finding them 'somewhat' or 'not at all'. But in spite of evidence suggesting that there is no one reliable source of information for teachers, it is clear that receiving a teaching qualification does not signal the end of learning for teachers. All qualified teachers surveyed had increased their understanding of Aboriginal values since qualifying by 'a great deal'.

While the central importance of Aboriginal values in determining educational outcomes for Aboriginal children is exemplified by these responses, when we look at other questions the picture becomes more complex. 'What other factors would you say have an important effect on educational success for Aboriginal students?' generated a list of 130 different responses which were broken down into five broad categories. Factors associated with the teacher were the most frequently mentioned, accounting for 42 per cent of the total. Factors associated with the child, some of which were linked with values issues, accounted for 34 per cent, and factors associated with the 'culture' of the school appeared in 14 per cent of the total. The other two areas identified – the presence of Aboriginal teachers and the child's language – accounted for 6 per cent and 4 per cent of the total respectively. The fact that few students had had experience of either working with Aboriginal colleagues or with children speaking an Aboriginal language might account for the infrequent occurrence of these two factors.

On interpretation, these 'other factors' become highly significant. First of all, that the teachers and student teachers surveyed were uncompromising in their acknowledgement of their own responsibilities indicates a high level of professionalism. This was reinforced by the response to another question: all agreed that teachers 'need to have particular personal characteristics to be able to work successfully with Aboriginal students'. Piecing together the separate responses reveals how the 'successful' teacher is characterized. As might be expected, particularly given the students' own empathic response to Ruby Langford's book,

affective skills such as sympathy, compassion, warmth, the ability to establish a friendly rapport with pupils were mentioned as being important, but far more significant were professional skills and the possession of a well-informed, political awareness. For example, the need to be 'non-racist' was mentioned often, also described as the need to 'critically analyse your own values' or 'identify and prevail over your own ingrained prejudices'. Preparedness to take action was also important: 'a readiness to combat any racism in your class or school' and 'a commitment to social justice'. Typical professional skills that were valued were 'being a "hands on" teacher' able to 'handle poor health problems' and 'flexible enough to adjust your teaching programme to accommodate the children's transience'. Additionally, teachers need skills in a range of teaching strategies, in choosing appropriate curriculum materials, particularly those which are culturally sensitive, and in being able to cater for the needs of different children in the class without clearly singling out Aboriginal children.

The students surveyed acknowledge that teachers have a vital role to play. However, teachers do not exist in social and political vacuums; nor do the children in their classrooms. It is in the respondents' often angry and despairing comments about the impact of the school's and the society's cultures on educational outcomes for Aboriginal children, and about the relevance of what children bring from outside into the classroom, that the major causes for these students' concerns seem to lie. The political realities for teachers and children are significant. Peer pressure on non-Aboriginal students to marginalize their Aboriginal classmates appears widespread, as does the racism of other teachers. 'The most difficult challenge I had to face was the racism of other teachers and students.' 'I could not comprehend that educated people in the teaching profession were not interested in the welfare of all students.' For one student, the solution was personal isolation: 'I decided not to talk about Aboriginal students with those (racist) teachers.' Official reluctance to take responsibility for problems was also significant, ('[i]t's hard to get people to take responsibility for a problem') as was the impact of 'educational cutbacks and beliefs of right wing governments'. There is a sense that many respondents feel they are fighting a lonely battle. 'Who do you ask? . . . I'm not remotely satisfied with the level of educational support provided.'

More important, it is the things that Aboriginal

children themselves bring to school (as well as the things they do not bring – pencils, books, paper) that show that the reasons why 'Aborigines encounter problems not faced by the majority of Australians' (Davies and McGlade 1982) at school go beyond Aboriginal values, and hark back to the colonial values so clearly exemplified in the discriminatory policies discussed at the beginning of this chapter. Aboriginal people remain on the margins not just culturally but also in terms of social justice. The damaging effects of poverty, ill health, violence in the home, and hunger on children's schooling are all catalogued, and links between these social realities and children's 'low self-esteem', 'alienation' and 'inattention and disruptive behaviour in the classroom' are inescapable.

Conclusion

These teachers and student teachers are prepared to confront their own lack of knowledge and expertise, are positive, enthusiastic, and eager to learn more, and are committed to doing the best job they can. They can learn about Aboriginal values, adjust their practice accordingly, try to get to know their pupils and their families better, involve parents in the life of the school. But while non-Aboriginal cultures continue to dominate socially and politically, there are limitations to what teachers can achieve. Exploring the values of another culture has been enlightening for the students who are the focus of this chapter. There are, however, two clear dangers in maintaining an uncritical acceptance of the importance of others' values, and hence of their difference. One is that too great a focus on 'difference' obscures that which is shared between cultures. The other is that focus on values differences make it easy to overlook the real differences: between poverty and wealth; between health and ill health; between the powerful and the oppressed. If, as the survey results indicate, children need nourishment, access to health services, protection from violence in order to be successful at school, and if racism remains embedded in schools and in the wider society, then teaching strategies, no matter how innovative or culturally sensitive they might be, will not be enough to make a difference; only a commitment to human rights is enough to do this. In deserving this, at least, everyone is the same.

Acknowledgements

I am extremely grateful to the students of the School of Education at Murdoch University who studied E420 in the first semester of 1996 for giving generously of their time to participate in this survey, and for their insightful comments.

Note

1 Since this chapter was first written, the Education Department of Western Australia has released another relevant policy document (EDWA (1998) Anti Racism Policy. Perth: Education Department of Western Australia). While this very brief document promotes the valuing and fostering of 'cultural diversity', and is warm and supportive in its rhetoric, it retains the same focus on surface strategies that its predecessor had, and still fails to address *how* schools and teachers can 'work towards racial harmony' (EDWA 1998: 8). What is also interesting is that while the front cover depicts five children, only one of them is white. Is the message conveyed by this that racism is not much about being white but more about being a person of ('other') colour?

References

Baker, L. (1996) Some major problems in Aboriginal Education today. Unpublished manuscript. Perth: Murdoch University.

Currie, J. (1995) *Aborigines and Education: Study Guide*. Perth: Murdoch University.

Davies, E. and McGlade, M. (1982) Cultural values affecting the child at school. In J. Sherwood, (ed.) *Aboriginal Education: Issues and Innovations*: 95–104. Perth: Creative Research.

Eckermann, A. K. (1988) Cultural vacuum or cultural vitality? *Australian Aboriginal Studies* 1: 31–9.

Garrigan, P. and Pearce, J. (1996) Use theory? Use theory! *Mentoring and Tutoring* 1 (4).

Groome, H. (1995) *Working Purposefully with Aboriginal Students*. Wentworth Falls: Social Science Press.

Harris, S. (1990) *Two Way Aboriginal Schooling. Education and Cultural Survival*. Canberra: Australian Studies Press.

Keefe, K. (1988) Aboriginality: resistance or persistence. *Australian Aboriginal Studies* 1: 67–81.

Langford, R. (1988) *Don't Take Your Love to Town*. Ringwood: Penguin.

Lippman, L. (1994) *Generations of Resistance*. Melbourne: Longman.

Malin, M. (1990) The visibility and invisibility of

Aboriginal students in an urban classroom. *Australian Journal of Education* **34** (3): 312–29.

Nannup, A. (1992) *When the Pelican Laughed*. Fremantle: Fremantle Arts Centre Press.

Pilkington, D. (1996) *Follow the Rabbit-proof Fence*. St Lucia: University of Queensland Press.

WA Ministry of Education (1991) *Social Justice in Education: Policy Guidelines for the Education of Aboriginal and Torres Strait Islander Students*. Perth: Ministry of Education.

3

The Pupil Control Ideology of Teachers in Culturally Diverse Settings: The Case of Arab and Jewish Teachers in Israeli Public Secondary Schools

ISMAEL ABU SAAD and BOBBIE TURNIANSKY

Introduction

This article presents a study of Arab and Jewish teachers' pupil control ideologies in secondary schools in Israel. The study setting provides the opportunity to explore this important dimension of teachers' values *vis-à-vis* the classroom in two separate and culturally distinct contexts.

Theoretical background

The values implicit in schooling and their effect on pupils is of great interest to researchers, practitioners and professional educators. The study of teachers' pupil control ideology (PCI) is aimed at eliciting the values underlying teachers' choices of classroom management and disciplinary styles, as well as pedagogical approaches. Willower, Eidell and Hoy (1973) developed a scale for measuring teachers PCI, based on the value systems of custodialism and humanism. These terms refer to contrasting types of individual orientations and the types of school organization that they seek to rationalize and justify. Prototypes of custodial and humanistic views towards discipline are presented below (Willower, Eidell and Hoy 1973).

Custodial orientation

A custodial pupil control orientation characterizes the traditional school, which provides a rigid and highly-controlled setting concerned primarily with the maintenance of order. Students are stereotyped in terms of their appearance, behaviour and parents' socio-economic status. Teachers who hold custodial views towards discipline consider the

school an autocratic organization with rigid pupil–teacher status hierarchy, in which the flow of power and communication is unilateral and downward. Students must accept the decisions of their teachers without question. Teachers do not attempt to understand student behaviour, but instead view misbehaviour as a personal affront. Students are perceived as irresponsible and undisciplined people who must be controlled through punitive sanctions. Impersonality, pessimism, and watchful mistrust pervade the climate of the custodial school.

Humanistic orientation

The prototype of the humanistic orientation considers the school as an educational community in which students learn through cooperative interaction and experience. Learning and behaviour are viewed in psychological and sociological terms, not moralistic terms. Self-discipline is substitued for strict teacher control. Humanistic views lead teachers to desire a democratic climate with open channels of two-way communication between pupils and teachers and increased self-determination. In addition, according to Fromm (1948), a humanistic orientation stresses the importance of the individuality of each student and the creation of an atmosphere to meet the wide range of student needs.

Some research findings

Much of the research on PCI has focused on identifying individual or organizational predictors of teachers' PCI orientations. Packard's (1988) review of twenty-seven separate studies revealed that one of the most frequently reported PCI findings is that female teachers are more humanistic or less custodial than male teachers. This finding has been tested and confirmed in a number of different cultures including the United States (Willower, Eidell and Hoy 1973), Australia (Smyth 1977), Israel (Abu Saad and Hendrix 1993) and the Caribbean (Richardson and Payne 1988).

Other individual-level characteristics shown to have a connection with PCI orientation include age, job and tenure. The PCI studies frequently reported an association between PCI and age, where younger teachers are more humanistic than older teachers (Smyth 1977, Willower, Eidell and Hoy 1973). Other studies have found that elementary teachers were more humanistic than secondary school teachers, administrators were more humanistic than teachers, counsellors were more humanistic than administrators, and teachers with fewer years of teaching experience were more humanistic than teachers with more years of teaching experience (Packard 1988, Richardson and Payne 1988, Smyth 1977, Willower, Eidell and Hoy 1973).

According to some researchers, organizational-level factors are also related to PCI. A number of researchers have found that teachers in low-socio-economic status SES schools were more custodial than teachers in middle- or high-SES schools (Andrews 1965, Gossen 1969), and Mitchell (1974) and Brayboy (1981) reported that the PCI of teachers in small schools is less custodial than the PCI of teachers who work in large schools.

However, these findings have not always been consistent. There have been a number of studies that have found no differences between the PCI orientations of elementary and secondary school teachers (Hardesty 1978, Hoy and Jalovick 1979, Helsel 1976), teachers and administrators (Murphy 1977, Seefa 1981, Voege 1979), or the socio-economic level of the students or school (Barfield and Burlingame 1974, Kelton 1976). In addition, Packard's review article (1988) reports that results over a number of studies generally do not support a relationship between school size and PCI.

The study

Israel is a multi-ethnic society consisting of a Jewish majority and an Arab minority, which constitute about 82 per cent and 18 per cent of the population,

respectively. Jews are clearly the dominant group and the political and educational systems are aimed at the realization of Jewish national interests and aspirations (Shavit 1990). Jews enjoy a greater relative and absolute share of the resources allocated by the state, as well as more favourable occupational opportunities (Al-Haj 1995, Zureik 1979).

The Israeli educational system, which is directed by the Ministry of Education, Culture and Sports in Jerusalem, is *de facto* divided into separate Jewish and Arab systems. In the 1953 Law of State Education, the aims of the educational system were set forth as follows:

> to base education on the values of Jewish culture and the achievements of science, on love of the homeland and loyalty to the state and the Jewish people, on practice in agricultural work and handicraft, on pioneer training and on striving for a society built on freedom, equality, tolerance, mutual assistance, and love of mankind.   (Mar'i 1978: 50)

These aims emphasize humanistic values, but have a strong Jewish orientation, which is not inclusive of other ethnic or religious value systems and groups. No parallel aims were ever set forth for the education of Arabs in Israel (Al-Haj 1995), and the lack of such aims has left the traditionally paternalistic, autocratic (i.e. custodial) values dominant in Arab culture today to dominate the school atmosphere as well.

The present study was designed to explore the relationships between PCI (dependent variable) and

1 ethnicity;
2 gender;
3 tenure;
4 educational level;
5 age (independent variables).

Method

The Sample

The sample was made up of 275 secondary school teachers working in five locations in the southern part of Israel, and included 173 Jewish teachers (53 male, 118 female, 2 missing) and 102 Arab teachers (70 male, 31 female, 1 missing) as shown in Table 3.1.

Table 3.1 Ethnic and gender composition of sample

Variable		
Ethnicity	Jewish	173 (62.9%)
	Arab	102 (37.1%)
Gender	Male	123 (44.7%)
	Female	149 (54.2%)

Instrumentation and data analysis

The instrument used was the PCI questionnaire developed by Willower, Eidell and Hoy (1973). The PCI measures an ideology about, or value-orientation towards, pupil control. The PCI questionnaire includes twenty items scored on a five-point Likert-type scale ranging from 1 (strongly disagree) to 5 (strongly agree). Scoring produces a bi-polar scale, ranging from custodial to humanistic. High scores (maximum of 100) indicate a custodial orientation and low scores (minimum of 20) a humanistic orientation. Information on the reliability and validity of the PCI is available in Willower, Eidell and Hoy (1973). The statistical methods for processing the collected data were descriptive statistics and MANOVA models using SPSS 6.0 for Windows.

Subjects were assigned educational tenure scores of low (less than 4 years), medium (4–10 years) or high (11 years or more) and were grouped into age clusters of 20–29, 30–39, and 40 years of age and older.

Results

As can be seen from Table 3.2, the demographic composition of the sample within each ethnic group is different. Non-parametric chi-square tests showed that, in general, the Arab teachers tend to be younger males with less tenure. The Jewish sample is composed of more female teachers and older teachers with more tenure. The two samples have fairly equivalent educational levels.

A multivariate analysis of variance was done using the PCI scores as the dependent variable with gender, education, tenure, age, and ethnicity as the independent variables. The analysis indicated significant main effects for ethnicity and gender but no interaction between the two variables. All of the other variables were non-significant. The results are shown in Table 3.3

The unweighted adjusted PCI means are shown in Table 3.4

As can be seen, Arab teachers are more custodial than Jewish teachers and in both ethnic groups, male teachers are more custodial than female teachers.

Table 3.2 Demographic characteristics

Variable		Jewish	Arab	Total
Gender *				
	Male	53 (31.0)	70 (69.3)	123 (45.2)
	Female	118 (69.0)	31 (30.7)	149 (54.8)
Education				
	Teacher's seminary	23 (13.5)	14 (14.3)	37 (13.8)
	Partial BA	17 (9.9)	14 (14.3)	31 (11.5)
	BA	92 (53.8)	48 (49.0)	140 (52.0)
	MA	26 (15.2)	10 (10.2)	36 (13.4)
	Other	13 (7.6)	12 (12.2)	24 (9.3)
Tenure *				
	Less than 4 years	40 (23.1)	48 (47.1)	88 (32.0)
	4–10 years	52 (30.1)	38 (37.3)	90 (32.7)
	11 years or more	81 (46.8)	16 (15.7)	97 (35.3)
Age *				
	20–29	31 (18.3)	65 (69.1)	96 (36.5)
	30–39	70 (41.4)	25 (26.6)	95 (36.1)
	40 and older	68 (40.2)	4 (4.3)	72 (27.4)

* Chi-square tests show differences between ethnic groups are significant at the .000 level. (Numbers in parentheses are within cell percentages.)

Table 3.3 MANOVA results – PCI

Independent variables	SS	df	MS	F	Significance
Gender	573.36	1	573.34	6.56	.011
Education	171.76	3	57.25	.66	.580
Tenure	229.11	2	114.56	1.31	.271
Age	214.59	2	107.30	1.23	.295
Ethnicity	1592.17	1	1592.17	18.23	.000
Gender × Ethnicity	96.05	1	96.05	1.10	.295
Within cells	19563.95	224	87.34		

Discussion

The findings of the present study with regard to gender are consistent with most of the literature, as well as with Abu Saad and Hendrix's (1993) earlier study in Israeli elementary schools. In both of these studies, male teachers were found to be significantly more custodial than female teachers. The PCI scores in Abu Saad and Hendrix's study were 69 for males and 55 for females, somewhat more polar than the scores of 63 and 57 found in the present study. The differences between men and women hold true for both the Jewish and Arab samples. Arab females have a more humanistic PCI than Arab males but are more custodial than Jewish

Table 3.4 Unweighted adjusted PCI means

Variable		Unweighted means
Gender		
	Male	63.16
	Female	57.48
Education		
	Teacher's seminary	60.86
	Partial BA	59.03
	BA	61.28
	MA	58.46
Tenure		
	Less than 4 years	59.23
	4–10 years	60.80
	11 years or more	60.34
Age		
	20–29	62.91
	30–39	59.43
	40 and older	57.10
Ethnicity		
	Jewish	56.99
	Arab	65.48
Gender × ethnicity	*Male*	*Female*
Jewish	60.18	54.77
Arab	66.83	63.72

males who are, in turn, more custodial than Jewish females.

The results of the present study also support the results from Abu Saad and Hendrix's study in Israeli primary schools, which found Arab teachers (mean PCI score 63) to be more custodial than Jewish teachers (mean PCI score 61). In the present study, the mean PCI scores for Arab and Jewish teachers are 65 and 57, respectively. So, each ethnic group displays the same tendencies that it showed in the elementary schools but to a greater degree.

The findings that the Arab teachers in the study have a more custodial PCI orientation are consistent with those of Andrews (1965) and Gossen (1969) who found that teachers in schools with students from lower-SES backgrounds were more custodial than middle- or high-SES schools. They are also consistent with the results of Appleberry and Hoy's study (1969), which found the PCI of teachers in rural settings to be more custodial than the PCI of teachers in suburban and urban settings.

The Arab teachers in the present study come from rural, low-SES areas. For the most part, rural Arab society in Israel is very traditional and, like other traditional societies, it has a well-defined system of hierarchical values and customs that regulates interpersonal and intergroup relationship within the society (Abu Saad 1991). In this society, control over the behaviour of individuals is external rather than internal. These values are more in line with the custodial PCI orientation, which emphasizes a rigid and highly controlled environment, than the humanistic orientation, which emphasizes self-discipline. In rural Arab communities schools are expected to be authoritarian and to reinforce traditional values and behaviours (Mar'i 1978). Schools tend to operate on a rigid time schedule with emphasis being placed on completion of the prescribed amount of material. Communication for the most part is unilateral and downward, flowing from teacher to student. In line with this approach, the instructional method employed is mainly lecture. Also in agreement with the custodial PCI orientation, the use of sanctions and corporal punishment in the school is accepted by both teachers and parents.

Regarding the effects of school level on teachers' PCI orientations, the findings of the present study do not present a consistent picture, as has been the case in a number of other PCI studies (Packard 1988). Among Arab teachers, the PCI of secondary school teachers was slightly higher than that found for elementary school teachers in Abu Saad and Hendrix's (1993) study; while among the Jewish teachers, the PCI scores of secondary school teachers were slightly lower (more humanistic) than those of Jewish elementary school teachers. Given the inconsistent findings in this and other studies, considerable caution must be used before drawing conclusions about the nature of schools at different levels accounting for the differences of teachers' PCI orientations.

Although no definite conclusions can be drawn, there is room for some speculation about why Jewish secondary school teachers have a more humanistic orientation than their elementary school counterparts. The PCI may be considered the outcome of the interaction between the students, the teacher, and the situation. The status of the Jewish Israeli teacher is low, as it is in many other Western countries. Teaching is considered to be a job for women and not for 'real men'. In the primary school setting, there is still a modicum of respect for the teacher. In secondary school, the situation is quite different. As the students get older, the problems the teachers must deal with change. The question is, what tools does the teacher possess for dealing with these problems?

There are not many formal options open to the teacher. His or her authority to impose sanctions on the students is limited. However, to do the job effectively, the teacher is dependent on the cooperation of the student, much the way a supervisor in any work setting is dependent on subordinates to enable him to 'get the job done'. In such a situation, the teacher must turn to other tools and these may include presenting a more humanistic orientation toward the pupils – more openness, more two-way interaction.

The results of the present study may make the Jewish secondary school teachers appear more humanistic. But what is uncertain, and deserves further study, is whether this is an internalized orienta-

tion or a learned response to a situation in which they feel they have no other options if learning is to be accomplished.

What does emerge clearly from the study, given the strong effects of ethnicity on PCI, is the major influence that the values of a teacher's culture and society have upon the values he or she brings into the classroom with regard to management, disciplinary and teaching styles.

References

Abu Saad, I. (1991) Toward an understanding of minority education in Israel: the case of the Bedouin Arabs of the Negev. *Comparative Education* **27**: 235–42.

Abu Saad, I. and Hendrix, V. (1993) Pupil control ideology in a multicultural society: Arab and Jewish teachers in Israeli elementary schools. *Comparative Education Review* **37**: 21–30.

Al-Haj, M. (1995) *Education, Empowerment, and Control: The Case of the Arabs in Israel*. Albany, NY: State University of New York Press.

Andrews, N. (1965) School organizational climate: some validity studies. *Canadian Education and Research Digest* **5**: 317-34.

Appleberry, J. and Hoy, W. (1969) The pupil control ideology of professional personnel in 'open' and 'closed' elementary schools. *Educational Administration Quarterly* **5**: 74–85.

Barfield, V. and Burlingame, M. (1974) The pupil control ideology of teachers in selected schools. *Journal of Experimental Education* **42**: 6–11.

Brayboy, L. (1981) *Teacher pupil control ideology and behavior and principals' ratings of teachers' discipline effectiveness*. Doctoral dissertation, Pennsylvania State University.

Fromm, E. (1948) *Man for Him Self*. New York: Farrar and Rinehart.

Gossen, H. (1969) *An investigation of the relationship between socioeconomic status of elementary schools and the pupil control ideology of teachers*. Doctoral dissertation, Oklahoma State University.

Hardesty, L. (1978) *Pupil control ideology of teachers as it relates to middle-school concepts*. Doctoral dissertation, University of Kansas.

Helsel, A. (1976) Personality and pupil control behavior. *Journal of Educational Administration* **14**: 79–86.

Hoy, W. and Jalovick, J. (1979) Open education and pupil control ideologies of teachers. *Journal of Educational Research* **73**: 45–9.

Kelton, B. (1976) *An analysis of the relationship between pupil control ideology held by professional staff children's belies in internal-external control*. Doctoral dissertation, University of Connecticut.

Mar'i, S. (1978) *Arab Education in Israel.* New York: Syracuse University Press.

Mitchell, C. (1974) *Pupil control ideologies of teachers and principals in small and large schools.* Doctoral dissertation, University of Illinois at Urbana-Champaign.

Murphy, S. (1977) *A comparison of the pupil control ideology of parents and school staff.* Doctoral dissertation, University of Arkansas.

Richardson, A. and Payne, M. (1988) The pupil control ideology of elementary and secondary school teachers: some Caribbean findings. *Education* **108**: 409–12.

Packard, J. (1988) The pupil control studies. In N. Boyan (ed.) *Handbook of Research on Educational Administration.* NY: Longman: 185–207.

Seefa, D. (1981) *An analysis of the pupil control ideology of principals and teachers in public elementary schools in the province of Sukhothai, Thailand.* Doctoral dissertation, North Texas State University.

Shavit, Y. (1990) Segregation, tracking, and the educational attainment of minorities: Arabs and oriental Jews in Israel. *American Sociological Review* **55**: 115–26.

Smyth, W. (1977) Pupil control ideology and the salience of teacher characteristics. *The Journal of Educational Administration* **15**: 238–48.

Voege, C. (1979) *Personal values, educational attitudes, and attitudes toward pupil control, of staffs and boards of religious-affiliated style and the level of pupil control ideology.* Doctoral dissertation, New York University.

Willower, D., Eidell, T. and Hoy, W. (1973) *The School and Pupil Control Ideology.* 2nd edn Pennsylvania State Studies No. 24. University Park, PA: Pennsylvania State University.

Zureik, E. (1979) *The Palestinians in Israel: A Study in Internal Colonialism.* London: Routledge and Kegan Paul.

4 The Kibbutz Children's Society and Cultural Diversity: Lessons from the Past and Present

YUVAL DROR

Introduction

Degania, the first kibbutz, was founded in 1910. Three kibbutz movements, Hakibbutz Ha'artzi, Hakibbutz Hameuhad, and Hever Hakvutzot were established in the mid-1920s. (Our article omits the Religious Kibbutz Movement.) A generation later, in 1951, an ideological and political schism led Hever Hakvutzot and part of Hakibbutz Hameuhad to unite to form Ihud Hakvutzot v'Hakibbutzim. Another thirty years would elapse until all three would form the United Kibbutz Movement.

The children's society, in which all the children of every kibbutz are divided into age groups that were an all-embracing framework for their lives, dates from the first kibbutz schools of the 1920s. Kibbutz education was part of the Labor Trend, the educational system of the Histadrut (Federation of Jewish Labor) that coexisted with other trends between 1921 and 1953, when a national education system replaced them. The kibbutz children's society was a model emulated throughout the Labor Trend and beyond it: hence its importance. The children's society became the youth society for adolescent age groups, but in this article the term "children's society" will be used inclusively for kibbutz children in general. The children's society institutions conducted the classes and work of its members on a day-to-day basis. As a group they marked local and national events, historical and current, together with or parallel to the adult society. While the framework was first and foremost local, it was also regional and national. Support came from local kibbutz education, from frameworks for children and youth in the kibbutzim in the area, from special projects, and from summer camps that were part of national youth movements.

In the 1950s, with the establishment of regional secondary schools, came regional children's societies, part of the day school system of what was to become the United Kibbutz Movement, or of the Kibbutz Artzi residential schools, further to the political left, which maintains its independence while cooperating ever more closely in education with the United Kibbutz Movement. This trend accelerated as many kibbutz elementary schools became regional schools in the last decade, *inter alia* because of the financial and social crisis of the kibbutzim.

We have then, a children's society as a sort of two-dimensional model. Activities take place in school, in the youth movement or in supplementary education (also called semi-nonformal education), and at the same time in the local and regional community: at times they are even nationwide. In the past we presented such a model for values education based on the kibbutz education in general (Dror 1995a). Here we apply it to the children's society, but go beyond it.

Kibbutz or communal education is a unique model, part and parcel of the kibbutz as a communal phenomenon, and at the same time deeply influenced by the educational and social system in Israel as a whole. Four main sources nourish the kibbutz educational system: the national liberation movement of the Jewish people (the Zionist movement, with its varied trends); the social liberation movement (varieties of socialism); the progressive education movement that developed in Europe and in the United States at the beginning of the century; and the free youth movement, German in origin, with its developments in the Jewish youth movements of Eretz Israel, as pre-state Israel was called in Hebrew (Dror 1995b). Zionist and socialist influence predominated in educational and curriculum content, but teaching methods as well were adapted to the values of settlement, secular Judaism, work and equality. Progressive education and the free youth movement affected kibbutz methods, for the most part in combination with European and socialist education. Kibbutz education principles, like those of Labor Trend education in general, combined all four sources, and were and are:

1 The child's personal and social development is the point of departure, no selection being applied. The community is responsible for educating and giving an equal opportunity to all its children.
2 The "educational environment" and "educational teaching". There is continuous daily contact with the community and its Zionist-socialist values, which include education through and for work.
3 Involvement of all those engaged in the educational process: child care workers, teachers, counsellors, local educational committees and their coordinators. To a lesser extent, parents and children are also included.
4 Combining classroom studies with social life and work, as well as formal with nonformal elements in kindergarten and especially in school curricula.
5 Individual and group learning is active, emphasizing the interdisciplinary approach, the worth of work and education for work.
6 The school is democratic. Students are autonomous in the children's society, teachers enjoy autonomy and local and national groups work together on curriculum development. Teachers have a close relationship with their students (Dror 1994).

This chapter describes and examines ideal and reality in kibbutz children's societies past and present, on the basis of activity frameworks and the circles of community in which they operate. Our main purpose is to arrive at a common denominator for past and present local and regional models of the kibbutz children's society, noting the cultural difference between the kibbutz and the life outside it. First we describe the growth of communal education frameworks. Then we detail the main children's society activities in the kibbutzim, the region, the youth movement, and in education for work and social integration. Finally, we evaluate the success of the children's society according to how far it

has put into practice the principles of kibbutz education. We also present ten educational dilemmas connected with kibbutz children's societies and their treatment of multi-cultural values education. Kibbutz ways of resolving these dilemmas afford lessons worth learning and applying outside those communities and beyond the borders of Israel.

Historical background: the growth of communal education frameworks

Socialization for kibbutz life is carried out through single-age educational groups, within which children learn from infancy how to live a collective, egalitarian life. In the past these groups served both as kibbutz school classes and as the basis for the children's society. These were primary groups, directed by child care workers who were responsible for all the children's food, clothing and health needs. To this day, nursery age groups number no more than 4 to 8. In the kindergarten, different age levels come together, child care workers assisting teachers to organize activities and care for the children. At school age, the day nurseries and kindergartens become children's houses, in which the group carries out the principle of combining the elements involved in education.

The all-embracing children's house of the past served one or sometimes two contiguous age groups as the place where they ate and slept; it was also the classroom and part of the local school, their social club and usually the meeting place for their youth movement. The child care worker was the intermediary between students, teachers, counsellors and parents, taking care of all the children's ongoing physical needs. In time, particularly in the 1970s and 1980s, there was a movement away from communal sleeping in nurseries, kindergartens, and children's houses, towards sleeping in the parental home. Concurrently, kibbutzim tended more strongly towards youth houses for junior and senior high school students in the individual kibbutz. At this time only some of the Kibbutz Artzi settlements had made the transition to family sleeping accommodation, and the transition from children's to youth houses in individual settlements was accompanied by the move to the residential secondary school of the region. The child care worker played an important role even among adolescents, though she was now less concerned with physical care and acted more as an intermediary between the youngsters and educational and social elements that touched on their studies, social life and work. The transition between communal and family sleeping accommodations was completed in the United Kibbutz Movement in the 1980s, while it grew stronger in the Kibbutz Artzi.

In 1991 came the Gulf War. Children spent the nights in sealed rooms in the homes of their parents, who (in the Kibbutz Artzi) afterwards refused to "return" them to communal sleeping arrangements. As a result, the Kibbutz Artzi completed the transition despite the lack of suitable accommodation. Throughout the kibbutz movement, the center of gravity in communal education shifted from the children's house to the parental home on one hand and the school, generally a district institution, on the other. The status of the child care worker diminished to the point where it no longer attracted kibbutz members, and the role had partly to be filled by staff hired from outside.

The revolutionary transition to sleeping with the family and the shortage of child care workers, and the economic difficulties of the 1980s and 1990s had a significant result. Age groups in the children's houses were amalgamated, even though socialization to kibbutz life, from the nursery years, had been designed to take place in small groups. The new groups had an age spread of two or three years, and were twice or even three times as large. This made for greater social variety, and more independence from the child care worker who previously was responsible for all the physical needs of a small group of children. It also reduced the influence of the primary peer group. Since most kibbutz children now attend regional schools from the primary grades, the children's house is no longer the all-embracing home in which the children spend almost the entire day. In most kibbutzim the children no longer have breakfast or dinner there but rather in the communal dining hall. Clothing is now generally a parental responsibility, so that child care workers are free to take on educational roles. What was once home in every sense has now become mainly a social club for limited after school hours: the noon rest period and afternoon recreation, before the children go to play, relax or sleep in their parents' homes.

In adolescence, too, changes are shifting the center of gravity to the family home. With the increase in deviant behavior in recent years, many kibbutzim have continued the practice of sleeping in the family home through adolescence, the youth houses having become social and cultural clubs, like the new style children's houses in scope. The educational institutions of the Kibbutz Artzi maintain their youth houses as full residential schools for this age group. In some regions the residential high school has become a day school with separate dormitories available, and the additional options of local youth houses or even living with parents until the end of Grade 12, as is the practice in the other kibbutz movements.

Changes in the children's and youth houses are evident not only in multi-age groups, but also in opening up to children from outside. In many kibbutzim, even nursery and pre-school groups admit outside children whose parents like the environment, to what is in effect a day care center. Residential schools admit day students, who often take part in extracurricular activities as well. Many are children of former members and others from a socio-economic status similar to that of the kibbutz, if only because their parents can meet the cost of communal education with its relatively high student–staff ratio. A larger number of outside children and youth groups come from families with serious problems: this type of student has been educated in kibbutzim since the 1930s, and will be described separately. Day students at the kibbutz school are a far-reaching innovation. This brings financial advantages that make it possible to broaden educational options, and enables kibbutz children to compare their own lives to those of a different peer group. The original kibbutz goal of raising its children away from "harmful" outside influences, has therefore changed in the relatively limited frameworks of these educational groups.

The kibbutz school, originally intended for the ideological education of its own children, faced from the start the dilemma of the desirable size for a commune. Where is the boundary between the need for an ideological community to be small and autonomous, and its need to cooperate with its surroundings in order to get services and to exert some influence there? The historic Kibbutz Hameuhad favored the school at home for all age groups and in all settlements, one that would be deeply involved with its local community. This model was only partially successful during the British mandate, which ended in 1948. From the 1950s there was a gradual transition to cooperation on a regional scale. On the other hand, the Hashomer Hatzair ideal was, from the start, a national residential institution in which all the youth of the movement would be educated, an independent "republic of youth" similar to their kibbutzim. This model lasted only thirteen years, after which it was replaced by smaller regional institutions which began to unite with their neighbors in the 1940s. In Hever Hakvutzot and its successor from 1951, Ihud Hakvutzot v'Hakibbutzim, there was no one obligatory model: pragmatic solutions regarding their secondary schools always predominated. These were usually regional, with varying degrees of cooperation that might include moshav and even city children (Dror 1995c). In retrospect, pragmatic solutions appear to have been the right ones, as they adapted to existing conditions, an attitude that prevails today in the entire kibbutz movement, even as regards elementary schools.

The main children's society activities in the kibbutzim

The children's society – local framework to regional association

Children's societies in the kibbutzim were very much alike from the 1920s to the 1960s. The general meeting was the supreme body, like the kibbutz general meeting. It made rules, enforced them and acted as judge, usually with the help of committees and office holders responsible to various cultural groups. Regulations were not overly specific. Work rosters for the children's residence and farm, as for work in the kibbutz itself, were drawn up with the help of the adults. Internal communication was carried out through a newspaper and a bulletin board, but most communication was immediate and direct. Groups were divided into junior (7–10), intermediate (11–15) and senior (16–18) age levels, like the divisions of the youth movements. Where numbers were small there were only two divisions. The older groups guided and directed activities in the younger one. Ceremonies and holiday observances from the children's society, its links to adult society in the kibbutz, and its youth movement activities were emulated in other Labor Trend schools, with the necessary adaptations.

The kibbutz children's society, past and present, had its central and occasionally overlapping goals:

1 Preparation for the direct democracy of the kibbutz, principally through their own varied and largely autonomous administrative bodies.

2 Preparation for adult life by helping the youngster find an appropriate place in the children's and youth society. This was a moratorium experience between the life of a child, protected by his or her parents, and competitive adult society.

3 Transmitting additional direct and indirect messages pertaining to values: combining studies and social life with work from an early age, and observing national and class holiday and other ceremonies.

Today there are various children's society models, adapted to their place and their activities. Local societies of elementary and secondary school children may complement those organized by regional authorities. The underlying assumption is that formal studies are the responsibility of the district school, the care of the child is that of the family, and that social education should be the professional responsibility of the settlements, with regional help. When some Hashomer Hatzair residential schools became day schools, their social activities too came under the aegis of the individual kibbutzim and the regional authorities.

The local model has several common features. The older age groups direct the younger children in Grades 4–6, even though the children's society is distinctly separate from the youth society. The coordinator for the youth groups works with their care worker, just as the child care workers for the elementary school group, with the education coordinator's help, are responsible for the children's social activities. Parents have assumed most of the care workers' former duties, and now serve as the main link between child and school. The education coordinator is generally an experienced care worker or teacher who serves as a link between school staff members, with whom she plans activities, maintaining contact with other groups, both in the school and elsewhere. Children now take community meals in the adult dining hall. The main communal meal is at noon, as many children prefer a light breakfast in their parents' home before they go to school. Care workers keep the children busy in the afternoon in the once all-embracing children's houses, which have now become clubrooms. They arrange transportation to sport and music groups that the children attend, and are responsible for homework and work on the children's farm. On short holidays there are special activities, and during the long vacation a summer camp, all run by the care workers.

The youth society in its own house is also directed by adult staff. The counsellor, the care worker and/or the coordinator for youth are in charge of the day-to-day operation of the clubhouse in the afternoon and evening, and of the group activities connected with the national youth movement. They help youth society office holders organize daily work, or a weekly day of work, for members, and participation in interest groups, holiday celebrations and excursions. In some kibbutzim, a teacher in the district school or another kibbutz member, is responsible for group activities and for contacts between school and parents.

Regional activities generally complement local ones, but sometimes replace it, and include rich and varied nonformal education such as:

1 youth movement activities;
2 semi nonformal activities under the aegis of the district school, for example, students' council, councils of kibbutz youth, and the development of all types of young leadership, not only for the youth movement;
3 supplementary enrichment education, weekend and vacation cultural activities, excursions, camps and sports days;
4 observance of holidays and significant current events in the community, sometimes with parental participation, community involvement through help to the elderly, to new immigrants, leadership in the local youth movement, and environmental projects;
5 active participation in such national endeavors as "Youth Says NO to Drugs" and overseas exchange programs;
6 in some districts, individual and social assistance outside the school, to marginal youth, for example helping them complete their basic education;
7 developing the professional staff necessary for the above projects – basic leadership courses, seminar days, workshops, written and audiovisual material and personal guidance at regional headquarters.

The regional framework has the advantages of integrating kibbutz children with those from other social milieus, affording social and academic variety that goes beyond that of the historic children's society, and linking all those involved in formal and nonformal educational frameworks in the kibbutzim and outside it.

Children's societies as the basis of kibbutz youth movements: from separate units to nationwide affiliation

From the first days of the Israeli state, the children's society in each kibbutz was the basic unit of the national kibbutz youth movement. From 1951 its members were part of the "Youth Division" of their respective kibbutz movements and were part of the Working and Student Youth. In the case of the Kibbutz Artzi, every educational institution to this day has its own Hashomer Hatzair branch. But the organizational setup has changed somewhat. Some local children's societies act as district branches of the Working and Student Youth and are directly linked to regional headquarters, no longer going through the generational division of the kibbutz movement. Hashomer Hatzair, too, has reinforced links between its kibbutz and city branches, making for greater educational and social integration. Parents encourage this: many know the importance of the city branches, either because they were once members, or they served as leaders sent from the kibbutz.

Since 1951, the United Kibbutz Movement has argued whether youth movement membership should be compulsory for their children. After the schism, the Youth Division was seen as an organization within the Working Youth, run by adults and complementing the school as a preparation for kibbutz life. As such, membership in it was compulsory. A contrary attitude, however, developed over the years, one that defined the Youth Division as a separate youth movement that cooperated with others of its own choice. This meant that membership in the youth movement of the kibbutz organization was voluntary.

It was quite different from school and based on voluntary regional and national frameworks that did not necessarily educate to kibbutz life. The dilemma continues as an argument about the link between youth movement and school, with viewpoints differing. Neither solution in its absolute form solved the problem, so the two were combined at the educational council of the United Kibbutz Movement at Yifat in 1986, and have been in effect since. The 1990s have seen the comprehensive "movement for youth" attitude as relating to all kibbutz children and as complementary to the school. There is also an optional activity, regionally and nationally organized, and designed to develop the future kibbutz leadership with the help of the movement's educational centers at Efal, Givat Haviva, Oranim and elsewhere. Combining the approaches relates fairly closely to the dilemma likely to be with us in the future, presented further on, of complementary education versus the youth movement, reality and ideal.

Education for work as a children's society activity

Education for work is an authentic example of the unique, two-way community education at the kibbutz, combining the basic elements of society, studies and work. For the kibbutz, work was a basic value of Zionist socialism, drawing first from Jewish sources and then from cooperative and egalitarian philosophies. Hence, its continuing and central importance. The kibbutz was influenced, too, by progressive education approaches, as well as by the economic need for children's work, especially seasonal work, as on farms everywhere. Today, too, students, particularly from the senior grades are "drafted" for quite a few days of farm work, although in some schools work time is eroded as matriculation examinations approach.

Kirschensteiner's and Dewey's progressive, activity-oriented education motivates education in the kibbutz, as did the heritage of the free youth movements of Europe. Work brings in the investigative approach, notably in the natural sciences, in individual, and in multi-age team and class groups. It also activates the educational group, making it possible for older groups to develop leadership by directing the younger ones, in a comprehensive children's society.

Work also provides a balance between intellectual and physical activities, as technological skills are acquired and all the child's senses are activated. It makes it possible to develop all types of children, including those who do not shine in theoretical subjects, and all facets of the individual personality. Work develops responsibility, autonomy and the desire to contribute without financial reward. The work of kibbutz youth contains twelve educational characteristics that have survived from the Mandatory period to this day, despite the pressure of secondary school studies. These divide into four groups, each embodying some link between work and the children's society.

1 **Time frame:** Work starts in the kindergarten with half an hour of daily chores, including the

garden and the care of the children's pets. By secondary school, the children are working six to eight hours a week, as part of their class timetable. In the senior classes they work a full day and study five days a week.

2 **Variety:** Students encounter different educational models. Besides parents and teachers there are the counsellors in charge of their social life, the coordinator of the branch they work in and their adult co-workers.

3 **Widening community circles:** Children can vary their work in the surrounding community as they grow up. They get to know not only peer group, children's society and kibbutz community, but from secondary school they are involved in regional work that has ideological, national and social implications.

4 **Curriculum:** Students' work has parallels to their classroom studies, and is integrated with them, as the children's society, work and studies are combined. Like their other activities, work is organized by the children's society. From elementary school, a student in each class or group of classes fits classmates into the work roster, coordinating between the adult kibbutz members in charge of production branches and the children who are to work in them (Bar-Lev and Dror 1995).

Integrating outside children and youth groups

Because the kibbutz is pluralistic, and all components of Jewish society in Israel are represented there, so is its children's society. Moreover, the outside children, taken in individually or in youth groups that parallel its own, make for a more extensive educational use of the children's society system. Children and adolescents have come into the kibbutz individually or through Youth Aliyah from 1933 onwards, on the eve of the Nazi period in Europe. Generally, they are from a problem family background and weaker socio-economic strata, and the kibbutz becomes an alternative home for them. Most of the children from 6 to 14 years of age are absorbed through the Training Program for Israel's Children, founded in 1943 by Recha Freier, who as early as 1932, before Youth Aliyah, sent children from Berlin to Israel. The condition for taking in an individual child is finding a kibbutz foster family that will be his or her family in every respect, and a reasonable chance that the child will find a place scholastically and socially among his kibbutz peers. In 1973, the Training Program came under the Ministry of Education's jurisdiction, but the scope of its activities has not changed. Some 150 boys and girls are brought up each year in foster families in 70 kibbutzim (a quarter of all 270 kibbutzim). Of these, 90 per cent remain until they enlist in the army at 18, which is an indication of the success of this project (Nevo 1994).

Youth Aliya began to function in 1934 with the arrival of youth groups at Ein Harod and the religious kibbutz, Yavne. These were made up of adolescents of the same age and until the late 1950s, numbered forty to fifty; now they are about half that size. Generally they study in separate classes in the kibbutz or in kibbutz secondary schools. Like their kibbutz peers, each such group has a counsellor and a care worker, besides the individual adoptive family. Members sleep in the same house, near that of their kibbutz peers, and have some joint social activities. Until the establishment of Israel as a state, the educational concept of Youth Aliyah combined studies, social life and work, with the kibbutz as an educating community, which the youth group growing up there would eventually join. The kibbutz then was the most desirable educational milieu along with moshavim and youth villages. Until the 1951 split in the kibbutz movement, 60 per cent of all Youth Aliyah wards were brought up there! After the state was established, the Youth Aliyah population came to consist for the most part of local adolescents with family problems. Immigrant youth groups came only with waves of immigration. From the early 1950s when 7,000 adolescents were growing up in some 150 youth groups in the kibbutzim, there was a steady and significant decline until the early 1970s, to 1,450 in 57 groups. There were several reasons for this. The schism, and the exodus from the kibbutzim after 1948, made the kibbutz movement less ready to take in outside children, as after long years of immigrant absorption it became more and more difficult to find foster families and the right kind of educators. Experience had shown that relatively few of these children actually joined the kibbutz, while the cost of maintaining youth groups soared. For the

Israeli children from weak backgrounds there were now alternatives where they could get vocational training or even full matriculation, which at the time the kibbutz movement did not provide. The situation was exacerbated by the educational reform, and the residential schools for talented children established for students from development areas. When the kibbutz movement once more took on national endeavors after the 1967 war, the number of outside children rose to 2,000 in about a decade. From the mid-1980s, with the recurrence of all the factors in operation in the state's first years, besides economic and social crisis in the kibbutz movement, the number once again dropped to a mere 1,000. In the 1990s came youth groups from the former Soviet Union, preparing for their families' immigration, and numbers rose once again, with 1,600 youngsters in 50 groups. The kibbutz contribution to absorbing the wards of Youth Aliyah stands at 60,000, a quarter of the total immigrant youth over more than sixty years, were educated in 170 of the country's 270 kibbutzim. Four thousand joined kibbutzim when they grew up; they founded twenty-five new kibbutzim, and were among the founders of forty others (Wolins and Gottesmann 1971, Gottesmann 1987).

The kibbutz movement's contribution in this area cannot be measured simply in numbers. Quantitative and qualitative research done in the 1970s and 1980s on members, present and past, of children's societies in the kibbutz and outside it, point to the value of kibbutz education in the lives of Youth Aliyah children. From the findings of Avnat, Rosner and Bareli (1988) and Kohlberg and his colleagues in research at the Anne Frank Haven in Kibbutz Sasa – to be discussed in our conclusion – these children have adjusted better to adult life, and become better citizens and more loyal Israelis. They have developed greater ability in moral judgement than siblings or peers not educated in the kibbutz. Even children's society graduates who have left, place a high value on the kibbutz contribution to their education, especially the relationship with their teachers, their adoptive parents, and members of the kibbutz in general (Ben-Peretz, Giladi and Dror 1992).

The children's society and kibbutz educational ideals: Failings and conclusions

1 Education of the individual child as a point of departure

The pluralistic kibbutz school is non-selective even today, allowing for individual solutions even for socially and scholastically deviant children. Avrahami and Getz (1994), who studied secondary schools in two kibbutz movements, again confirm this, despite the conspicuous focus in the schools today on formal education and preparation for matriculation. The individual kibbutz, responsible for educating all its children, finds individual solutions outside the district school for those having special difficulties, while at the same time keeping them in their original children's society. Larger schools and more comprehensive curricula, as previously stated, make more pluralistic education possible in Israel today, and the basis for this is local and regional children's groups and societies.

2 Educational environment, educational teaching and close, continuous community links

On the basis of a prolonged visit to kibbutzim in 1982, Jack Quarter (1986) developed a model that he called Kibbutzim versus Socialism. "Pragmatic" kibbutz children sense loyalty and emotional attachment to a particular kibbutz, and not to the socialistic way of life that is insufficiently clear to them, and they left in large numbers in the crises of the 1970s. Alongside this problem evident in numerous studies, as yet unresolved, there are achievements: prolonging the education stage past the age of 18, and establishing nationwide young adult societies as a continuation of the children's society.

Since the 1950s, the kibbutz has maintained a stratum of "extended youth" to which a third to a half the 18- and 19-year-olds belong when they do a community service year before joining the army. Here they serve as youth movement leaders in the kibbutzim and the cities. Some experience life in special task-oriented communes that assist new or weak kibbutzim; physical work and group leadership in an urban commune in a development town; or combine leadership in the movement with

theoretical studies in communes near kibbutz educational centers like Oranim and Efal.

Avrahami's research shows that value related and collectivist motives for undertaking the communal service year combine with personal ones of seeking meaningful work and comparing kibbutz and city life (Avrahami and Dar 1993). This is very positive, and many young people from the cities have joined the communes. Moreover, since the 1980s there have been nationwide educational groups of young adults from the kibbutz and city, for those who have finished army service. Their purposes are the same as those of the younger group, and some are even direct continuations. In many cases their activities parallel university studies, even on the same campus as is the case in Oranim. Some participants continue these activities even beyond the age boundaries of youth as members of urban kibbutzim, or in the educational centers of the kibbutz movement. Here there are weekly study workshops of a day and a half, that deal with educational, political and Jewish-Zionist themes. Participants direct younger groups of secular Jews in formal and non-formal frameworks. There are workshops and continuing education courses in Judaism and society, traditional festivals and holidays in Israeli culture; "Bar Mitzva" programs for boys and girls, parents and educators in town and country and Jewish studies in the kibbutzim and other communities. Such subjects may form the basis of new school curricula and programs for new immigrants. Most participants grew up in youth movements and kibbutz children's societies, and in effect are continuing these in group activities with a multi-age structure, while enforcing their multi-cultural aspects.

3 Bringing in participants in the educational process
4 Combining studies, formal and nonformal, with social life and work

These activities have moved from the all-embracing children's house of the past to the district school. There, Avrahami and Getz (1994) found they do not always take place. Despite the difficulties involved, the process of bringing all those connected with education into the process, and combining its formal and the nonformal aspects, which is unique to the kibbutz, has nationwide and worldwide significance. Kahane (1983) cites the numerous socialization agents, besides parents and teachers, to whom the adolescent can turn, as characteristics of the coordination within the kibbutz, characteristics that have broader implications. Marshak (1980) examined the parent–child relationship in the United States during the Rebellion of Youth period using the kibbutz as a possible model for a stable application of youth movement culture. Comparatively speaking, she found that the rebellion was substantially less in the kibbutz for two reasons. First, from an early age, identification foci were divided among parents, the care worker, peer group members and other significant adults, including teachers. Research supplies substantial proof that in many areas, parental advice to adolescent children in the kibbutz carries weight. Second, the children's society of the youth movement offers kibbutz adolescents relative autonomy.

The children's society, educating to work, has significance beyond the kibbutz. In international terms, the process is called, *inter alia*, "work education", "career education" and "work experience". Experts in the field, whether in Europe, the United States, Canada or the former Soviet Union, regard the ideal model as a combination of studies and work, with at least some practical experience. Differently from those countries, where the reality is mainly a curriculum and limited practical experience, in the kibbutz work is studied through Zionist and settlement history, but mainly through practical experience from an early age and in varied settings, as an individual and on teams chosen by the children's society. The kibbutz child is educated toward a future career by choosing a branch of the adult economy and exposure to the complexity of social and community life there, not merely by classroom simulations and discussions (Bar-Lev and Dror 1995).

5 *Active individual and group learning, interdisciplinary emphasis*

Nonformal, active teaching and educational methods as applied in the "theme" and "process" methods are now a thing of the past. However, much teaching initiative still exists, due to teacher autonomy. To the credit of the kibbutz is the initiative taken in secondary schools despite the pressure of matriculation examinations. An example that could be followed elsewhere is the computerized greenhouse, an up-to-date, sophisticated version of the children's farm. The first such project was started by the artist and educator Avital Geva in 1977 at Mevo Eron, the Kibbutz Artzi regional educational institution. It combines agriculture, service to industry and a computer system for theoretical studies, stressing teamwork and research skills. Some fifty children from Grades 7–12 participate, and may credit individual work hours there to the school curriculum requirements. The greenhouse with its multi-age work teams that prepare projects connected with their studies under the direction of adult experts, serves the kibbutz. Experimental crops planted in the greenhouse aids kibbutz agriculture and the community as a whole. Moreover, computer programs are prepared for branches of agriculture and of local industry, and computer services offered to the kibbutzim that are partners in the school. Some teams work with farming and industrial specialists outside the kibbutz, including university people assaying new systems with the help of youngsters who are computer experts. The model has been tried in other Israeli schools, and was presented as an example of educational activity combined with environmental art at the Biennali in Venice in 1993 and at the Kunsthalle Museum (Dusseldorf, Germany) in 1996 (Dror and Bar-Lev 1992).

6 *The democratic school – student and teacher autonomy*

By the very nature of the kibbutz school, relationships between educators and students are close and informal. Research has shown, however, that it has been overdone and interferes with the demands of formal studies. Particularly in the residential institutions of the Kibbutz Artzi, boundaries between the formal and informal tend to blur. The variety in the children's society today indeed expresses student autonomy, but in fact, social activity in the schools as well as in many kibbutzim and some districts has actually declined. On the other hand, there has been an increase in the number and variety of educational frameworks over the past twenty years. The international lessons are that it is now possible to attend formal and nonformal activities outside the community, regional and national as well as local frameworks are available, new school populations have contributed to the increase in size from nursery age to young adulthood, and there is two-directional interaction between the educational system and the community (Dror 1993).

From an international perspective, the Anne Frank Haven at Kibbutz Sasa in upper Galilee has been studied as an outstanding example. In the 1970s and 1980s Kohlberg, a luminary in the moral education field, investigated the integration of kibbutz youth with Youth Aliyah groups with his students, who later continued their own independent research. The moral development of the "disadvantaged" Youth Aliyah children, was close to that of the kibbutz children, and substantially different from their siblings and peers not educated in the kibbutz. The "secret" proved to be the sustained work of both groups of youth, with their adult counsellors, in translating day-to-day problems into moral terms. Kohlberg and his team learned from the kibbutz example and the children's society, where the educators developed their own system, the "Just Community" system based on the democratic school, where students and teachers together carry out value related activities. This system is applied in Israeli schools outside the kibbutz, and in schools throughout the world. In 1980 the Anne Frank Haven was studied again, this time by an Israeli group from Haifa University, who found another generally applicable principle for the success of integration there: local and regional communities were involved in the activities of the kibbutz and outside children, the first year serving the two groups to get acquainted, in the interests of cultural pluralism (Dror 1995d).

Conclusion: what can be learned from multi-cultural values education at the kibbutz children's society?

The kibbutz children's society, as stated before, operates as a two-dimensional model: activity frameworks in the kibbutz and outside it distributed through local, regional and national communities. We now develop the theoretical model, presenting ten dilemmas and kibbutz solutions to them as lessons generally applicable both outside the kibbutz and outside Israel. The first two are directly linked to the two-dimensional model, and the others are related to them.

1 Nonformal social education in the school and outside it

The kibbutz example shows that variety involving social education both in and outside the school is

the preferred solution. There are unique advantages to a children's society that supplements school activities, which differ from the advantages of a youth movement based on the children's society or on community centers.

2 The local or regional children's society

The prevailing and desirable tendency is to combine frameworks, with a trend towards increased regional activity. Besides the regional branches of the youth movements in the kibbutz, there are nationwide activities linked to semi-nonformal education in district schools: excursions, study days and national conventions with an ideological theme in Grades 11 and 12, all of which are the responsibility of the school social coordinators and carried out in cooperation with kibbutz education departments.

3 Social education for all and/or selecting an elite (i.e. semi- or completely nonformal social education)

Traditionally, the kibbutz has tended to combine supplementary education, which has a broader popular base, with the more élitist youth movement. This continues today, with the increase and growth of regional and national frameworks. This formula is recommended for social activity in a varied population of children, adolescents and young adults.

4 A role for the children's society in studies and work, or just a social role

The kibbutz experience indicates that combining different types of activities carries a great educational potential, so is suitable for a pluralistic society. Even if no work is available in non-kibbutz frameworks, combining the children's society with classroom studies is essential, as the Anne Frank Haven and the "Just Society" system indicate.

5 Children's and youth societies: a school or community responsibility

Despite the basic perception of social life, studies and work as linked, and perhaps because it is so difficult to apply it today, the schools of the 1990s concentrate on teaching and studying. At the same time, the kibbutzim, with aid from their regions, are responsible for social life after school hours. This dilemma does not appear to have a solution, except in adaptation to the schools and communities of a specific region, even though combining the children's society with life in the classroom has the great advantage of concentrating professional and financial resources.

6 *The total residential framework as against the day school*

Is a total school, like the Kibbutz Artzi residential institution, with the traditional children's society, preferable to a day school that has only a students' council? Here too the answer lies in adaptation of the school to the communities involved, not forgetting the obvious educational advantages of a residential institution in which all types of children's societies work together.

7 *Activities for children, adolescents and young adults*

Kibbutz experience indicates that in this era of prolonged maturation, there is room for children's, youth and young adult societies with progressive degrees of pluralism. Nonformal activities take place outside the kibbutz, particularly during childhood and adolescence. The young adult stratum can be added at the student level, in times when so many people seek to acquire at least one university degree.

8 *Combined or separate authorities in children's society education for democracy*

Here the kibbutz can serve as a negative example. The children's society meeting is generally the legislative, judiciary and executive power, although these are separated in all committees. It seems desirable to adapt more at different levels to the separation of powers, following the practice in the democratic institutions of the adult society that it emulates, as a better expression of social pluralism.

9 *Loose and open structure or institutionalized children's society*

Kibbutz experience shows the advantages of structural flexibility, changes and larger frameworks which have developed in recent years, *vis-à-vis* the pluralistic society outside. At the same time, each stage requires some institutionalization to assure continuity since staff turnover, like membership changes, are frequent and rapid in children's societies.

10 *Protecting insiders or opening up*

The kibbutz children's society, despite earlier tendencies to live within themselves, has opened up to enable members to meet peer groups with other life-styles. This integrative and pluralistic principle was applied in the absorption of outside children and youth groups and in broadening school and youth movement frameworks, formal and nonformal, as befits children's societies that are in principle pluralistic and integrative.

Kibbutz children's society experience, including the drawbacks and emphasizing the advantages that research has affirmed, offers varied practical models, applicable outside the kibbutz and beyond Israel. The dilemmas mentioned and their resolution against the background of kibbutz reality, serve as a kind of educational and social laboratory that points out directions both in research and in the actual practice of education.

References

Avnat, A., Rosner, M. and Bareli, C. (1988) The influence of kibbutz education on second generation immigrant youth of oriental origin. In M. Gottesmann (ed.) *Cultural Transition – the Case of Immigrant Youth*. Jerusalem: Magness Press, The Hebrew University: 121–39.

Avrahami, A. and Dar, Y. (1993) Collectivistic and individualistic motives among kibbutz youth volunteering for community service. *Journal of Youth and Adolescence* **22** (6): 697–714.

Avrahami, A. and Getz, S. (1994) *Kibbutz School in the Tension of Change*. Efal: Yad Tabenkin (Hebrew).

Bar-Lev, M. and Dror, Y. (1995) Education for work in the kibbutz as a means towards personal, social and learning fulfilment. *Journal of Moral Education* **24** (3): 259–72.

Ben-Peretz, M., Giladi, M. and Dror, Y. (1992) The Anne Frank Haven: a case study of an alternative educational program in an integrative kibbutz setting. *International Review of Education* **38** (1): 47–63.

Dror, Y. (1993) Community and activity dimensions: essentials for the moral and values educator. *Journal of Moral Education* **22** (2): 125–37.

Dror, Y. (1994) Social education – bridging between education and social systems: Owen's utopian education and kibbutz education today – a comparison. *Utopian Studies* **5** (2): 87–102.

Dror, Y. (1995a) (ed.) The kibbutz experience: implications for moral education. *Journal of Moral Education* **24** (3). Special issue.

Dror, Y. (1995b) The kibbutz children's society – ideal and reality. *Journal of Moral Education* **24** (3): 273–88.

Dror, Y. (1995c) School size as a function of uniqueness, autonomy, integration and comprehensiveness: an historical model with current implications. *Journal of Educational Administration and History* **27** (1): 35–50.

Dror, Y. (1995d) The Anne Frank Haven in an Israeli kibbutz. *Adolescence* **30** (119): 617–29.

Dror, Y. and Bar-Lev, M. (1992) "Education and Work" in Israel: a comparison of kibbutz and non-kibbutz organization and ideology. *British Journal of Education and Work* **5** (2): 19–42.

Gottesmann, M. (1987) *Youth Aliyah: Continuity and Cange*. Tel Aviv: Tcherikover (Hebrew).

Kahane, R. (1983) The committed: preliminary reflections on the impact of kibbutz socialization pattern on adolescents. In E. Krausz (ed.) *The Sociology of the Kibbutz*. New Brunswick (USA) and London (UK): Transaction Books, 319–29.

Marshak, M. (1980) *Parent–Child Interaction and Youth Rebellion*. New York: Gardner Press.

Nevo, M. (ed.) (1994) *The Training Program for Israel's Children 1943–1993*. Jerusalem: The Ministry of Education and Culture (Hebrew).

Quarter, J. (1986) Intergenerational discontinuity in the Israeli kibbutz. *Communal Studies* **6**: 1–27.

Wolins, M. and Gottesmann, M. (eds) (1971) *Group Care: The Educational Path of Youth Aliyah*. New York: Gordon and Breach.

5 Adolescence, Education and Personal Values in Five Cultures

CYRIL SIMMONS

Introduction

The aim of this chapter is to seek to understand the personal and moral values of young people from five countries in the context of their diverse educational and cultural experiences. This will necessitate some discussion of the relationship between developing concepts of adolescence and education in England and the United States, differing educational systems designed for young people in Japan, Saudi Arabia and Arab-Israel, and the expressed values of adolescents in five countries.

Adolescence and education in Europe and The United States

Adolescence is a period of life which, throughout history, has begun with rapid physical growth and has been accompanied by less obvious but equally dynamic sexual, social and cognitive developments. However, the adolescent growth spurt, the onset of periods in girls, voice deepening in boys and, in non-Muslim societies, the first experience of sexual intercourse in both sexes have taken place earlier in the latter part of the present century than in the earlier (Rutter and Smith 1995). This quickening of the pace of adolescent physical development in the twentieth century has been accompanied by an equally speedy maturation of the *idea* of adolescence as a distinctive stage of human development characterized by turbulence and requiring special attention from educationists and other agents of society.

The 'invention' of adolescence – Jean Jacques Rousseau

In Europe in the eighteenth century by the time young people had experienced puberty most had already assumed many adult roles and were used to wearing adult-style clothes and taking part in adult activities. However, for Jean Jacques Rousseau, the eighteenth century philosopher and essayist, the early initiation of young people into adult society was seen as a precocious activity and one that should be arrested rather than encouraged. Rousseau's chosen method for inhibiting adolescent development was to withdraw young people from adult town life, keep them in ignorance of sexual matters and subject them to prolonged schooling in their own homes (Boyd 1965). Rousseau, by attaching a new significance to puberty and to the education of teenagers, was signalling an end to the notion of adolescence as a seamless development from childhood to adulthood and the beginning of the idea of adolescence as an extended childhood and a delayed adulthood. But he also wished to flag up, in colourful and emotive language, his conviction that the adolescent years, far from constituting a calm passage from one stage of life to the next, comprised a transition that was full of emotional turmoil. The following passage, for example, gave strong support to the view that adolescence was necessarily and ineluctably linked with bizarre behavioural characteristics:

> Man is not meant to remain a child for ever. At the time prescribed by nature he passes out of childhood. As the fretting of the sea precedes the distant storm, this disturbing change is announced by the murmur of nascent passions. A change of mood, frequent tantrums, a constant unease of mind make the child hard to manage. He is a lion in a fever. He

mistrusts his guide and is averse to control. (op. cit.)

Nineteenth-century developments – the English public schools

Rousseau's cure for precociousness, the use of education to extend childhood and delay adulthood was, to prove perspicacious and influential. Gillis (1974), for example, maintains that 'the discovery of adolescence belonged essentially to the (English) middle classes' precisely because they sent their sons to the reformed public schools to live in school houses under the supervision of schoolmasters who were in *loco parentis* and who kept their charges from adult town life and from a knowledge of normal sexual development. By these means adolescent peer groups were isolated as far as possible from normal patterns of social development and in Gillis's own words the élite secondary school became 'the real crucible of the age-group's social and psychological qualities' (op. cit.).

Twentieth-century developments – G. Stanley Hall

Hendrick (1990) on the other hand identifies the 'crucible' not with élite nineteenth century boarding schools for the sons of the English middle classes but with the twentieth century's 'economic and social critiques of young wage-earners, and with the child-study movement, especially the work of the American psychologist G. Stanley Hall'. Hall was a prodigious and eclectic writer, as his two volume magnum opus on adolescence published in 1904 makes abundantly clear. Not surprisingly some of his most memorable ideas were drawn from Rousseau. For example, he took over not only the notion of adolescence as a time of emotional turmoil but used the German expression *Sturm und Drang*, with its literary connotations of revolt against convention, to dignify it. Further he followed Rousseau in declaring that young people were 'leaping rather than growing into maturity' (op. cit.) and that one solution to this precocious behaviour was to withdraw them from town life, prolong their childhood and extend their education. Hall's writings and lectures, therefore, were a 'crucible' for a powerful mixture of ideas that inspired a whole generation of teachers, doctors, social administrators, youth workers and parents

with the belief that adolescence was not only a social fact but one that possessed a new scientific vocabulary eminently suitable for the twentieth century. In Hendrick's words Hall 'offered an analysis which provided a comprehensive explanation of youth while simultaneously telling the professions that they were imperative for its proper development' (Hendrick 1990). In addition, Hall broadened the concept of adolescence to embrace not only pupils attending élite public schools but also working-class lads or 'boy labour' as he called them.

Adolescent girls

As these new concepts developed it became clear that adolescent girls were perceived very differently from boys. Thus, in the second half of the nineteenth century while middle-class boys were sent to the reformed public schools to enhance their career prospects, their sisters were kept at home to be schooled in household matters by their mothers and governesses. As Dyhouse (1981) observed 'Victorians educated boys for the world, girls for the drawing room.' Again, in the early part of the twentieth century Hall's sexist views on adolescence were so blatant that they were roundly criticized in his own day. He argued, for example, 'that woman at her best never really outgrows adolescence as a man does' and that 'bookishness was a bad sign in a girl . . . and that prodigies of scholarship are always morbid' (op. cit.). Finally, however, it was working-class girls who, even when education became compulsory in England and Wales in 1880, had fewer opportunities than most young people to enjoy a moratorium between childhood and adolescence. Sharpe (1976) points out that school boards turned a blind eye to the absences of 'little mothers' who were known to be at home looking after their younger brothers and sisters while their own mothers were out at work. Furthermore, if the 'little mothers' snatched a few hours of freedom while their parents were away from home they ran the risk of being thought precocious by the social commentators of their day. Curiously working-class girls, when they became adolescent, were thought to be full of subversive energy while their middle-class counterparts were thought to be in need of rest and quiet in order to conserve their stamina. As Dyhouse comments, 'middle-class girls could be seen to have problems because they were adolescents; working-class girls because they grew up too soon' (op. cit.). It is curious that in the twentieth century the move to delay adulthood in order to curb youthful precocity was overtaken by the recognition that the very act of extending childhood created problems of its own for adolescents. To paraphrase Gillis (1974), the image of youth shifted from trouble-maker to troubled.

Adolescence and education

In the twentieth century the school leaving age was raised by a succession of education acts, which led inevitably to young people increasingly having their childhood prolonged and their adulthood delayed. This extension of education for young people was matched by parents, throughout the social spectrum, becoming increasingly willing to extend their children's years of dependence in the hope of achieving long term educational and economic benefits. It is notable, however, that the dependence of young people on their parents into late adolescence as measured by attendance at university was very much the perquisite of the middle classes in the United Kingdom. Reid (1986) aptly comments that 'post-school education presents the starkest picture of the relationship between social class and education'. Hence, at the end of the twentieth century the children of the middle classes, because of their long academic careers, are the gilded youth of the age because 'they are fully adult in every sense but the economic – namely sexual, intellectual, political' (Gillis 1974). Indeed the growth in access to co-educational universities and colleges in industrialized countries in the latter part of the twentieth century has caused some writers to speak of the end of adolescence in terms that would have been recognizable to Hall and to postulate instead the emergence of 'postmodern youth' (op. cit.). In Europe and North America the extension of the time young people spend in education has not, of course, been the only agent of social change. Factory Acts, Youthful Offenders Acts, Children and Young Persons Acts, too, have played their part in separating adolescence into periods of life distinct from childhood on the one hand and adulthood on the other. Nevertheless, today in both the United Kingdom and the United States it is education that is high on the national agenda despite,

or because of, the difficulties of educating large and differentiated populations in a climate of fiercely competing demands for limited public resources.

Adolescence and education in Japan

In Japan there is no equivalent word for adolescence in the European and North American tradition nor is it customary to regard young people as a special group who are likely to experience emotional and behavioural problems in their teenage years (White 1987, 1993). On the contrary, high school students in Japan are called children (*kodomo*) and are treated as such by their teachers (Rohlen 1983) in that they are constantly reminded of their duties to school, family and society and are obliged to submit, happily in most cases, to levels of control in dress and behaviour, that Western teenagers would not contemplate or tolerate. It is notable that in Japan young people do not reach the age of majority until they are 20. This goes some way to explain why in Japan there is no developed youth culture of the sort that is familiar in the West. This is not to say that Japanese young people do not read youth magazines, enjoy friendships with other young people, have romantic dreams and want to dress in the latest fashions when they are out of school. But it is to make the point that the sort of social relationships that are beloved of Western teenagers are much more difficult to maintain in Japan. This is because same-sex friendships are usually formed during the years of compulsory education from 6–14 years of age in schools in the immediate locality but are disrupted by the transition from junior to senior high school. Old and new friendships at senior high school are more difficult to maintain because many pupils commute to them from homes where there are not sufficient rooms for entertaining visiting friends at weekends or during the holidays. Friendship cliques or groups are less common in Japan than in the West because unsupervised groups outside school are unusual. Same-sex friendships, therefore, are likely to be close and long-lasting while opposite-sex friendships are not likely to be serious before college entrance has been achieved. However, for that 40 per cent of the population that leaves school at 18, adolescence is likely to be less restricted than the above account would suggest.

Education in Japan, as a direct result of the occupation of Japan in 1946 by the Allied Powers under General Douglas MacArthur, is based on the American 6–3–3 system of co-educational and comprehensive schools. However, whereas in the United States high schools are characterized by open admission and a mix of academic, vocational and general courses, Japanese high schools are ordered in a strict hierarchy with access to the academic high schools determined by success in entrance examinations. In other words, Japanese schools reflect not social and academic diversity but social and academic segregation and stratification. At the same time because of its enormous popularity, contemporary Japanese education fulfils, to a very considerable degree, Rousseau's ideal of postponing maturity in the young. Thus, after completing compulsory education at lower secondary school at the age of 15, 95 per cent of Japanese teenagers, attend upper secondary school voluntarily until the age of 18 (Katsukata 1996) and over 50 per cent of high school students succeed in gaining places in institutions of higher education (Nishimura 1985). As if this were not enough, there exists in Japan, in addition to the formal education system, the most highly developed informal system of cram schools (*juku*) in the world. *Juku* are designed primarily to enhance academic performance and are open six or seven days a week from the time regular schools close until late at night. Furthermore, because social status in Japan depends to a considerable extent on academic background, *Juku* succeeds in attracting over half the child population at a cost of more than $1,000 a year for each pupil. Understandably, *Juku* is blamed for pushing an already highly competitive education system to even greater heights of competitiveness and for interfering with the normal life and cultural activities of children. Educational pressures on young people in Japan culminate in two distinct bouts of *juken jigoku* or examination hell. The first *juken jigoku* involves 14-year-old students competing for entrance to the best upper secondary school in their locality and the second occurs three years later when most young people are preparing for entrance examinations to university. In an attempt to lessen the pressures on Japanese young people it was decided, after much debate, that all public (i.e. state schools) should allow children at least two free Saturdays a month. However, the granting of this concession was delayed until April 1995 because of fears that any free time allowed by the public schools at weekends would be utilized immediately by *juku*. This delay tells us much about the value that is placed on education in Japanese society and on the strategies that are believed to lead young people to educational success.

The values of persistence, endurance and cooperation in Japan

The very high take-up rates for education at all levels in Japan together with very low drop-out rates are contrasted by Blinco (1993) with the situation in the United States where around 30 per cent of students leave high school before graduation. The reason most commonly advanced for explaining this difference in cultural attitudes is the very high valuation placed by the Japanese on the qualities of persistence and endurance. Indeed, according to Duke (1986), this value is encouraged at every step in life starting in the home, developing in the school and continuing throughout a company career. White and Le Vine (1986) further explain that in Japan it is believed that people will remain self-centred and immature if they do not experience hardship. It follows therefore, as night follows day, that if enduring hardship is virtuous, then adolescents in Japan will be urged to continue to study intensively throughout their school careers and never to drop-out. This difference in cultural values is thrown into sharp relief by the experiences of Japanese children whose parents take them abroad on foreign postings. The children discover that, when they re-enter Japan after time spent in Europe or North America, they have not only fallen behind the gruelling academic pace set by Japanese schools but they have aquired a foreign 'script for success in school emphasising independence, explicitness and uniqueness – quite un-Japanese values' (Azuma 1986). These values which are central to Western-style individualism are literally quite foreign to Japan-style 'groupism'.

According to Duke (1986), loyalty to the group is 'the stuff of "being Japanese"' and, like perseverence, is learned from a child's earliest years. Certainly Japanese children spend more time each day and every year with their *kumi* (class or group) than their European or North American counterparts but, unlike their foreign peers, they also take an active part in small groups or *han* into which *kumi* are sub-divided. Each *han* of four to eight pupils elects a *hancho* or leader who assists the teacher in managing the group for academic and disciplinary purposes. In this way most children in Japan gain experience in exercising leadership and understanding small group processes in achieving common goals. Indeed the more senior the pupil the more likely they are to experience decision making at the level of school government and to be prepared for later leadership roles in industry where Japanese managers customarily work alongside their staff and obtain consensus by means of discussion rather than by imposing 'executive' decisions.

Adolescence in Japan, then, is very different from the European and North American experience. In Japan educational aspirations prolong childhood and ensure a more home-based and study-centred life than that of their Western peers. The latter generally prefer the society of friends of both sexes and the freedoms of early adulthood to a life devoted to education. However, young people in Saudi Arabia do not fall neatly into either of these categories.

Adolescence and education in Saudi Arabia

Education in Saudi Arabia is provided by the government free of charge to all Saudis and children of Arabic speaking residents from kindergarten through elementary school (6–12) to secondary school (intermediate 12–15 and high school 15–18). Despite education not being compulsory, young people have voted with their feet and have attended schools in large numbers and at all levels over the last twenty-five years. In 1960, for example, there were just fifteen primary schools whereas in 1986 there were 3,155 (GPGE 1988). Also in 1986, 56 per cent of all children aged 6–11 attended elementary school and 31 per cent of 12–17-year-olds attended secondary school (UNESCO 1989). The General Directorate of Education for Boys, the first government department responsible for education in Saudi Arabia, was founded in 1926. In 1954, as a result of increasing oil revenues, it became the Ministry of Education but still did not concern itself with the education of girls. In fact it was not until 1959 that the government, in consultation with the Uluma or religious scholars, finally addressed this question.

The education of girls in Saudi Arabia

The education of females in Europe and North America began later in time than that of boys and was usually of a different kind. This characteristic of girls' education is illustrated once again most clearly in Saudi Arabia. In Saudi the first private school for girls was founded in 1941 by immigrants to Mecca who came originally as pilgrims but decided to stay on. Later, Saudi Arabians founded three schools for girls in Mecca (1947), Jeddah (1956) and Riyadh (1955). The latter was supervised by three of King Saud's daughters and offered to girls, for the first time, the curriculum that the Ministry of Education had devised for boys alone. However, without any doubt the biggest step forward in the education of girls in Saudi Arabia came about in 1959 when King Saud delivered a royal decree on the subject. Significantly, the decree followed a decade in which Saudi men who had been educated abroad would, in some cases, prefer to marry educated foreign women rather than illiterate Saudi women. This led many Saudis to fear for the future of their society in general and their daughters in particular, but at the same time it gave the advocates of education for women their strongest card yet (Al-Baadi 1982).

The King's decree needed to be diplomatic because his subjects were divided over the wisdom of permitting the education of women in Saudi. Some parents would permit their daughters to study the Qur'an and to learn about their duties to God but were reluctant to permit them any sort of formal education. Others were more comfortable with formal education so long as it comprised religion and stereotyped subjects for girls such as home economics and embroidery. Finally, a few parents wanted their daughters to receive a full and formal education up to and including higher education. Although this last group was the smallest, it was important not to offend it by ruling out of court its aspirations for its daughters. At the same time the other two groups had to be reassured that girls' education was compatible with the traditions of the time. Even so, some parents refused to let their daughters go to school on the grounds that they would lose respect for the home-based role of women in Saudi and others feared that the very foundations of morality and family life would be undermined if girls were educated (Parssinen 1980). As a result, the goals for girls' elementary education were very conservative and aimed to prepare them for little more than running a home and learning how to sew and cook (Ministry of Education 1980). Nevertheless, great advances in the provision of basic literacy and numeracy were achieved and the opening of the first intermediate schools and the very first high school in 1964 was an acknowledgement of a wider role for girls than that of domestic duties. Once secondary education had been opened up for girls then the possibility of a university education for women was assured, if for no other reason than the secondary schools themselves needed to be staffed by female graduates. Despite these advances, the textbooks used in the elementary schools in Saudi emphasized the traditional place of women in the home and warned girls about the deceptive liberty of Western women. At the same time they omitted any reference to women studying in order to become doctors, teachers and civil servants and referred only to women practising domestic skills (GPGE, 1988b).

Girls in Saudi Arabia have been able to realize their education aspirations in recent years but only in the face of widely held conservative attitudes. These attitudes have arisen not so much because of the influence of Islam *per se* but rather because of the traditions that have grown up around it (Waddy 1980). In Saudi Arabia the two sexes never meet after they leave kindergarten except in their own home and family. Courtship does not occur and marriages are arranged. Male Saudi adolescents are relatively mobile and may drive the family car or even have a car of their own (Boyd and Najai 1984) but female Saudis are not allowed to drive cars at any age and female adolescents are expected to stay at home and learn traditional tasks such as cooking and child care. Adolescence in Saudi Arabia, therefore, takes place in the context of an Islamic country that has only recently acquired the infrastructure of a modern society but is nevertheless determined to educate all its people both male and female.

Adolescence and education in Arab-Israel

Arabs living within the borders of what became the state of Israel in 1948 are indigenous Palestinians who comprise about 17 per cent of the population. Most are Sunni Muslims but a small number are Christians and Druze. Whilst Israeli-Arabs are 'technically Israeli citizens their integration and participation in Israeli society is neglible' (Franks 1987). This is because the Israeli-Arab population is located in enclaves or villages and is a minority group that is excluded from decision-making in areas such as labour relations, security and education.

The education of Palestinians has rarely been under their own control. From 1517–1917 Palestine was part of the Ottoman Empire and from 1917–1948 it was under the British mandate. According to Reshef and Silbert (1983) the British attempted to operate a fair policy in the education of Jews and Arabs and indeed British-funded schooling was seen by many Arabs as a route to a white-collar job and some degree of status in a predominantly peasant society. However, Mahshi and Bush (1989) point out that although the British increased the number of schools for Palestinian Arabs, less than half the Arab population had schools to go to. They further claim that the schools the Arabs did attend were not only underfunded but that they actively encouraged Palestinian Arab pupils to believe that Palestine was the natural homeland of the Jews.

Israeli independence in 1948 led to the incorporation of Arabs within the Israeli borders into the state education system. The Arab Education Department was a separate entity within the Ministry of Education and Culture but with a Jewish-Israeli at its head. However, one of his deputies and most of his supervisors, teachers and administrators were Israeli-Arabs. The Arab and Hebrew education systems run in parallel but the State Education Law of 1953 clearly defines the aims of Jewish schools in terms of developing love for the homeland and keeping alive memories of the Holocaust while having no correspondingly clear aims for Arab schools. The school system is of the 6–3–3 variety, as in Japan and Saudi Arabia. School is free and compulsory up to the age of 16 although pre-school education, which is generally available in Israel to Jewish children, is attended by less than half of 3- and 4-year-olds in the Arab sector. Most Israeli-Arab 5-year-olds attend kindergarten but once they enter primary school they study what is essentially a Jewish-Israeli syllabus. This is most obvious in religious studies where Israeli-Arabs study Islam through the Qur'an but are obliged to spend twice as much time studying Judaism. The Arab Mayors have pointed out (Habib-Allah, 1991) that Arab–Jewish relationships would improve if young Arabs studied less

Hebrew history and young Jews began, for the first time, to study Arab language and culture.

The most famous Arab adolescents in the West Bank and Gaza Strip in recent years are the children of the *intifada* (uprising). However, the behaviour of these 'children' was always very different from that of their peers living within the green line that continues to divide the occupied territories from Israel proper. For example, whenever the Palestinians called a strike in support of their claims to become an independent state their children would boycott school while, at the same time, their Israeli-Arab peers would continue to attend lessons because they 'have to take exams like everyone else in Israel and if they can't pass the exams they are losing' (Fields 1989). This comment by an Israeli-Arab professor indicates that attitudes toward education among Arabs in Israel have changed little since their ancestors sought social mobility through the schools of the British mandate. Furthermore Arab-Israeli citizens presently living in their homeland are not involved in fighting for independence and would be unlikely to leave their homes to seek citizenship in a Palestinian state. The children of Palestinians, however, would benefit immensely from stability in the schools of the West Bank and Gaza Strip which for too long have been overcrowded and underfunded (Mi'ari *et al.*, 1992).

Personal and moral values in five countries

Over the last decade I have had the opportunity of conducting surveys with young people in each of the countries discussed above, starting with a major English study in 1981 (Simmons and Wade 1984). The aim of this survey was to portray what young people in middle adolescence (mean age 15) thought, felt and believed about important aspects of their lives using as evidence their own written statements. Those who took part were assured that their anonymity would be preserved, that their views would not be criticized and that they would be given time and space to express themselves freely. To this end a questionnaire was devised comprising six sheets of A4 paper that contained ten unfinished sentences. The sentences or prompts were designed to elicit the subjects' responses about their ideals (The sort of person I would most like to be like . . .), their least ideals (The sort of person I would least like to be like . . .), their most

preferred companions (The people I am happiest with are . . .), their least preferred companions (The people I am unhappiest with are . . .), their use of solitude (When I am by myself I . . .), their *summum bonum* (What matters to me more than anything else . . .), their most desired outcomes (The best thing that could happen to me . . .), their least desired outcomes (The worst thing that could happen to me . . .) and, finally, their nascent philosophies both positive (The best thing about life is . . .) and negative (The worst thing about life . . .).

Two methods were used to analyse the written responses. First, the number of references to individuals or *themes* was totalled. Thus, in the 1984 English survey in response to the second prompt 50, or 6 per cent, of the 820 subjects chose Margaret Thatcher by name as the person they would least like to be like. The second method of analysis is described below under 'comparative values'. The 1984 English survey was the first in time (1981) and the largest (820 subjects). The Japanese survey (283 subjects) followed in 1986 (Simmons 1989), the Saudi-Arabian (89 subjects) in 1991 and the Israeli-Arab (118 subjects) in 1992 (Simmons and Habib-Allah 1994). The American survey (126) took place in 1994 (Simmons, 1999). Two small English and English-Muslim studies were completed in 1992 (Simmons and Simmons 1994).

Comparative themes

A striking example of a consistent and dominant theme running through responses is in the Saudi-Arabian survey where a common *ideal* is a religious person ('his eminence the Mufti of the Kingdom of Saudi Arabia, because of his great knowledge of Islamic religion and Sharia' (law)) and a *least ideal* is the irreligious ('the singer [pop star] because singing takes us away from our religion and prayer and it is a bad habit among people'). Furthermore, religious people are *preferred companions* ('those who do not commit sins and do good deeds') although strict religious leaders can be *least preferred* companions ('my teacher of *Hadith* (tradition), Qur'an and interpretation because he is very stern'). Self-examination is cited as a *use of solitude* ('I think of all that I have done during the day and reckon myself') and serving Allah is the subjects' *summum bonum* or their best thing about life ('my duties towards Allah and my religion'). The *best outcome* is to be a good Muslim ('praying all prayers and that Allah accept my repentance') and the *best thing about life* is Islam ('the love of Allah and The Prophet'). The *worst thing about life* would be to disobey Allah ('enjoying life and forgetting the Day After').

An equally salient theme running through the Israeli-Arab responses was the importance of education as a means to social mobility. Thus the *ideal* is to be an educated person ('educated persons who help others like doctors, engineers, lawyers, judges') and the *least ideal* is to be an uneducated, dependent person ('ignorant people whom I despise because they had the opportunity to learn and study – but they became a burden on society'). Furthermore, *preferred companions* are 'intellectual people who participate in life development and progress and educate the coming generation' while *least preferred companions* are 'uneducated and ignorant people'. Education is the *summum bonum* 'to succeed in all my education and make my parents proud of me' while the *worst outcome* is 'failure in education (because) that means failure in life.' Finally, education is the *best thing about life* because 'without education there is no progress in life and we would not be able to face difficulties in life'.

The Japanese sample revealed a similar zeal for education. The *summum bonum* was clear – 'entering the prefectural high school and progressing to my favourite university' – as was the *best outcome* – 'passing the high school entrance exams'. The last writer added with a certain amount of national pride: 'I don't think there are many students in countries other than Japan who are pushed into high school entrances so I think that passing the exams is the best thing that could happen to me.' Finally the *worst outcome* as one girl put it, would be 'failing all the entrance examinations to all the high schools I have tried for'.

By contrast the English and American surveys contain no evidence of strong religious affiliations and some evidence of negative feelings towards school. An English girl sums up the humanistic dilemma of many when responding to the second prompt:

> I can only hope that I don't feel empty about my life. I don't want to regret my life and what I think is important. I wouldn't want to go through life without a belief, not necessarily religious, but a belief in yourself and something that reassures you about the importance of life. I wouldn't want to become old and think, 'That's it, that's my life over, what a waste, I need more time.'

All surveys contained positive opinions about education but the Japanese, Saudi-Arabian and Israeli-Arab surveys contained no negative comments about school. It is left to an English teenager to write that the worst thing about life is 'school every bloody day, day after day, for eleven years or more'.

Another striking difference between the surveys is the strong sense of self in the English and American reponses to the first prompt and the almost complete absence of 'myself' choices in the Japanese survey. 'Myself' choices (i.e. wanting to be oneself rather than anyone else and thereby rejecting the need to personify one's ideals) are commonplace in the English and American surveys ('I do not want to be someone else or do something else. I like myself as I am. I am not perfect, but then who is?'). Thus this concept, beloved of existentialist philosophers and humanistic psychologists, is now very much a part of popular culture in the West but in Japan such an unambiguous declaration of selfhood would be considered grossly ill-mannered. Only one Japanese boy completed the first prompt by writing 'myself, now' although it was clear from the rest of his paper that he regarded himself as a rebel who was impatient with the social and language conventions of his time.

Striking similarities between the surveys are found in response to the third sentence where, in every case, friends are cited as *preferred companions* and the family, which usually means parents, take second place. However, when subjects were asked about their *summum bonum*, the family is placed before friends in all the surveys apart from the one conducted in Japan. It is possible that the pressures on the young in Japan to succeed at school have made the home and family seem less attractive than to their peers elsewhere.

Comparative values

In the second method of analysis, responses were assigned to six categories from materialistic through to altruistic according to the dominant *values* expressed in them. The following are examples of responses from the five surveys:

Material:
> I would most like to be a very successful person who makes an annual income of over 100,000 dollars, with a wife and two kids, maybe one, live in a nice neighbourhood with nice cars and have a cool

dog too. I guess this is an all American Dream but this is what I would like to see in my future, however, I will probably end up struggling all my life making 30,000 a year at best. Life's a bitch. (American Survey)

Physical:
I would like to be slightly taller and thinner than I am at the moment and have paler skin and auburn hair. (English Survey)

Friendly:
A person who is kind to the elderly, who gets on well with friends and uses honorific language to superior people. (Japanese Survey)

Honest and Reliable:
My father because he is generous, brave and does not fear death. (Saudi-Arabian Survey)

Cooperative and Helpful:
The person who works hard to give and help others with all the knowledge he has, e.g. a doctor saving lives, teachers who build a good generation of children. (Israeli-Arab Survey)

Altruistic and Religious:
A person like Malcolm X, the black American Muslim leader. He brought blacks and Muslims many rights, he brought many reforms and he was a martyr for human rights. (English-Muslim Survey)

This analysis demonstrated that in the first English study (op. cit.) there were striking differences between the values expressed by the two sexes. In response to seven out of the ten sentences it was clear that English girls were much more likely than English boys to respond with interpersonal rather than materialistic values. Similar differences were found in the Japanese and Saudi surveys but in only one sentence was the result statistically significant. In the Israeli-Arab study there were no significant differences at all between the responses of the two sexes. In the more recent English and American studies differences between the sexes were less marked, probably because of the smaller samples involved. Turning from intra to inter-study comparisons, there are no clear overall patterns but rather differences caused by individual prompts. Thus the Japanese cite fewer materialistic values in the first four sentences than the English but in sentence 6 they clearly value entering high school more than they value friends and family. With the English the

reverse is the case. Another reversal occurs in the last four sentences, where the English make more material responses than the Japanese in response to sentence 7 but fewer in response to sentences 9 and 10. In the latter they express more interpersonal, social and humanitarian concerns than their Japanese peers. A similar pattern emerges when comparisons are made between the most recent English study and the Israeli-Arab and Saudi Arabian surveys. The English oversubscribe to material values when responding to the first and seventh prompts but oversubscribe to friendship and reciprocal relationships when reacting to the sixth and eighth prompts. Finally, the English and American adolescents are similar in their values, with both being more materialistic and less altruistic than their peers in Arab-Israel and Saudi Arabia.

The holding of values

A short historical and comparative study of this sort reveals that not only is 'adolescence' a social construct that is flexible and adaptable to changing employment, educational and political pressures but that many adolescent values are similarly susceptible to cultural, ideological and religious influence. Following Kitwood's (1980) analysis it is postulated that many beliefs that young people hold are *taken for granted*. This is because beliefs held since childhood have for so long been regarded as absolute that by the time an adolescent realizes that they are, in fact, relative he or she is very much a product of the self-same values. *Taken for granted* values, therefore, are frequently expressed by those who hold them as universal truths. Indeed, such values may not be consciously 'held' at all because they have for so long been uncritically accepted.

The holding of religious values is a case in point. In Saudi Arabia religious dissent is forbidden and religious beliefs are accepted uncritically. Consequently, religious beliefs that many English young people would regard as relative are treated by their Saudi peers as absolute. Certainly religious beliefs dominate every prompt in the Saudi questionnaires partly, perhaps, because Saudi Arabia is the cradle of Islam and therefore 'every student who receives an education in Saudi Arabia has the whole of the Islamic past around him' Navdi (1981). Interestingly in Arab-Israel, where there are reports that the Iman are becoming more influential and are introducing Islamic practices against Western style freedoms for women, religious convictions were rarely expressed perhaps because of the burning ambition of Israeli-Arabs to advance socially and politically through education. The English-Muslims are also interesting in this respect in that they not only subscribe to more religious values than their English and American peers but also more than their Arab-Israeli equivalents. It may be that living in England, where educational opportunities are well established, adherents of Islam will express a greater regard for their religion than in Arab-Israel where Islam has been practised for centuries but educational and political opportunities still need to be won.

Education is valued by the young in each of the five surveys but in Japan the pursuit of education most nearly resembles that of religious zeal. Educational success is the holy grail that makes bearable the endurance of hardship, particularly that of 'examination hell', at the ages of 14 and 17. Surely only in Japan could a pupil, in all seriousness, conclude writing about her *summum bonum* with the words 'I will never forget the final words of a teacher when he retired from school last year: Life until death is study.' The children of Japanese business executives involved in inward investment in Western countries must, therefore, be all the more surprised to be confronted by the strongly held individualism of their foreign peers, their more relaxed attitudes to dropping out of education and their lack of respect for teachers. More surprising still, perhaps, is the Arab-Israel survey where the participants outdid even the Japanese in response to the sixth and seventh prompts, with over half citing education as their *summum bonum* and their best outcome. However, maybe the motivation of Arab-Israelis in seeking to gain political power through education in order to solve the Arab-Israeli problem in their homeland is greater than that of the Japanese in their desire to gain a greater gross national product than their competitors in the Pacific rim. In the most political of the surveys the best thing about life for nearly half the Israeli-Arabs is peace (prompt 9): 'Peace between Jews and Arabs – it is important as a key to have all our rights and not to be discriminated against.'

In England and America there has been much reform in recent years in a quest for higher standards in education, spurred on by the demonstratively superior scholastic achievements of European and Pacific rim countries (Maclure 1988, NCEE 1983). However, the most often cited

summum bonum in England and North America is not education but family and friends. This contrasts sharply with Saudi Arabia where serving Allah is the supreme good for the majority of respondents. In the literature of adolescence (e.g. Coleman and Hendry 1990) the importance of having friends during the process of psychological disengagement from parents is well attested to and it may be that in cultures without strong paternalistic religions the parents of adolescents are still seen as the most important guarantors of meaning and purpose in life.

In the West the provision of mass secondary and increasingly tertiary education in the second half of the twentieth century has led to the coming of age of the concept of adolescence in terms of delaying independent adulthood. This concept is allied to strong beliefs in individualism and the importance of self-expression whereas in other cultures these beliefs are not valued as highly as religion, 'groupism' and national or ethnic identity. R. S. Peters (1966) pointed out that it is possible 'for individual men and women to live together in society without any clear consciousness of themselves as persons' but that 'in our society being a person matters very much'. Education, therefore, is conceived differently in different cultures with differing aims and objectives. It is also valued differently by the participants according to the values of their society and to their personal needs. If, as is likely the continuity of values between generations has been underestimated, then the views of the young quoted in this chapter give a strong indication of the dominant values in the society in which they have been reared.

References

Al-Baadi, Hamad Muhammad (1982) *Social change, education and the role of women in Saudi Arabia.* Unpublished doctoral dissertation, Stanford University.

Azuma, H. (1986) Why study child development in Japan. In H. Stevenson *et al.* (eds) *Child Development and Education in Japan.* New York: W. H. Freeman.

Blinco, P. M. A. (1993) Persistence and Education: a formula for Japan's economic success. *Comparative Education* 29 (2): 171–83.

Boyd, D. A. and Najai, A. M. (1984) Adolescent TV viewing in Saudi Arabia. *Journalism Quarterly* 61: 295–301.

Boyd, W. (1965) *Emile for Today.* London: Heinemann.

Coleman, J. C. and Hendry, L. (1990) *The Nature of Adolescence.* London: Routledge.

Duke, B. (1986) *The Japanese School: Lessons for Industrial America.* New York: Praeger.

Dyhouse, C. (1981) *Girls Growing Up in Late Victorian and Edwardian England.* London: Routledge and Kegan Paul.

Fields, R. M. (1989) Children of the Intifada. *Migration World Magazine* **17** (3–4): 12–19.

Franks, L. R. (1987) *Israel and the Occupied Territories. A Study of the Educational Systems of Israel and the Occupied Territories and a Guide to the Academic Placement of Students in Educational Institutions in the United States.* World Education Series. Washington DC: American Association of Collegiate Registrars and Admission Officers.

Gillis, J. R. (1974) *Youth and History: Traditions and Change in European Age Relations, 1770 – Present.* New York: Academic Press.

GPGE (1988a) *Administration of Educational Research and Statistics, Talim Al Banat Bain Al Madhi wa Hadhr.* Riyadh: GPGE.

GPGE (1988b) *The Sixth Year Reader (with Poetry for Memorization)*, 16th edn. Riyadh: GPGE.

Habib-Allah, M. (1991) Education for the Arab Minority in Israel: issues, problems and demands. Proceedings of the *Third Arab Education Congress,* Shfar-Am.

Hall, G. S. (1904) *Adolescence its Psychology and its relations to Physiology, Anthropology, Sociology, Sex, Crime, Religion and Education.* New York: Appleton.

Hendrick, H. (1990) *Images of Youth.* Oxford: Clarendon.

Katsukata, S. (1996) The class of '96: education today. *Look Japan* **42** (486): 4–8.

Kelly, G. (1955) *The Psychology of Personal Constructs.* Norton: New York.

MacClure, S. (1988) *Education Reformed.* London: Hodder and Stoughton.

Mahshi, K. and Bush, K. (1989) The Palestinian uprising and education for the future. *Harvard Educational Review* **59**: 470– 83.

Mi'ari, M., Ghassas, A. and Mohammed, H. (1992) *Reading and Reading Comprehension among Pupils of Elementary Schools in the West Bank.* A Pilot Study Report commissioned by The Israel Section of Defence for Children International, P.O. Box 8028, Jerusalem.

Ministry of Education (1980) *The Evidence of Development in the Elementary School System in the Kingdom of Saudi Arabia over the Past Eight Years.* Riyadh: Centre for Educational Documentation.

Navdi, A. H. A. (1981) Education and society in Saudi Arabia. In Wasiullah Khan (ed.) *Education and Society in the Muslim World.* King Abdulaziz University, Jeddah: Hodder and Stoughton.

National Commission on Excellence in Education (1983) *A Nation at Risk: The Imperative for Educational Reform.* A Report to the nation and the Secretary of Education. United States Department of Education, Washington: US Government Printing Office.

Nishimura, H. (1985) Commissioning a master plan. *Japan Quarterly* **32** (1): 18–22.

Parssinen, C. (1980) The changing role of women. In W. A. Beling (ed.) *King Faisal and the Modernisation of Saudi Arabia.* London: Croom Helm.

Peters, R. S. (1966) *Ethics and Education.* London: George Allen and Unwin.

Reid, I. (1986) *The Sociology of School and Education.* London: Fontana Press.

Reshef, S. and Silbert, Y. (1983) The Palestine government and Jewish education 1920–1933. *History of Education* **12**: 14–30.

Rohlen, T. P. (1983) *Japan's High Schools.* Berkeley: University of California Press.

Rutter, M. and Smith, D. J. (1995) (eds) *Psychosocial Disorders in Young People.* Chichester: Wiley.

Sharpe, S. (1976) *Just Like a Girl, How Girls Learn to be Women.* Harmondsworth: Penguin.

Simmons, C. (1989) Adolescent attitudes in England and Japan. In J. P. Forgas and J. M. Innes (eds) *Recent Advances in Social Psychology: An International Perspective.* Amsterdam: North-Holland, Elsevier: 21–30.

Simmons, C. (1999) A comparative study of educational and cultural determinants of adolescent values, *Journal of Beliefs and Values,* Vol 20, No 2, 1999 in press.

Simmons, C. and Habib-Allah, M. (1994) English, Israeli-Arab and Saudi Arabian adolescent values. *Educational Studies* **20** (1): 69–86.

Simmons, C. and Simmons, C. (1994) A comparative study of English and Muslim adolescent values. *Muslim Education Quarterly* **12** (1): 16–28.

Simmons, C. and Wade, W. (1984) *I Like To Say What I Think.* London: Kogan Page.

UNESCO (1989) *Statistical Yearbook.* Paris: UNESCO.

Waddy, C. (1980) *Women in Muslim History.* London: Longman.

White, M. (1987) *The Japanese Educational Challenge: A Commitment to Children.* New York: The Free Press.

White, M. and Le Vine, R. (1986) What is an Ii Ko (Good Child)? in H. Stephenson, et al. (eds.) *Child Development and Education in Japan.* New York: W. H. Freeman.

White, M. (1993) *The Material Child.* New York: The Free Press.

Part Two

Institutional Issues

6 Governing Institutions in Contexts of Cultural Diversity

JANE MARTIN

The postmodern world is typically believed to be characterized by different cultural traditions whose values are said to be chronically rival and incommensurable, compounded by a poverty of recognition and mutual understanding.[1] The challenge for our time is to develop new forms of governance and intermediary institutions that create the conditions for cooperative action in a civil society characterized by the valuing of such difference.[2]

In this context, many schools are a microcosm of the predicament facing the postmodern polity. The challenge for an institution, as for society, is to discover processes that can reconcile the valuing of difference with the need for shared understanding and agreement about public purposes. Purposes that challenge and eradicate prejudice and discrimination.[3]

Yet schools are a microcosm with a difference. Whereas in a civil society there may be the hope for understanding of difference, within formal institutions such as schools there must of necessity be reconciliation or shared agreement about values: without this there can be no coherent institutional purpose or policy. For learning is a culturally defined concept and in contexts of cultural diversity there will be competing conceptions of learning derived from competing cultural values. The governance of institutions thus depends upon shared understanding and agreement about those values before it can flourish. Therefore, governance in contexts of cultural diversity must recognize competing cultural values, represent them and mediate between them in the interests of achieving agreement.

The experience of cultural difference can also be one of otherness and exclusion. Cultures codify the essential boundaries of social classification. To be placed in a different world is thus to experience the deep codes of society: who is to be included as members, who excluded as alien sets the boundaries of the social order; the identities of self and other, of sacred and profane are defined within the moral order; while the relations of power, of super and subordination, constitute the political order. Systems of social classification so embody the relations between communities that to be regarded as other, outside, profane is to experience the greatest disadvantage – to be denied the dignity, and thus the sense of agency, that derives from being acknowledged, as a fellow citizen with shared rights and responsibilities. Yet because these classifications, of who we are and what we can become, can be recognized as social constructions we can also learn that they are amenable to revision, supported by the appropriate institutional formation in the public domain.[4]

The governing body is the public arena where mediation is achieved through deliberation that leads to a judgement about the values and purpose to be expressed in and through the institution. By way of this public judgement the process of policy-making becomes the manifestation of the achievement of shared values. In order to exercise such public judgement on behalf of the communities they serve, the governing body must be sure to connect with the public and reflect their views. In contexts of cultural diversity this will require more sophisticated mechanisms of local democracy which facilitate public dialogue and negotiation. Particularly in contexts of cultural diversity, the essentially political processes of governing an institution – of local democracy – are paramount in connecting the public to the institution.

In this way schools and their governing bodies illustrate in a particularly powerful way the nature of the intermediary institutions which, it is argued, are the precondition for the well-being of an emerging civil society. This situates governance at the centre of the movement to improve our schools in order that public values (about learning) can be properly reflected in the public management of our institutions. Governors sit at the boundaries between community and institution and between governance and management.

This chapter will suggest that just as the conditions for civil society must be characterized by public discourse that acknowledges mutuality and reciprocity, so the governance of schools must facilitate local democracy that is open and deliberative in order to reach shared understandings about educational values. It will be argued that this is particularly the case in contexts of cultural diversity. The discussion will draw upon empirical case studies carried out as part of a recent Economic and Social Research Council (ESRC) research project, part of the Local Governance Programme.[5] This material will highlight the changing nature of school governance in schools serving culturally diverse populations. The role of the governing body is argued to be critical to the process of bridging the internal culture of the school and the external cultures of the community and central to the effective management of the school.

Intermediary institutions for a civil society

Public institutions are needed to strengthen civil society against the incursions of an increasingly powerful state and to mediate the emergent differences of cultural tradition. The idea of a civil society has gained in prominence, historically at times of political change and uncertainty. Now, in the turbulence of the late twentieth century, a considerable literature has grown to review and develop the analysis of a civil society appropriate for our time. Three organizing ideas shape the concept of a civil society.

Institutional structures for counterbalancing state and society

A civil society is defined by institutional conditions which create a network of non-governmental intermediary institutions between the family and the state that facilitate social cohesion in society. These conditions are most usefully described by Gellner.[6]

> Civil society is that set of diverse non-governmental institutions which is strong enough to counterbalance the state and, whilst not preventing the state from fulfilling its role of keeper of the peace and arbitrator between major interests, can nevertheless prevent the state from dominating and atomising the rest of society.

Civil society does describe a particular relationship between the individual in society and the state. Indeed, the existence of civil society may be a necessary prerequisite for a coherent social order by which state domination may be controlled and called to account by an active citizenship and by which, in turn, the state may support the free association of citizens in a plurality of economic and social spheres. Whilst the existence of a civil society may therefore create the conditions for a liberal democracy[7] it will not be enough just to recognize that such intermediary institutions exist in our society – as indeed they do. It will be the configurations of power in and around those institutions that determine individual and collective freedoms. Without the active democratization of the institutions of civil society, however, built *with* state power rather than *through* state power,[8] there will not be the possibility of empowering less powerful citizens and thus preventing the atomizing effects of private markets. Civil society depends upon such a defining relationship between society and the state rather than the separation of society and the state. As Shils[9] puts it: 'Civil society does not include the state but it presupposes its existence. It presupposes a particular kind of state, namely a state of limited powers.' (p. 9)

We would suggest that parallel conditions have been embodied in the programme of legislative reform in education. Reform that, as Keane[10] points out, was predicated upon a need to redraw the boundaries between state and civil society which had become blurred through corporatist forms of state intervention in social life. In short, the creation of 'self-governing' (locally managed as well as grant maintained) schools has arguably begun to establish some of the conditions for civil society to develop.

Practice of mediation through the art of association

We regard the intermediary institutions of the civil society not only as an essential prerequisite for an active democracy but also as an inclusive network in which all citizens may voluntarily associate. This presupposes a moral idea of the public and the sovereign authority of a community.[11] By community, however, we do not mean the bounded community reliant upon cultural homogeneity of which Gellner speaks, and which Tester[12] mistakenly takes as the failure of civil society, but an inclusive community or rather inclusive communities. Indeed, the plurality of spheres with permeable boundaries is a necessary condition for the free association necessary to civil society. In the same way as de Tocqueville highlighted the importance of the art of association in the civil society, Shils[13] describes the hallmark of a civil society as the autonomy of private associations and institutions characterized by a pluralism which 'comprises the partially autonomous spheres of economy, religion, culture, intellectual activity and political activity . . . these spheres are never wholly autonomous in their relations with each other; their boundaries are not impermeable' (p. 9).

I would assert that such a network of intermediary institutions creates the domain in which private meets public; a public sphere where private interests are reconciled in the context of the public good. As such the civil society will not be just a space to be colonized but a process of mediation as Kumar[14] puts it: 'The "concrete person" of civil society differs from the isolated subject of the sphere of morality in that he gradually comes to recognize himself as a member of society and realizes that to attain his ends he must work with and through others'. The institutional arrangements within civil society that recognize different interests and accommodate cultural diversity will strengthen the public sphere through political mediation.

Codes of civility

Civil society is distinguished from society itself through an adherence to the civilized condition. Tester[15] explains the development of the civil society as that which allows for 'symmetric reciprocity between strangers' so necessary in modern societies in particular in urban and cosmopolitan contexts

where equal relationships need to be accommodated rather than relationships between unequals in the natural state (pp. 28–34). However, whilst Tester is right to make the historical distinction that 'civil society was the creative and homogenous world as distinct from the passive and heterogeneous state of nature' (p. 51), he stops short of redefining civil society for the postmodern condition where cultural difference once again needs to be articulated.

The civility to which we allude is not that which the eighteenth century thinkers interpreted as merely manners, 'whereby some social groups posses the cultural resources to define their manners as civil whilst others are in need of civilization'[16]. Rather, it is a way of articulating private interests in the public sphere which, as Bryant[17] puts it, allows for, 'the equable treatment of others as fellow citizens however different their interests and sensibilities. It is of special relevance wherever people of different interests and sensibilities congregate – notably in cities' (p. 339). This requires a social order of citizenship, as Kumar[18] puts it in the classical tradition, 'one where men (rarely women) regulate the relationships and settle their dispute according to a system of laws; where civility reigns and citizens take an active part in public life' (p. 377).

Reason emerges through dialogue with others, through which we learn not necessarily 'facts' but rather a capacity for learning, for new ways of thinking, speaking, and acting. It is Habermas[19] who articulates the conditions for such communicative rationality as being 'ideal speech contexts' in which the participants feel able to speak freely, truly, sincerely. The possibility of shared understanding, however, requires individuals not only to value others but create the communities in which mutuality and the conditions for agency can flourish. The conditions for this depend upon the creation of arenas for public discourse – the final and most significant democratic conditions for the creation of the civil society.

Civil society and the governance of education

These layers of ideas within the concept of the civil society provide an appropriate frame for interpreting the tensions that underlie recent changes to the government of education. For, although it can be argued that the programme of reforms from the mid-1980s has been designed to strengthen intermediary institutions in support of a civil society, the contradictory pressures that underlie the legislation are frustrating its purposes. Schools, on the one hand, are expected to enter into competition for consumer choices (the 1988 Education Act on admissions) which confounds mediation and erodes civitas (cooperative action). On the other hand, however, schools have been required to enter into a 'partnership' with parents and the community in the governance of the school (the 1986 Education Act on governing bodies and annual parents' meetings) in support of reaching shared agreements. The need to strengthen the relationship between schools and their parent communities has been the focus of policy development and practice since the late 1970s and formed the central proposal of the 1986 Education Act on school governing bodies and annual parent meetings.[20] In contexts of cultural diversity this raises particular issues since the parent community cannot be regarded as an homogenous group. The community itself will often be a site of contested values which raises questions about traditional representative forms of governance.

Schools acknowledge the importance of reaching out to their parent communities to support the learning needs of young people, especially in contexts of difference and disadvantage, yet lack the appropriate institutional mechanisms. The annual parents' meeting is cast in the legislative mould of an end of year financial report, inappropriate for involving parents in consideration of the broader life and purpose of the school.[21] However, the governing body, because of its traditionally formal role, does not allow opportunities for more deliberative exploration of issues presented by different parent communities.

In contexts of cultural diversity schools cannot proceed effectively as educational institutions without the agreement of their different parent communities. There is evidence of some schools beginning to develop new mechanisms which complement the statutory arrangements and enable the necessary processes of mediation. Such schools have a keen understanding of their local communities and the social and cultural factors affecting the education of their young people. What characterizes them, however, is their attempt to seek to reach agreement with parents and in so doing to win their consent for a shared educational purpose.

There is clearly an acknowledgement of the different deeply held cultural traditions of multi-racial school communities and the particular cultural boundaries which they can create. However these schools are building on their understanding of their local communities in order to actively dissolve the boundaries of otherness. But the role of governors and the political processes of governance play a key part. Three case study illustrations highlight the innovative ways in which this can be brought about.

School A

School A is in a vigorous market environment and has just gained grant maintained status in April 1992 (before which time the school was threatened with closure).

The pupil population is spread over a wide geographical area – usually described as split between local families, mostly Asian middle class high aspirational parents, and the predominantly Afro-Caribbean pupils from the estates further afield. The major 'client-group' are the highly aspirational Asian middle class families – the supportive families who represent a steady supply of high achieving pupils for the school. The school also recognizes, however, that pupils come from a number of other ethnic communities including Afro-Caribbean and Somali. Indeed, there are up to forty different languages spoken by pupils in the school. Since the positive GM ballot, parental support for the school has fallen away through the traditional channels (Parent–Teacher Association) at a time when the school particularly needs to retain the consent of parents for its future development.

The key manifestation of the school's desire to regain the support of parents is through the revival of the PTA in a new format. Described as the Friends of School A Association, Year 7 and Year 8 parents have been invited to form an open forum for the development of links between parents and the governing body. While the traditional concerns such as fund raising will remain on the agenda, there is a desire on the part of the school to make it clear to parents the responsibility that the governing body has for the school due to grant maintained status and to emphasize that they have a voice on that body. Such a link would also seem to emphasize the notion of the parent body having representation through parent-governors.

The forum was set up in the summer term of 1994 by the headteacher, the community link tutor and a parent-governor. The first meeting was held in November 1994 and was attended by the Chair of Governors, all parent-governors and some community governors. About thirty-five parents invited from Years 7 and 8 also attended. The emphasis at this first meeting was the governing body and the link through parent-governors, 'these friends here are your representatives there and if they are going to represent you they've got to meet with you sometime' (community link tutor).

The initial contact was used to disseminate information about the governing body, including contact telephone numbers. The intention was to make governing body minutes available for parents with meeting agendas in advance to encourage their active contribution to issues as they arose – not just for information after the event. However, the conversation was not just one way; parents responded to the meeting with offers of help with fund-raising events and reading groups. The steering group for the forum were sensitive to creating a parent-friendly atmosphere with a good deal of informal discussion time – particularly for those parents who would feel uncomfortable in a formal setting. The importance of encouraging parents to contribute in small groups and in a comfortable environment was uppermost, in the knowledge that other meetings had been too formal. The current suggestion is to meet once every half-term as it is felt that monthly meetings would be too much of a commitment to ask of parents. Social meetings have been suggested and the school newsletter will be used in future to raise issues from the governing body.

The school acknowledges that such a forum provides an opportunity for all parents from all community groups to become involved and that there might be a danger of certain groups taking it over. The forum will be an important start in breaking down the communication barrier and dispelling the apprehension of parents but it is realized that it will be difficult to get an input from parents from different backgrounds. One key concern is to enable parents to contribute who wouldn't normally feel confident to do so. With this in mind the forum will start to make contact with parents on 'simple issues like keeping your child safe, drugs, family life, health related exercises' (parent-governor).

School B

School B has a strong tradition of community links with immigrant communities and has recently set up a forum for the Somali communities that it serves. School B is situated in a multi-racial city where many of the inhabitants are second generation immigrants from Africa or Asia. More recently, however, the school has been serving an increasing number of Somali refugees and has a large population (200) of Somali children in the school. The city has become essentially socially segregated and School B serves an area that is predominantly multi-racial black and white working class. The market in education would appear to be reinforcing the social boundaries as the aspiring middle classes gravitate towards schools in the north of the city. The context of a Welsh host community – and the Welsh components of the National Curriculum – only serves to contribute to the sense of 'otherness' experienced by School B and its students.

Due to its traditions of communicating with immigrant groups School B is sensitive to cultural issues that can create unnecessary barriers. A respect for the traditions of the Somali community is illustrative of this. As the community tutor told us, 'Somali parents' main concern is that they get the best for the children – for their sons to do better than they did. They are concerned, for example, to get pupils back to school when there has been an exclusion' (community tutor). Usually Somali parents will come to see teachers without an appointment. The school is therefore careful to have an open-door policy which includes a member of staff being able to meet parents on this basis rather than offend and inconvenience parents by turning them away.

The community tutor identified that there had been 'a significant increase in Somali pupils into the school and I [was] not at all happy (a) with the curriculum that they were being offered and (b) that the links with the community were sufficient to sustain a quality educational experience.' The need for dialogue with this increasing community came in to sharp focus with an incident between a Somali pupil and a white boy which escalated to such a degree that 'after school they [Somali pupils] were touring round in mini buses and so on trying to get at the boy who sort of was the main instigator, the white boy, and police were involved', so much so that 'things were getting out of hand' (community tutor).

Subsequently the school made contact with the local religious leader for the Somali community. He came to the school to speak to Somali pupils and ask them to exercise restraint. It was decided then to develop contacts on a regular basis rather than just meeting when 'fire fighting' was required. As a result the elected representative for the Somali community was contacted. At this point it became clear that dealing with the 'right' people on behalf of a community is a delicate matter:

> That's when things unfortunately really began to fall apart. We thought we had it right and we had nothing right at all, because all of a sudden then we started having messages to the effect that didn't we realize that no one would respect this arrangement and that we were doing it all wrong, that they were not representative of the Somali community, that you were dealing with a faction, and the faction was not respected and so one becomes, I became isolated, the Head became isolated because of the vociferous comments that we were receiving. (Community tutor)

The school had inadvertently stumbled across factional interests within what they had thought was a homogenous group of Somalis and had not realized that such factional interests transcended the elected political representative. As the community tutor put it: 'warring factions in the homeland are carried over here without using weapons'. A Somali representative on the governing body was then contacted. He advised that the school convene a meeting for all interested parties within the community from amongst whom elected representatives could be sought for a standing committee.

Meetings with the community tutor, a governor representative and eight 'elders' from the Somali community took place followed by a meeting for parents, after which, a formal group was convened with three community representatives who would act as a direct link with the community, visit the school regularly and assist with particular concerns regarding Somali pupils. Since then the group has dealt with a number of issues which have been raised either by the group representatives or by teaching staff. As a result the school has improved the environment for Muslim prayers, at the request of the group. The community tutor has mediated with religious leaders over religious objections to pupils drawing the human body, which was causing concern to members of teaching staff. The school has now agreed to amend some of the tasks which

children were refusing to do. Incidents which had become confrontational in the classroom have thus been resolved due to an improved understanding of the religious code to which pupils must adhere. A further meeting is planned for the group to meet with the Head of Religious Studies and other staff are now requesting meetings with the group.

School C

School C currently has over 75 per cent black pupils, predominantly from Asian families, and serves a community with a high proportion of 'outer ring' grant maintained schools in an area that also has a strong independent school sector. The key forum for renegotiating the boundary with parents is the governing body.

A new headteacher has strong personal values about working with the families of students, is a strong supporter of comprehensive education and cares deeply about schools addressing the under-achievement of black students. She is originally from Bangladesh herself and has an understanding of the cultural tensions between the Bangladeshi and Pakistani communities from which most of the families have come. Her choice of wearing traditional dress sends strong signals to families of her cultural identity, and her decision to establish an open surgery on Monday evenings underlines her availability for parents. She articulates well her perceptions of the tension between what the school wants to do and what parents will accept, and sees her role as the leading professional able to mediate between the two positions. However, her strong sense of the educational values that the school must uphold clearly direct her strategy in meeting the culturally-defined wishes of parents. While she acknowledges the need to negotiate, she describes this as 'giving way on the little things' – such as granting parental wishes to organized single-sex PE groups. Her personal understanding of the 'generation gap' and the position of girls in Asian families, and her ability to see 'both sides' of Western and Asian cultures enhances her position as mediator and negotiator.

With a high proportion of 'outer ring' grant maintained schools in the area as well as a strong independent sector, awareness of competition is expressed and the reputation of the school with parents is an issue. Senior management are aware of what parents like to see in schools – the traditional things like uniform and homework – and are prepared to meet parents half-way. This reveals the motivation to work with parents in order to satisfy a 'client group'. We might speculate that the school is endeavouring to carve out its niche as a school that promotes high achievement for black pupils and that the developing understanding of the culturally-defined wishes and needs of parents will be a significant factor.

Staff are aware that the cultural background of students and their families can be a key barrier to developing the relationship with parents, not least through language and communication difficulties. One task for the senior management is the urgent development of coherent policy and practice on parental involvement. The current strategy is for a small number of staff to 'handle' parents, with the aim of developing a more integrated partnership. Staff sensitivity to cultural issues and learning is clear. We have been told that students 'swap identities between school and home' (classroom teacher) which has implications for teaching and learning styles. An example of this is the unquestioning manner in which students learn by rote in the Mosque School. Generational cultural conflict is summed up as 'parents still looking back to the traditional culture of the old country when pupils need to look forward' (classroom teacher). A strong sense of mediating between the school culture and the home culture is articulated.

The school seeks to engage with parents proactively and describes the relationship as close, but recognize that they are only 'working towards' parental involvement. In general the response of parents to school overtures is slow, which appears to result from traditional hierarchical power structures. This is reinforced by Asian cultural traditions. Parents are not described in any way as assertive and the school is working with governors to 'change parental opinion through community leaders' in order to 'influence the community' (classroom teacher).

Current practice indicates that the governing body is the key forum for negotiation on behalf of parents. Parent-governors are an extremely supportive group but will assert their interests as shown when Muslim parents requested that girls have the opportunity to wear headscarves as part of the school uniform. This request was contested in the governing body, but agreement was reached to accommodate parents' wishes. As a result the wearing of headscarves is no longer an issue and, in fact,

few girls do so. The governing body is described as 'well-balanced' with Muslim and black governors representing parent viewpoints. It appears to be at once a forum that supports the headteacher's values of raising expectations, but also a body with which the head needs to press certain issues, such as particular instances of the community use of the premises. The headteacher, nevertheless, recognizes the importance of the support of the governing body. Elsewhere the governing body is recognized as a negotiating forum to reach shared agreements with parents. The role of the headteacher and her senior management team seems to have become pivotal in maintaining the balance of power between the parent voice on the governing body and the interests of professionals.

The processes of governance

In attempting to reconcile competing values in contexts of cultural diversity, it is clear that it is the processes of governance that are key. The illustrations above point up a new politics of governance – for mediating between diversity of interests and values is a matter of politics. The new politics of governance must be characterized in the same way as the necessary associations of civil society, by relations of cooperative action which will depend upon the capacity of the public domain to generate the necessary qualities of shared understanding and agreement in contexts of constraint and difference. Such processes – which must secure social trust and cohesion – suggest a politics of communicative rationality[22] secured by a democratic public domain.[23] The political processes of school governance, not uniquely, must therefore be characterized by conditions of openness and dialogue leading to shared understanding and judgement within a local participative democracy.[24]

Reaching shared values can only be achieved if we are open to wider horizons. In our relationships with others and in contexts of cultural diversity where we are confronted by different perspectives and views, a prerequisite of any common understanding is openness to mutual recognition. We must learn to be open to difference and to allow our prejudices to be challenged. The key to this is dialogue, whereby participants are led beyond their initial positions to take account of others. Through conversation we learn by listening, as well as speaking. Through processes of dialogue with others we learn to take a wider view and thus the possibility arises of a more widely defined community of shared understanding which in turn creates a richer capacity for judgement about what is to grow out of the understanding.[25]

Mechanisms for participative democracy are therefore required to allow all to contribute to public discourse, enabling the public to express its voice about educational values, to take each other's needs and claims into account, and to learn to develop through shared understandings.[26] These are the only processes that can connect a culturally diverse public to public institutions and effectively reconcile competing cultural values in a way necessary for effective public management.

Achieving shared values through governance

The challenge facing the management of schools and public services more generally, is to construct a new public management, and thus a new professionalism, which acknowledges the centrality of governance.

In education, in particular, we know that a public service must connect with the public it serves. We know that young people only achieve their potential when pupils, teachers and parents reach shared agreement about the values which are to shape the educational purposes of the school. An education cannot just be professionally delivered. To do so would run the risk of remaining detached from an understanding of the wider public purpose and, moreover, the conditions required to achieve that purpose.

This is the work of governance. It is the domain of agreement about public value. It is a domain invested with public accountability. Such an analysis suggests that governance must lie at the centre of the movement to improve our schools, particularly in contexts of cultural diversity. But this brings implications for the way we govern and manage our schools.

To govern is to exercise judgement and take decisions on behalf of others. It is an essential part of our political process. At one level, our current structures of school governance mirror the traditional system and invite clear boundaries between those who make the rules – who govern – and those who administer them – who manage. Put in this way, we should require nothing more from our

governing bodies than the ability to participate and make sound judgements on behalf of the communities they serve. Thus, the expertise of the headteacher and senior staff – a professional administration – is acknowledged and valued for enabling and supporting the processes of governance.

If governors do concentrate their efforts on becoming effective in making sound judgements, actively participating and connecting with those they represent, then the implications become clear. To make sound judgements governors need clear and concise management information; they need to reflect the views of the customer and the community. To participate actively they need support mechanisms that enable them to get to meetings and get to grips with the business. To connect with others they need public acknowledgement that they are performing a worthwhile function in the interests of the local community. It becomes the role of the professional to ensure this information, support and public acknowledgement, such that the processes of governance are efficient and effective.

However the reality is not so clear cut. For in the delivery of a modern public service the managerial tendency cannot be ignored. We do not need our schools to be run in line with modern management techniques. Quality teams and target-settings should all have their place. The interface between management and governance becomes blurred as we try to distinguish between policy-making and policy implementation, strategic decision-making and day-to-day management. For the reality is that governance and management are interdependent, so the interface between governance and management must also be characterized by openness, discourse and judgements that mediate competing values. The role of the governing body is crucial in this regard, since governors bridge the internal culture of the school and the external culture of the community.

As we have seen in this case study data, governors must reach out to their communities but they must also be allowed to connect with the management of the school. In this way the governing body also becomes the forum for dialogue between headteachers, senior management and governors where professional and public views can be reconciled. Only in this way can a partnership be created that enables the very necessary dialogue between the representatives of the public, the recipients of the service, and the professionals charged with delivering that service. In processes of governance which depend upon shared values there can be no boundaries – only respected territories where difference itself is valued.

Acknowledgements

This paper draws substantially on a previous paper published in *Local Government Studies* Vol. 22, No. 4 (Winter 1996) pp. 210–28 entitled 'School governance for the civil society: redefining the boundary between schools and parents', which was jointly authored with Stewart Ranson, Penny McKeown and Jon Nixon. I am extremely grateful to them for permission to use the material again here.

Notes

1 Gray, J. (1995) *Enlightenment's Wake: Politics and Culture at the Close of the Modern Age*. London: Routledge; Gray, J, (1995) *Berlin*. London: Fontana; Owen, D. (1995) *Nietzsche, Politics and Modernity*. London: Sage.

2 Dunn, J. (ed.) (1992) *Democracy: The Unfinished Journey*. Oxford: Oxford University Press.

3 Mouffe, C. (1992) *Dimensions of Radical Democracy: Pluralism, Citizenship, Community*. London: Verso; Mouffe, C. (1993) *The Return of the Political*. London: Verso; Phillips, A. (1995) *The Politics of Presence*. Oxford: Oxford University Press; Young, I. (1990) *Justice and the Politics of Difference*. Princeton: Princeton University Press; Yeatman, A. (1994) *Postmodern Revisionings of the Political*. London: Routledge.

4 Ranson, S. and Stewart, J. (1994) *Management for the Public Domain*. London: Macmillan; Ranson, S. (1994) *Towards the Learning Society*. London: Cassell.

5 ESRC Project No. L311253003 *The New Management and Governance of Education*. Directed by Stewart Ranson, Professor of Education at The University of Birmingham with Jane Martin, Research Fellow in the School of Education, The University of Birmingham; Penny McKeown, Lecturer in Public Administration at the University of Ulster and Jon Nixon, Professor of Education at the University of Christ Church, Canterbury.

6 Gellner, E. (1995) The importance of being modular. In Hall, J. (ed.) (1995) *Civil Society*. Cambridge: Polity Press (p. 32); Gellner, E. (1994) *Conditions of Liberty: Civil Society and its Rivals*. London: Hamish Hamilton.

7 Gellner (1995) ibid.

8 As is supported by Keane, J. (1988) *Democracy and Civil Society*. London: Verso.

9 Shils, E. (1991) The virtue of civil society. *Government & Opposition* **26** (1).

10 Keane (1988) ibid.

11 Seligman, A. (1995) Animadversions upon civil society and civic virtue in the last decade of the twentieth century. In J. Hall (ed.) (1995) *Civil Society*. Cambridge: Polity Press.

12 Tester, K. (1992) *Civil Society*. London: Routledge.

13 Shils (1991) ibid.

14 Kumar, K. (1993) Civil society: an inquiry into the usefulness of an historical term. *British Journal of Sociology* **44** (3).

15 Tester (1992) ibid.

16 ibid.

17 Bryant, C. (1993) Social self-organization, civility and sociology: a comment on Kumar's 'Civil Society'. *British Journal of Sociology* **44** (3); see also Bryant, C. (1995) Civic nation, civil society, civil religion. In J. Hall (ed.) (1995) *Civil Society*. Cambridge: Polity Press.

18 Kumar (1993) ibid.

19 Habermas, J. (1984) *The Theory of Communicative Action, Volume One, Reason and the Rationalisation of Society*. London: Heinemann Educational Books.

20 Martin, J. and Ranson, S. (1994) An opportunity for partnership: annual parents' meetings. In A. Thody (ed.) *School Governors: Leaders of Followers*. Harlow: Longman; Martin, J., Ranson, S. and Rutherford, D. (1995) The annual parents' meeting: potential for partnership. *Research Papers in Education* **10** (1).

21 Martin, J. *et al.* (1995) ibid.

22 Habermas (1984) ibid.

23 Ranson and Stewart (1994) ibid.

24 The stages of development from open dialogue to understanding and judgement are explained in Ranson, S. (1997) Citizenship and trust in civil society. In S. Baddley and A. Coulson (1997) *Trust and Contract in the Public Services*. London: Policy Press.

25 Ranson (1994) ibid.

26 Ranson, S., Martin, J. and Nixon, J. (1997) A learning democracy for cooperative action. *Oxford Review of Education* **23** (1).

References

Bryant, C. (1993) Social self-organization, civility and sociology: a comment on Kumar's 'Civil Society'. *British Journal of Sociology* **44** (3).

Bryant, C. (1995) Civic nation, civil society, civil religion. In J. Hall (ed.) (1995) *Civil Society*. Cambridge: Polity Press.

Dunn, J. (ed.) (1992) *Democracy: The Unfinished Journey*. Oxford: Oxford University Press.

Gellner, E. (1994) *Conditions of Liberty: Civil Society and its Rivals*. London: Hamish Hamilton.

Gellner, E. (1995) The importance of being modular. In J. Hall (ed.) (1995) *Civil Society*. Cambridge: Polity Press, p. 32.

Gray, J. (1995) *Berlin*. London: Fontana.

Gray, J. (1995) *Enlightenment's Wake: Politics and Culture at the Close of the Modern Age*. London: Routledge.

Habermas, J. (1984) *The Theory of Communicative Action, Volume One: Reason and the Rationalisation of Society*. London: Heinemann Educational Books.

Keane, J. (1988) *Democracy and Civil Society*. London: Verso.

Kumar, K. (1993) Civil society: an inquiry into the usefulness of an historical term. *British Journal of Sociology* **44** (3).

Martin, J. and Ranson, S. (1994) An opportunity for partnership: annual parents' meetings. In A. Thody (ed.) *School Governors: Leaders of Followers*. Harlow: Longman.

Martin, J., Ranson, S. and Rutherford, D. (1995) The annual parents' meeting: potential for partnership. *Research Papers in Education* **10** (1).

Mouffe, C. (1992) *Dimensions of Radical Democracy: Pluralism, Citizenship and Community*. London: Verso.

Mouffe, C. (1993) *The Return of the Political*. London: Verso.

Owen, D. *Nietzsche, Politics and Modernity*. London: Sage.

Phillips, A. (1995) *The Politics of Presence*. Oxford: Oxford University Press.

Ranson, S. (1994) *Towards the Learning Society*. London: Cassell.

Ranson, S. (1997) Citizenship and trust in civil society. In S. Baddley and A. Coulson (eds) *Trust and Contract in the Public Services*. London: Policy Press.

Ranson, S., Martin, J. and Nixon, J. (1997) A learning democracy for cooperative action. *Oxford Review of Education* **23** (1).

Ranson, S. and Stewart, J. (1994) *Management for the Public Domain*. London: Macmillan.

Seligman, A. *(1995)* Animadversions upon civil society and civic virtue in the last decade of the twentieth century. In J. Hall (ed.) (1995) *Civil Society*. Cambridge: Polity Press.

Shils, E. (1991) The virtue of civil society. *Government & Opposition* **26** (1).

Tester, K. (1992) *Civil Society*. London: Routledge.

Yeatman, A. (1994) *Postmodern Revisionings of the Political*. London: Routledge.

Young, I. (1990) *Justice and the Politics of Difference*. Princeton: Princeton University Press.

7 Race Awareness and School Ethos: Reflections on School Management Issues

JEAN M. BIGGER

This article reflects on the process of innovation and change in a secondary comprehensive school for girls serving an inner city area. Originally a grammar school, it became a large comprehensive school that has suffered in recent years from falling rolls. The school had remained open largely due to the efforts, at a critical moment, of the local Asian community which wanted single sex education for their daughters. The school had a city-wide intake, with about a quarter of the pupils coming from ethnic minority groups; in the majority were pupils from Pakistani Muslim families. Only a small number of these pupils went on to higher education. There were no full-time teachers from ethnic minority groups when I took up my post; a part-time Pakistani teacher employed under Section 11 was paid on instructor rate to teach English and Urdu.

I became a deputy head after completing a Masters degree in educational management. This course had emphasized team-building and the process and management of change in its exploration of education policies and strategies. My new school provided an opportunity to see if the theories explored in the Masters degree would work in real life teaching situations. As well as having to learn the written and traditional practices of the new school and a new education authority, there was the chance to meet a very different client group of pupils from those with whom I had worked before.

My previous large rural comprehensive school had very few students who were not white and English in origin during the thirteen years I was there – I remember one Afro-Caribbean family, one Hong Kong family, a small group of Vietnamese and two brothers from the Philippines. My awareness of multi-cultural issues was consequently not high: as Head of Careers two incidents in particular come to mind. One of my pupils, when applying to join the Armed Forces, was required to be able to swim before he could enter but could not do so. He said he did not enjoy going to the swimming pool: I imagined that this was because he did not like the water and was surprised to discover that it was because he was bullied at the pool for being Afro-Caribbean. A pupil of Philippine origin was initially turned down for a place on a technician course because he was a year too old at 17: his achievement in rapidly mastering English was not recognized. Without an advocate he would not have been able to enter his chosen career.

Despite having been brought up in Bradford, Yorkshire alongside a large and rapidly growing diverse cultural population, and having travelled outside Europe, neither experience seemed to prepare me well for the first days in my new multi-cultural school. I was very much a beginner and felt the 'strangeness' of the girls in their *salwar kameez*. This chapter charts my own learning curve as I took responsibility for pastoral work of the school and sought to initiate a review of the school's approach to multi-cultural matters. The theoretical framework was that of Fullen (1982a, 1982b) who distinguished between initiation (the initial decisions), implementation (the first stages, covering a few years, of introducing change) and institutionalization (the process whereby the change is fully incorporated into the system). The analysis below covers only the first two stages. Institutionalization is not a short-term prospect and was not realized in this context.

Teacher attitudes

On the whole there was little integration between

Asian pupils and others except when they reached the sixth form. Asian pupils tended to be found in bottom sets and predominated in Needlework and Child Development classes. These were skills that Asian parents regarded as essential for their daughters to acquire, but the classes often contained white pupils identified as less able who had been counselled into these subjects because they might better be able to cope with the work. Pupils with special educational needs and pupils learning English were withdrawn from mainstream classes, which tended to restrict the number of external examinations they could take in Year 11.

A number of staff commented that pupils spent too much time going 'home' to Pakistan and their education was wasted because they would be married as soon as they left school. Some staff were reluctant to talk to parents over the telephone as they felt that neither party would understand what was being said; they also noted that many parents did not attend evening meetings to discuss their daughter's progress. Few Asian pupils went on to higher education and some staff felt that some Asian pupils were unrealistic about their career aspirations as they would not achieve the qualifications. Other staff were very supportive in helping the girls achieve their ambitions. They were aware that the girls had to help their mothers in the evening and that this affected their ability to do justice to homework. However, many of the pupils did not obtain the required level of qualifications for higher education courses.

It was argued that Asian girls were difficult to place on work experience because they insisted on wearing their own clothes and not Western style dress that it was believed employers would prefer; and that they could not work with men in the same office. However, many of the girls said that dress was not an issue and that they were not prevented from working in a mixed office. One sixth form student triumphed in achieving sexual and racial equality on her work experience at an airport. As the employers were not familiar with Asian names they had assumed she was a boy and had offered her a placement in engineering. When this very attractive young woman arrived they immediately suggested that she would be better placed in the office. She said that as she was planning to study engineering at university she would prefer the engineering shed. Her week was a great success apart from the long journey to find the ladies' toilet.

Asian pupils were often thought to be badly behaved, swearing and fighting and receiving temporary suspensions from school. Parents wanted their daughters to remain in school during the lunch hour: however, this was the only opportunity girls had to meet young men of their own choice who picked them up in their cars at the back gate. Catching these miscreants proved something of a dilemma for staff as the girls said they would be beaten if their parents found out. Some staff did not inform the pupils' families, which led to distrust between home and school and provided pupils with a chance of playing one group off against another as they led the life of a dutiful daughter at home while pursuing clandestine relationships at noon. These friendships were always doomed and ended in tears as arranged marriages were the norm. Girls who left home expected to be shunned by their families and cut off from the support systems of the community.

Some staff talked about the 'Asian' girls as a group and did not appear to make an effort to recognize them as individuals and by name. A number of staff and pupils said that the girls 'smelled' because they did not change their clothes often enough (my own experience contrasts strongly with this contention which seemed to be the product of a common 'ethnic' prejudice). It was said that holidays for the Eid festivals went on too long, without acknowledgement that families might be travelling to visit relatives who lived in other areas of the country in order to celebrate together. Pupils speaking in mother tongue were assumed (without good reason) to be talking in a derogatory manner, so this was actively discouraged. The good results obtained by Pakistani pupils in GCSE Urdu were explained as being because the examination was easy to pass: it was not understood that the majority of pupils had to learn Urdu since Punjabi was the language used at home. It was not always appreciated that pupils for whom English was a second language, but spoke standard English quite well, might have difficulties in comprehension and in written English. There were misconceptions about the difference between pupils with learning difficulties and those for whom English was their second or third language.

Some staff said they felt unable to discipline a pupil from an ethnic minority group as that pupil would accuse them of being racist. There was a tendency to refer all matters concerning Asian pupils to the part-time Section 11 teacher as they were regarded as her pupils and she would understand their background and be able to speak to their parents. This led to a marginalization of the issues by mainstream staff

Pupil attitudes

I noted only a few close friendships between the Asian pupils and the other girls. The Asian girls could be openly hostile to staff. Soon after I started one angry pupil called me a 'white bitch'. Name calling took place between white and Asian pupils and between Asian pupils themselves. Pakistani girls said that they walked with their heads down in the street to avoid people shouting out racist comments at them. One girl on her way to school said that a man had stopped his car, got out and punched her without provocation. An Asian sixth form boy (there was shared sixth form provision) worked as a waiter: a white customer refused to pay his bill and began to threaten the boy, who picked up a wine bottle to defend himself. The police were unable to charge the man because the boy had held an offensive weapon. In school one of the places where girls from ethnic minorities could be most bullied was on the games field. Staff were generally unaware of this and believed that their reluctance to take part in sport was because they disliked games or were lazy. Other examples of similar racial harassment in other schools can be found in Troyna and Hatcher (1992) and in reports from the Council for Racial Equality (CRE 1988a, 1988b).

For many girls home and school was their whole life. School was their recreation and they wanted to have an opportunity to have places to chat to their friends, listen to music, watch films and enjoy the occasional lunch-time party. Halal food was not provided for lunch, so they had to eat vegetarian food; Christmas dinner for youngsters usually so fond of meat was a disappointing event and caused friction.

Behaviour in school

An equal opportunities adviser, who had previously worked at the school prior to my arrival, had brought the number of temporary suspensions of Asian pupils to the notice of the headteacher as they were numerically by far the largest group receiving them. It was agreed to monitor the numbers of suspensions and to be less rigid in the reasons for why pupils were suspended. For example, swearing was

an automatic suspension and it was agreed that Asian girls, who acquired many of their perceptions about the 'correct' Western behaviour from television might not realize that it was not acceptable behaviour to swear in everyday conversations. Time was spent counselling pupils who were in dispute to get them to solve their differences by discussion. This led to a drop in suspensions and a better standard of control became evident.

The appointment by the Authority of a school educational social worker who came from the local Asian community and who had been a former pupil of the school helped to provide a support for the girls and to improve links between home and school. However, after she returned from maternity leave, she was given responsibility for other schools. Sadly, there were no members of the community in the local police force or social services who could have given some insight to their colleagues into the life of the Asian community. In one meeting it was stated that a Pakistani girl under discussion might be sent back 'to India'. This confused the girl's father who thought they were planning to send her to a foreign country.

The pupils needed to voice their concerns and to have someone to take an active interest in their way of life. They brought tapes and films into school to use during the lunch hour and had the occasional party. Staff and non-Asian pupils were free to attend and it was a good way to hold informal discussions. Like all school children they complained about the dinners; having to eat vegetarian food was not popular. At Christmas the former Pakistani Section 11 teacher (who by this time had been given a full-time post at the school) suggested that she would provide halal chicken for the meal. The rest of the meal would be provided by the school dinner staff and eaten with the rest of the school in the dining room. This, however was found not to fit in with the regulations regarding school kitchens. Lengthy negotiations took place with the school meal service to see if halal meat could be provided for all school dinners. At an early meeting one of the school meals service stated that the provision was unnecessary as Asian pupils did not eat meat! There were local halal butchers who were willing to provide meat but only frozen carcasses are allowed in school kitchens. The approved way was for frozen meals packed in trays to be purchased from an Asian supplier. This depended upon whether viable numbers of pupils required them. Many girls said that they did not mind Western food – they just wanted to be able to eat meat. In the end, special provision could not be made.

Physical Education (PE) staff allowed pupils to change in the toilets if pupils felt that the changing rooms were not within the bounds of modesty. The wearing of head-covering in science and technology lessons was not an issue so long as these were tied back to prevent them becoming a safety risk with, for example, the Bunsen burners. Winning the confidence of the pupils was all part of the process of improving behaviour. This meant fairness but not letting pupils get away with inappropriate behaviour and trying to play school off against home. Parents were contacted if their daughters were found leaving the school during lunch time. This seemed to increase the trust between home and school.

Staff development: in-service education

Staff were encouraged to find out more about their pupils by attending courses set up by the Multi-cultural Centre. They were also invited to attend events at the Asian Cultural Centre and the weddings of former pupils. As the school let out its premises for public events, some pupils used their former school for family celebrations. Some staff were more comfortable with this than others.

In-service training was given to explain the different special needs of second language pupils when compared to those pupils with other learning difficulties. The importance of the use of mother tongue was explained as a tool for enhancing the understanding of concepts in English as well as giving recognition to the value of cultural diversity. Although students may use flawless spoken English, they do not always feel confident in using complex English sentence structure. Rubric on examination papers can seem confusing and the language used in examination questions can make it unclear to the student as to what information is required. The correct style used for answering an examination question in England may not be the one that students were originally taught. (As the numbers of students who have English as a second language increase in the higher education sector, in-service training for lecturers will also need to expand correspondingly. This is especially important for those involved in teacher education since these students will themselves be the next generation of teachers in school. Many students in teacher training and their

lecturers have had little experience of working alongside people who have English as their second language.) The staff at school were encouraged to examine the content of their courses and to look at the relevance of material used for a culturally diverse school. The English department obtained a small grant towards the purchase of books by authors from outside Europe. A group of staff interested in equal opportunities was asked to form a group to develop a school statement. This was a positive experience for us all, and the following text was hammered out and refined:

> Our school endorses the County's Equal Opportunities Statement. One of the main functions of school is to assist students to become fully participating members of society. Sadly, our society is one which discriminates against individuals because of race, gender, creed or disability. It is our intention to raise awareness of such prejudices, and evolve strategies for dealing with ignorance, misunderstanding and intolerance, to help create a society based on the principles of equality of opportunity for all.

> 1 Each individual will be equally valued and entitled to feel secure and to have equal access to the best possible education.
> 2 The Curriculum

> - The curriculum will encourage and reinforce equality of opportunity.
> - The content of the curriculum will reflect and respect the varied composition of society and be appropriately designed to dispel ignorance and misunderstanding.
> - Teaching materials and subject matter will be reviewed and amended in order to avoid stereotyping or bias in matters of race, gender or disability.
> - Opportunities will be created as far as is possible for students to experience non-traditional subjects.

> 3 Classroom practice and activities within the school

> - will encourage and reinforce equality of opportunity.
> - will reflect and celebrate cultural diversity and the customs of all students. The use of mother-tongue will be seen as a natural occurrence and as an asset to the learning process.
> - will reflect the equality between the sexes. Girls will be valued equally with boys in their access to the curriculum, to career opportun-

ities and to all aspects of the life of society as a whole.

- will display a commitment to increasing the student's self esteem and acknowledge their achievements.

4 Policy and Practice

- Equality of opportunity cannot be expected to occur spontaneously. There need to be agreed guidelines and strategies by which this policy can be implemented.
- The staff will regularly review their strategies by which this policy can be implemented.
- Racist, sexist and other discriminatory behaviour will not be accepted by staff or students. Sufferers of discrimination and harassment will be aided and supported whilst offenders should be counselled into understanding why their actions are unacceptable. Such matters should be considered for their impact on the school as a whole, for the families involved and for our society.

This statement was held to be important by the group that produced it but the rest of the staff and the pupils had not been a part of it. No strategies were evolved for monitoring whether it was being used or what would happen if it were ignored. The group tried to educate by example. With colleagues who said that there was an 'Asian' student at the staff-room door they asked if they would please go back and find out the name of the pupil. These staff encouraged their colleagues to regard festivals such as Eid as important events in the life of their students. The two Muslim and the Jewish teachers were given paid leave of absence to celebrate their major festivals.

Staff appointments

Initially the school's only Pakistani teacher was attached to the school on a part-time basis as a member of the Section 11 team. She was taken on as a full-time member of staff teaching English and Urdu after pressure was brought to bear to get her Qualified Teacher Status. She taught English initially to GCSE level and subsequently to A Level. This was not without complaint as one parent was concerned that his daughter was being taught by a 'foreigner'. She achieved acceptance because of her knowledge and her style of teaching, which captured the interest of her pupils. She later taught

religious studies alongside an enthusiastic teacher whose main subject was PE: their results were excellent. She subsequently became Head of Special Needs and obtained a Special Needs Diploma and for one year she took on the temporary appointment of Head of Year 11. Her teaching expertise, her interest in all her pupils and her fairness in relationships made her a very popular teacher and head of year. A second appointment was made to the English department of an Asian teacher born in England whose speciality lay in Drama. These Muslim teachers represented both a traditional and a less traditional stance as role models to the pupils. Other staff appointed were questioned about their attitudes and their experience in working with students from a diverse cultural background.

Raising achievement

The policy of withdrawing second language pupils from mainstream classes in order to give them extra English lessons was examined. Time lost from subjects denied them the opportunity to sit for some external examinations. It was argued that pupils remaining within subject classes were receiving English teaching and were stretching their knowledge through acquiring a specialist language set within the context of the subject. Accordingly the policy of providing support in the classroom was introduced for pupils whatever their special needs.

The policy of setting pupils when they entered the school was also discussed. The three ability sets were decided upon by written reports from their previous schools and by visits from the head of year to talk to class teachers. Asian girls tended to be in the lower sets. A positive effort to spread the intake more evenly across the groups was made. A number of the Asian pupils had not learned English until they had started at their nursery or first school: this had proved a disadvantage and had led them being placed in lower ability groups. Children who start in lower groups during their school lives can tend to remain in them because of their own and their teachers' expectations. Some teachers' feel that they must not pressurize second language children too much because they feel sorry for them and because they believe that the children really do not understand. This 'kindness' can be the worst thing that can happen and have devastating consequences, because without pressure and the expectation that they can achieve, children may drift along without focus, not making the necessary effort.

Staff were also encouraged to move away from rigid setting of top, middle and bottom towards a top set and two parallel groups. Some staff went on to choose mixed ability classes while others continued to prefer setting. Arguments will always rage in education about these differing approaches, but perhaps those who follow setting should look more closely at why they are putting pupils in lower sets. Second language difficulties should not be equated with lack of ability.

In the school Pakistani students taking A Levels were not always gaining the number of points necessary for entry into higher education (HE). As the majority had achieved good grades in GCSE Urdu, it was decided to introduce it as an A level subject. This provided the route to a degree for a number of girls. On occasions I have been asked by higher education staff if it is a 'proper' A level. I explain that a good grade in Urdu is a demonstration that they are good linguists. Their linguistic skills should be transferable and should help them to solve any problems they have with written English. Of course, they can only develop properly if their grammatical and structural errors are pointed out.

A number of Asian parents were reluctant to allow their daughters to leave home to go to college or university. They expressed fears for the moral and physical welfare of their children. Parents did not want their children to be affected by what they perceive, through the media, to be a corrupt Western society that has lost its family values. These were in the main parents who themselves had not been through higher education. Links were formed (called a 'compact' agreement) with a nearby college of higher education, where female students were in the majority. The college specialized in teacher education and was keen to have more students from ethnic minority groups. Sixth form students and their parents were invited to visit the college, and the girls were offered a taster week in which they were able to attend lectures, meet students and find about the life and work of the college. A numbers of students were offered places conditional on their A level results. Only one student took up this offer, a white English girl who wanted to continue living at home. Traditionally teaching is not regarded as a high status occupation by Asian families: the majority of the Asian girls involved in this link went on to higher education

elsewhere, some remaining in the city but others being allowed to study away from home. Not all parents were persuaded in this way and it often took hours of discussion to dispel fears. Some parents would let their daughters go on to university only if they married first. Often Asian girls will undertake long daily journeys to university in order to comply with their parents' wishes that they continue to live at home.

The school had a policy to raise educational achievements using its links with industry. All pupils in Year 11 and in the sixth form undertook work experience. Other year groups had industrial awareness weeks where industrial visits were made and people from industry came into school to work with the pupils on projects. A 'compact' scheme developed locally to create links between schools and industry under the aegis of the Training and Enterprise Council. They work together on strategies that aim to raise pupil achievement and career aspirations, and to increase their understanding of the world of work. It seemed an ideal opportunity for the school to become involved, and to formalize the links already made with local firms through work experience. The purpose is to help to raise achievement by motivating students and offering the additional support of a mentor from a local company. Mentors undergo a police check to screen out offenders against children. Their role is to work with pupils in Years 10 and 11 (ages 14–16) to encourage pupils to have good attendance and to achieve their full academic potential. Discussions focus on the world outside of school in terms of both career prospects and leisure pursuits and to explore ways in which school can help them to fulfil their ambitions. The mentors learn how to cope with young people and can have the satisfaction of seeing a pupil gain in confidence and improve their life chances. In return, the mentors gain an insight into the current education system and also an opportunity to improve their own personal skills and lead to possible promotion.

In the first year of 'compact' mentors were recruited to work with groups of three or four Year 10 pupils. All the pupils in the year group were a part of the scheme. Asian girls may feel very uncomfortable dealing with men they do not know and this shyness at interview can prejudice their chances of being offered a particular post or gaining a place in higher education. I decided that, unless it would have been far too difficult for the girl or if the parents disapproved, the girls should have the opportunity of having a male mentor especially if his career matched the pupil's aspirations. Two Muslim mentors were also recruited. Parents were kept in touch throughout the development of 'compact' and at the end of the year there was an informal evening in which pupils introduced their mentors to their parents. Knowing if 'compacts' can raise achievement in pupils is a long term process, but there is evidence from other 'compacts', such as in Birmingham, that they can be instrumental in improving achievements.

Home–school links

Before new pupils entered the school they were invited with their parents to an informal interview with one of the senior members of staff. The majority of parents attended. Asian fathers or a close male relative usually came. Some school staff do not understand that if the father can not attend it is quite appropriate for another male relative to take his place. After this meeting some of the parents did not visit the school again. A number of staff felt that this showed a lack of interest on their part not realizing that many of the parents were at work during the time parents' evenings were held. Also, there is a general attitude amongst Asian parents that at secondary level education is in the hands of the school and so parents should not interfere. School staff can be reluctant to contact a parent over the telephone as they become embarrassed if they do not understand what a parent is saying.

Asian mothers rarely visited school. The importance of the role of the Asian woman within the home can be misunderstood in Western society, being regarded as a stumbling block towards progress rather than a cultural norm. She is respected for this vital part she plays in running the home and bringing up the family, and through her society achieves its strength and continuity. We invited a group of Asian mothers to visit the school for an afternoon. They were offered transport and the visit was timed to end so they could be home when their younger children returned from school. A few were able to come, but this did not seem to be a appropriate strategy for the future. Home visits seemed a more effective way of improving home–school links. Some staff feel a reluctance to do this in case they are not welcome. Initially I went with a Pakistani colleague and always received a warm welcome and friendly hospitality. Taking sick pupils home was always a good way of keeping up links and there were frequent informal contacts while shopping in town. Attendance at community events provides another important way of keeping in touch with families and former pupils. Acquiring a few words of someone's language is much appreciated, even at the level of simple greetings. This helped to build up confidence and an increasing number of women began to come with their daughters to the informal interview before the girls started at the school. They usually were accompanied by an elder daughter or a relative who had been educated in England acting as a go between; together we all found out the answers to information we needed to know.

I was invited to visit Pakistan to stay with a colleague's family. This gave me far more feeling for the way of life for my pupils and their families than any tourist holiday could have done. Another benefit was to experience how non-English speakers must feel when they first come to England. Trying to make sense of conversations in Punjabi could be frustrating and tiring. However there is a sense of triumph when one begins to tune in to certain parts of the conversation. Unfortunately, few teachers can receive such a good in-service course.

The Asian community in the city formed an Educational Group to discuss issues in their children's education. Some teachers and members of the careers service were invited and came. One parent expressed his concern that although he had been told that his child was doing fine at school when it came to the SATs (Standard Attainment) tests this did not prove to be so. Clearly as teachers we need to have an honest dialogue with our parents and give accurate information. We need, both as reflective teachers and as researchers, to be aware of the importance of triangulating our observations and views with politically aware members of minority communities, to allow their voice to be heard.

Reflection

I left the school in 1994 and have subsequently had the opportunity to teach multi-cultural education to BEd students during teacher training, to supervise them on school experience and to recruit students into higher education.

Reflecting on the work we tried to carry out in the school, I now feel that much was very token. Eating samosas and having fashion shows where pupils could show off the latest style in *salwar kameez* was not tackling the issues of the two societies that existed within the school. The majority of pupils continued to operate on the basis of us and them. We tried the softly-softly approach of teaching by example, hoping that our own attitude would change the ethos of the school. The majority of pupils and staff liked and respected the two Asian teachers; but as teachers, without understanding their culture and communities. The Asian pupils felt some of the teachers in the school to be racist. Our own example and the Equal Opportunities Statement did little to change it. We were too diffident to tackle issues head on. It is hard to be certain whether a more proactive approach would have had greater success. With the pupils we had no procedures for dealing with racial prejudice or harassment. Telling someone that such behaviour is unpleasant and explaining why you think it is so can have very little effect on those who acquired their racial prejudices at an early stage in their lives.

Outside the school many of the attitudes pupils encounter will serve to back up their feelings. Racism is widespread and appears in many forms. As a child in Bradford I heard many silly and naïve explicitly racist remarks about the (then) new immigrants from Pakistan. They, the stories went, smelled, had lots of wives, lived with large numbers in each house, ate cat food and so on. On a recent visit to Malaysia, a white Australian in Penang airport told me she had not enjoyed her holiday because there were 'too many brown people on the island'. Others are implicit in attitudes and may seem innocent until they are considered more thoughtfully. A teacher colleague said that she knew that she was wrong but a year after they had left school she could not remember what her Asian pupils had looked like. A Roman Catholic colleague disapproved of Muslim students covering their heads, although it was presumably acceptable for nuns, who also wish to be modest.

I recently taught students in their final year of teacher training who opted to take a course on multi-cultural issues. The rest of the cohort received only one main session with the expectation that it would permeate the rest of the course. Students could also ask to be placed in a multi-ethnic school for a school experience, but the majority go to all white schools and will go on to teach in similar schools. Many future teachers will be unprepared for coping with cultural diversity and will be unsure of the backgrounds and needs of ethnic minority pupils. Racial harassment can be a major problem in mainly white schools with only a few non-white pupils (Troyna and Hatcher 1992). All teachers are required to address multi-cultural and equal opportunities issues and to develop in the minds of their pupils a respect for all people and their way of life. For all teachers to examine their teaching strategies and their curriculum remains as relevant today as it did after the Swann Report (DES 1985). Teachers, and teachers in training, need to develop understanding and competence. So also do OFSTED inspectors.

How future teachers respond to the varied needs of ethnic, religious and linguistic minorities depends a great deal on teacher education. The issues need to be *fully* understood by *all* student teachers who need to be informed at their own level and come to face their own prejudices. This understanding needs to relate to class management, teaching and learning, and the curriculum. It needs to encourage and enable teachers and future teachers to learn how to empower pupils, and to understand, respect and accept their ethnic, religious and linguistic backgrounds. Key to this is meeting people on their own ground and thereby learning to listen.

Tokenism in schools and teacher education can breed misunderstandings. Students enter teaching unaware of what they do not know and unaware that they may be perpetuating harmful practices. One danger is stereotyping: not only the type that inappropriately depicts all Eskimos living in igloos, and Africans in poverty and mud huts; but also stereotyped views of religious groups, of bilingual pupils, or of supposed ethnic characteristics. Student teachers need to view other cultures as normal and ordinary, not exotic, quaint, different and bizarre. This openness will affect their relationships with pupils by developing real interest in their backgrounds and being prepared to ask and listen – and to apologize where appropriate. Professionalism means not having favourites but applying educational criteria to all circumstances. The educational standards demanded will not be affected, for better or for worse, by ethnicity: setting easier tasks for students because they are black or bilingual will not do these pupils any favours.

Teaching needs to attract more students from ethnic minorities to act as role models for children (white as well as black), but there are issues. Teaching needs to be made attractive to these groups.

Racism needs to be eradicated from the power relationships between black student teachers and their school and HE mentors. Black students have encountered prejudice throughout education, meet it again in higher education, and once more in school from colleagues, parents and possibly children, and this can undermine their confidence. They may be unsure of their place in the educational hierarchy, or whether to use mother tongue (in which they may be fluent – but would the school approve?). They may find that their own cultural expectations are not recognized, that for example deference to authority is interpreted as lack of initiative, and that their position and status in the classroom can be undermined by insensitive colleagues and parents.

Student teachers also need the skills to support bilingual pupils. This involves a recognition of the value of mother tongue in language and concept development, in learning and in the development of self esteem, identity and belonging. Bilingual pupils warrant specialized teaching skills which teachers often do not have, so this area of work is marginalized into the work of Section 11 language support teachers (even this support has now been eroded). A pupil's work might be assessed in their weaker language, using criteria that lay greater stress on mistakes than on their potential. Penalized as pupils, it is harder to achieve higher education entry qualifications, and harder to master the complex language that higher education requires.

My experiences have led me to seriously question if multi-cultural education is enough. Telling pupils about other people's lives and beliefs seems to reinforce their 'foreignness': this way of looking at people can in itself be racist. We can interest pupils by giving then books to read by black authors, have traditional meals from other countries, visit different places of worship, and listen to music from other lands, but we should be alert to the question of whether this really creates a more universal society where racial prejudice no longer exists. At one equal opportunities meeting I attended, a black teacher said that she did not want to go to her son's school to hear steel drums. She could hear them whenever she wanted to and she would rather know how he was getting on in school. Multi-cultural events and activities can be an easy way out, a way to seem to be doing something without fear of being controversial. If the 'soft' approach of multi-cultural education has not achieved sufficient success, we perhaps need a greater emphasis on anti-racist teaching. This seeks to face head on why people have prejudices and why these are wrong. The substantial shift in this direction in the 1980s (Mullard 1982, Troyna and Williams 1986, Modgil et al. 1986, Troyna and Carrington 1990) was met by considerable opposition but the issues have not gone away. Both teachers and pupils need to examine their personal attitudes before they can move forward to a new standpoint. Some would fear that this is too radical and might increase racism in the short term; and certainly the strategy needs long-term planning to be successful, and needs to be in the hands of experienced and skilful practitioners. This has implications for teacher, initial and in-service, training. Multi-cultural and anti-racist approaches have been explored for a generation. My experience shows that we cannot rightly claim that it has yet been sufficiently part of teacher education, nor that it has been effective.

References

Council for Racial Equality (1988a) *Living in Terror.* London: CRE.

Council for Racial Equality (1988b) *Learning in Terror: A Survey of Racial Harassment in Schools and Colleges.* London: CRE.

DES (1985) *Education for All: The Final Report of the Committee of Inquiry into the Education of Children from Ethnic Minority Groups, Cmnd 9543.* London: HMSO.

Fullen, M. (1982a) Research into educational innovation. In H. L. Gray (ed.) *The Management of Educational Institutions: Theory, Research and Consultancy.* Lewes: Falmer Press: 245–61.

Fullen, M. (1982b) *The Meaning of Educational Change.* Toronto/New York: OISE/Teachers College.

Modgil, S., Verma, G., Nallick, K. and Modgil, C. (1986) *Multicultural Education: The Interminable Debate.* London: Falmer Press.

Mullard C. (1982) Multi-racial education in Britain: from assimilation to cultural pluralism. In J. Tierney (ed.) *Race, Migration and Schooling.* London: Holt, Rinehart and Winston.

Troyna, B. and Williams, J. (1986) *Racism, Education and the State: The Racialisation of Education Policy.* Beckenham: Croom Helm.

Troyna, B. and Carrington, B. (1990) *Education, Racism and Reform.* London: Routledge.

Troyna B. and Hatcher R. (1992) *Racism in Children's Lives: A Study of Mainly White Primary Schools.* London: Routledge.

8 Parents, Schools and Values

PETER LANG

> Imagine an education system where none of the educators is trained, indeed, where training is seen as a sign of weakness. There is no curriculum, but the amount to be learnt is vast and it is assumed that everyone knows what it is. There is no assessment, but if people fail the penalties are severe. This is not any old education system, but the foundation for every course, job profession in the country. It is of course the family. Parents are the most important educators in any person's life, yet they get most of the blame when things go wrong and the least support and training to ensure that all children get the best possible start in life.
>
> Titus Alexander 1996: 15

Introduction

This chapter considers some of the implications of this statement for the contribution that parents make to the values and attitudes that their children develop. Its starting point is that though the way parents undertake this aspect of their role is clearly of key importance, it is normally only discussed at a superficial level and likely to be something for which they are ill prepared. Values and attitudes are understood as follows:

> Values are the principles that inform judgements as to what is morally good or bad. Attitudes are the dispositions and inclinations we hold toward other people and their actions, and are largely dependent on what we 'value'. Both inform and influence behaviour, and hence are fundamentally important both to school life and wider society. (SCAA 1996: 8)

It asks how parents should contribute to children's values and attitudes and whether schools should support them in this? What should the relationship between these two agents be and what are the problems and complicating factors involved. In the light of the answers to these questions it suggests what the possibilities for collaboration might be.

The discussions, surveys and publications resulting from the work of The National Forum for Values in Education during Autumn 1996 generated considerable controversy and media coverage, of which the following are two examples.

> Gillian Shepherd has joined the chorus of complaint against a new moral code of values for school children that ignores the virtues of family life.
>
> The education secretary is threatening to rip up the government sponsored report, which is intended to teach children the difference between right and wrong.
>
> Mrs Shepherd acted after The Mail on Sunday revealed concerns last month over the final draft of the National Forum for Values in Education and Community report.
>
> The report ordered by the schools Curriculum and Assessment Authority, is due to be published this week.
>
> Mrs Shepherd described it as 'ludicrous', adding 'There ought to be clear indication that traditional family values are things we want the curriculum to support.' (*Mail on Sunday* 27 October, 1996)

> The commendably terse statement of values on two sides of paper was compared tongue-in cheek by Sir Ron Dearing, chairman of the Authority (SCAA), to the tablets brought from the mountain by an earlier moral guide. Moses had run into problems at this point he reminded the press conference yesterday.
>
> Certainly the code of values has already provoked controversy at the omission of marriage as an essential element, and Nick Tate, the Authority's chief executive, sighed that charity had been in short supply in the last few days.

Although drawn up for schools, the statement of values was really directed at the whole of society. 'Schools are very moral places . . . what they need is general public backing for what they do' said Dr Tate. Agreeing on shared values was of great symbolic importance and would give schools the confidence to promote those values.

Dr Tate denied the project was over ambitious and irrelevant to parents. 'They want to feel the values they are promoting at home are being supported in the school. They do not have a narrow and limited view of education.' (Donald MacLeod, in the *Guardian* 31 October, 1996)

Apart from illustrating the level of controversy the work of the Values Forum generated, these quotations reflect a tension that has underlain much popular educational debate in the area of moral education and values in the 1990s, a tension which, as in this case, has been highlighted at regular intervals when particular points have been focused on by the media. The notion of traditional family values has for example had a particularly good airing, as has support for the need for real punishments to be administered to the young, in particular physical punishment.

The tension can be seen as existing between two strongly opposed views. The first is the idea that there are indeed traditional family values and effective means of firm discipline, both of which have been allowed to decline at a significant cost to the quality of life both in ethical and practical terms, and that these are common sense and unproblematic and best left in the hands of parents and possibly of teachers of a traditional kind (contrasted with the stereotyped progressive educationalists and other do-gooders). The second is a view that suggests that the nature of morality and values is not simple or unproblematic, particularly in a socially and culturally diverse society in which there may be a need for some recognition of value differences. An important dimension of this view is that any attempts to promote a set of values must take into account the reality of society as it exists now, though not necessarily to condone this. The argument here being that we need to start from where people are if progress is to be made, not where they might have been in some speculative golden age in the past.

Thus, on the one side Gillian Shepherd defends traditional family values while on the other Dr Nick Tate suggests that the fact that it has been possible, after considerable effort, to produce a set of shared values is in itself a great achievement and that far from the traditionalist view of schools as seed beds for sloppy progressivism, they are actually very moral places and it is society and, implicitly, families that need to support them. However, he did not go on to note that it was an achievement made possible through casting each value at a very general level and in most cases avoiding those values where significant cultural differences exist in how they are interpreted, though this had been recognized during the work of the Forum itself.

The work of the Values Forum has now received approval from the government and a press release from SCAA dated 19 May, 1996 stated, 'Ministers have approved plans by the School Curriculum and Assessment Authority (SCAA) to take forward work on values education.' It quotes Estelle Morris MP and Parliamentary under-secretary of State for Education as saying, 'The spiritual, moral, social and cultural development of our children is just as important as academic knowledge. We encourage schools to take forward SCAA's work in this area.' The quotations from Nick Tate and Estelle Morris include assumptions with which this chapter is concerned. Estelle Morris reinforces the view that schools have an important contribution to make in promoting values and Nick Tate makes two significant assumptions, that parents do actively promote a set of values that they see as appropriate for their children, and that they see the school as supporting them in this.

If, then, both schools and families have roles to play in promoting the development of values in children and young people, what should the relationship between these two agents be? Can they work together; should one or the other take the leading role, or are their concerns so different that they must operate independently? Given the diverse nature of schools and families in our socially and culturally plural society is anything more than the most superficial of collaborations possible? Indeed, is it possible, or realistic to seek to suggest what the relationship between the roles of schools and families in development of values in the young should be? As will be discussed below, there are a number of things that make this very difficult. This is the reality of the current situation, but it is a reality that reinforces the need for discussing how things might best be approached, for without dialogue and debate little is likely to change. The opening quotation suggests the centrality of parents' roles in the development of their children, and it is to this we now move.

Understanding parents' contributions to the development of their children's values

In the opening quotations both Gillian Shepherd and Nick Tate implicitly supported the idea that not only do clear values exist in families, but that these will be effectively transmitted by parents to their offspring. Disagreement about this common-sense view of the family have tended to focus on different family structures and ignored the issues raised by the different cultural backgrounds involved. Further, this popular common-sense belief about families and values, apart from being grossly simplistic is only one side of the confused and contradictory views and expectations of families. These have characterized popular debate at least since the time of the Maria Colville case when a young girl, whose family was being monitored by Social Services, was abused and eventually killed by her parents.

The most recent manifestations are clearly identified in this comment by Wyness:

> The convergence of public order policy and educational reform in Britain has generated compelling, if inconsistent images of the 'responsible parent'. On the one hand, parental responsibilities are invoked as legitimate socialising powers set against the 'collectivist' influence of the educational establishment. On the other hand, these same responsibilities are implicated as part of an ever-tightening alleged causal chain which links delinquency and child abuse to inadequate parenting. What we are not offered are realistic images of how parents themselves routinely negotiate what Bronfenbrenner (quoted in Popenoe 1988, p. 330) calls the 'enduring irrational emotional involvement' with children.   (Wyness 1996: 1)

Recently we have been subjected to much talk of 'family values' and appeals to the practical common sense of parents. Sections of the media, particularly the tabloid press, have appeared to suggest that the normal British family knows best on matters as far apart as the EC and whether children should be smacked. At the same time there has been talk of curfews for out of control primary age children and ways of making parents take responsibility for their children's actions. There has been disagreement

about what parents can or can't do, and claims made that children behave the way they do because their parents are too preoccupied to control them or can't be bothered to tell them the difference between right and wrong.

One thing that this confused popular debate makes clear is that, what ever else may be appropriate, treating families and parents as if they were a homogenous group is not. Apart from the social and cultural diversity it is certain that within every group there will be families who are more or less competent in the tasks involved in child-rearing.

In the quotation from Wyness above his reference to Bronfenbrenner draws attention to the fact that we know very little about the way parents actually operate both in terms of beliefs and actions in the day-to-day business of child-rearing. So, if we ask the question what constitutes an effective family, we get answers that don't deal with how they actually operate and instead list characteristics of effective families (see, for example, Tizard and Hughes 1984, Pugh and De'Ath 1984).

Traditional theories of moral development (Piaget 1932, Kohlberg 1976) have never been of much help to those seeking to develop practical strategies in schools (especially in multi-cultural situations) and this is true of the roles of schools and families in the development of values. There are, however, instances of work with a more psychological base that could provide limited insights into the way families may operate effectively in areas closely related to that of the development of values. Studies of the way parents can influence the level of social competence and effective interpersonal relationships in their children provides an illustration of this.

> Social competence may be, in part, a product of parents' internal working models of attachment caregiving, which influence parents' caregiving ideas and their processing of information in caregiving situations. The more blocked is parents' processing of affective information, the less is their ability to notice, freely communicate about, and appropriately respond to their own and their children's emotions in caregiving situations. These effects may interfere with parental sensitivity, promote the development of felt insecurity in the child, and foster the development of peer relational difficulties.

We described some encouraging empirical evidence for this pathway from parents' caregiving ideas to their children's social competence. Mothers who believe social competence is important, who recognise their child's need and capacity for autonomous learning, and who think external factors are responsible when difficulties occur tend to have children who demonstrate social competence. (Mills and Rubin 1993: 115)

In this chapter we have proposed that parents 'teach' children about interpersonal relationships tacitly through their style of interacting with their children and explicitly through their verbal communications regarding social relationships. We have speculated that the messages conveyed through these two channels affect separate, but perhaps overlapping, aspects of children's social competence. Data from our pilot study support the contention that parent–child synchrony and parent coaching of social skills make independent contributions to children's social competence with peers. (Pettit and Mize 1993: 151)

These two extracts offer a number of points about the development of social competence and effective interpersonal relationships which might be extrapolated to the development of values and attitudes. They suggest that the way that parents influence the development of values and attitudes in their children is likely to be complex and multi-faceted. Significantly, it will be a process that will involve both conscious and explicit actions and behaviour where the effect is not recognized. The ideas and perceptions of parents about what should be involved, the models they themselves offer and their conscious efforts to instruct may all play a part. These points can only be seen as a starting point. 'Social competence' is itself a relative concept tied to the cultural milieu in which it is exercised. The work referred to in these extracts is clearly informed by a particular notion of social competence. Thus, in using these findings to illuminate values and attitude development there is a danger of applying a culturally specific model to a culturally plural situation. Nevertheless, two key points have emerged: if attempts are to be made to help and support parents in this area, it will be a complex undertaking and one where exactly which aspects of the process are being engaged with must be made clear; given these difficulties, what schools can contribute will be quite limited and would need to be fairly specific and sharply focused.

The complexity can be seen in terms of transmission – there is a difference between parents being committed to a set of values and possessing a model of how they should be developed. In the case of outcomes, parental expectations may range from

the intentional implanting of a set of unquestioned values to values developed rationally and at the other extreme emphasizing the development of critical thinking ability in their children to enable them to make rational decisions about values for themselves.

A limited enquiry involving discussions with some twenty parents supported the typology above. Some of the parents saw themselves as dealing with a clear set of values while others saw their nature as more problematic. When it came to how these should be passed on some parents appeared to have no coherent view while others offered a very simplistic one that amounted to stating the values and punishing when the child's behaviour ignored the values that had been presented to them. Where parents saw the process as a more complicated one, none responded with the development of an overall strategy. Instead they focused on specific aspects such as the need for consistency, providing an appropriate behavioural model and discussing value issues in an open and neutral way. Those parents from ethnic-minority backgrounds were not significantly different in terms of their responses.

In spite of our limited understanding of the processes involved, the picture that has emerged is one where the complexity of the processes involved both suggest the need for support for parents and that the form that such support should take will be difficult to determine. What models of support currently exist?

Supporting parenting

Some writers are quite unequivocal about the need for support:

The idea of the home as a deliberate agent of education, especially for democracy and its values, as a centre of creative, responsible, co-operative activity in which young and old share a common life, contributing as they are able, and respected as integral members of its community – this is rarer than it used to be. It is a trend that must be reversed; schools are indispensable, but the best of them cannot compensate for defective homes; the teacher is no substitute for the parent, this means educating for parenthood and family life. It is sometimes supposed by those without experience of it that rearing children is a simple task for which instinct alone is necessary . . . the successful rearing of children in a modern democracy requires knowledge and skills such as only specific training can supply, knowledge not only of hygiene, psychology and household management but of the values by which our society lives and the qualities it requires in its citizens.   (F. Garforth 1985: 168)

Garforth is less clear about the form this 'explicit training' should take. Currently ideas for the development of parenting skills generally takes two forms, either courses for adolescents run as part of the school curriculum or courses for those who are already parents. The arguments for the need for support in the development of parenting skills tend to fall along a continuum whose polarities imply very different responses in terms of action. At one extreme the need is based on the view that certain groups of parents possess at best the most rudimentary skills, and are therefore unable to exercise proper control over their children's behaviour – in this case the need is seen as one of society. At the other extreme the need is perceived by parents themselves and involves developing higher order skills to enable their children to develop as competent and emotionally mature individuals. Here the need is seen in terms of individual parents and children. Somewhere between these two extremes is a need, again often perceived by parents themselves, that arises from the difficult and often exhausting nature of parenting. Here what is sought are practical strategies for survival. Thus, the picture is again a complex one, one where the emphasis in terms of need ranges from the control of the potentially delinquent to the promotion of social and emotional competence. There is no real emphasis on the issue of values or attitude development.

As opposed to a concern about what is needed, what is actually available to parents? Tizard and Hughes (1984) are critical of courses that involve attempts by professionals to alter the way in which parents carry out their educational role and go on to suggest: 'Indeed in our opinion, it is time to shift the emphasis away from what parents should learn from professionals and towards what professionals can learn from studying parents and children at home' (op. cit.: 63). Twelve years later Alexander, while supporting the views of Tizard and Hughes, draws attention to the responses which involve initiatives from parents themselves:

> Yet there has been a growth in different kinds of parenting education in response to parents' needs. These courses or parents groups provide opportunities to share experiences and learn practical strategies for dealing with everyday problems.

Programmes like *Parent Link* and *Family Caring Trust* are not run by professional agencies, but by parents or volunteers who have trained to use parents' own experiences and a package of materials with groups. Unlike the professional parent education courses criticised by Tizard and Hughes, which are mainly targeted at parents considered 'deprived' or 'inadequate', these courses are more available in middle class areas where parents can afford to pay. These parents see the value of improving parenting and are less likely to fear intervention by social services or other professionals than in many poor areas. But many of these materials are also being used successfully by working-class, African Caribbean and bilingual Asian parents, as in the London Borough of Waltham forest.   (Alexander ibid: 21)

Pugh et al. (1994) conducted a comprehensive survey of policy and practice in parent education of this kind. They listed the main features of such programmes; some points they identify are:

• a belief that 'good enough' parents are responsible, authoritative, assertive, positive, democratic and consistent;
• they are not autocratic, authoritarian or permissive;
• parents' strengths should be reaffirmed, building on confidence and self-esteem;
• experience feelings and relationships are as important as knowledge, with the emphasis on understanding and enjoyment.   (76–7)

Certainly the features of parenting programmes presented here suggest an approach where the inclusion of a values dimension would be appropriate. Currently they do not contain any discussion of values or attitudes or how they might be developed. Thus the Parent Link approach, while stressing that all in the family have rights and providing strategies for dealing with 'unacceptable' behaviour, does not consider the basis upon which rights might be established or what counts as 'unacceptable'. A brief survey of popular handbooks concerned with the development of various aspects of parenting skill reveals a very similar situation; for example in one such book Faber and Mazlish (1982: 139) list the ways autonomy may be encouraged:

1   Let children make choices.
2   Show respect for a child's struggle.
3   Don't ask too many questions.
4   Don't rush to answer questions.

5 Encourage children to use sources outside the home.
6 Don't take away hope.

They do not consider why autonomy is worth achieving, but simply present it as a way of overcoming dependency.

Apart from their neglect of values and attitudes there is another important point about these approaches: they are not themselves value free, they all reflect a humanistic ideology and are influenced by the precepts of humanistic psychology. This implies a need for a certain degree of caution when considering if they are an appropriate basis for development into the area of values. The humanistic perspective is closely identified with certain class and cultural perspectives, and in spite of Alexander's claim above, might not be the only approach appropriate in culturally plural situations.

Though existing approaches to parent education do not deal with values and attitudes this does not mean they should be ignored. There is evidence that these humanistically-orientated approaches are effective in relation to other aspects of parenting and might provide a suitable basis for extension into these areas.

The school's contribution

There are those who see the school as central to values development:

> unless schools take seriously this aspect of education, the values conveyed to children are simply those of the adults who happen to wield power in the environment in which they grow up. The question then becomes whose values. This turns out to be a very complicated matter indeed, and one which, as regards this child or that, requires the acknowledgement of immense diversity. What can we therefore do about it? We can accept this and encourage schools to attend to the one person who needs to cope with the particular package of values presented to him or her – the child. Education need to be radically person centred. (Watson and Ashton 1995: 20)

Towards the end of their book these writers comment:

> Overall, we stress the importance of a system of education which has as its cornerstone a commitment to help pupils to discriminate between the conflicting values which operate so pervasively

throughout society. For such a system to be effective, education in beliefs and values will need to infiltrate every element of school life, both within lessons and outside them. (Ibid.: 149)

To achieve this they argue for an approach that involves a form of values clarification where the values involved are explicitly acknowledged. In this book parents are barely mentioned, and issues connected with pluralism and cultural difference not considered at all. A very similar situation is found in Bottrey's (1990) otherwise valuable book *The Morality of the School*.

So far as the literature is concerned there is little that seriously considers parents in relation to the school's role in developing values and attitudes in its pupils. There is certainly nothing that addresses how schools and parents might collaborate with and support each other. Apart from the fact that the potential for such collaboration has not been considered, there are issues concerning home–school links that may also create problems. One problem which, though created by the policies of the previous government, does not look likely to change with the new one is identified by Tomlinson.

> This chapter started from the premise that improving children's educational performance, enhancing their personal and social development and creating genuine home–school links could happen only if the current stress on parents as consumers of education and agents of competition gave way to a belief that parents must be partners in the educative process. (Tomlinson 1995: 245)

Not only does Tomlinson argue that genuine partnership is unlikely to develop while a free market model is imposed on education, she also stresses that partnership between schools and ethnic minority groups is generally a very long way from being achieved.

> There has long been a mismatch of expectations between what minority parents expected of education and what teachers felt they could offer. Minority parents, Afro-Caribbean, Indian, Pakistani, Bangladeshi, Chinese and others – have all indicated that they not only want their children equipped with the credentials and skills on a par with white pupils, they also want their backgrounds and cultures taken seriously in school, they want racism and racial harassment eradicated. (Ibid.: 239–40)

Again, an essential element of partnership is that both parties involved would have a right to express their views and contribute to the way things develop, something that Vincent and Tomlinson (1997: 366) assert does not take place: 'Therefore, it is possible to conclude that there are few opportunities for collective parental participation at any level of the education system. Even the opportunities for the exercise of individual 'voice' are dependent to some extent upon local circumstances.' Indeed, they argue that the very concept of 'partnership' has been transformed into a means of social control of both pupils and parents.

> However, recently, aspects of the widespread educational restructuring have served to translate the 'soft' language of partnership into a disciplinary mechanism that is more overtly controlling of children's home lives. Contracts have become rearticulted as a means, not of provoking and supporting parents–teacher dialogue about ways in which they could co-operate (their original 'cuddly concept' [MacLeod, 1996] but as a mechanism for enforcing school discipline.   (Ibid.: 369)

In this section it has been shown that the current situation is not a promising one so far as the development of collaboration or mutual support is concerned. This is both because there is little existing work or writing to inform it and because generally relationships between schools and parents are of a kind that would inhibit or prevent meaningful work being undertaken.

Possible ways forward

Though the writers quoted above all make valid points, it seems likely that there is a larger middle ground than is recognized. In my view this is typified by the views of the staff of a large multi-cultural primary school in Coventry. In a discussion about values and parents they said they felt there was moral ground in the middle and that they had not encountered problems in relation to the different belief systems represented amongst parents. They saw the value of shared values and a fully developed Personal and Social Education (PSE) policy, but felt other pressures had prevented them getting round to detailed work in these areas. When asked about a possible contribution to value development in the home, the headteacher made an important point that parents, unlike schools, are not organizations and that with all the goodwill in the world, it

is actually very difficult for a school to engage with parents as a body. There was goodwill at this school but a greater priority would have to be given and a sharper focus provided before collaboration with parents in relation to developing values would be possible.

One way of initiating collaboration would be to focus on the qualities that the school should seek to develop in its pupils. If parents could be involved in discussions about this, consideration of values would inevitably be involved. There are many key qualities such as fairness, honesty, empathy, concern for the environment, respect for tradition, etc. that appear not to be culture bound. In research in which I have been involved, representatives of thirteen European countries drew up a list of twenty qualities which all agreed it was important for the school to seek to develop in its pupils. Shown to multi-cultural groups in Singapore, groups in China and a group of Israeli–Arabs, support for all twenty qualities was also forthcoming. Identifying qualities could be followed by a consideration of how they might be developed in school, this in turn could move on to discussion of ways the home might contribute.

Haydon stresses the need for teachers to discuss their values:

> Whatever their background, teachers have to respond to diversity of values among the people they are teaching and among parents, some of whom may hold values with which a teacher profoundly disagrees. At the same time, teachers have to educate people in such a way that they will themselves be able to cope with conflicts of values within the society. If teachers are not able to face openly and with tolerance their own differences in values, they will hardly be able to help others to do so. This means that discussions between teachers, in which their own differences are honestly explored, ought to be an essential part of the expectations which the profession has of itself.   (Haydon 1997: 155)

My own research has shown that where schools build on Haydon's suggestion and go on to identify what values they can agree about, the development of these shared values can have a very positive effect on the schools' overall effectiveness. Here again parents could be involved in some parts of these discussions. For parents alone, schools could set up well organized, unthreatening forums in which they could discuss these issues together, find how much they share with other parents, gain support and develop confidence and possibly consider strategies.

Through such initiatives parents would come to appreciate the complexity of an area that they may well not think about or take for granted. Teachers and parents from all cultural backgrounds would benefit and come to understand each other better. Though what is described in this last section would be little more than a consciousness-raising exercise and would be unlikely to reach all parents, for those involved, heightened awareness would be likely to result in a more considered approach to the development of values and attitudes in their own children.

References

Alexander, T. (1996) Learning begins at home: implications for a learning society. In J. Bastiani and S. Wolfendale *Home-School Work in Britain: Review, Reflection and Development.* London: David Fulton.

Bottery, M. (1990) *The Morality of the School.* London: Cassell.

Bronfenbrenner, U. (1970) *Two Worlds of Childhood.* New York: Touchstone.

Faber, A. and Mazlish, E. (1982) *How to Talk So Kids Will Listen and Listen So Kids Will Talk.* New York: Avon Books: 139.

Garforth, F. W. (1985) *Aims, Values and Education.* London: Charity Gate Press.

Haydon, G. (1997) *Teaching About Values: A New Approach.* London: Cassell.

Kohlberg, L. (1976) Moral stages and moralisation: the cognitive-developmental approach. In T. Lickonia (ed.) *Moral Development and Behaviour.* New York: Holt Rinehart and Winston.

MacLeod, D. (1996) Would you sign this? *Guardian* 15 October.

Mills, R. and Rubin, K. (1993) Parental ideas as influences on children's social competence. In S. Duck (ed.) *Learning about Relationships.* London: Sage.

Popenoe, D. (1988) *Disturbing the Nest.* New York: Aldine de Gruyter.

SCAA (1996) Discussion Papers No. 6. *Education for Adult Life: The Spiritual and Moral Development of Young People.* London: SCAA.

Pettit, G. and Mize, J. (1993) Substance and style: understanding the ways in which parents teach children about social relationships. In S. Duck (ed.) *Learning about Relationships.* London: Sage.

Piaget, J. (1932) *The Moral Judgement of the Child.* Harmondsworth: Penguin.

Pugh, G., De'Ath, E. and Smith, C. (1994) *Confident Parents, Confident Children: Policy and Practice in Parent Education and Support.* London: National Children's Bureau.

Tizard, B. and Hughes, M. (1984) *Young Children Learning: Talking and Thinking at Home and at School.* London: Fontana.

Tomlinson, S. (1995) Home–school links. In R. Best, P. Lang, C. Lodge and C. Watkins (eds) *Pastoral Care and Personal and Social Education: Entitlement and Provision.* London: Cassell.

Vincent, C. and Tomlinson, S. (1997) Home–school relationships: 'the swarming of disciplinary mechanisms'. *British Educational Research Journal* 23 (3).

Watson, B. and Ashton, E. (1995) *Education Assumptions and Values.* London: David Fulton.

Wyness, M. G. (1996) *Schooling, Welfare and Parental Responsibility.* London: Falmer Press.

9 Racist Bullying: Creating Understanding and Strategies for Teachers

KEITH SULLIVAN

Introduction

At Burnage High School in Manchester, England, in 1986, Ahmed Ullah, a 13-year old Asian boy was murdered in the playground by a white teenager who had a history of bullying and disruptive behaviour. For many ethnic minority children, racist intimidation and bullying is the gauntlet that they have to run in the classroom, the playground and the world at large on a daily basis; incidents like the murder of Ahmed Ullah stand as a symbol of what could happen to them.[1]

In recent years, school bullying has become a prominent international educational issue. The efforts of a large number of researchers and practitioners have been expended on understanding the dynamics and characteristics of bullying in its various forms and in finding ways to deal practically and effectively with it. (See, for instance, Olweus 1993 [Sweden], Smith and Sharp 1994, Sharp and Smith 1994, Cowie and Sharp 1994, Tattum and Herbert 1993, Maines and Robinson 1992, Besag 1989, 1992 [UK], Rigby 1996a, Slee 1996 [Australia], Rubin and Pepler 1989 [Canada], O'Moore and Hillery 1989 [Ireland], and Sullivan 1997 [New Zealand].) Similarly, much energy has been spent on understanding and countering racism in schools (see, for instance, Alton-Lee, Nuthall and Patrick 1987, Banks 1994, Brandt 1986, Donn and Schick 1995, Foster 1990, Gaine 1987, Gillborn 1990, Hessari and Hill 1989, Hingangaroa-Smith 1990, Jeffcoate 1985, Jones 1991, Modgil *et al.* 1986, Sullivan 1993, Troyna and Hatcher 1992).

The subject of this chapter is racist bullying, the area where racism and bullying meet. In exploring racist bullying, I will provide a definition and an overview of contemporary themes that have emerged both internationally and in my own set-

ting of Aotearoa/New Zealand. I will also provide a framework for finding effective solutions for reflective teachers, that is, solutions that provide theoretical perspectives and clear information as well as useful and practical ways of dealing with racist bullying on a day-to-day basis and in the long term.

Defining racist bullying

As thinking about bullying, harassment and racism has developed, problems have arisen over terminology and meaning. When people use the same descriptors but with different meanings, then confusion arises, with the result that people 'talk past each other'.[2] This section will consider the variety of interpretations and posit a definition of racist bullying.

Spoonley (1988) defines racism as 'prejudice plus power' (p. 42). He describes prejudice as negative, inflexible and stereotyped attitudes towards others supported by notions of genetic, intellectual and cultural superiority. When such negative attitudes are combined with power and the ability to discriminate against individuals from another ethnic group, this is racism. It can be argued that racism has three main manifestations: it can be individualized, that is, practised by one individual against another or others; collective, when it is practised by a group of people against an individual or a group; or institutionalized, when it is embedded within the structures and institutions of society.

Rigby (1996b) defines bullying as the 'repeated oppression, psychological or physical of a less powerful person by a more powerful individual or group of persons' (p. 303). He points out that bullying, whether physical or psychological, lives in the mind of the victimized person, not only at the time of being bullied but in anticipation of bullying and after having been bullied, and that a central feature is the imbalance of power between the bully or bullies and the victim. He also points out that bullying takes many forms: physical, such as hitting and kicking which occurs mainly amongst boys; verbal abuse and name-calling; cruel and continued teasing; removing and hiding belongings; and purposely excluding, the last occurring more amongst girls.

While the British use the term 'bullying', the Americans refer to the same range of phenomena as harassment (Rigby 1996b). On the other hand, in Australia, these terms are often used interchangeably but harassment is also used with reference to sexual or racial annoyance or aggression, and to minor forms of bullying. Rigby suggests that there is a distinction between harassment and bullying: racial harassment occurs because of prejudice and wrong information and can be addressed through providing a corrective educational solution, whereas bullying occurs because the bully takes pleasure in carrying out the act of bullying. In this case any ethnic/racial dimension is merely one consideration, one aspect that makes the potential victim vulnerable.

In the UK, Kelly (1994) interprets harassment as a group phenomenon and bullying as a personal experience. She describes harassment as:

> distinguished by the fact that it can be legitimated by reference to an ethos which supports hierarchies of dominance, exclusion and mistreatment of those who are made into objects of mistrust, dislike, even hatred. Harassment is also tied in with group dynamics – the bonding of the in-group, the disarray of the out-group; and with the social world outside the school in which the same values thrive. (p. 66)

On the other hand, she suggests that bullying is a personal experience inflicted on individuals with limited social skills.

> Bullying causes deep pain because it comprises an intensely 'personal' mistreatment, usually of individuals by means of secret, calculated and often prolonged forms of abuse. The victims are isolated and instructed in helplessness. The bullies learn and practise distorted interpersonal skills. Bullies and victims are locked into relations of dominance and subordination, intimidation and threat. The observers collude in the submission of the victims and the gratification of the bullies.   (Kelly 1993: 146)

While Kelly's descriptions of the group ethos attached to racist harassment seem valid, I would argue that although bullying can be one on one it often occurs with the direct support of co-bullies or the intimidation or acquiescence of bystanders. The creation of in-groups and out-groups is central to bullying dynamics (see Hargreaves 1973, Sullivan 1998). Therefore I would argue that there is sufficient overlap in the two terms, bullying and harassment, that they can be used interchangeably. Similarly, although I accept that there are differently motivated forms of bullying and harassment, as defined by Rigby, this is more useful as a guide to remedying the situation rather than an apposite semantic breakdown.

For the purpose of creating a workable mechanism, I will define racist bullying as an abuse of power that involves either physical or psychological bullying (including name-calling and exclusion) or both to demean or harm a person from another ethnic group. Racist bullying can occur on a one-to-one basis, which can be termed individual racist bullying; can be carried out by a group of people, which is collective racist bullying; or can occur because of the societal structures, which is institutional racist bullying.

The issues in racist bullying

Research on racist bullying is relatively sparse and our understanding of this form of bullying is very limited as a result. The scholarship does not often detect forms of bullying as racist apart from racist name-calling because disentangling the bullying and the racism is often difficult. There are issues that need examination, however, and I will discuss these individually.

Individual and collective racist bullying

Issue one: racist name-calling as bullying
In a survey of over 6,000 British school children, Whitney and Smith (1993) state that of those being bullied, 14.8 per cent in junior/middle schools and 9.4 per cent in secondary schools reported 'being called nasty names about my colour or race'. The subjects of this study were not identified by ethnicity so it is impossible to tell what percentage of the sample were from ethnic minority groups. However, in a smaller study by Moran *et al.* (1993),

the researchers focused on thirty-three pairs of Asian and white children (who were matched for gender, age and school) and found that although there was no significant difference in the level of bullying between the groups, there was a significant difference for racist name-calling by ethnicity. They reported that 'one-half of the bullied Asian children, but none of the bullied white children were called names about their colour. This racist name-calling appeared hurtful to the recipients and was often the reason for disliking other children' (p. 431).

Similarly, in their evaluation of the New Zealand *Eliminating Violence* anti-bullying programme, Moore et al. (1997) report a very high incidence of racist name-calling. They carried out case studies in three Auckland secondary schools and administered a questionnaire on three occasions – before the programme was initiated, half-way through (at six months), and at the end of the programme (one year after the first questionnaires had been administered) – and questioned both victims and perpetrators of bullying.

In School 1, 46 per cent of the students reported having been a victim of bullying before the programme was introduced. This had dropped to 34 per cent at the time of the third questionnaire. From answers received for the first and third questionnaire, 35 per cent and 31 per cent respectively reported having been 'called names because of race/colour'. From questionnaires answered by those who bullied, 28 per cent and 26 per cent respectively reported having 'called names because of race/colour'.[3]

In School 2, of students responding to the questionnaire on the first and third occasion, 76 per cent and 62 per cent respectively reported having been bullied. At these times, 47 per cent and 42 per cent respectively reported having been 'called names because of race/colour' (p. 54). For those who bullied, 48 per cent and 42 per cent respectively reported that they had 'called names because of race/colour'.

In School 3, of students responding to the questionnaire on the first and third occasion, 76 per cent and 72 per cent respectively reported having been bullied, and 45 per cent and 43 per cent respectively reported having been 'called names because of race/colour'. For those who bullied, 27 per cent and 23 per cent respectively reported that they had 'called names because of race/colour'.

According to the above research findings, racist name-calling is widely experienced by ethnic minority children in both the UK and New Zealand. It is by far the easiest racist bullying to identify, to respond to and therefore to educate against. It is also probably an indicator of the presence of other forms of racist bullying that are not so easy to detect.

Issue two: more pernicious forms of racist bullying
The British Sheffield bullying project (see Sharp and Smith 1994, and Smith and Sharp 1994) entailed a massive amount of government funding and is perhaps the most extensive project on bullying to date. Its findings and the perspectives it has chosen to highlight have created an anti-bullying cutting edge. Although there is an increasing body of evidence that racist name-calling is rife, research into other areas of racist bullying, that is, physical and psychological bullying, are more difficult to identify. From an anti-racist perspective, Loach and Bloor (1995) caution that in being subsumed under the umbrella of bullying, racism could be seen in a simplistic way that detaches it from its often brutal reality and that treating it as bullying rather than racism could allow this complex issue to be misunderstood, ignored or even hidden. They warn, 'Bullying is a convenient way for institutions to acknowledge the *fact* of the conflict within their walls without having to face the *meaning* of that conflict' (p. 18). Consequently they can be diverted into dealing with symptoms rather than the underlying problem of racism. The authors agree a more simple approach would be acceptable:

> if it were possible . . . to differentiate between occasions when physical abuse from a white child to a black child was *racism* and when it was simply *bullying*. However, this differentiation does not and cannot happen in practice, so that what we are left with in this research and in the received wisdom of the teaching and the social work world is the 'knowledge' that when one child hits another child then that is an act of bullying not an act of racism or sexism or ableism. At best, the decision as to whether the act is racism or not is left to the discretion of the teacher making the judgement. If an adult perpetrates an act of violence against a black adult, the courts and public opinion still seem to have trouble deciding whether or not to call the act racism. When it is a white child acting against a black child the difficult question is avoided altogether since by definition this activity must simply be bullying.   (p. 19)

Loach and Bloor's concern is that the physical intimidation, exclusion, humiliation and physical assault of racist bullying – the extreme of which is presented by the murder of Ahmed Ullah – can be easily misread, inadequately acknowledged or totally misunderstood and the complex and racist context can thus be ignored. This is bound to lead to deficient problem-solving.

Troyna and Hatcher (1992) provide an interesting analysis of predominantly white schools with a minority of black children (2–6 on average) per class in Britain. To all intents and purposes, these schools appear to be good examples of what Troyna and Hatcher term the 'contact hypothesis' – that the positive experiences of the white and black children being together do away with discriminatory behaviour and racial prejudice. They observe, however, that a closer investigation shows that racism emerges as a significant feature of the culture of such schools and they identify racist name-calling as by far the most common form of racism.

I would argue that it is the tip of the iceberg and an indicator of less easily identified forms of racism. It can be detected categorically because of its clarity and concreteness, while identifying other forms of bullying as specifically racist is more difficult. When bullying is expressed as physical violence or is exclusionary and isolating, this may be due to racial hatred, but if the act is a physical or psychological one the fact that it may be racially motivated is often difficult to prove. This can be exacerbated because psychological bullying through marginalization and exclusion often relies on strategies of disempowerment through providing either false or incomplete information. For instance, an excluded child may be told that the shoes they own are not cool. In order to try to please the perpetrators of their bullying, the victimized child may convince her parents to buy the brand of shoes that the perpetrators claim to be cool, only to be told that they are no longer cool; the bullying children may then choose to focus on the uncoolness of the victim's clothes, thereby shifting the supposed rules.

This type of psychological cruelty may have been put in place because the child is from an ethnic minority, and the same bullying acts may also be applied to another child who has been excluded for other reasons. Further to this, if a child is told that she is being excluded because of ethnicity or skin colour, she has something tangible to deal with, and the bully loses the power of unpredictability and control over ever-changing and apparently random 'rules'. Part of the insidiousness of bullying in all its forms is the comparison in power-holding

between the victim and the bully, and much of the power of the bully resides in the persistence and unavoidability of the attacks. The factors which lead to racist bullying – the racism of the bully and the ethnicity of the victim – are static and it is therefore likely that the disguise of the forms that the bullying takes are a convenient cover for the deep structure of the racism that lies underneath.

Issue three: racist bullying of members of 'easy target' ethnic groups

Troyna and Hatcher (1992) suggest that some ethnic groups are seen as easier targets than others for racial harassment or bullying. For instance, in England, Afro-Caribbeans are seen as physically able to stand up for themselves and are well-represented in sports and athletics so amongst those with racist tendencies there is even a grudging respect. It is therefore easier to pick on Asians as they are seen as weak and easily intimidated. Troyna and Hatcher document the extensive 'Paki' bashing that has occurred over the years in England which backs up this impression.

Although research has not been done in this area in New Zealand, Maori and Pacific Island groups are seen as similarly tough and are well represented on sports teams. There is also a sub-culture that emulates Afro-American attitudes, ways of speaking and music and the tendency to form gangs. On the other hand, Chinese and Indian communities are small in New Zealand, have a reputation for getting themselves well educated and are regarded as a financial threat to the ordinary New Zealander. Although information is anecdotal and inconclusive, Asians are perceived as unaggressive and 'easy targets' and are increasingly becoming victims of racist bullying (see Ku 1992, for an elaboration of this syndrome).

Institutional racist bullying

Issue four: 'symbolic violence' as institutional racist bullying

David Corson (1992) in his article 'Minority cultural values and discourse norms in majority culture classrooms' focuses on the learning experiences of indigenous groups – Maori, kooris (Australian aboriginals), North American First Nations peoples and Hawaiians – and draws the following conclusion:

Often culturally different students will approach discourse activities in majority culture classrooms in ways that are inconsistent with school norms but consistent with their own cultural norms and values. The evidence confirms that teachers can and do make incorrect assessments of their students' ability because of this problem which affects all modes of language and which is clearly more likely to occur when the distance between the teacher's culture and the child's is greater. I need not elaborate on the social justice issue involved here: more than simple miscommunication results from these misassessments; life chances are often reduced and the cultural interests of entire groups of children can go unrecognized.   (p. 473)[4]

Two excellent examples of what I would call institutional racist bullying from New Zealand researchers can be used to illustrate Corson's point, Alton-Lee, Nuthall and Patrick (1987) and Jones (1987, 1991). Alton-Lee et al.'s 'Take Your Brown Hand Off My Book' presents an interesting array of challenges in terms of racism in the classroom. The researchers used remote microphones in order to record children's classroom conversations and were able to describe events of the living culture of the classroom that are usually outside the realms of experience not only of researchers but also of teachers. As a result, they were able to detect and describe how the hidden curriculum is so powerful that in the case of a curriculum item designed specifically to increase children's valuing of cultural diversity, it ended up, unbeknownst to the teacher, having the opposite effect: it increased the sense of superiority of the dominant culture and 'created a classroom where racism was unconsciously validated' (p. 4).

Alton-Lee et al. describe how, in the case of a particular Maori boy, racist name-calling undermined both his sense of the worth of his own culture and his self-esteem, and also led to his being seen by the school as a trouble-maker. It was only through his size and ability to retaliate physically that the racist name-calling decreased. In the eyes of the school, however, children who make an aggressive stance to counter racist name-calling may become seen as disruptive or even as bullies; in this scenario the original perpetrators of the aggression are never identified. This suggests that racism is implicitly condoned and acted upon institutionally, so that members of ethnic minorities are more likely to be judged guilty rather than assumed innocent; and

the victims of this racism, both personal and institutional, become anti-social as a result of their disempowerment and their experience of the lack of social justice.

Alison Jones (1987, 1991),[5] in a case study carried out in an Auckland girls' secondary school, illustrates the different experiences of two classes of fifth form girls, one middle-class and largely European (5 Simmonds), and one working-class and largely of Pacific Island Polynesian descent (5 Mason). In relation to this scenario, she explores Bordieu's concept of symbolic violence ('those cultural processes through which schooling helps ensure the failure of subordinate groups', 1991: 146), examining how these two classes are treated differently, with 5 Simmonds girls having access to success and 5 Masons to failure.

In her case study she shows how the 5 Simmonds girls are able to use the teacher as a vehicle for obtaining knowledge and to question and challenge received knowledge, in other words, to be active learners who receive 'valuable' knowledge; whereas the 5 Mason girls tend to learn passively and the knowledge they acquire is not 'valuable' knowledge.[6] They want the teacher to give them work to copy so that they can gain the knowledge the teacher has and get good jobs. The Pacific Island girls do not challenge the teacher because in their cultures the teacher, like a minister of religion, is a person who should not be challenged or asked questions of as this would be seen as disrespectful. It would also show that the questioner was not listening or had missed the point the first time around. Jones argues that the school 'hides its role in this selective distribution of knowledge and skills to particular groups of students. Because the school implicitly maintains it is neutral, it does not recognise this political role, nor how this role reflected in what happens in the classroom' (1987: 4). Jones then sees symbolic violence as committed against the 5 Mason girls as their patterns of learning do not provide them with the means to pass the exams that they will need to continue their education; instead they are prepared only for low-paying jobs where they will be expected to follow orders and to carry out tasks which require little ability. On the other hand, the 5 Simmonds girls acquire the skills that allow them to succeed in the exam system and beyond; and to have the confidence and ability to function in management positions.[7]

Important foundational issues

Issue five: the importance of context: human rights vs cultural relativism, a New Zealand example

In terms of interpreting events and finding appropriate solutions to racist bullying, it is important to understand issues to do with the culture and values of the groups to which the victims and bullies belong. In Moore et al.'s (1997) evaluation of the Eliminating Violence scheme, one of New Zealand's three major initiatives in the bullying area, the researchers identified that a major source of potential conflict that has implications for bullying is a cultural difference between the views of European and Polynesian New Zealanders on the physical disciplining of children. As part of the study, authors interviewed parents of children in their case study schools. Parents all felt that violent behaviour in schools, as with some forms of bullying, was a result of the way that children were brought up and that there was a distinct cultural difference in the way that violence was or was not used as a way to discipline children and to instil respect. While physical punishment is condoned in some Pacific societies it is deemed unacceptable in New Zealand society in general:

> In our Samoan way you should smack the child out of love not out of anger. There are good values in our culture, but with my personal upbringing, a problem is that my parents would have smacked me more out of being angry, rather than smacking me for doing the thing that is not right.

> Back in the Islands, the majority of Pacific Islanders know how to bring up their children over there, because society dictates to them how, but the measure of violence is not the same with New Zealand society. What to us is normal is not normal to the rest of the country.   (p. 123)

In this situation, there is a conflict between what is deemed acceptable in some Pacific nations' cultures and the human rights of individual children as members of New Zealand society who may be subjected to physical violence as a result of these attitudes.[8]

Issue six: creating a safe environment, including cultural safety

The issues that have been discussed up to this point have related specifically to racist bullying. I would argue that the most fundamental remedy against bullying of any kind is the creation of a safe environment. From a racist bullying perspective, there is also an added dimension which can be termed cultural safety. Research on bullying shows that victimized children are more likely to have low self-esteem, suffer high levels of depression and have poor general health, are two to three times more likely to consider suicide, are more likely to be frequently absent from school and are likely to be socially isolated (Rigby 1996b). Seriously bullied children have been driven to take their own lives; at best, the experiences of seriously bullied children lead them as adults to have lowered self-esteem and to suffer from depression (Olweus 1993, Farrington 1993).

In Maslow's (1970) needs hierarchy theory of personal adjustment, he argues that people have five levels of needs and that these are hierarchically organized. He terms the first three levels deficiency needs and suggests that if individuals grow up within an environment in which these needs are not met that they will be stopped from functioning as healthy and well-adjusted human beings. The first level of needs are physiological, that is, satisfying the basic biological drives: the need for air, food, water and shelter. The second level entails safety needs, the need to feel secure from physical or psychological threat; and the third level includes basic social needs, that is, satisfying the need to be loved and accepted by others. The fourth and fifth level needs are termed esteem needs and self-actualization needs. Esteem needs relate to the desire to achieve success, have prestige and be recognized by others. Self-actualization needs relate to self-fulfilment, to reaching one's potential. Maslow posits that these fifth level needs are only actualized after the other four levels have been realized.[9]

Research on isolated children carried out by me (Sullivan 1998) supports the notion that it is very difficult for children to learn if at least the first two of Maslow's identified needs are not met. If children are bullied, their safety needs are not met and higher level needs such as relationship and self-esteem needs are seriously undermined. Bullying then has cognitive and socio-emotional, as well as human rights, implications. Bullied children are often emotionally disabled as a result of being bullied and their ability to learn effectively is seriously impaired.

The New Zealand term 'cultural safety' is useful when considering issues of safety and racist bullying. Cultural safety means that in the school setting ethnic origins and cultural needs and perspectives are acknowledged, respected and accommodated. It can be argued that, as with Maslow's needs hierarchy, if individuals do not feel safe physically, psychologically or culturally, their ability and potential to learn are seriously threatened.[10]

Discussion: effective ways to deal with racist bullying

The issues identified in this chapter are intended to provide a starting point and focus to allow schools to address racist bullying as a phenomenon and to set about putting into place strategies to deal with it. The intention of this part of the chapter is to suggest an approach to solving incidents of racist bullying in schools by their adoption of a well-considered and community-owned philosophy that is built on and complemented by creative problem-solving responses which encourage teachers as both theorists and practitioners, and which freely utilize any strategies that are available. Such responses should go through a series of regular evaluations, always striving for improvements.

While some educationalists have addressed racism in the school, there is a fear amongst them even as they go about their analysis that work in this area is high on theory and low on practice.[11] For the teacher, it is true, problems in the classroom and also in the playground need immediate solutions, and the 'real world' of the classroom may seem many steps removed from theory. However, I would argue that while it is important to have good and implementable practice to deal effectively with racist bullying, it is equally important to have a good grasp of theory in order to nurture the ability to challenge and debate ideas and to re-visit and revise thinking regularly in terms of new experiences (as in Aristotle's notion of praxis which Freire has resuscitated to good effect). This is central to training the teacher to be a reflective practitioner. Teachers with such skills are useful not only to themselves and their schools but are also able to model this way of thinking and functioning in the world for their pupils, our future generations of leaders and citizens.

Therefore I would argue that in order to be effective in its strategies against racist bullying, a school needs to adopt a two-tiered approach. In the first instance it needs to be clear about its fundamental character and value system, those characteristics that inform its culture, by:

1 having a clearly articulated and inclusive school philosophy and values statement that is the foundation upon which any programme or response is built;
2 attempting to understand the issues in the areas of racism and of bullying, how they overlap and how they differ.

Thus, if a school has a transparent culture, and its values are agreed upon and disseminated by the school community, adherence to or rejection of the values as expressed in rules and contracts will be easily identifiable as functional or dysfunctional. Consequently, an agreed set of responses or actions can be instituted to deal with any breakdown of the value system. Numerous bullying researchers (for instance, Smith and Sharp 1994, Rigby 1996a) advocate the key importance of developing a whole school policy. From the point of view of having both a deep understanding of the issues and a sense of ownership, members of the school community – that is, the teachers, administrators, support staff such as playground supervisors and cleaning staff, the pupils, parents and members of the community – need to be involved in the development of a philosophy and of policies and programmes that grow out of the philosophy.

An important issue in developing a school philosophy is that the process should be open and seen to be open. For instance, often in ideologically-loaded discussions, such as in relation to racism and bullying, a 'politically correct' response can quickly emerge and all other discussion and opinions can be quickly suppressed. Arguing from an anti-racist perspective, I feel that policies and programmes that unmask and deal with the actual and implied racism in society are appropriate and that these responses, rather than being radical and of the extreme left as they are labelled, are actually realistic and reflect the accepted status quo of the school. I believe, however, that it is better to argue things through and let people who disagree with me have time to think about issues that they may not have been exposed to before, rather than bashing them on the head with arguments so that they go away momentarily silenced but resentful (and with a closed mind) but not expressing this as they would be seen to be racist (which at that point they may be). If a 'politically correct' attitude is adopted through undemocratic processes, the seeds of resentment will be sown and may end up undermining the process.

In a similar vein, Macdonald et al. (1989) write the following:

> In the field of education, the basic assumption behind many current anti-racist policies is that since black pupils are the victims of the immoral and prejudiced behaviour of white students, white students are to be seen as 'racist' . . . Racism is thus placed in some kind of moral vacuum and is totally divorced from the more complex reality of human relations in the classroom, playground or community. (p. 402)

I would argue that in the microcosm of the school, race/ethnicity is one of a set of variables that children come into contact with, and although some parents may be racist and their children may have the potential also to be racist, the school can play a part in providing positive and alternative ways of understanding the world. Maines and Robinson's (1992) no-blame approach is a useful philosophical starting point. In the no-blame approach there is an assumption that if people are pushed into corners they will react defensively and will not listen to reason or change their opinions or ways of doing things. If, on the other hand, a solution is found without blaming, by looking at the issues and by trying to get the child to empathize, to feel what it would be like to be at the receiving end, then there is the basis for non-threatening and humane problem-solving.

Schools need to address and debate issues relating to bullying and racism in order to formulate a shared philosophy and to develop effective policy and programmes that are owned by the school and its community. Troyna and Hatcher (1992) discussed how pupils in one primary school gained confidence in anti-racist messages promoted through assemblies and perceived that the headteacher had implemented the school's anti-racist policy, but their experience was that this was not practised by the majority of staff. Similarly, Blatchford (1989) found that playground monitors were acting in racist fashions that may have been in contradiction to school policy. A whole school policy supports the development of a safe school where everyone knows and utilizes the same set of guidelines.

The first part of a whole school approach, then, is about developing a school philosophy and a safe school setting, culturally and in other ways. It is also concerned with developing an active learning and problem-solving approach to issues such as racist bullying. In order to make these strong foundations effective, the second part of a school's approach should complement these theoretical philosophical aspects with pragmatic and implementable strategies that should entail the following:

1 having access to resources that have been developed to deal with bullying and racism;
2 having a plan of action that includes regular updating and is 'owned' by the school.

Over recent years in anti-bullying and anti-racist work, various means have been identified for dealing with racism and bullying. For instance, in New Zealand in relation to bullying there are three major programmes that can be accessed: the New Zealand Police's *Kia Kaha*, the Foundation for Peace Studies Aotearoa/New Zealand *Cool Schools Peer Mediation Programme* and the Special Education Services' *Eliminating Violence – Managing Anger* programme. A similar list could be given for Australian, British, Irish, Canadian and Scandinavian contexts. In line with the problem-solving approach of the first part of a school's philosophy, it would be useful to have available a range of strategies in order to address a range of scenarios.[12]

It is also now widely recognized that an important part of any strategy is that there are regular evaluations of the success or failure of a programme and that it is necessary sometimes to fine-tune programmes that are generally working well. This is also a useful way of using school experiences to identify the types of situations that occur and to share learning experiences amongst members of the school so that everyone benefits and so that the sense of school community ownership of the approach is nurtured and maintained.

Conclusion

Although the purpose of this chapter has been to examine the issue of racist bullying by providing a definition, discussing some of the underlying issues and providing a blueprint for effectively dealing with it, an underlying concern has been to address the issue of cultural pluralism and how to approach this in schools and to provide a set of values to counter racism through education. Intolerance and racial hatred and the bullying and violence that this often brings, both at school and in the outside world, are unacceptable. Within the school, if an atmosphere of safety, trust and a nurturing of respect for others is the foundation, then there is hope that racist bullying and bullying itself will abate.

Notes

1 Troyna and Hatcher (1992) discuss the nature and incidence of 'Paki bashing', and Gillborn's (1995) documentation of the reports of racial harassment including bullying, gang warfare and incidents of grievously bodily harm and murder underlines the seriousness of racial bullying.

2 See Metge and Kinloch (1984) who describe situations in New Zealand and the Pacific where different cultural meanings for body language and attitudes can cause cross-cultural misunderstandings. The authors call this 'talking past each other '.

3 A problem that has arisen in relation to evaluating the success of anti-bullying programmes is that the process of introducing such a programme increases awareness and results in a greater ability to identify bullying and a greater willingness to report incidents. This means that at the end of the programme, the incidence of bullying can seem as high, or almost as high, as at the beginning and give the impression of failure.

4 For an elaboration of cultural and social class differences in language acquisition, see Sullivan, 1984.

5 Increasingly research on Maori and Pacific nations educational issues has been taken over by researchers from the ethnic groups under investigation. People such as Alison Jones who is Palagi (a Samoan term for European) are criticized for a lack of an internal perspective and are seen as making culturally inappropriate observations and conclusions. Although this may be partially true, I would argue that Jones' observations about the variation between strategies of the two groups of girls and the resultant disadvantaging of the Pacific Islands students are generally correct. It has also provided a focus out of which has emerged these culturally-centred responses. For an example of such a critique that suggests alternative ways of developing research for Pacific nations people, specifically from a Samoan perspective, see Tupuola (1993).

6 See Landbeck (1992) for an interesting overview of passive and active learning.

7 Educational statistics back up Jones' more qualitative observations, as consistently and significantly, Pakeha/ Palagi (European) and Asian students outperform Maori and Pacific Island students in School Certificate, Sixth Form Certificate and Bursary examinations (national and largely externally-assessed examinations sat in the third, fourth and fifth years of high school respectively).

8 There are also members of Pacific Island communities who argue that physical violence is unacceptable. Wuillemin, Richardson and Moore (1986) in a study in Papua New Guinea showed that there was a disjunction between the urban and rural settings with the rural populations having different standards from the national judicial system. They further found that when rural dwellers had immigrated to the cities and lived there for a period of time, their values changed, moving towards those represented by the judicial system. In other words, with the passage of time, they adapted to the requirements of their new situation. The debates occurring in New Zealand Polynesian communities suggest that this may be happening in relation to the use of corporal punishment in that context.

9 Maslow's theory is a global theory and can be criticized for over-generalising. However, it does ring true. Alderfer (1972) developed a theory that is both less rigid and a refinement of Maslow's theory. He simplifies Maslow's needs from five to three classifications: existence needs (which incorporate physiological and safety needs), relatedness needs (which equates with social needs), and growth needs (which includes esteem and self-actualization needs).

10 In New Zealand, cultural safety has become an issue in relation to Maori students in essentially European schools. It was highlighted by a recent conflict in a nursing course at Christchurch Polytechnic (see Horton and Fitzsimons 1996, and Ramsden and Spoonley 1993).

11 Foster (1990), Banks (1994) and Brandt (1986) have attempted to remedy a perceived imbalance between practice and theory. Brandt asks 'is anti-racist teaching practicable or is it simply an academic or political exercise generated by political militants and by academics who are so far removed from the "chalk face" that they have no sense of the real issues facing teachers and teaching and have little sense of what is operable?' (p. 1).

12 Amongst contemporary anti-bullying scholars and practitioners, there are tendencies to favour one or two approaches over the other options. There is also a difference of opinion between those who think bullies need consequences or punishment (Tattum and Herbert 1993), and those who are of the opinion that blame results in further repercussions and does not solve the problem and who prefer to find solutions without attributing blame (Maines and Robinson 1992). My own response is that a toolbox is more useful, so that the appropriate 'tool' can be used for each particular situation; for instance, for introducing a no-blame solution or a peer support network (see Cowie and Sharp 1995) or an approach that is designed to be behaviouristic and concerned with behaviour modification. All of these approaches have ideological undertones and this is where disputes arise. What is most important is to deal reflectively with events as they arise rather than to adhere to one philosophical stance.

References

Alderfer, C. P. (1972) *Existence, Relatedness and Growth.* New York: Free Press.

Alton-Lee, A., Nuthall, G. and Patrick, J. (1987) 'Take your brown hand off my book': racism in the classroom, *Set*, No.1, Item 8.

Banks, J. (1994) *Multiethnic Education* (3rd edn). Boston: Allyn and Bacon.

Besag, V. (1989) *Bullies and Victims in Schools: A Guide to Understanding and Management.* Milton Keynes: Open University Press.

Besag, V. (1992) *We Don't Have Bullies Here.* Resource Materials for INSET and Further Developments, for Primary Schools and Secondary Schools and Colleges. London: Calouste Gulbekian Foundation.

Blatchford, P. (1989) *Playtime in the Primary School. Problems and Improvements.* Windsor: NFER-NELSON.

Brandt, G. L. (1986) *The Realization of Anti-Racist Teaching.* London: Falmer Press.

Corson, D. (1992) Minority cultural values and discourse norms in majority culture classrooms. *The Canadian Modern Language Review/La Revue Canadienne des langues vivantes,* **48** (3) (April/Avril): 472–96.

Cowie, H. and Sharp, S. (1994) Tackling bullying through the curriculum. In P. K. Smith and S. Sharp (eds) *School Bullying: Insights and Perspectives.* London: Routledge.

Cowie, H. and Sharp, S. (1996) *Peer Counselling in Schools: A Time to Listen.* London: David Fulton.

Donn, M. and Schick, R. (1995) *Promoting Positive Race Relations in New Zealand Schools: Me Mahi Tahi Tatou.* Wellington: Research Section, Ministry of Education.

Elton Report (1989) *Discipline in Schools.* London: HMSO.

Farrington, D. P. (1993) Understanding and preventing bullying. In M. Tonry and N. Norris (eds) *Crime and Justice* vol. 17, University of Chicago Press.

Foster, P. (1990) *Policy and Practice in Multicultural and Anti-racist Education.* London: Routledge.

Foundation for Peace Studies Aotearoa/New Zealand (1994) *Cool Schools Peer Mediation Programme Training Manual* (2nd edn). Auckland.

Gaine, C. (1987) *No Problem Here: A Practical Approach to Education and Race in White Schools.* London: Hutchinson.

Gillborn, D. (1990) *Race Ethnicity and Education, Teaching and Learning in Multiethnic Schools.* London: Unwin Hyman.

Gillborn, D. (1995) Racism, Modernity and Schooling: New Directions in Theory and Practice. First Draft. Paper presented at the annual meeting of the American Educational Research Association, San Fransisco.

Hargreaves, D. (1973) *Social Relations in a Secondary School.* New York: Routledge and Kegan Paul.

Hessari, R. and Hill, D. (1989) *Practical Ideas for Multicultural Learning and Teaching in the Primary Classroom.* London: Routledge.

Hingangaroa-Smith, G. (1990) Taha Maori: Pakeha Capture. In J. Codd et al. (eds) *Political Issues in New Zealand Education.* Palmerston North: Dunmore Press.

Horton, E. and Fitzsimons, P. (1996) The cultural safety debate and the Conservative restoration in Aotearoa/New Zealand. *New Zealand Journal of Educational Studies* **31** (2): 171–88.

Jeffcoate, R. (1985) Anti-racism as an educational ideology. In M. Arnot (ed.) *Race and Gender: Equal Employment Opportunities in Education.* Oxford: Pergamon.

Jones, A. (1987) What really happens in the classroom?, *Set*, No. 2, Item 7.

Jones, A. (1991) '*At School I've Got a Chance'. Culture/Privilege: Pacific Island and Pakeha Girls at School.* Palmerston North: Dunmore Press.

Kelly, E. (1993) Gender issues in education for citizenship. In G. K. Verma and P. Pumfrey (eds) *Cultural Diversity and Curriculum* vol. 2, London: Falmer Press.

Kelly, E. (1994) Racism and sexism in the school. In P. Blatchford and S. Sharp, *Breaktime and the School: Understanding and Changing Playground Behaviour.* London: Routledge.

Kelly, E. and Cohn, T. (1988) *Racism in Schools – New Research Evidence.* Stoke-on-Trent: Trentham Books.

Ku, J. (1992) Asians as Victims. *Diversity and Division* **2** (1): 11–13.

Landbeck, R. (1992) Beliefs about Learning. *Pacific Curriculum Network* **1** (1): 1–5.

Loach, B. and Bloor, C. (1995) Dropping the bully to find the racist. *Multicultural Teaching* **13** (2): 18–20.

Macdonald, I., Bhavnani, T., Khan, L. and John, G. (1989) *Murder in the Playground: The Report of the Macdonald Inquiry into Racism and Racial Violence in Manchester Schools.* London: Longsight Press.

Maines, B. and Robinson, G. (1992) *Michael's Story: The 'No-blame' Approach.* Bristol: Lame Duck Publishing.

Maslow, A. (1970) *Motivation and Personality* (2nd edn). New York: Harper & Row.

Metge, J. and Kinloch, P. (1984) *Talking Past Each Other: Problems of Cross Cultural Communication.* Wellington: Victoria University Press.

Modgil, S., Verma, G. K., Mallick, K. and Modgil, C. (eds) (1986) *Multicultural Education: The Interminable Debate.* Lewes: Falmer Press.

Moore, D., Adair, V., Lysaght, K. and Kruiswijk, J. (1997) *Eliminating Violence From Schools Evaluation Project: Final Report.* Wellington: Education Department, University of Auckland for the Ministry of Education.

Moran, S., Smith, P., Thompson, D. and Whitney, I. (1993) Ethnic differences in experiences of bullying: Asian and white Children. *British Journal of Educational Psychology* **63** (3): 431–40.

New Zealand Police (1992) *Kia Kaha.* Wellington.

Olweus, D. (1993) *Bullying at School: What We Know and What We Do.* Oxford: Blackwell.

O'Moore, A. M. and Hillery, B. (1989) Bullying in Irish Schools. *Irish Journal of Psychology* **10**: 426–41.

Ramsden, I. and Spoonley, P. (1993) The cultural safety debate in nursing in Aotearoa. *New Zealand Annual Review of Education, Te Arotake a Tau o te Ao o te Matauranga i Aotearoa* **3**: 161–8.

Rigby, K. (1996a) *Bullying in Schools; And What To Do About It.* Melbourne: The Australian Council for Educational Research.

Rigby, K. (1996b) Preventing peer victimisation in schools. In C. Summer, M. Israel, M. O'Connell and R. Sarre (eds) *Selected Papers from the 8th International Symposium.* ACT: Australian Institute of Criminology: 303–9.

Rubin, K. and Pepler, D. (eds) (1989) *The Development and Treatment of Childhood Aggression.* Hillsdale, NJ: Lawrence Erlbaum.

Sharp, S. and Smith, P. K. (eds) (1994) *Tackling Bullying in Your School: A Practical Handbook.* London: Routledge.

Smith, P. K. and Sharp, S. (eds) (1994) *School Bullying: Insights and Perspectives.* London: Routledge.

Slee, P. (1996) *The P.E.A.C.E. Pack. A Programme for Reducing Bullying in our Schools.* Adelaide: Flinders University, School of Education.

Special Education Services (1995) *Eliminating Violence.* Wellington.

Spoonley, P. (1988) Are you racist? – You'd be much nicer if you weren't. In W. Hirsh and R. Scott *Getting it Right: Aspects of Ethnicity and Equality in New Zealand Education.* Auckland: Office of the Race Relations Conciliator.

Sullivan, K. (1984) *Social class and cultural differences in the acquisition and comprehension of Wh-Question words.* Unpublished M.Phil. thesis, Department of Education, University of Cambridge.

Sullivan, K. (1993) Bicultural Education in Aotearoa/New Zealand: Establishing a Tauiwi Side to the Partnership. *New Zealand Annual Review of Education, Te Arotake a Tau o te Ao o te Matauranga i Aotearoa* **3**: 191–222.

Sullivan, K. (1998) Isolated children, bullying and peer group relations. In P. T. Slee and K. Rigby (eds) *Children's Peer Relations.* London and Washington: Routledge.

Tattum, D. P. and Herbert, G. (1990) *Bullying – A Positive Response.* Cardiff: South Glamorgan Institute of Higher Education.

Tattum, D. P. and Herbert, G. (1993) *Countering Bullying.* Stoke-on Trent: Trentham Books.

Troyna, B. and Hatcher, R. (1992) *Racism in Children's Lives.* London: Routledge.

Tupuola, A. M. (1993) Raising research consciousness the Fa'a Samoa way. *New Zealand Annual Review of Education, Te Arotake a Tau o te Ao o te Matauranga i Aotearoa* **3**: 169–220.

Whitney, I. and Smith, P. K. (1993) A survey of the nature and extent of bullying in junior/middle and secondary schools. *Educational Research* **35**: 2–25.

Wuillemin, D., Richardson, B. and Moore, D. (1986) Ranking of crime seriousness in Papua New Guinea. *Journal of Cross-Cultural Psychology* **17** (1): 29–44.

10 Whose Knowledge? Values Education across National Boundaries

JOAN STEPHENSON

The enjoyment of the rights and freedoms set forth in this Convention shall be secured without discrimination on any ground such as sex, race, colour, language, religion, political or other opinion, national or social origin, association with a national minority, property, birth or other status.

(Article 14 of the European Convention on Human Rights)

One of the major aims of values education must be to make the above declaration work in practice. In the belief that teachers, their beliefs, attitudes and actions are central players in this endeavour, any study of their current knowledge and future needs must be of help in reaching this aim. This chapter expresses one person's views on a selection of the most common issues found in values education across several continents. Findings from a research project involving initial and serving teachers from six countries (Australia, Eire, Israel, Slovenia, Switzerland and the United Kingdom; Stephenson et al. 1997) is used alongside the work of others to explore some of the attitudes, beliefs and practices of teachers in the classroom to challenges raised by values education. An attempt is made to set this within the present demands being made of schools and teachers in the areas of social and moral education in an increasingly diverse and shrinking world.

Moral health, attitudes and values have become an increasingly verbal concern of the media and general public across much of the developed and developing world. The role of education at large, and the school and individual teacher in particular, in the forming or nurturing of values and attitudes of children and young adults is an open debate. Various sections of society blame the perceived lack of discipline and 'good example' in schools for the rise in anti-social behaviour amongst young people.

Most are agreed that schools should play a part in what can be loosely termed 'values education'. This can be said of most nations. In a sense it could be said that in the developed world at least, the school has taken over the traditional role that the family and extended family played in an earlier society, before the mobility of the workforce and the financial and social independence of young adults, particularly females, made the cohesive hold of previous generations less influential. The form this school-centred role should take, and the nature of the values and the philosophy and purpose underlying such programmes, produce less consensus or in some cases are even ignored. Even less is known about what the 'average' teachers actually say they believe and do in their classrooms despite the recent directory of resources and research in values education (Taylor 1994), which has no less than 113 entries. The gap between the rhetoric and the reality lies largely unexplored. This is true not only of the United Kingdom, but also, from the evidence of our study, across the teaching population at large to a greater or lesser extent.

The focus of this chapter comes from answers given by pre- and in-service teachers to three questions asked as part of a wider research project across several countries. These concerned the nature of the knowledge upon which teachers and prospective teachers based the values education they sought to introduce into their classrooms and their attitudes to the accessibility of this knowledge to pupils they were teaching. The questionnaire was followed up by interviews and observations in the classroom of a selection of those taking part. In all some 300 practising or intending teachers in six education systems gave their personal and individualized views concerning moral, social and cultural values which they saw as pertinent to themselves and the context in which they operate. These responses immediately raised several issues that I will begin to deal with here.

First, while there was a wide measure of surface agreement between respondents as to what they saw as the principle 'values' they would wish to see in any programme developed and delivered to children, the description, interview and observation evidence would suggest that an expression of intent did not carry through into practice, at either the macro or micro level, as a matter of course. Examples of 'do as I say' rather than 'do as I do' were present. This would suggest that the picture given by any study based on questionnaire evidence alone must be tempered by the knowledge that it is in some part the 'ideal' state that those replying would like to believe exists. This 'ideal' may reflect, among other things, the 'self-image' the teacher aspires to for themselves and the influence upon the teacher of the statutory or hidden requirements of the society in which they operate.

The 'value laden' or 'value free' nature of education is a second major issue raised. In the United Kingdom, the statutory National Curriculum for England and Wales, while presently laying down no subject area under the title of 'values education', does expect schools and teachers to promote the spiritual, moral and cultural development of children in their charge. The Office for Standards in Education (OFSTED) requires its school inspectors to evaluate the performance of teachers not only through their pupils' progress in National Curriculum subjects areas (ten in primary, fourteen in secondary schools) but also through how the school promotes these other aspects and how the pupils respond (OFSTED 1994, Part 2: 22, Part 4: 15/16). When talking or writing about values education in England, the National Curriculum Council (NCC) guidelines of 1993 are usually quoted; they suggest a fundamental connection between the act of teaching and consideration of values:

> Values are inherent in teaching. Teachers are by the nature of their profession 'moral agents' who imply values by the way they address pupils and each other, the way they dress, the language they use and the effort they put into their work.   (p. 8)

There is no uncertainty here, at least about the value-laden nature of life in the classroom. What or whose those values are, whether they are conscious or unconscious thought through agreed categories or bodies of knowledge, individual or school-wide, pertaining to the community as a whole or sections of it, methods by which they are to be presented or how they are received by the pupils, is less clear.

Equally unclear is the real purpose of education within society today as opposed to its stated purpose. An obvious aim of education is preparing the young to play an effective role in the social context to which they belong. Increasingly we find a sophist view of education emerging, where the finished product must meet the various demands of the 'market place' where qualities that are most highly valued are those skills which technology and business demand in the rapidly changing workplace. This is to be a largely value-neutral process; a stance recognizably similar to that being argued against by Socrates. Another and more commonly labelled 'liberal' view of education would regard this former definition as training rather than education, seeing their aim as the drawing out and nurturing of the child's development not only in directly marketable knowledge and skills but also in a knowledge of self, worth, and those affective sides of personality applicable to life, if not necessarily directly to their future function as an employee or model citizen. If it is this last conception of a teacher's role that includes directly influencing the lives, attitudes and beliefs of their students then it is difficult not to ascribe a moral education function to the job he or she does. This is a view supported by Starkey (1995: 20–1):

> Education is essentially about helping people to find fulfilment in civil society. Schools have important instrumental functions of helping young people to achieve qualifications related to future employment. Schools also have the function of initiating students into the expectations of society and transmitting fundamental values.

On the other hand, a wider view of education is taken for instance by Shapiro (1985: 46–7):

> we have viewed schooling primarily in the context of reproducing the social relations of the production – the transmission of an ideology that is apposite to the 'culture' of work in our society. Such 'economic' socialization is, however, only a partial description of the school's ideological function. Education, it must be remembered, is a component not of the economic 'infrastructure' but of the state 'apparatus'.

But what do the teachers, who are charged with putting the programmes or the expressed objectives of their governments and authorities into practice, actually believe and do? Leaving to one side for another occasion the question of how this is to be achieved, is it enough that they as citizens of that country can be assumed to have the fundamental values that are to be transmitted? This raises many questions about the 'morality' of defining a society's 'values' and to what extent the teacher acts as a mirror reflecting or even indoctrinating 'received' views required of them by the dominant 'caste' or adopts the often criticized liberal stance of accepting all values as valid even when they are at variance with the official line. In reality this is most often a matter of degree rather than absolutes, but for the teacher in the classroom, or certainly in the British secular classroom, it can become a source of conflict with colleagues, parents and the community. The students and teachers, surveyed in the recent international study on which this chapter draws (Stephenson et al. 1998), all saw the main source/ resource for any teaching, active or passive, that they did in the area of values education, as being their own knowledge. If such a high reliance is placed upon it, then its nature and possible consequences are important for us all, for we all have a vested interest in the beliefs and practices of the rising generation.

As a result of the findings in our study, I would agree with Haydon when he says:

> Teachers should not simply be left to get on with the job of values education – far from it. That people entering teaching have values of their own does not necessarily mean they have thought extensively about them; that they can readily articulate and defend them; and that they know how to respond when encountering others with contrary values. In all these respects, the educators may themselves need educating.   (1996: 4)

And I would add to this that they are the values that the next generation necessarily will either reject or subscribe to in their new developed context.

There was little evidence to suggest that the teachers in our project had thought deeply about their particular set of values and, more importantly, they had little understanding of where those values were derived from. Their response to a question about the accessibility of the knowledge being taught to their pupils illustrated this clearly when over 90 per cent of those replying indicated that they felt the knowledge was equally accessible to all the children in their care. This was so over a variety of contexts, involving schools that had high multi-

ethnicity, in a variety of socio-economic strata and under a cross-section of the political regimes, ranging from old, established democracies, through societies where a dominant organized religion had lately been or was presently very influential in defining standards, to emerging democracies where nationalistic concerns were a prime feature of the change in which they are found, are they influenced by or do they influence attitudes? Along with Shiebe I believe that '[T]o talk of an individual's values is to refer to a system of learned beliefs' (Shiebe 1970: 42). Many of our respondents were not aware of any influence on the structuring of their beliefs and attitudes, or how these in their turn affected their dealings with children. This was particularly so when these views, because of differences of culture, gender or class were likely to be at conflict with other influences on the children. Their view that the knowledge needed was their own and that it was equally accessible to all is based upon a number of assumptions; a major one of these being that all decent people bring up and have expectations of their children that mirror those they themselves experienced. This is patently not true. Each set of teachers from the various countries, which themselves differ, held this to be so – illustrating that even when using the same words, an assumption of like-mindedness is dangerous. There is a contradiction here between the teachers 'valuing' of 'own knowledge', the respect for others views, which they gave as one of their major tenets, and the perceived accessibility.

Attitudes to values education activities, variously labelled under religious education, personal and social education, citizenship education, moral education, civics, etc., differ greatly according to which country we are talking about. In some, as in Australia for instance, at least some of the states have a well-developed curriculum content and criteria for action, together with supporting materials for teachers to draw upon in schools. In others (Ireland and Israel serve as examples) the religious and cultural life of the country so pervades everyday life that values and morality are, or perhaps in Ireland it should be said *were*, and have been intrinsically bound up with the practice of education as a whole, that teaching and moral assimilation are bound together. In Israel, there is the added dimension of forging solidarity against clearly perceived and defined counter-interests in a diverse population, many of whom are recent comers to the country if not to at least part of the culture. Similarly, in

Ireland it could be argued that a retention of a special and prized identity has been safeguarded and nourished by the attitudes and practises of cultural moral values in schools. For countries emerging from what is seen by the majority population as the suppression not only of culture but also nationality, by a larger neighbour as in the former eastern-bloc countries, values are seen as synonymous, to some extent, with the shedding of that which was imposed by the retreating power and reassertion of the attitudes, beliefs and knowledge that are specific to the re-emergent national identity. Slovenia, with its changes in curriculum content in history, away from the exploits of eminent Russians to a more nationalistic chosen élite, gives one example of this change in what is valued within the culture and therefore the schools. The United Kingdom with a multi-cultural population of long standing, might be supposed to have insight, openness and a tolerant attitude to values from a number of cultures. Recent insistence in the National Curriculum on corporate acts of worship having to display a predominantly Christian ethic, and the Muslim community's call for denominational schools to include provision for an emphasis on Muslim beliefs, to give parity with Anglican, Roman Catholic and Jewish provision, puts a somewhat different complexion on the expectation. In all countries it could be seen that while diversity was expressed as a strength, in practice at an official and unofficial level it is often seen as a threat. As Starkey puts it so succinctly:

> There is a political consensus in Europe, at a rhetorical level, of the importance of education for democratic and human rights values. Politics, however, is about priorities and choices and the same leaders who proclaim their commitment to human rights may also espouse economic and social policies which involve discrimination and increased inequality. (1996: 33)

The measure of the 'official' attitude to educating children in whatever chosen values is reflected in values education's place inside or outside the official curriculum. With the exception of some states in Australia, as has already been mentioned, only Slovenia and Israel of the others had even suggested programmes. In Slovenia under the communist government 'Social and Moral Education' was a curriculum subject. Not surprisingly the present curriculum is in a state of flux, but the present minister for education sees the teaching of 'Ethics and Society', not religious education, replacing the former programme. He is adamant that public schools must be legally neutral. In Israel, while there is a set of guidelines published by the ministry of education, these were in fact drawn up by a teacher training college, and reflect the views of a particular section of society. If we look further into the situation across other countries in the European Union, then the position of a diversity of practice looks little different. France devotes one hour per week to civics education for all ages. They have a strong historical commitment to education for Human Rights. The syllabus is detailed and support for teachers includes non-statutory guidelines and a wide range of text books, manuals and other resources. Staying in Northern Europe, Germany has a civics education curriculum, the practice differs from *Land* to *Land*, whilst in Denmark, although there is no official curriculum in place, individual groups of schools form their own syllabus and practice. Moving to Southern Europe, Portugal has a personal, social and civics education component across all ages. However, we find in Greece that inter-cultural values, when and if they arise across the curriculum, are those introduced through the text books laid down by the government. In Italy the stance differs in respect to the age of the child, with values education being part of the secondary but not the primary programme. The situation in respect of unofficial attitudes is more difficult to judge, and in the UK at least, has moved to individual accountability at the official level, rather than the corporate emphasis on team work and shared responsibility that is a long-standing characteristic of the ethos of most British schools.

The responses from all the countries in our study expressed a view that is often laid against liberal education. This concerns the teachers' reluctance to express any firm views of their own; holding all principles as being valid, and not taking a stance against what the critics see as inherently wrong or evil. This raises the question of the objectivity as opposed to the subjectivity of values. Is it possible to agree on beliefs or actions that are always 'good' or 'evil' whatever the values systems of the culture? Some of our respondents believe this to be so. There is a marked consensus in the desirability of 'tolerance' as a major tenet of belief across all the values systems of our respondents. However, to unpick the word further, beyond an also universally expressed principle in our study, that of respect for others' views, raises the issue of whether all views are equally tolerable. Are the views of a racist to be given the same weight as those of, say, a pacifist? How do the teachers feel about and deal with instances of these dilemmas within their own beliefs and their classrooms? As West puts it, 'schools find themselves caught between political and popular control' (West 1993: 17).

This raised problems for some of our teachers in that any strongly expressed views might bring accusations of bias against or undue pressure being put on those sections of society who did not share those views. However, as long ago as 1983 the Inner London Education Authority (ILEA) included the following statement in guidelines to teachers: 'It can be very helpful for pupils to know their teachers' views providing these are offered as one among many possible perspectives on an issue with no more weight on "truth" than any other' (ILEA 1983: 48).

This issue of possible indoctrination was raised by some of our respondents and completely ignored by others, a measure perhaps of the 'self-view' and 'dominant society view' alluded to earlier. Indoctrination is, our respondents believe, not only permissible in some cases but even desirable. There are some cases when not to indoctrinate would be seen as failing in one's duty to society, the State and the individuals concerned. In no case was there an example of what a teacher would do if required to teach some quality to which they did not subscribe. Nor, except in a very few examples was there any questioning of the social mores of the society to which the teacher themselves belonged. This again underlines the points made by Haydon above.

In a sense, looking at things simplistically, it could be argued that all 'education ' is indoctrination, as its process will change the outlook and experience of both the one being 'educated' and the educator. In as far as this is the transference of the knowledge/beliefs of one or a collection of individuals (i.e. society) to another, however willingly accepted, it interferes with the formation of personal views by the individual him or herself. Hare makes this statement:

> teachers are indoctrinators. The debate will then shift to the discussion of *which sorts* of indoctrination are acceptable.... much of traditional schooling is indoctrinatory, and we must face up to this. It is a testimony to the success of this schooling that many people believe indoctrination to be exemplified in Communism, or pacifism, but not in their own beliefs.   (1976: 25)

There are teachers in our schools whose perceptions would fit into both parts of this statement.

There are others who separate values education from the debate on indoctrination because of the empowerment it gives to children to verbalize and back up their own beliefs.

> Some people automatically assume that changing behaviour means indoctrination or social engineering, and this is anathema to most educators . . . values education is not about indoctrination. (Robb 1996: 6)

For him this implies that the main task for teachers is to 'direct or change behaviour'. Although he does go on to acknowledge that indoctrinating young children against things that will do them harm is permissible, he holds the view that:

> Values education has nothing to do with persuasion, let alone inculcation or indoctrination. In the values education class only, young people are empowered to say what they think as long as they can give reasons. The values education teacher's job is not to convince pupils that the teacher's view is right or best, but to ensure conditions that enable youngsters to arrive at their own realization of what is good for self and others. (Ibid.: 22)

This view of the role adopted by teachers when pursuing values education in the classroom is not supported by our study. The overwhelming consensus that the knowledge underpinning their behaviour and teaching was their own, that this knowledge was equally accessible to all children in their class and their insistence on they themselves having the major influence as a role model illustrated for us a different situation. Debate and discussion with children was indeed cited in another part of our study as one of the most common methods of facilitating values education, but other sections showed it was the teacher who in fact did most of the talking, and a high percentage of that was in the interests of social control. While only a few respondents did not acknowledge the importance of other factors and influences on the children, most presented as conformers who saw it as part of their job broadly to uphold the status quo. This is not surprising given the fact that schools are part of the prevailing social fabric. They are of necessity striving to be calm and ordered places, where at best standards of behaviour are maintained through consensus and debate, or are of necessity imposed at least for the safety of others. Many, while reluctant to call it indoctrination would fit in more closely with Costello who sees three categories of values that should or should not be indoctrinated; category A, beliefs where there is no justifiable alternative, e.g. triangles have three sides, they 'represent the state of knowledge as it is or we believe it to be at the time'; category B, those beliefs where 'it is possible for two people who are both equally well-informed about the nature of aesthetics, morals, politics, and religion, to disagree about the issue without either party necessarily being regarded as mistaken (or, at least, not mistaken in the sense in which someone who asserted that "Rome is the capital of France" would be mistaken), warrantable alternatives are offerable'; and category C in which the beliefs a child is indoctrinated with in his or her early years, are 'certain moral beliefs concerning which we might want older children (and indeed adults) to have closed minds. For example, having attempted to indoctrinate a group of children with a belief such as "torturing animals is morally wrong", with the result that they accepted the belief, we should not be happy if those children considered that "reopening the issue (was) a permanent possibility" (Costello 1987: 25).

Hyman and Wright, commenting on the work of George S. Counts (1932) [George S. Counts, *Dare the Schools Build a New Social Order*, the John Day pamphlets, no.11 (New York, John Day). p. 10], address the indoctrination issue, pointing out that 'no one applies the word "indoctrination" when the schools try to teach most facts and accepted bodies of knowledge. This is regarded not as any unwarranted "imposition" but as a duty' (1979: 66). The responses of at least the teachers in our study would imply this holds as true today as it did then.

It is perhaps a further measure of the general conformity of the teaching profession in all the countries taking part and a function of the socio-economic section of society from which they are in general drawn, that causes this general acceptance of being an arm of society bearing a responsibility to fit the next generation into that society, to be so widespread. As Watson and Ashton observe:

> schools are like litmus paper, reflecting the state of society, and this places teachers in a highly vulnerable position. There is a great temptation for them to draw back from changes which might endanger their fragile status.   (1995: 11)

Some of our teachers did express an uncertainty and dilemma over teaching values education at all. For some this was because they felt it to be an intrusion into private territory and intrinsically not desirable, others because they were unable either to define what the words meant, did not see values as 'facts' or were reluctant or unable to promote one set of values rather than another. None of these reactions are new phenomena and were raised during the first flowering of the values education movement in the United States. As Hare says, 'Since moral judgements are not statements of fact or pieces of information, they cannot be taught out of a text-book like the capitals of European countries' (Hare 1974: 66).

Choosing between values is an issue faced by other areas of life as well as schools and teachers. As Pring put it:

> Part of the present moral and social climate is a distrust of authority, especially in the realm of values. Without an agreed tradition of values it is not easy to see how one can promote with confidence one particular set of values rather than another.   (1987: 27)

It is likely that over the intervening twelve years the situation has become more complex rather than less.

Other issues raised by our study also concerned the personal efficacy of the teacher as a model, arbiter, purveyor or guide in the areas covered by values education and the general effectiveness of formal values education programmes as a whole. A leading question for them was 'Who should decide what moral values are taught?' Children will 'catch' values from a variety of sources (parents, peers, press etc.) it could be argued that the function of the teacher therefore becomes: 'a clarifier and facilitator of the valuing process. The main emphasis here is on the inculcation of a valuing process rather than on the inculcation of a particular set of values' (Cross 1987: 10). Studies in the United States have indicated the overriding influence comes from families and peer groups on promoting actively tolerant attitudes. In the case of our respondents, while acknowledgement of the influence of others was present, particularly amongst the practising teachers, a much higher level of teacher influence was perceived than was borne out some time ago in studies elsewhere:

> in other realms . . . the domain of values and morals, the child has his first learning and possibly his most persuasive learning earlier and elsewhere.

In these areas, it may be that the best the school can do is engage the instruction of the other educators and to seek to strengthen or complement or correct or neutralise or counter-educate. (Cremin 1976: 36)

In the United States where programmes that would come under a 'values education' umbrella were prevalent during the late 1970s and early 1980s, with the emergence of both the Kohlberg moral development approach and Values Clarification, their experience could be of some guidance here. Purpel and Shapiro writing in 1985 highlight the 'halo' effect witnessed. They also point out some positive outcomes:

> Suffice it to say that there is general agreement that such efforts have been enormously beneficial . . . They have helped to restore the moral dimension as a significant aspect of educational theory and practice, . . . However, there is also a sense in which the specific moral education programs have experienced results parallel to other curriculum reforms, i.e., a history of initial enormous interest of a fad-like quality followed by either rejection or absorption of specific programs into mainstream school life. . . While the relative failure of these programs *per se* to make for significant change is clear, the net effect of such efforts has been to keep the moral issue on the agenda, at least for a large number of educational theorists. (p. xiii)

Writing in 1997, Purpel stresses the 'swirling and confused' state of values education in the country in the 1990s. In his view the system sees no place for formal values education programmes within the schools. The only exception to the general discrediting of the whole area, he feels, lies not in attempting to provide open choice-laden unprescriptive programmes, but in an approach that encourages pupils to behave in line with tried and tested principles including, honesty, civility, responsibility and respect for authority. The call for a return to 'family values', described by him has its echo in the developed world. Writing with hindsight and experience of a number of initiatives, he addresses some of the dilemmas which have arisen for our respondents in this chapter:

> I want to say rather emphatically that some of the important dilemmas implicated in values education are best left in tension and to remain unresolved. The conflict between individual rights and social order, between personal creativity and cultural continuity, and between individual fulfilment and social responsibility are inherent, inevitable, and I dare say, eternal dimensions of human existence. Our constant challenge is to reinterpret the particular configuration of these conflicts in the context of a particular time, place and setting, knowing that circumstances will determine our most thoughtful, albeit temporary, response. The genuine threat to this struggle lies much more in certainty than in uncertainty, for certainty precludes the necessity for reflection, humility, and forbearance (Purpel 1998: 204).

It is a message which we as teacher educators would do well to consider.

All our respondents, both practising teachers and student teachers, felt that their training courses had not adequately prepared them to confront the issues raised in considering values education. In-service training was felt to be similarly inadequate. In the United Kingdom, certainly until comparatively recently, a paternal attitude to values teaching held sway. As Carr, when discussing the expectations of society of the moral standing of the teachers themselves, saw it: 'this traditional picture of the teacher as occupying a custodial role with respect to the values and moral practices of society held great sway in mainstream teacher training and education . . .' (1993: 196).

He goes on to express the current attitudes to this stance which perhaps go some way to explaining the lack of direction teachers now perceive in their training: 'this sort of paternalism as applied to conceptions of professional educational preparation and training must now appear to most of us to be quite unacceptable – even morally repulsive' (ibid.).

This raised the question of what we as responsible persons should be doing to address this. While in no way disagreeing with this verdict, at least from my own experience in the United Kingdom, I would venture to suggest that part of the problem is caused by the relative lack of awareness of philosophical questions, logical thinking and, to use a discredited Kohlbergian notion, level of moral development on the part of the students and teachers themselves. This situation is probably true of a high proportion of adults in the general population as well as among educators. There has recently been a move towards the introduction of philosophical thinking, in a practical and accessible way, into even primary classrooms. Some of the reported consequences are proving most interesting. However, given the general levels found within our study, if this is to grow and develop, enhancing the likelihood of the exploration of values in our schools and society, and fulfilling the aims of Article 14 through the medium of values education, then we must agree with Costello not only in his desire to see further development of philosophy in schools but also in his analysis of the desired outcome for teachers:

> initial and in-service teacher education programmes should prepare them to undertake work whose aim is to promote critical thinking in the classroom. . . . In seeking to enhance reasoned reflection in the adults of tomorrow, we must begin with the teachers of today.   (1996: 142)

How we, across our various countries and common issues, are to do so in an already overcrowded programme remains the topic for another chapter.

References

Carr, D. (1993) Moral values and the teacher: beyond the paternal and the permissive. *Journal of Philosophy of Education* **27** (2).

Costello, P. (1987) Indoctrination in the classroom. In M. Bottery (ed.) *Issues in Moral and Values Education, Aspects of Education no. 37.* University of Hull, Journal of the Institute of Education.

Costello, P. J. M. (1996) Values and the teaching of philosophical thinking. *Curriculum* **17** (3).

Cremin, L. A. (1976) *Public Education.* New York: Basic Books.

Cross, M. (1987) The never ending story: moral valuing as an important approach to moral education. In M. Bottery (ed.) *Issues in Moral and Values Education, Aspects of Education no. 37.* University of Hull, Journal of the Institute of Education.

Hare, R. M. (1974) Adolescents into adults. In B. I. Chazan and J. F. Soltis (eds) *Moral Education.* New York: Teachers College Press.

Hare, W. (1976) The Open-minded teacher. *Teaching Politics* **1**.

Haydon, G. (1996) Values in the education of teachers: the importance of recognising diversity. In C. Selmes and W. M. Robb (eds) *Values in Teacher Education: Volume One.* Aberdeen: Navet/CAVE.

Hyman, H. H. and Wright, C. R. (1979) *Education's Lasting Influences on Values.* Chicago/London: The University of Chicago Press.

ILEA (1983) *History and Social Sciences at Secondary Level,* Part III. London: ILEA.

National Curriculum Council (1993) *Spiritual and Moral Development.* York: NCC.

Office for Standards in Education (1994) *Handbook for the Inspection of Schools* (Consolidated Edition). London: OFSTED.

Pring, R. (1987) Implications of the changing values and ethical standards of society. In J. Thacker, R. Pring and D. Evans (eds) *Personal, Social and Moral Education in a Changing World.* Windsor: NFER-NELSON.

Purpel, D. E. (1997) Values education in the United States. In H. J. Stephenson, E. Burman, M. Cooper and L. Ling (eds) *Values in Education.* London: Routledge.

Purpel, D. E. and Shapiro, H. S. (1985) (eds) *Schools and Meaning: Essays on the Moral Nature of Schooling.* Lanham/London: University Press of America.

Robb, W. M. (1996) *Values Education for More Effective: Moral Education, Religious Education, Citizenship Education, Health Education, Sex Education, Environmental Education, Alcohol Education, Multi-cultural Education, and Personal and Social Education.* Aberdeen: CAVE.

Schiebe, K. E. (1970) *Beliefs and Values.* New York: Holt, Rinehart and Winston.

Shapiro, S. (1985) Education and the unequal society: the quest for moral 'excellence', in D. E. Purpel and H. S. Shapiro (eds) *Schools and Meaning: Essays on the Moral Nature of Schooling.* Lanham/London: University Press of America.

Starkey, H. (1995) From rhetoric to reality: starting to implement education for European values. In G. H. Bell (ed.) *Educating European Citizens: Citizenship Values and the European Dimension.* London: David Fulton.

Taylor, M. (1994) *Values Education in the UK: A Directory of Research and Resources.* Slough: National Foundation for Educational Research/Gordon Cook Foundation.

Watson, B. and Ashton, E. (1995) *Educational Assumptions and Values.* London: David Fulton.

West, S. (1993) *Educational Values for School Leadership.* London: Kogan Page.

11 Ethics and Values in Schools: Philosophical and Curricular Considerations

TERENCE J. LOVAT

Introduction

I wish to propose three avenues of investigation relevant to a concern about ethics and values in schools. These three avenues take us all the way from, on the one hand, important though seemingly remote issues related to varying conceptions of goodness, right and justice to, on the other hand, highly practical and applied concerns with curriculum adaptation. To deal with issues at one end of this spectrum to the exclusion of those at the other is to risk, at one end, an overly theoretical and impractical consideration and, at the other end, unreflective practical action. The three avenues of investigation I name as, first, **Different Ethical Positions**, second, **Professional Ethics for Teachers**, and, third, **Ethics in the Curriculum: A Case Study**.

I will argue that attention to all three dimensions is essential to the quest for a balanced and complete values education. **Different Ethical Positions** provides a philosophical framework for an approach to ethics and values that is multi-dimensional. Such a framework is a necessary foundation for a values education that is ultimately to cater for the range of differences (dispositional, cultural, gender and class, to name a few) which are to be found in ethical awareness, values attenuation and the classrooms of the average society. This becomes a particular imperative for the classrooms of an increasingly multi-cultural society. **Professional Ethics for Teachers** provides a framework for a code of conduct for the teaching profession. Whether through a formal or more integrated code, public recognition of this level of accountability on the part of the profession is necessary to the authenticity of values education in schools. **Ethics in the Curriculum: A Case Study** provides an example of bridging the theory and the practice of values edu-

cation. At some point, the rhetoric of, and witness implied in, values education must also take shape in a curriculum form. As the paper proceeds to elaborate these three dimensions, I will continue to attempt to draw out the connections between them as well as the implications and ramifications for practical school contexts of all three.

Different ethical positions

It is important to recognize that ethical thinking can be done in a variety of ways, drawing quite different conclusions. If this were not so, there would be little or no contention about ethical matters. Except for the morally perverse, there would be common agreement about the full range of important ethical issues, and agreement across time and place. As it is, this is clearly not the case: people of upright intention disagree about the 'moral ought' associated with particular issues, and difference is evident along several lines, including, most importantly, those of culture. Taylor (1985) contrasts the values positions of ancient and modern cultures, while King (1976) spoke eloquently of the challenge of drawing the various cultures of contemporary USA together in a common push for justice. Charlesworth (1993) suggests that, beyond the most primary values related to autonomy and justice, it is impossible for the modern multi-cultural society to come to a consensus on most of the practical values that guide everyday living. These are important understandings for teachers in multi-cultural settings. While it is beyond the scope of this work to provide a full analysis of the phenomenon of cultural difference in values perspectives, it may be helpful simply to identify a number of clearly different ethical positions that have been proposed and followed in the course of history.

One position is seen clearly in the platonic world view. In Plato's *Republic* (cf. 1987), the sage paints a picture of society as hierarchical and uneven. Certain people are born to superiority and others to inferiority, this inequitable state being according to divine mandate. All knowledge, including knowledge of the Good, the Right and the Just, comes from the gods. A properly ordained ruling class, consisting of the wise ruler and the philosopher kings, constitute the sole interpreters of ethical rights and wrongs. The social system, having been designed by the gods, is by nature a moral entity, and a good one at that. Ethics and the morality of practical living must be assessed in this context. Ethical good is that which contributes to the system, while ethical wrong is that which detracts from it. Individual morality is judged almost exclusively in terms of its contribution to the greater good of the whole, the whole being conceived as a perfect society. In this scheme, there is clearly little room for oppositional thought.

One can see that the powerful institutions of pre-Enlightenment society, especially the Roman Empire, the Christian Church and the many monarchies of medieval times, made use of such an ethical framework, with the most unforgiveable crimes being those of treachery, heresy and the like. One can also see that much of this ethical framework is still well utilized today: all organizational systems make some use of it in providing internal cohesion, maintenance and loyalty. The hallmark of an ethics based on such thinking is its concentration on a systemic morality which emanates from outside of individuals and which impels a necessary conformity. Private morality matters only because it assists in the preservation of this conformity, and so to the stability of the system. The 'common good' is likewise judged by its relevance to the whole, rather than its impact on the majority of individuals.

While elaborating this position may not explain dispositional, cultural or generational difference, it does at least highlight the tenets of a form of ethical thinking that is clearly more convincing to some than to others and it is most likely that at least some of the lines of division fall along those of disposition, culture and generation. With regard to the latter, there is ample evidence of a decline in the power of formalized religion to affect ethical thought and action and so, granted the obvious predilection of religions with this prescriptivist

form of ethics, it is reasonable to suppose that, on average, fewer young people of today are inclined to this way of thinking and acting than was the case a generation or two ago.

We find a clearly alternative ethical view in the thought of the ancient sophists, and especially in the work of Protagoras (cf. Plato 1989). This latter sophist railed against the dominant systemic thinking of his day by proposing a relativism that placed control in the hands of each individual. He was intent on deflating the claims of the privileged few to be the guardians of all knowledge. In this thinking, ethics is essentially something decided on by individuals. Here, the 'common good' can only be the one that serves the good of the majority of individuals. In many ways, this kind of thinking was suppressed by the dominant institutions of pre-Enlightenment times for some 2,000 years. It began to reassert itself in the period known as the Enlightenment.

Within Enlightenment philosophy, we find a strong move towards individual rights and notions of justice which are individually, rather than systemically, orientated. The social philosophy of John Locke (cf. 1962) suggests that individuals adhere to the thing called the state for their individual betterment, rather than that of the state. Individuals coalesce to form the state by choice and because they believe this coalition will serve their individual best interests. There is no commitment to the state, nor an inherent good in the state, beyond this function. The important good is that which pertains to individuals. Morality in society turns on self-respect and respect for the rights and property of others. One of the abiding purposes of society is to advance the protection of this mutual respect.

One can see that it was largely a movement towards this kind of thinking that underpinned the overthrowing of the old empires of Church and State in the Reformation and revolutions of Europe, and their replacement with the more democratic and/or communitarian societies with which we are familiar. While this kind of ethical framework has been with us now for a long time, in many ways it is only in our own time that it is coming to fruition. The various individual rights-orientated legislations that are embedded in most modern Western societies, such as anti-discrimination, equal opportunity, freedom of information and privacy laws, are indicative of this kind of ethics.

Again, we may well find clues to the ethical differences we note around us by exploring an ethical frame like this one. Because of its anti-establishment spirit, it may well suit some dispositional, cultural and generational contexts more than others. In terms of the latter, it is no doubt more likely to take root in a generation which lacks the kind of strong formal religious influence that was more characteristic of the past. Additionally, it may well suit better a generation that is generally more persuaded by individual intuition in ethics than by the generic 'moral ought'.

Lest the entire scheme be conceived too simply, it is not merely a matter of positioning an earlier generation with Platonism and the contemporary generation with sophism. Too many truths would be left uncovered by this, not least those of individual difference which tend to subordinate dispositional, cultural and generational differences. Additionally, and in many ways more importantly, there is a new ethics emerging for our own time, and it is one that itself may well captivate as many of an older generation as it does those of the current generation. It will do this because, while new and different in itself, it captures much of both a Platonic and sophist world-view.

As suggested, this new ethics is only now being constructed. While incorporating the strengths of both older forms, it moves beyond them to a vision of human responsibility that is genuinely global in its outlook. It resembles Platonic ethics in its concern for the whole, rather than individual parts, and in its compliance with the world-view of major religions. On the other hand, it is like the sophist view in that it urges a response from each individual and, when it does make use of religious injunction, it is a multi-cultural and multi-faith religious urge, rather than an ethnocentric version, to which it gives voice. So, the ecological ethos of Hinduism becomes at least as important to the Christian as anything to be found in the home tradition. In a word, this is an ethical framework that synthesizes the social and individual consciences of the other two forms and brings them together in an ethic of action for the global community and environment.

The new ethics highlights the fact that one can live a life of self-respect, respect for others, and be socially correct in all things, but the wider world, or important sections of it, may still be suffering or even crumbling. Each individual is somehow connected to each other individual across the globe; each society is linked to every other society. One cannot merely look to one's own best interests, nor

even to the good of a particular society. If other individuals, other groups and other societies are suffering, or the globe as a whole is being neglected, the Good is not being pursued. There can be only one true 'common good' and that is a comprehensively global one. This ethics has radical implications for such moral issues as sexism, racism, ageism, faithism, as well as all aspects of bioethics and ecoethics, including animal rights and the ethics of inanimate nature (cf. Beauchamp and Walters 1994, Birch 1993, Birke 1994, Brody 1993, Bytheway 1995, Charlesworth 1993, Clark 1990, Freire 1993, Fraser 1994, Jolly and Holland 1993, Jupp 1991, Healey 1992, Hughes 1995, Mellor 1992, Mies and Shiva 1993, Mitchell et al. 1996, Singer 1994, Thomasma and Kushner 1996).

Exploring this latter example serves to remind us that, while many of the differences of ethical thought can be found in our tradition, and have therefore been around for a long time, there is also always the possibility of something entirely new developing. This underlines the dynamic nature of all thought, including ethical thought. The wise teacher will be alert to both the fact of age-old differences and of newly evolving possibilities. The shrewd teacher will see all of these things alive in any typically homogeneous group of students, as well as in their parents. Lack of understanding of these things will render a teacher less effective in the specific roles of life mentor and curriculum practitioner. It is to these latter roles that this chapter now turns, in the first instance to the role of life mentor.

Professional ethics for teachers

In an age of increasing professionalization, it has become common for specialist areas of public service to develop codes of appropriate conduct by which professionals in a particular field should offer their service. The need for this has increased with the growth of individual-orientated rights legislation of the kind mentioned above. These have rendered professionals in service of the public far more liable to civil and legal action if their service is not conducted properly. Codes of conduct, and the entire phenomenon of a professional ethics, are therefore also protective of the profession. The best example we have of a fully developed code of conduct based on classical ethical principles is that of biomedical ethics (Beauchamp and Childress 1994).

Within biomedical ethics, four age-old ethical principles have come to be definitive. These are **autonomy**, **justice**, **non-maleficence** and **beneficence** (cf. Mitchell et al. 1996). When these four principles are applied to practices within the medical profession, they serve as parameters for proper conduct and action for the profession. It seems a reasonable and useful line of argument, therefore, to suggest that these principles may have application to a similar range of practices in the teaching profession. I will attempt to outline below what these might mean in this context.

In the broadest sense, **autonomy** is contrasted with the notion of heteronomy, or, literally, 'rule by others'. In ethical contexts, the concept of autonomy connotes independence and self-determination. It implies a duty on the part of individuals to do all in their power to be capable of autonomous action and a duty on the part of others to ensure that each individual is so capable. It is a principle which assumes that the individual is responsible for, and most properly should determine the direction of, his or her own life. Autonomy impels that the intentions and actions of individuals be essentially self-motivated, demanding coherence and intellectual wholeness from within, and free of undue pressure or manipulation from external sources (Langford 1985).

Cultural shifts in thinking have elevated the importance of the autonomy of the patient in medical practice over the past few decades (Mitchell et al. 1996). Similarly, the implications for teachers have been recognized for some time (Peters 1972, Crittenden 1978). Teaching was once regarded as a prescriptive craft, with the teacher possessing all knowledge and transmitting it through teacher-centred, student disempowering curricula. Coupled with this, the teacher possessed liberties to engage in such heavy-handed discipline practices as were considered necessary for good management of these curricula, including the practices of corporal punishment. There has been a shift which recognizes far better the subtleties and complexities of learning and, consequently, much of the weakness of heteronomous modes of learning (de Bono 1970, Stenhouse 1975, Costa 1981, Biggs 1987, Salomon 1994). There has also been a shift which rejects violence as appropriate to solving social problems, including the violence of corporal punishments. Indeed, within many Western legislatures, parents and teachers place themselves at actionable risk if they engage too freely in such punishments.

There are other aspects of autonomy which impinge on teaching and schooling practice. New privacy laws in Western societies tend to highlight the autonomous rights of the clients of public education, who are firstly the students themselves, and away from the paternalistic rights of teachers and educational bureaucrats. These laws would seem to render practices that were common in the past, such as unfettered access to student files for whatever purpose, or the free and unattended use of students for curriculum experimentation, to be ill-advised and possibly illegal.

In the general sense, **justice** refers to expectations that a society holds concerning relations between the members of that society and, furthermore, concerning that which is considered to encapsulate 'due rendering' to any member of that society (Benn and Peters 1959). Quite beyond the laws which govern any society, there are standards and mores which suggest how people should live up to their obligations to one another. The general sense of justice is normally taken to connote 'equality'; the just person is, therefore, one who treats all persons as equal. It is in this sense that philosophers speak of 'justice as fairness' (Urmson 1988).

Within the context of the teaching profession, 'justice as fairness' is not meant to bind the teacher to offer every student identical service and treatment. It does, however, usher in the notion of 'due care' to ensure that all students are offered the maximum of that proper service which accords with their educational needs. Furthermore, it promotes the idea that this service should be available to all at the same rate and within the same reasonable time, irrespective of wealth, power, status, religion or other affiliation. Such a notion militates against such teacher practices as favouritism, overly casual preparation and unvalidated grading, as well as ethnocentric and biased curriculum design and implementation.

Non-maleficence establishes a duty on all who would be ethical not to harm or injure, or impose risks of harm or injury on, others. In biomedical ethics, it has taken on central importance (Beauchamp and Childress 1994). Within the Hippocratic medical tradition, the dictum, *primum non nocere* ('above all, do no harm') is regarded as the virtual corner-piece of all ethical parameters for the medical practitioner. It sets clearly before the practitioner the role that society expects she or he should play, that of someone who scrupulously avoids any action which might lead to the harming of others. Such actions might include invasive treatment for the purposes of science, rather than for the benefit of the patient, all forms of mal-practice and any lack of proper attention to the patient's real needs.

If Hippocrates' great interest had been education rather than medicine, he might well have uttered the same caution. Though the care rendered by teachers is of a different kind, it has the same capacity to build up or tear down. While much of the physical and health care proper to a doctor is actually shared by the teacher, the teacher's responsibilities go beyond this to the intellectual sphere as well. In other words, in a sense, the teacher is in a position to achieve even greater harm than the doctor. Like doctors, teachers can achieve physical harm for their clients by imposing unwarranted or unwise requirements on them in curricular and extra-curricular situations. This is especially the case in areas of teaching where physical safety is in question, such as physical educa-tion, outdoor education and science. More peculiar to the profession, however, is the fact that teachers can also achieve intellectual harm through a variety of means, including poor preparation and implemen-tation of curriculum, unfair assessment and evalu-ation practices, and through general lack of due care.

The principle of non-maleficence also cautions the teacher against what can amount to detraction of a pupil. Teachers possess enormous power over the reputation and good name, and hence the self-image, of pupils in their care. In their frustration, teachers can engage in detraction of their pupils, either to their face or to others in public places, in a way which most would find alarming were it com-mon practice among medical practitioners and other professionals.

Like all the other principles, **beneficence** has a general ethical sense, proposing that every person who hopes to be ethical has a duty to engage in conduct that is aimed at the good and well-being of others. In biomedical ethics, beneficent action is considered to be a mandatory minimum in terms of the professional's duty (Beauchamp and Childress 1994). Similarly, when the principles of bioethics are applied to teaching, it should be considered as part of one's duty that all efforts be made to advance the good and well-being of the students in one's care (Peters 1972). This goes beyond those duties implied by non-maleficence to include duties related to promoting the physical and intellectual well-being, and guarding the reputation, of the teacher's clients, both pupils and their parents.

Consideration of more highly developed profes-sional ethics for teachers can only assist in the over-all growth and enhancement of the profession. Endorsement of such a code of conduct would sig-nal a new maturity for the profession and bring it into line with other high status professions, both in terms of its inner conduct and in terms of its responsiveness to new ethico-legal parameters in public service. It also denotes the kind of ethical base that must be in place if any effective school-based values education is to proceed. Ethical train-ing, more than most training, requires consistency of theory and practice, ideas and action. An effect-ive teacher of values must be one who speaks of values in every public word and action. One would go so far as to say that a teacher who displayed no sense of professional ethics in public conduct would be incapable of effective teaching in the area of values education. In turn, it is the grappling with issues of values, and the public recognition of this, that will inform the quest of classroom-based values education. It is to this highly vexed and most practical aspect of values education that the paper now turns. The vexed question is, however care-fully defined by dispositional and cultural difference, and however carefully prepared for by practitioners with high personal moral sense and sharp public recognition for same, can we actually teach in this area in a way that makes a difference (Straughan 1988)?

Ethics in the curriculum: a case study

Many Western public education systems have spent much of the past century caught up in a form of secularism that has tended to exaggerate the divi-sions between religious and non-religious educa-tion settings. Together with a subservience to ideas about learning which placed marked emphasis on notions of objectivity and detachment, public sys-tems of education have often taken pride in being centres of value neutrality. That is, in contrast with religious systems of schooling, public systems strived to reveal the objective and unbiased truth. This has left little room in their schemes of learning for values education. In our own time, one senses a change of heart.

The past decade or so has marked a turning-point for moral and values curricula in Western public education. In Australia, the New South Wales Department of School Education document, *The*

Values We Teach (NSW, 1991), states: 'Public schools are not value free. They aim to inculcate and develop in students entrusted in their care those educational, personal, social, moral and spiritual values which are shared by the great majority' (p. 55). Here, we need to recall the earlier proposition of Charlesworth (1993) that consensus on anything but the moral fundamentals is not possible in a multi-cultural society. In this light, it was a bold and potentially highly contentious move that saw *The Values We Teach* set out a core of values for the practical attention of schools. The core revolved around values to do with *education* (focusing on the inherent value of learning, knowledge, curiosity, logical and critical thinking, truth, and life-long learning), *self and others* (focusing on values such as self-acceptance, responsibility, cooperation, honesty, respect for others, health and fitness) and with *civic responsibilities* (concerned with values such as respect for the rights and property of others, as well as social justice and the elimination of discrimination). These are said to be central to school-based values education. Indeed, the document goes so far as to say that public schools should 'work actively and consciously to help their students acquire [these] values . . .' (NSW 1991: 4). Clearly, these values would need to be dealt with everywhere in a way that is sensitive to the multi-cultural dilemma identified above.

A recently conducted Australian Research Council funded project (Lovat and Schofield, 1998) has used *The Values We Teach*, and a resultant values education programme, as the basis for determining whether a school curriculum can modify and change perceptual awareness in relation to ethical matters. The ultimate aim of the study was to determine whether it was possible to change the stated values held by children in a positive direction by means of direct curriculum intervention. The project involved a number of discrete elements, the first of which was the need to devise a reliable and valid scale to measure the values held by primary school aged children. The second element, the actual intervention, was in the form of a 'values education programme', devised by the researchers following the guidelines established by *The Values We Teach*. Finally, an attempt was made to evaluate the 'felt' effects of the programme, and to determine from both students and staff the perceived value of the programme. I will address each of these in turn.

First, an instrument was trialled over a number of months on approximately 500 students in Years 5 and 6 of primary school. In the actual project, 1,050 students from the same age range (approximately half each in experimental and control groups) were pre- and post-tested across a six month period. The instrument highlighted thirty-three stated values (e.g. 'I never take things that are not mine'; 'I like having people from other countries living in Australia') which reflected the values set in each of the three categories (i.e. education, self and others, civic responsibilities) identified in *The Values We Teach*. Each item was measured on a six-point Likert scale.

From the investigators' point of view, the instrument was consistent in its make-up with the philosophies expounded in the two sections above. Its items were sufficiently varied, both in terms of content and style, so as to allow for the varying responses one might expect from groups characterized by a range of differences, including dispositional, multi-cultural and gender differences. Hence, item reversal caters for a range of responses that might result from dispositional, cultural and even gender differences. Items in question included: 'If I was caught doing something wrong, I would try to blame someone else' and 'I always tell the truth.' Items that variously place the centre of moral responsibility and decision-making on self, parents and/or others were also designed to cater for dispositional, cultural and possibly gender differences. Items in question included: 'I would be happy to be best friends with someone from another race' and 'My parents would be happy if I was best friends with someone from another race.' Items that variously placed men and women at the centre of the issue were also designed to allow for these differences. Items in question included: 'Men should be able to stay at home and look after children while their wife works, if they choose' and 'Women should be able to do whatever job they want.' The items also reflected, in most cases, the types of items that one would expect to characterize a professional code of conduct for teachers. Hence, one finds across the three categories items that speak of personal commitment ('I like to do my best in everything'), personal integrity ('If I say I'm going to do something, I keep my word') and civic consciousness ('I think we should help people who don't have much money').

Second, the intervention consisted of a formal values education programme delivered across the same six month period which was contained by the pre- and post-testing. The parameters of the programme were tailored to ensure they matched the goals and objectives of *The Values We Teach*, as well as the items represented in the instrument. Hence, the same points made about the connection between the measuring instrument and the philosophies expounded in the two earlier sections of this chapter also can be made about the intervention programme. The programme dealt with matters that allowed for difference and was consistent in its tenor with what one would expect to find in a professional code for teachers.

Teachers were in-serviced on the programme, and asked to spend at least ten minutes a day on it. This was often integrated with other lessons, with the result that the intervention often permeated much of the overall teaching programme. Teachers were asked to focus on the range of moral issues and dilemmas arising from *The Values We Teach*, and to use a variety of teaching strategies, including discussion, role play, games and audio-visual stimuli as catalysts for ongoing involvement and learning. Throughout the programme, teachers were encouraged to ensure they acted as role models relative to the values under discussion. Where teachers observed specific benefits flowing from the programme, such as in areas like cooperation, these benefits were highlighted and the behaviour was reinforced. In this way an attempt was made to combine elements of the cognitive (cf. Kohlberg 1976), social learning (cf. Bandura 1991) and psycho-analytic/affective (cf. Eysenck 1976), theories of moral development, since it was considered that any programme of moral education should operate at all of these levels (cf. Rest and Thoma 1986).

Third, the 'felt' effects of the programme were measured by an evaluation instrument in the case of students, and logs and anecdotal feedback in the case of teachers. In the case of the students, feedback from the evaluation not only confirmed very high ratings for general enjoyment (4.51 on a scale of 6) and belief in the worthwhileness of the programme (5.05), but very positive reporting about the impact that the programme had had on a range of issues, including those associated with a multi-cultural society (for example, 'I am now more aware of problems that people from other cultures have when living in Australia' = 4.64). Student feedback also spoke about the importance one should place on values (5.4), their willingness to discuss such issues in class (4.73) and the levels to which such discussion assisted in resisting peer pres-

sure (for example, 'In class discussions, I usually agreed with my friends, even if I didn't really believe in what they were saying' = 2.73). Anecdotal teacher feedback reported perceptions of effectiveness, changes of behaviour on the part of students, and confirmed the general view about overall levels of enjoyment, both their own and those perceived in the students.

Results of the project were mixed. The primary aim of the study was to determine whether the intervention programme produced significant improvement in the attitudes and values of the intervention group. A series of two-way Analysis of Variants (ANOVAs), with intervention group and sex as the grouping variables, were calculated. A significant (F = 6.64, p < .01) main effect was observed for the first factor, education, with the intervention group showing a significant improvement over the intervention period. This would seem to indicate that the intervention programme was most successful in relation to those issues that related to the specific school/educational environment. By contrast, the programme was not so obviously successful in relation to the other two factors, which may represent more generic and perhaps abstract issues of integrity and equity. Even here, however, while no truly significant factor differences were observed, there was identifiable movement in individual items, especially in those which accorded with the more significant discussions identified by the teachers. These discussions tended to centre on items to do with such topical issues as sexism and racism (eg. 'Women should be able to do any job they want'; 'I like having people from other countries living in Australia'). This may indicate the possibility of effective intervention, provided the intervention is sufficiently strong.

While difference was catered for in ways described above, the factor of cultural difference in response did not manifest itself in an obvious way, possibly owing to the relatively homogeneous make-up of the majority of schools in the particular region in question. Indeed, movement on those items that emphasized multi-cultural awareness was consistent across all intervention groups. The one factor of difference that did manifest itself very clearly was that of gender. Very large and significant differences between males and females in both intervention and control groups were observed for the factors of self and others (F = 79.40, p < .001) and civic responsibilities (F = 45.73, p < .001), with females having much higher scores on both of these variables. This suggests that, although there was no greater benefit for one sex over the other from the intervention programme, all females were starting from a much higher base-line level on these issues.

In general terms, children were extremely positive about the course, were very strongly of the opinion that values were important in their lives, and believed that they were able to resist peer pressure in the formulation of their values. They were also strongly of the opinion that all children should get the opportunity to discuss these issues in their class. In very general terms, Year 6 students were more positive in their support of the course than Year 5 students, suggesting an added factor of greater maturity. Given the earlier findings of major sex differences on two of the factors, responses to this instrument were also examined to determine whether males and females differed in their perceptions of the programme. Significant sex differences were found for thirteen of the seventeen items, with females being more positive about the programme than males in every case. This difference was most marked in areas of peer resistance (eg. 'In class discussions, I usually agreed with my friends, even if I didn't really believe in what they were saying' = 2.47 [girls], 3.01 [boys]) and multi-cultural awareness (eg. 'I am now more aware of problems that people from other cultures have when living in Australia' = 4.84 [girls], 4.42 [boys]).

A number of major conclusions can be drawn from the modest success of the intervention study. The first and most important is that a curriculum intervention in the area of morals and values can produce a statistically significant change in stated attitudes with regard to both broad groupings and specific issues, and so would appear to comprise an important adjunct to the ethical training responsibilities of teachers described above. The second conclusion is that, for an intervention to maximize its success, it must focus on the very basic school-related environment and real-life experience of the child and/or be sufficiently strong in its impact to break through the boundaries created by the natural interests and concerns of a particular age group. Third, the findings revealed that there are pronounced gender differences in relation to issues of values. Fourth, it is important to note that students generally enjoyed, valued and endorsed the experience of learning and discussing in this area. Indeed, it is fairly unusual to find such strong endorsement from this age-group for an exercise like this which was, after all, purely classroom-based

and essentially cerebral. Responses to the evaluation instrument would seem to indicate that the programme was regarded as a novel and welcome exercise and one which might be further exploited by the education system.

Conclusion

This chapter has proposed that effective ethics and values education must begin with some exposure to the many and varied ways in which ethics can and has been conceived and acted upon in history. Even if the teacher of values lacks a full socio-historical theory, at least understanding that there are fundamentally different ethical positions will presumably enhance tolerance and greater acceptance of difference. As indicated within, this is an especially important perspective for a multi-cultural generation. In turn, the chapter has proposed the need for the development of professional ethics for teachers, whether by formal code or informal acceptance, on the basis that such public accountability and recognition is a necessary artefact for a profession charged with responsibilities for values education in the public curriculum. It is recommended that this development might take light from recent developments in other professions with similar public service profiles. Finally, and in a highly applied fashion, the chapter endorses the possibility of enhancing in children knowledge about and perceptions of moral matters through direct curriculum intervention. As suggested above, the rhetoric and witness about values education implied in the first two sections of this chapter can amount to nought if the matter of effective curriculum implementation remains unaddressed. The argument in this chapter is that these three dimensions need to be attended to in concert for the teaching profession truly to advance in ethics in its self-understanding, its public face and its effective curriculum practice.

References

Bandura, A. (1991) Social cognitive theory of moral thought and action. In W. M. Kurtines and J. L. Gerwitz (eds) *Handbook of Moral Behavior and Development*, vol. 1. Hillsdale, NJ: Erlbaum.

Beauchamp, T. and Childress, J. (1994) *Principles of Biomedical Ethics*. New York: Oxford University Press.

Beauchamp, T. and Walters, L. (1994) *Contemporary Issues in Bioethics*. Belmont, CA: Wadsworth.

Benn, S. and Peters, R. (1959) *Social Principles and the Democratic State*. London: George Allen and Unwin.

Biggs, J. (1987) *Student Approaches to Learning and Studying*. Melbourne: Australian Council for Educational Research.

Birch, C. (1993) *Regaining Compassion for Humanity and Nature*. Sydney: NSW University Press.

Birke, L. (1994) *Feminism, Animals and Science: The Naming of the Shrew*. Philadelphia: Open University Press.

Brody, E. (1993) *Biomedical Technology and Human Rights*. Aldershot, UK: Dartmouth.

Bytheway, B. (1995) *Ageism*. Bristol, PA: Open University Press.

Charlesworth, M. (1993) *Bioethics in a Liberal Society*. Melbourne: Cambridge University Press.

Clark, M. (1990) *A Defiant Celebration: Theological Ethics and Gay Sexuality*. Garland, TEX: Tangelwuld Press.

Costa, A. (1981) Teaching for intelligent behaviour. *Educational Leadership*, **39**: 29–32.

Crittenden, B. (1978) Autonomy as an aim of education. In K. Strike and K. Egan (eds) *Ethics and Educational Policy*. Boston: Routledge and Kegan Paul.

de Bono, E. (1970) *Lateral Thinking*. New York: Harper and Row.

Eysenck, H. J. (1976). The biology of morality. In T. Lickona (ed.) *Moral Development and Behavior*. New York: Holt, Rinehart and Winston.

Fraser, N. (1994) *Critical Politics: From the Personal to the Global*. Melbourne: Arena Publications.

Freire, P. (1993) *Pedagogy of the City* (trans. D. Macedo). New York: Continuum.

Healey, K. (ed.) (1992) *Animal Rights*. Sydney: Spinney Press.

Hughes, B. (1995) *Older People and Community Care: Critical Theory and Practice*. Bristol, PA: Open University Press.

Jolly, B. and Holland, I. (1993) *Facing the Future: Ecopolitics VII Conference Proceedings*. Brisbane: Griffith University.

Jupp, J. (1991) *Immigration*. Sydney: Sydney University Press.

King, M. (1976) The future of integration. In L. Habermehl (ed.) *Morality in the Modern World*. Belmont, CA: Wadsworth.

Kohlberg, L. (1976) Moral stages and moralization: the cognitive-developmental approach. In T. Lickona (ed.) *Moral Development and Behavior: Theory, Research and Social Issues*. New York: Holt, Rinehart and Winston.

Langford, G. (1985) *Education, Persons and Society*. London: Macmillan.

Locke, J. (1962) *Two Treatises of Government*. Cambridge: Cambridge University Press.

Lovat, T. and Schofield, N. (1998) Values Formation in Citizenship Education: A Proposition and an Empirical Study. *Unicorn*, **24**: 46–54.

Mellor, M. (1992) *Breaking the Boundaries: Towards a Feminist, Green Socialism*. London: Virago.

Mies, M. and Shiva, V. (1993) *Ecofeminism*. Melbourne: Spinifex Press.

Mitchell, K., Kerridge, I. and Lovat, T. (1996) *Bioethics and Clinical Ethics for Health Care Professionals*. Sydney: Social Science Press.

NSW (1991) *The Values We Teach*. Sydney: Department of School Education.

Peters, R. (1972) *Ethics and Education*. London: George Allen and Unwin.

Plato (1987) *The Republic* (trans. D. Lee). Harmondsworth: Penguin.

Plato (1989) *Protagoras* (trans. C. Taylor). Oxford: Clarendon Press.

Rest, J. and Thoma, S. J. (1986) Educational programs and interventions. In J. R. Rest (ed.) *Moral Development: Advances in Research and Theory*. New York: Praeger.

Salomon, G. (1994) *Whole Individuals in Complex Settings: Educational Research Re-examined*. Invited Address at the Annual Conference of the Australian Association for Research in Education, Newcastle, Australia.

Singer, P. (1994) *Rethinking Life and Death: The Collapse of our Traditional Ethics*. Melbourne: Text Publications.

Stenhouse, L. (1975) *An Introduction to Curriculum Research and Development*. London: Heinemann.

Straughan, R. (1988) *Can We Teach Children to be Good?* Milton Keynes and Philadelphia: Open University Press.

Taylor, R. (1985) *Ethics, Faith and Reason*. Englewood Cliffs, NJ: Prentice Hall.

Thomasma, D. and Kushner, T. (ed.) (1996) *Birth to Death: Science and Bioethics*. New York: Cambridge University Press.

Urmson, J. (1988) *Aristotle's Ethics*. Oxford: Basil Blackwell.

12 The Purpose and Context of Multi-cultural Education and its Justification in the Curriculum of Mono-cultural Schools

HEATHER FIONA WAINMAN

> The reality of British society, now and in the future, is that a variety of ethnic groups, with their own distinctive lifestyles and value systems, will be living together.[1]

From this identified reality, the Swann Report went on to advance the concept of 'Education for All', stating that good education must reflect diversity, encourage understanding of various cultures and lifestyles and avoid an 'anachronistically Anglo-centric view of the world'.[2] The Swann Report thus advocated that education should encourage a commitment to shared values and should enable pupils to respond positively to these. Therefore, one of its main goals is 'to change attitudes among the White Majority, and to develop a pattern of education that enables *all* pupils to give of their best'.[3]

It is thus against this background that consideration will be given to the nature of multi-cultural education (referring to matters pertaining to many cultures), its aims, objections to it, responses to such objections, ways in which it can be delivered, and its position in relation to mono-cultural schools (referring to establishments dealing with one culture, primarily an 'all-white' culture).

What is multi-cultural education?

The nature of multi-cultural education has not always been clearly defined, but some key aspects have been established which include that it should be for all pupils in all schools, and that it should thus enable pupils to appreciate the diversity of cultural experiences available to them. There are two main ways in which such education can be addressed in schools. First, schools can attempt to respond to the cultural requirements and sensitivities of children and parents from various ethnic backgrounds, promoting respect for religious and cultural beliefs. They could also aim to make educational use of the experiences they bring to the school. Alternatively, multi-cultural education can be considered as appropriate to all pupils if they are to be adequately prepared for life in a pluralist society.

These approaches are linked, but have important distinctions and repercussions with regard to multi-cultural and mono-cultural schools. Both raise the profile of multi-cultural education, but while the former seeks to react to the multi-cultural make-up of a school, the latter moves away from the solely reactive response and places multi-cultural education at the heart of education for all, regardless of the cultural balance of the school. Such education transcends the nature of the educational establishment, and moves into the realms of using education as a means of preparing all pupils for the pluralistic nature of society. The contribution made to society as a whole by multi-cultural education requires it to pre-empt, rather than merely react to, the cultural make-up of the school.

What are the aims of multi-cultural education?

Having looked at the nature of multi-cultural education, it is now important to consider its aims. Again referring to the Swann Report, it appears that its aims are to provide a means of 'educating *all* children from whatever ethnic group, to an understanding of the shared values of our society'.[4] This is not, however, to suggest that multi-cultural education should aim to produce a society in which only similarities with regard to ethnic groups are highlighted. The aim is not to produce an amorphous mass which is educated only about what is common to various groups. Thus multi-cultural education goes beyond the drawing out of shared values and encourages 'an appreciation of the diversity of the lifestyles and cultural, religious and linguistic backgrounds which make up this society and the wider world'.[5]

The aim is to acknowledge unity while at the same time celebrating diversity. Multi-cultural education must therefore seek to facilitate an understanding of this in order to prepare pupils for life in a culturally and ethnically pluralist society. It must give pupils an education that reflects the multi-racial and multi-cultural make-up of British society. In relation to this, it is important to give pupils the knowledge necessary to address issues of myths and stereotypes and so develop in them the skills needed to allow them to contribute positively to society as a whole.

Further to this, the aims include developing a curriculum with a global and international content, to avoid the possibility of an insular curriculum based solely on Britain and its values. British society contains a variety of social and ethnic groups and this should be made clear to pupils in the information offered to them. Other cultures and nations have their own validity and should be described in their own terms and not be judged against British or European 'norms'. The danger is that, when describing other cultures, we do not do so in their own terms, but from the perspective of our own values. This is what leads to such judgements being made. We look at other cultures, not from the inward understanding of that culture, but from an outward assumption of British values. Thus British values are seen to transcend all others and a true understanding of other cultures is not gained. Only by getting inside that culture and understanding it from that perspective can this aim be met. It is clear then that education must play a leading role in establishing such criteria and the aim of multi-cultural education should be to facilitate harmonious pluralism in which ethnic minority communities maintain their distinct identities within a common framework. In preparing pupils for such a society and in educating pupils for such an understanding of society multi-cultural education meets its aims. At the same time, however, this raises another question: are we looking at the aims of multi-cultural education, or are we actually considering the aims of education in a multi-cultural society? The difference is subtle but important and will be returned to later.

Common objections to multi-cultural education

Despite the moves towards multi-cultural education, and despite suggestions that such education is essential given the pluralist nature of society, there have been criticisms of it, or at least moves against it which have made its implementation difficult, some of which will be considered here.

Government legislation

While clearly not being openly critical of multi-cultural education, there have been certain ideas written into government legislation that tend away from a multi-cultural style of education and toward an Anglocentric view. This implicit shift has had a major influence on the readiness of, and indeed on the opportunity for, schools to offer multi-cultural education. The 'nationalist' perspective of such government legislation, and in particular of that contained in the 1988 Education Reform Act and National Curriculum guidelines, has done much to oppose moves toward 'education for all' in terms of multi-cultural education. The legislation has directed education firmly towards a British perspective and thus perpetuates the narrowly 'white and English' notion of education, and the values of a distinctly British society. The 1988 Act has therefore been described as: 'An Act based on a political and economic philosophy of individualism in a capitalist free-market, an Act which attempts to reconstruct through education a national identity based on a narrowly defined notion of "Englishness" '.[6]

Such moves towards an Anglocentric curriculum can be seen, for example, in legislation on history, religious education (RE) and collective worship, and on modern foreign languages. The National Curriculum guidelines on history have always had a distinctly British slant and recent publications suggest that if anything this is to be increased. Until now, teaching, especially for infant children, has been based around developing historical skills and awareness by considering stories from different periods and cultures. By starting this at an early age, pupils should have had the opportunity to see all cultures as being equally valuable and also to begin the process of stepping into a culture and accepting it at face value before preconceived ideas about British 'norms' had been established. However, it appears now that, as part of the National Curriculum, British history will be placed at the core of what is taught: 'Children will have to learn about the great events and people of British history from the age of five under government plans to ensure all pupils know the country's heritage'.[7] The revised curriculum has increased the proportion of time devoted to the delivery of British history. By doing this, pupils are conditioned into British values and the danger of this is that when other cultures are later introduced, they are alien and are thus regarded as inferior in comparison to the perceived norm. In relation to Key Stage 3, for example, certain aspects of British history have to be covered, such as the medieval realms, the making of the United Kingdom and the two world wars. Where study has the potential to move into other cultures – when looking at wars, or expansion, trade and industry – the supporting information places a strong emphasis on the Anglocentric perspective. Study of the First World War is covered under the notion of Britain and the Great War. Expansion, trade and industry draw primarily on British developments. Clearly this need not be the case, and it does lead to the development of society as a whole being seen from a narrow perspective. Other areas of study do draw on experiences from other cultures, such as the Roman Empire, Islamic civilizations and Native Indians, but these take up much less curriculum time than British history does. By placing the study of history in this perspective, opportunities for multi-cultural education are at best limited.

The legislation with regard to RE and collective worship again emphasizes this Anglocentric approach. British law has made it difficult for RE to make a substantial contribution to multi-cultural education. Historically, the confessional nature of RE made reference to other faiths superfluous. There was a trend towards looking at other faiths, but acknowledging them as inferior to Christianity. Clearly, the secular and multi-faith nature of society could not have been foreseen by the makers of the 1944 Education Act, but it is interesting to note that, despite the now obvious make-up of society, the 1988 Education Reform Act resisted the recommendations of the Swann Report and re-emphasized Christianity as being the basis for RE teaching and collective worship. Hence, in relation to RE section 8 (3) of the Education Reform Act states: 'New locally agreed syllabuses must reflect the fact that religious traditions in Great Britain are in the main Christian whilst taking account of the teachings and practices of other principal religions represented in Great Britain.' While clearly encouraging pupils to consider the beliefs and practices of world religions, the Act also firmly places Christianity at the centre of such teaching, thus perpetuating an Anglocentric view which may not be fully conducive with preparation for an increasingly pluralistic society.

The issue of culture is touched upon in guidance on the implementation of the act given in DES circular 3189, section 1 (7) which refers to one aim of RE being to: 'promote the spiritual, moral, cultural and physical development of pupils and of society'. The issue of culture is closely linked to RE as the customs, values and beliefs of any society are at least partly defined by religious ideas. Religion thus influences those parts of culture linked to rites of passage, types of worship, the celebration of festivals, spirituality, behaviour and morality. However, given the balance suggested by the Act, blending the multi-cultural into the dominant culture has proved problematic and has led to a great deal of debate and consideration of what the government has referred to as the 'mish-mash' of RE. This was not intended to protest against the teaching of world religions, but rather as a comment on a multi-faith approach that the government felt contrived to teach things together in a way that made them meaningless. Thus, an attempt to avoid the 'mish-mash' was sought by attempting to define the nature of a multi-faith syllabus, with column 630 stating that such a syllabus would: 'provide for flexibility of emphasis in areas where the vast majority of pupils are from other faiths'. This would allow local Standing Advisory Councils for Religious Education (SACREs) to produce, in areas deemed appropriate, syllabus information related to the particular needs of the locality. However, it was stressed that this should not lead to pupils being taught in faith groups.

This was clearly established in the 1991 debate on the Education Reform Act, which established RE as essentially educational, appropriate for all pupils and incorporated into one curriculum for all pupils which would allow proper exploration of all faiths. It is clear, therefore, that RE does contribute to multi-cultural education, but it is equally clear that legislation is designed to slant the teaching of RE in favour of one particular culture. It is equally significant that, despite living in a pluralist society, special permission is needed, even in areas where a non-Christian faith dominates, to study this as the prime religion. This anomaly is also seen in legislation related to collective worship. It is of course possible to opt out of single faith worship, though again legislation can make this difficult, but: 'it is significant that schools will have to apply to "opt out" and are not required to "opt in" to the provision of a single faith act of worship in a multi-faith society'.[8]

The assumption inherent behind such legislation tends against uninhibited multi-cultural education. The common thread running through this legislation on RE and collective worship is that British values come first and should be upheld, and that reference to other religions or cultures should be simply added on where appropriate. This assumption relegates such religions or cultures and gives an impression of inferiority in relation to the British/Christian values and norms. Giving Christianity such a prominent role also makes it difficult for pupils to step into another culture without judging it against the dominant culture. For example, most agreed syllabuses see Key Stage 1 as introducing Christianity only, with other religions being held back to Key Stage 2 or even Key Stage 3. This allows pupils little opportunity of objectivity and little chance to form unbiased opinions. All of this serves to perpetuate a problem of balance in relation to multi-cultural education.

A similar message is given with regard to modern languages in the 1989 DES document 'Modern Foreign Languages in the National Curriculum'. In this, Welsh is recognized as a core curriculum subject in Wales, but other 'living' languages of Britain, in some schools representing the majority of children, are relegated to 'schedule 2' status whereby they can only be offered as options – as opposed to 'schedule 1' status which is *required* and which covers the European Community working languages. It is clear, therefore, that, although not directly criticizing multi-cultural education, government legislation has done as much, if not more than its more outspoken critics, to ensure that education in Britain is Anglocentric as opposed to multi-cultural.

Educational nationalism

Linked to government legislation has been opposition on a more complex political level related to the question of who belongs within a British 'national identity' and whose version of British heritage and culture should be accepted as authentic. Such opposition has centred on the need to present British imperial history in a way that will encourage British culture and patriotic pride. Thus, nationalism in educational terms becomes an ideology in which citizens are encouraged to believe that their national past marks them out as being different from others:

> Educational nationalism asserts that minorities have complete choice and opportunity to join the British nation and assimilate into a 'British way of life' and that their own intransigence and that of their multi-cultural supporters hinders the process.[9]

This approach assumes that the education system is designed for a white majority and that assimilation by ethnic minorities is both possible and desired. Such a system again argues against a multi-cultural form of education, and places British values as being something that should be aspired to by members of other cultures. By definition, this also devalues their cultural identity.

Honeyford's criticisms

One of the names most readily associated with criticism of the multi-cultural approach to education is that of Honeyford. Primarily he criticizes the approach to multi-cultural education that sees it as a way of responding positively to the cultural requirements of children and parents from minority groups. He argues that making such concessions to cultural groups inevitably undermines some of the fundamental principles on which the British education system is based, such as equal opportunities. Thus when a Muslim father tried to withdraw his daughter from swimming lessons on religious grounds, he saw it as a direct clash with educational principles:

> I had to run a school which was obliged both from conviction and legal necessity to ensure equal opportunities for girls. And denying a little girl the right to swim clearly violated *our* principle . . . I had no right to restrict her human possibilities in the way her father wanted.[10]

He claimed that his aim was to liberate pupils from the restricting cultures of their parents. The crux of his argument lay in the fact that he saw concessions made on cultural grounds as being socially divisive in that they destroyed the possibility of integration by emphasizing diversity and accentuating cultural and racial differences. If schools are to do society justice they should play a part in establishing social cohesion and integration, laying emphasis on the common needs of all children and applying the same rules and policies to them all. So multi-cultural education, far from preparing for a pluralist society, perpetuates and adds to the divisions inherent within it. According to this view, it achieves the opposite of what it sets out to do and therefore fails in its objectives. This would be equally true in either a multi-cultural or a mono-cultural school or environment.

Mono-cultural objections

While government legislation clearly influences all schools, other more explicit objections to multi-cultural education were relatively muted until it became clear, after the Swann Report, that issues of multi-cultural education were not confined to multi-ethnic schools but were intended to address education as a whole, even where the school was exclusively mono-cultural. The Swann Report referred specifically to visits to 'all white' schools and its findings stated that the preparation in such schools for life in a multi-cultural society was highly inadequate:

> The insularity and parochialism of many teachers and pupils in these 'all white' schools is dismaying in its implications for the preparation of all pupils both for life in a multi-racial society and an interdependent world.[11]

The reasons behind this lack of preparation for a multi-cultural society seem to lie in the perceived irrelevance of such education to all white schools and communities, and also owe much to the previously mentioned nationalist view of education. Such specific objections took the issue to a new dimension and increased the objections to multi-cultural education. It added to the debate about whether multi-cultural education is acceptable in its place, i.e. in schools that draw pupils from a range of ethnic backgrounds, or whether it is something that is educationally acceptable in all schools operating in a multi-cultural society, regardless of the make-up of the school.

Answers to the criticisms

The Swann Report went straight to the heart of the criticisms levelled at multi-cultural education in adopting the following position: 'The fundamental change that is needed is the recognition that the problem facing education is not how to educate children of ethnic minorities, but how to educate all children'.[12] By placing it firmly in the realms of something that should happen in all schools, the issues of mono-cultural education and educational nationalism are clearly addressed. The fundamental principle remains that multi-cultural education is necessary both in a pluralist society and in an interdependent world.

With specific reference to all white schools, the traditional view that such education is irrelevant because 'almost all the pupils are white and there is a feeling among staff and pupils that there is, therefore, no problem concerning "race" at the school'[13] is challenged. Indeed it is often suggested that, far from there being no problem in such schools, the problem is at its greatest here and, far from being irrelevant, multi-cultural education is in fact essential. The evidence from such schools often contradicts the idea that there is no race problem, with racism and prejudice being prevalent, if not on the surface, then just beneath it. Many pupils from such schools 'still leave school with no real understanding of and a reluctance to accept ethnic minorities as their equal and fellow citizens'[14] and are thus ill prepared to take their place in a modern pluralistic society.

While it is very difficult to address the problems inherent in government legislation, partly because of its implicit nature and partly because of its legal standing, key points have been made with regard to the necessity of a curriculum that is more open and diverse than the Anglocentric one currently being promoted. By looking at ways in which multi-cultural education can be delivered, regardless of the ethnic weighting of the school, some of these points will be considered.

Cultural education

One suggestion is that pupils should be made aware of the notion of 'culture' itself and its influence on thinking. Whether or not a school is mono-cultural, pupils need to be aware of their own conditioning in order to study culture or religion effectively. Western (British) conditioning, advanced since the Enlightenment, has placed Western thought on a very scientific and reasoned footing. Thus, there are two worlds in the mind of the West – the religious and the secular. This must be understood clearly by a pupil before he or she tries to consider the culture or religions of the East, which can be seen as being influenced less by science than by the role of God. Without understanding such cultural differences, there is a danger that a mind more familiar with the Western type of thinking will automatically see this as superior to that of the East, leading not only to a lack of understanding, but also to the possibilities of racism.

> (scientific/reasoning) is seen by many as bearing the torch of progress, safeguarding human autonomy, and governing by rule of reason. (religion) is seen by many as outdated, a barrier to progress, a threat to human autonomy, and a challenge to the supremacy of reason.[15]

Without understanding and acknowledging these differences, it is difficult to go on to consider religions that fit into a society with different truths and values. Without such understanding and consideration of context, pupils will usually go on to compare unfavourably the practices of cultures and religions to their experiences in British society. Such value judgements are clearly unhelpful to the formation of a pluralist society. Thus, cultural education should be taught to all pupils to aid their understanding of themselves as well as of others. Such educational aims could certainly be deemed as relevant to all pupils.

Moral education

Aspects of multi-cultural education can be delivered through moral education, whether moral education is something that is inherent in the whole school curriculum or something that is delivered through RE or Personal and Social Education (PSE). Whatever form it takes, moral education is concerned with encouraging pupils to hold 'right' attitudes and to act accordingly. Morality requires that people should be treated equally. It would follow then that moral education would include reference to the injustice of all prejudice, including racial

prejudice. One of the aims of moral education could therefore be seen as the elimination of racial prejudice. In addition to this, moral education is also concerned with developing an understanding of 'person', and this will also contribute to education for a multi-cultural society, especially with regard to issues of justice. While making very little reference to moral education, the Swann Report promotes an ethical dimension with regard to 'education for all', stating that it should:

> seek to identify and remove those practices and procedures which work . . . against pupils from any ethnic group, and promote through the curriculum an appreciation and commitment to the principles of equality and justice on the part of all pupils.[16]

Thus the sound educational practices of moral education – encouraging awareness of values as a basis for judgements, feelings and behaviour, the understanding of moral concepts such as equality, fairness and the notion of 'person'; the development of emotions such as empathy, and the ability and willingness to act for the right reasons – need to be encouraged throughout the education system, and can be seen as a means of facilitating both multi-cultural education and education appropriate for all in a pluralistic society.

Pastoral education

Pastoral education, like moral education is something that can take place either as part of the whole school ethos, or in a specific time-tabled subject (PSE). Most information on personal and social development often, however, ignores the issue of multi-cultural education, usually assuming personal development occurs regardless of race. This confidence may be misplaced as it would appear that the two issues should not be seen as independent of each other. In order for effective pastoral care and education to take place, an understanding of the cultural background of the pupils is essential. This must be a true understanding, based on clear knowledge of what it means to be a member of that group, and not an assumed understanding based on a notion of a British view of that culture. The ability to step into a culture, to view it from the perspective of that culture, must be the aim of anyone working in this field. This understanding must also take into account the fact that there is often conflict related to the values held with regard to education between the school and the home. Effective counselling must take into consideration the inherent values of these often diverse perspectives. It is thus that pastoral education and multi-cultural education are inextricably linked:

> By asking the question 'what kind of society do we want?' and by providing an answer in terms of pluralism and plural education, Swann's argument bears directly onto a number of concerns which have traditionally been considered as 'pastoral'.[17]

The well-being of pupils, their families, the role of parents, a sense of personal worth and learning to value others are the concerns of both pastoral and multi-cultural education: 'a pluralist education which pays due attention to the needs and concerns of pupils and their parents will develop as the application of a pastoral curriculum is re-interpreted in the context of a multi-racial society'.[18] Again, such education appears to be relevant, if not vital, to pupils in all schools, regardless of the school's ethnic balance.

Religious education

As has already been noted, the law relating to RE has limited the contribution the subject can make to multi-cultural education. Despite this, however, it can have a major role to play if dealt with sensitively.

The Swann Report did mention RE in the context of making a positive contribution to multi-cultural education but did so only by placing moral education firmly in the context of RE due to their shared values:

> The 'moral' dimension of RE also relates directly to some of the fundamental concerns raised by the multi-racial nature of our society, most notably perhaps the need to tackle racism and injustice and to seek to create true equality of opportunity for youngsters from all ethnic groups, which we would see as central to 'education for all'.[19]

Addressing the question of racism tends to be an area considered in RE, particularly at Key Stage 4. Whether working towards GCSE, or meeting the guidelines of a locally agreed syllabus, many pupils will be encouraged to consider issues of morality, including the question of racism. Thus, pupils are introduced to the question of what racism is and how it develops and are encouraged to understand the concepts of prejudice, discrimination and stereotyping. In order to get a balanced view of this, it is important that racism is not just considered from a white/British perspective. Pupils could be encouraged to look at why prejudice might exist, but should then go on to consider how the victims of such prejudice might feel and why they should object to acts of discrimination. In order to do this, pupils would have to try to see racism from both sides, understanding it from more than one perspective. They would need to step into various cultures and try to understand the implications of racism from different points of view. In conjunction with this, pupils could also investigate how different religions respond to racism, drawing out shared and different beliefs, values and attitudes. For example, Christianity, Hinduism and Islam all condemn racism, and indeed all forms of prejudice, and this common aim could be addressed by pupils. Introducing pupils to this through the teachings of the holy scriptures can provide a useful starting point:

> So there is no difference between Jews and Gentiles, between slaves and free people, between men and women; you are all one in union with Christ Jesus.　(Galatians 3:28)

> I look upon all creatures equally; none are less dear to me and none dear. But those who worship me with love live in me and I come to life in them.　(Bhagavad Gita 9:29)

> Allah does not look upon your outward appearance; He looks upon your hearts and your deeds.　(*Hadith*)

By drawing out such similarities, pupils can begin to appreciate that the issue of racism is a problem that cuts across cultural boundaries and becomes an issue for everyone in a pluralistic society. The Swann Report also recognizes the progress towards multi-cultural education made by the phenomenological approach to RE, involving pupils of all backgrounds trying to put themselves into the 'shoes' of those from another religion and experiencing what it means to be a part of that religion. This can be done in many ways. Visiting a place of worship with a group of pupils can be enlightening in terms of bringing to life what such a building is like. However, the visit can be enhanced if a member of the faith community talks about what the place of worship means to them. Telling pupils in a classroom, for example, that the Sikhs remove their shoes on entering a Gurdwara gives pupils knowledge, but to actually remove their shoes on entering a Gurdwara and to have the significance of this explained by a Sikh adds the vital component of understanding. It helps pupils experience something of what it means to be part of the religion, as opposed to just finding out about that religion. This should be a major contribution of RE. It should allow pupils to explore from inside rather than just consider from the outside.

If such visits are not possible, pupils can still enter into a religion in the classroom. When considering infant baptism, acting out the ceremony, particularly if a local clergyman agrees to participate, takes pupils into the realms of what it is like to be part of a religion. It gives a greater insight than reading about such an event can. Videos are also a useful tool. When looking at how festivals such as Diwali or Passover are celebrated, a video that has members of the relevant religious community explaining what is celebrated, how it is celebrated and the significance of the celebrations gives a believer's perspective. If pupils are encouraged to write as if they were sharing the celebrations from the perspective of a member of that group they can gain a real insight into cultural beliefs and values. By encouraging pupils to enter into cultures and beliefs in this empathetic way, it may be possible to avoid the negative comparisons that can come with simply learning about a religion.

It is important that pupils also learn from the religion. Particularly in mono-cultural schools, there is a danger that Christianity is seen as the 'norm' and that the other five world religions are compared unfavourably to it, being seen as unequal alternatives to 'our' practices. The only way to avoid this is for pupils to understand all religions from the perspective of a believer. This is not to say that they should become believers themselves as this is clearly not the aim of present day RE. However, for them to understand all religions, they must develop a feeling of what it is like to be part of a faith and a culture. While this approach can make a significant contribution to multi-cultural education, it must be used with care. It is possible that such multi-faith RE may be a token gesture to multi-cultural education and may in fact do it a disservice by allowing pupils to 'spectate' religions, rather than coming to any real understanding about them. It can only be successful if pupils are able to make the transition of learning about, to learning from a religion.

Within the obvious constraints of government legislation, RE can make a positive contribution to multi-cultural education, if used properly, and can also do much to prepare all pupils for life in a pluralistic society.

Political education

The Swann Report puts emphasis on political education as a way of encouraging multi-cultural education without becoming tied up in the cultural clashes that have led to disharmony. Thus political education is seen as a way of encouraging:

> the ability to accept a range of differing and possibly conflicting points of view and to argue rationally and independently about the principles which underlie these, free from preconceived prejudices or stereotypes, and to recognize and resist false arguments and propaganda.[20]

It would, of course, as previously mentioned, be necessary for pupils to have an understanding of the foundations of belief and the world-view of the various cultures in order to facilitate such a meeting of minds as described above. Pupils must understand their home culture in order to be able to reflect critically on other cultures. Only then can culture clashes be dealt with in such a way as to make multi-cultural education effective.

Most of the examples thus far have involved the sort of education which, rather than being subject specific, is cross curricular. However, the following example will show that it is equally possible to deliver useful multi-cultural education through more traditional subjects.

Mathematics

The implementation of principles derived from multi-cultural education can lead to the enhancement of mathematical skill and a better understanding of the application and development of mathematical knowledge. This approach is again based on the assumption inherent in the Swann Report that schools should encourage the development of understanding the contributions to knowledge made by other cultures. In the 1950s, mathematics was linked to experience covering things like bank interest, profit margins and probability. Reference to Pythagoras and Pascal and the development of mathematical ideas and solutions established the cultural background of progress, achievements and mathematical understanding as being primarily European. However, it would be equally possible to draw examples from a range of cultural sources as a means of extending and reinforcing mathematical skills and understanding. For example, reference could be made to contributions made to mathematical development by other cultures, such as an example from China where the equivalent of what is commonly referred to as Pascal's triangle was used some 300 years before Pascal's birth, and one where a solution was used for simultaneous equations some 500 years before European equivalents: 'In addition to providing a more accurate understanding of the development of mathematics than a Euro-centric interpretation, these methods of teaching incorporate valuable ways of constructive repetition which can enhance the interest and understanding of pupils'.[21] In other words, as with the other examples, the work presented is valuable for its educational contribution, not simply for its contribution to multi-cultural education.

The key, therefore, to answering criticisms levelled at multi-cultural education is to look at the educational contribution of the work and ask whether it is educationally justifiable in its own right, or if it depends on the school's ethnic status. Claiming the backing of the Swann Report, critics of Anglocentric education argue that pupils can only be fully educated, and can only be prepared for life in a pluralistic society, whether they are educated in a multi-cultural or mono-cultural setting, if they receive not good multi-cultural education, but good education in the context of a pluralistic society. It is thus that the critics of multi-cultural education are answered.

Conclusions

The purpose of multi-cultural education, and indeed its relevance to all schools, including those of a mono-cultural nature, was stressed quite clearly by the Swann Report. It stated that education should be for all, and its main points emphasized that:

- as Britain is a multi-cultural society, pupils should be enabled to understand what this means;
- the education system should not be changed to accommodate pupils from ethnic minority backgrounds, but should be changed to provide

appropriate education for all in a pluralistic society;
- such education is necessary for all pupils, not just those in schools with pupils from ethnic backgrounds;
- education has to be more than a way of reinforcing the beliefs and values a pupil brings to the school;
- it should be a way of combatting racism;
- it should identify common values while at the same time celebrate differences;
- it should prepare the way for harmony in a pluralistic society.

By thus giving multi-cultural education a purpose which is educationally viable, as opposed to culturally distinct, the justification for its inclusion in the curriculum transcends debate about whether it is appropriate for mono-cultural schools. If multi-cultural education is desirable for society as a means of preparing pupils for life in a pluralistic society and an interdependent world, it is desirable for all pupils, regardless of the ethnic weighting of the school they attend. Thus multi-cultural education should be delivered in all schools, including mono-cultural schools, in order to produce a future society which is balanced and accepting of the diversity within it:

> We consider that a multi-racial society such as ours would in fact function most effectively and harmoniously on the basis of pluralism which enables, expects and encourages members of all ethnic groups, both minority and majority, to participate fully in shaping the society as a whole within a framework of commonly accepted values and procedures, whilst allowing and where necessary assisting the ethnic minority communities in maintaining their distinct ethnic identities within this common framework.[22]

Multi-cultural education is therefore relevant and important in all schools in order to encourage social stability and an understanding of the nature of society. In thus preparing for a pluralist society, pupils are encouraged to go beyond their own world view and through an understanding of diversity enrich their experience in terms of respect for and knowledge of beliefs and values different from their own. This should not be seen as a departure from educational principles, nor should it be seen as a way of cutting pupils off from their culture. Rather it should be seen as a way of broadening the scope of education and as a way of opening up the minds of the pupils:

> If education is concerned to develop such basic human capacities as curiosity, self-criticism, capacity for reflection, ability to form an independent judgement, sensitivity, intellectual humility and respect for others, and to open the pupil's mind to the great achievements of mankind, then it must be multi-cultural in orientation.[23]

Mono-cultural education is therefore rejected as being a system that discourages curiosity about societies and cultures, and thus discourages the use of the imagination, which is unlikely to develop critical awareness and which can develop a dangerously insular world-view. Its educational effects are therefore detrimental, not only to the pupils of minority backgrounds by marginalizing their culture, but also to the majority by narrowing their possibility of experience. In short, mono-cultural education 'damages and impoverishes all – black or white',[24] while multi-cultural education releases pupils from the constraints of ethnocentric philosophy.

It is clear, therefore, that the notion of the purpose of multi-cultural education, and the question of its relevance to mono-cultural schools, should not be understood or represented as an educational response to issues of race or ethnicity only. Multi-cultural education, its purpose and justification in all circumstances, should be understood as an educational response to a changed situation within society. Multi-cultural education is thus justified and its purposes are fulfilled when they are redefined in terms of a valid and positive educational experience for all pupils, regardless of their background, in preparation for life in a pluralist society.

Notes

1 See the *Swann Report*, page 324.
2 See the *Swann Report*, page 318.
3 See the *Swann Report*, page 769.
4 See the *Swann Report*, page 316.
5 See the *Swann Report*, page 316–17.
6 See Gill, Mayor and Blair (eds) 1992, page 113.
7 See Hymas 1994, page 25.
8 See Gill, Mayor and Blair (eds) 1992, page 113.
9 See Tomlinsom 1990, page 169.
10 Halstead 1988, page 205.
11 The *Swann Report*, page 71.
12 The *Swann Report*, page 363.
13 See Goodhew 1987, page 175.
14 Tomlinson 1990, page 168.
15 See Norcross, P. 1989, page 88.
16 The *Swann Report*, page 320.
17 See Garnett and Lang 1986, page 162.
18 ibid., page 163.
19 The *Swann Report*, page 470.
20 The *Swann Report*, page 334.
21 See Todd 1991, page 71.
22 The *Swann Report*, page 5.
23 Halstead 1988, page 226.
24 Todd op.cit., page 26.

References

Brown, C. (1988) The 'White Highlands' . . . anti-racism? *Multi-cultural Teaching* **6** (2), Spring.

Chauhan, C. (1988) Anti-racist education in all-white areas – a black perspective. *Multi-cultural Teaching* **6** (2), Spring.

Garnett, B. and Lang, P. (1986) Pastoral care and multi-cultural education. *Pastoral Care in Education* **4** (3): 162.

Gill, D., Mayor, B. and Blair, M. (eds) (1992) *Racism and Education: Structures and Strategies*. London: Sage Publications.

Grace, G. (1988) Multi-cultural education: an agenda for teacher education. *University of Cambridge Faculty of Education: Readings For Situations and Themes*. Cambridge: Cambridge University Press.

Goodhew, T. (1987) Personal and social education and race. *Pastoral Care in Education* **5** (3): 175.

Gow, D. (1988) Glimmer of light in the racist gloom. *Education Guardian*, May.

Halstead, M. (1988) *Education, Justice and Cultural Diversity*. London: The Falmer Press.

Hymas, C. (1994) Britain put at history's heart. *The Sunday Times*, May.

Jones, M. (1986) The Swann Report on 'education for all': a critique. *Journal of Philosophy of Education* **2** (1).

Leicester, M. and Taylor, M. (1992) *Ethics, Ethnicity and Education*. London: Kogan Page.

Norcross, P. (1989) The effects of cultural conditioning on multi-faith education in the mono-cultural primary school. *British Journal of Religious Education*: 88.

Pelleschi, A. (1986) Screening pupils in a multiracial school. *Pastoral Care in Education* **4** (3).

Report of the Curriculum Working Party For Multi-cultural Education, March 1991.

Singh, M. G. (1988) Three orientations to inequality and multi-cultural education. *Multi-cultural Teaching* **7** (1) Winter.

The Swann Report (1985) Department of Education and Science.

Taylor, M. J. (1986) Education for all. Some ethical dimensions of the Swann Report. *Journal of Moral Education* **15** (1), January.

Todd, R. (1991) *Education in a Multicultural Society.* London: Cassell.

Tomlinson, S. (1990) *Multi-cultural Education in White Schools.* London: Batsford.

Troyna, B. and Carrington, B. (1987) Antisexist/antiracist education – a false dilemma: a reply to Walkling and Brannigan. *Journal of Moral Education* **16** (1).

13 Valuing Diversity in Schools: Transforming Education through Humanistic Policy, Pedagogy and Practice

KATHERINE HANSON and MARIA PAZ AVERY

Introduction

How does a school system create an educational environment that values diversity and directly addresses racism, sexism, classism, handicap, and other forms of institutionalized beliefs and behaviors that present barriers to student achievement? For the last five years, Valuing Diversity in Schools has worked to create fundamental change in the educational paradigm and practice within several school districts in the United States. This chapter describes the process and outcomes in one urban school district, where its Valuing Diversity in Schools program recently won national recognition at the national conference of American Association of School Administrators. It offers a glimpse of the potential for a transformative approach that focuses on social justice, sees diversity as central to democracy, and links the context and practice of the classroom with that of the larger school system and community.

As individuals long committed to equity and diversity, we have worked in a number of arenas including community organizations, city agencies, mental health centers, and schools. For many years now we have been a team at Education Development Center, Inc.'s (EDC) Center for Education, Employment and Community (CEEC). CEEC's focus is working with schools and educational organizations in order to strengthen equity and diversity in education. The work described here is an overview of five years of intensive involvement in one community where we functioned in the overlapping roles of technical assistance provider, change agent, confidante, and action-reflection participant. Since this was not a research project our description of our philosophy, approach, work, initial outcomes,

and implications remain anecdotal. We hope, however, that they give you the sense of what a community can do, with some resources, a lot of creativity, and even more commitment.

Our approach, called Valuing Diversity in Schools, is a comprehensive, systemic approach to educational restructuring that places the unique strengths and demands of our increasingly diverse student population at the core of schooling. Making student diversity central to all aspects of the schooling experience compels adults – administrators, teachers, parents, non-certified staff, and members of the community – to be constantly mindful of the consequences of their actions and decisions, especially on categorical groupings of students who, for historical, political, and social reasons are denied the opportunities and benefits of this society.

Valuing Diversity in Schools provides a structure to examine how the structures, policies, and interactions of an educational system, intentionally or unintentionally continue to replicate the social inequities of the larger society. This self-examination encourages constructing inclusive solutions and ways of working that create a vision of what can be and that lead to equitable, quality education for all. This framework explicitly examines racism, sexism, classism, handicap, and all other forms of institutional discrimination and personal bias as major contributing factors to the failure and underachievement of youth, and seeks to create communities of learning grounded in critical pedagogy and social justice. It proposes that equality is not simply the equal distribution of resources but must include all resources required to make success possible for each and every student. We begin with a brief description of the general context of education reform, followed by the beliefs and assumptions that underpin our work and a brief historical context of the project, ending with a description of the work and some indicators of how things are changing in one community.

Education and culture

Horace Mann saw the public school in the United States as the "great equalizer." Yet, for many children the public school has supported an anti-democratic system of discrimination and bias. The education system serves a role defined by the political culture of a society making classrooms vulnerable "not only to political and economic forces, but also to the inhumane and anti-egalitarian beliefs and biases in the culture at large" (Freire 1985). Schools are open systems, permeable institutions: beliefs about race and gender, about class and language, about intelligence, ability, and achievement emerge in the classroom (Rose 1995).

Unfortunately, rather than approaching reform from this larger context, much of the current discussion about improving academic achievement treats education as a technical issue (Giroux 1992).[1] Such a perspective explains academic under-achievement of certain groups methodologically and mechanically – the result of the "lack of cognitively, culturally, and/or linguistically appropriate teaching methods and educational programs" (Bartolome 1994, p. 173). Because education exists within a socio-cultural reality, solutions cannot be reduced to "finding the 'right' teaching methods, strategies, or prepackaged curricula that will work with students who do not respond to the so-called 'regular' or 'normal' instruction" (p. 174).

Within the United States, hundreds of school districts are attempting such "methods," including site-based management, school improvement plans, assessment, parent involvement, curriculum development, teacher collaboration, new student support services, and schools of choice. Most are separate, unconnected efforts, implemented as additions rather than as integral components of a comprehensive plan. These restructuring efforts tend to fall into four general areas:

1   student experiences;
2   the professional life of teachers;
3   school governance;
4   collaboration between schools and community,

with most concentrating on student and teacher experiences (Prager 1992).

This often leaves classroom teachers without the systemic or administrative support necessary to sustain classroom innovation and multi-cultural education. When the focus is only on the classroom, the attendant issues are not addressed, such as assessment and grouping, school values and norms, parent involvement, staff development, and other policy concerns. In addition to examining the classroom and the larger system, restructuring efforts must build a system of "cultural education in the Freirian sense—where people first deeply understand their own culture and cultural identity in social, historical, and political context before they propose to teach or learn about other cultures in an unexamined and uncritical way" (Murrell 1997: 49).

For school systems and their communities such restructuring involves addressing a combination of factors simultaneously and over time: leadership, a shared mission, school goals, resources, the promotion of colleagueship, and professional development. Roles of teachers, principals, and central office administrators must change so that teachers function as learners and leaders, principals as learning leaders, administrators as resources and school boards as directors. Additionally, we envisioned an approach that clearly linked education restructuring and democracy, confronting directly what historian James Anderson (1988) defined as a critical duality:

> that within American democracy there have always been classes of oppressed people and that there have been essential relationships between popular education and the politics of oppression. Both schooling for democratic citizenship and schooling for second-class citizenship have been basic traditions in American education.   (p. 1)

In order to construct a paradigm that moves away from this duality and embraces a multi-cultural democracy, in which individual groups' concerns must be pre-eminent at different times, we drew on the concept of "unity in diversity." Freire (1995) said that

> this idea of Unity in Diversity is critical . . . so various oppressed groups can become more effective in their collective struggle against all oppression. The more each oppression is contained in its own historical location, as defined by the oppressors, it is very difficult to effectively oppose oppression. The

label "minority" hides the reality that so-called minorities actually constitute the majority while the oppressors represent a dominant but small minority.

Valuing Diversity is a way in which individuals and groups within education and beyond could stand in solidarity with one another, challenge one another, and empower themselves in ways that did not diminish others.

Guiding assumptions

Valuing Diversity works on both the policy and practice level to develop structural conditions that sustain constructive responses to current and emerging education concerns. It focuses on student diversity as the core factor from which all components of an education system are examined. From this core we can examine implications for the specific components. Moving more deeply, we can overlay one individual component with student diversity, returning to examine the implications of these two intersections on other aspects of school life. Including the disaggregation of as a third overlay develops a comprehensive sense of what currently exists, what needs to change, and a sense of direction for that change.

A significant concept in our work is the understanding of culture. Education is one of the primary carriers of our macroculture – norms, values, beliefs, attitudes, and behaviors. Cultures are complex, dynamic social systems that involve both individuals and institutions in a state of constant growth and change. Culture is that part of human interactions and experiences that determine how we feel, act, and think; how we decide what is right, wrong, good, bad. Transmitted from others, culture defines our shared human experience, which may or may not reflect individual differences. Individuals are both immersed in and impacted by culture, but individuals also impact and change the larger culture. Making our cultural assumptions and systems transparent enables us to critique and, when necessary transform the culture.

This idea of a living, changing culture is important to understanding how critical schools are to changing our stereotypes, biases, and negative paradigms. For example, if within society inequality is defined and maintained by the culture, people play a key role in the maintenance of that inequal-

ity. While institutes within a culture help form the individual appropriate for that society, individuals also interact in dialectic fashion with their culture, being formed by and at the same time creating culture. This dialectic interaction is at the core of our process to co-construct a new social order that goes beyond tolerance and coexistence to collectively creating new solutions to the problems of life within a truly democratic society. With this focus on understanding the process of culture, Valuing Diversity effectively balances the tension between individual rights and community responsibility, a concern as we move to a new form of cultural inclusion. Several assumptions, developed from this perspective, guide our work, including:

- Organizational structures and social relationships must recognize and affirm the interdependence of individuals and groups.
- Personal/group efficacy and social justice are inextricably linked, and individual freedom is tied to the larger good. Efficacy is connected to a set of "competencies of power," defined as the skills, attitudes, and behaviors that enable an individual or group to participate in society, including academic skills, personal/collective advocacy, and political competencies, economic/work skills, and the ability to envision and create the future.
- Diversity is the foundation for all creativity. It is from the authentic exchange across difference that new ideas, new structures, and new ways of interacting develop.
- Action/reflection is key to learning. The change process has to occur at both a personal and an organizational level; and all authority (even one's own) interrogated. It provides an opportunity to broaden one's perspective of the potential for change by asking new questions.
- Change is a process over time and change is a norm. Change continues over the professional life of teachers, administrators, and the school life of the students. Individuals adjust their vision to reflect changes around them, often without knowing it. But the understanding that time is not static, that the future always shifts, allows for the conception and realization of multiple futures. But this also requires a fluidity, an ability to live with ambiguity, that can create confusion, unless one is strongly grounded in a strong ethical framework.
- Transformation must be a public priority, with

strong support from key stockholders and a sense of public accountability on the part of all.

- All levels of the school district and community must be involved, and adults and students engaged actively and respectfully in the process.
- District administration must play a public leadership role in setting the agenda with the larger community, creating new kinds of partnerships and shared accountability for outcomes with major institutions in the community. District administration models valuing diversity in its policies, structures, and operational procedures and support schools in their efforts to reach high standards for all their students.
- Individual schools are the locus of change that most directly affects students. Staff and administration must be empowered to engage in those practices, methodologies, and interactions that will meet the unique learning needs of all their students.

Grounding theory in practice

Valuing Diversity in Schools began in 1991 as part of a middle school reform effort already under way in sixteen urban schools in one Midwestern state. The initiative is part of a larger national movement to create separate schools for young adolescents between the ages of 11 and 14, in which policy, pedagogy, practice and curriculum focus on what works best for young adolescents. Responding to requests for assistance from these schools, Valuing Diversity began five years of ongoing work. In that time, we expanded beyond a focus on middle school reform to comprehensive districtwide restructuring.

Critical elements of our approach include: the participation of district and school teams in an experiential framework-setting conference, trained peer facilitators who guide both district and school teams through the process, climate surveys and data collection models that allow for both self-reflection and solid analysis, action plans that enable teams to create an infrastructure for restructuring, and technical assistance to the individual districts or schools to help maintain and strengthen work over time.

Valuing Diversity radically broadens the traditional concept of education restructuring. Instead of the narrow definition of a primarily classroom-based add-on approach, in which diversity is important only to "students and faculty who are different," Valuing Diversity grounds academic excellence for all in the synergy of different perspectives and experiences. Based on the assumption that transformation makes the greatest permanent impact when it permeates all levels and all content areas, it places diversity at the center of system-wide restructuring. As such, it looks at the totality of the school and its environment and seeks to ensure that each component from the formal to the hidden curriculum, to teacher–student interactions, to district policy, to the politics of decisions supports a vision of individuals in all their differences living, learning, and working in community.

The experience of one community

One community, in particular, embraced Valuing Diversity. For the last five years, this consolidated school district and its surrounding community have worked to make the policy and practice of Valuing Diversity a reality. This community, located in the north central Midwest, is a mid-sized urban center in a highly conservative region. The community, with its changing demographics, crumbling infrastructure, decreasing tax bases, and public distrust of education, is representative of hundreds of mid-sized urban and suburban centers throughout the US. The school corporation, with five feeder districts, serves almost 22,000 students in five high schools, five middle schools, and twenty-five elementary schools. Of the 1,379 teachers, 151 are African American, 6 Asian, 5 Latino, and 2 Native American. The schools represent a growing diversity of students. The kindergarten through high school (K-12) student population is .5 per cent Native American, 30.2 per cent African American, 1.6 per cent Asian, 4.7 Latino, and 63.1 per cent European American. Within the elementary and middle schools, students of color are now almost 40 per cent of the school population.

Administrators, teachers, and staff are all eager to engage in efforts to enhance education for all. Several critical factors contributed to their readiness to make this approach integral to their systemwide efforts. Among these factors were:

1 the ongoing involvement of the district in the nationally recognized middle grades improvement project, with its focus on diversity;
2 leverage funding from a national foundation that encouraged the district to take this project

on and which instigated significant funding from the school budget;

3 initial support from the superintendent who provided resources to begin the process;

4 a forward-looking, risk-taking acting director of curriculum and instruction who took the challenges to the school board;

5 strong support both from community organizations and from school board members.

Valuing Diversity struck a responsive cord in the community, but had to contend with a history of suspicion about diversity work. The school district had undergone a difficult transition when they voluntarily desegregated schools in 1981. At that time many school personnel felt they had little assistance in addressing the issues that arose with integration. Some of the suspicion and negative experience from that situation needed to be overcome in the process. Another concern was the integration of Valuing Diversity with the Performance Based Accreditation (PBA) process, a state-mandated system for strategic planning and accountability that had direct implications for funding of individual schools. However, the foundation provided by the earlier involvement in the Valuing Diversity conferences and the middle grades initiative demonstrated the kinds of changes that were possible in the teaching and learning process and in the structures that supported the delivery of instruction and helped overcome resistance.

We worked closely with a district office team to develop and facilitate a districtwide, community-partnered process that would make Valuing Diversity in Schools a K-12 integrative focus of reform. Strategic planning meetings defined the parameters of the initiative, including a professional development plan. Central to this process was the participation of the two middle schools that had participated in early Valuing Diversity conferences, and representatives from the central office, bilingual education and special needs programs, teachers union, bus drivers union, support service staff, parents, civic and social service leaders, and business leaders. They became the communication system for the project, building and extending support for the initiative throughout the community and providing important feedback and direction to the planning process. Eventually, many of these individuals became a formal part of the process when they served on a permanent community advisory council.

Building on the premise that school systems and their surrounding communities have permeable boundaries and need to be integrally connected (Rose 1995), we consciously engaged major stakeholders from the community in a synergistic and public collaboration with the school district. A major event, the Community Day of Discussion on Diversity, was created, bringing together a range of school personnel with city leaders for a day of structured experiences and conversations that highlighted the changing demands on education. Originally designed as a one-time event that drew 125 people, the Day of Discussion grew each year, with attendance in 1996 reaching 500 people.

Together the community and school district focused on developing a thoughtful multi-year plan for restructuring. By the end of the first year they had:

• a school board resolution charging the district to execute a three-year professional development plan to "prepare all employees to effectively educate **all** students through the development of **awareness**, **acceptance**, and **affirmation** of student diversity";

• a three-year professional development plan forged by the synergistic collaboration of major stakeholders;

• School Board approval of the plan and a budget allocation to support it;

• training of school-based administrators to prepare them for the three-year professional development diversity initiative;

• implementation of the first all-day, interactive, experiential in-service for each of the districts' five feeder systems, publicly introducing the school districts' commitment to Valuing diversity in Schools to all 3,500 employees;

• training of school diversity teams from each of the 33 schools through a focused Valuing Diversity framework conference.

In that first year, several spin-off activities resulted from the collaboration. For example, the YMCA and the Girl Scouts created a program called HEROES, to work with a group of youth during the times they were out of school for all-day in-service training. The program of HEROES paralleled that of Valuing Diversity. Additional professional development opportunities were supported by community groups: the State Department of Education provided prejudice reduction workshops; the Jewish Federation helped to bring the nationally acclaimed program Facing History and Ourselves to the community; and corporation funds sponsored teachers to receive Gender/Ethnic Expectations and Student Achievement (GESA) training.

The strength of these initial outcomes withstood the buffeting of a teachers' strike during the second year and the subsequently difficult negotiations. While we chose not to continue any activities during the strike, the spin-off activities flourished, school conversations about diversity, and planning for future activities continued. The opportunity to explore difficult issues in a safe, structured environment provided a foundation that helped heal the rifts created by the strike much more quickly than many had expected, as one school principal explained:

> I'm quite sure that without Valuing Diversity, we'd still be fighting over the strike. My teachers all went out on strike. When the strike ended they were able to pickup and move on. Folks here are still carrying around anger and pain from the strike in the sixties – you hear them talk about it all the time. But Valuing Diversity helped us put a lot of stuff on the table safely before the strike. We were talking about things that had remained hidden before. We could say things, learn things, and begin to trust one another in ways we couldn't before. We're really working toward making sure that each child is valued and that everyone receives the best education.

Technical assistance

With the resolution of the school strike, we rejoined the district and schools. Now, rather than organizing and presenting conferences and workshops or facilitating strategic planning sessions, we shifted our role to a more invisible role of technical assistance. As consultants, we played a complex, exciting, and sometimes invisible role; as the ancient wisdom says, when the work is done the people will say "amazing, we did it. All by ourselves." At planning meetings, we listened, facilitated difficult discussions, guided, questioned, and challenged. Because we were external to the system, we could see things and provide insights that those immersed in the day-to-day operations could not. We challenged the status quo, asking the question "why not" when objections were raised to changing the pattern of how things were done. Respecting and liking the people with whom we worked, we sought to move gently but honestly, a process

acknowledged by comments from a school board member who said: "By helping us to really pay attention to our own differences, to value those, and to decide to use them as strengths, you've moved us to a whole new way of doing business".

As facilitators, we helped design and conduct strategic planning meetings and formative evaluation sessions. As experts, we provided training on specific topics, provided access to current literature and national resources, and created instruments and tools to gather relevant data. As mentors, we coached the district team and key personnel to think through strategies, plan agendas and meetings, and look at possible anticipated and unanticipated consequences of actions and decisions – always keeping a focus on the ultimate goal of increasing the chances for success for all students. We often acted as knowledge brokers, sharing resources with teachers, administrators, counselors, parents, linking the district and schools with other trainers and specialists, and developing new partnerships. During the last two years of the initiative, we worked with individual schools and the district office in two areas: strengthening the infrastructure, and broadening the base of support.

Strengthening the infrastructure

Innovation at the school building level is difficult to sustain if the rest of the system constantly puts obstacles in the way and does not actively support the innovation. Based on the systems principle of interdependence, we sought to ensure that the central administration consistently upheld a clear, shared vision and mission for the district as a whole, while supporting the flexibility of means needed by the individual schools to make the vision and mission relevant to their unique characteristics. During in-services, the schools had the opportunity to explore the district's vision against the realities of their unique strengths and needs. During that time, each school had the opportunity to develop their own set of goals and strategies that would best meet these needs and build on their strengths. Our ongoing task was to work with the surround that would make it possible for the schools to do what they needed to do.

We met regularly with the superintendent and with key staff from curriculum and instruction, bilingual education, and community relations to initiate processes that moved the restructuring agenda forward. Together, we candidly evaluated the social and political status of the community's educational system, and identified the strengths and barriers to reform. We developed strategies to strengthen relationships with the teachers' union, to reach out to more parents, and to gain the support of additional central office and building staff.

A recurring theme was the importance of keeping a clear, coherent, and focused direction. One of the foibles of school systems is the tendency to keep adding more and more programs and expect that systemic reform will somehow occur spontaneously. To help keep them focused, we repeatedly asked:

- How does what exists contribute to or obstruct the chances of success for all students, including those who have been historically disenfranchised?
- If there are factors that are obstructing success for specific categories of students, what needs to be done to remove them?
- What are the anticipated and unanticipated consequences of a particular change for different groups of students?
- How will this new thing, this new activity contribute to the achievement of the goals of diversity that you have set as a district and/or a school?

For example, when schools were asked to develop an action plan to address diversity, the immediate response was, "You're asking us to do yet another plan on top of the PBA, Goals 2000, and so on?" Our task was to assist the district team in reinforcing the notion that this was not an add-on but rather a different habit of mind for looking at what was and what could be. Schools that caught on to this idea quickly merged their other planning teams and the diversity teams. Together they examined their existing program goals, asking whether these goals were appropriate to the diversity of students in their school population, and then identifying the gaps and devising strategies that addressed the strengths and weaknesses in their school. There is now an ongoing, conscious effort to look at all changes and new programs, both at the district and school levels, in light of the vision and mission statements of the district. The success of such a large-scale effort rests in large part on the stance that principals take toward planned activities. Our experience showed that those schools where the principal was deeply involved and saw the relevance

of the conceptual framework and its practical applications, were more likely to respond positively and actively. For this reason, the co-chairs of the district team (representing both the authority and commitment of the school district) met regularly with the principals to solicit their input and/or apprise them of what was planned at different stages of the initiative. At key junctures the executive director of curriculum and instruction accompanied them, reinforcing the message that this initiative was a district priority. A critical aspect of these conversations with the principals centered on helping them see the links among the different aspects of education reform and school change.

In preparation for each teacher or staff in-service day, diversity team and other facilitators were provided with training on the objectives of the day and the tools to promote focused discussion. This empowered them both to skillfully guide work done in the in-service, to continue to build their leadership skills, and expand the capacity of the school to engage in ongoing reflection and action.

Articulation, detracking, and data disaggregation

This work came together in one of the five feeder districts that made up the comprehensive district. This feeder district was selected to create a K-12 articulation of curriculum, practice, and policy that saw the middle schools as the lynchpin for system change. While this district would be the pilot site, the other middle schools agreed to begin planning and preparation for a similar move in their districts. Additionally, this feeder district was chosen to serve as the pilot for a K-12 focus on "detracking." Articulation of expectations and curriculum across the K-12 spectrum and the need for disaggregated data were identified as necessary conditions for detracking to be successful.

Struggling together with a number of consultants, the five principals, central office staff, the five middle school principals and staff began to move toward a new way to organize their work – not as a series of separate projects but as a comprehensive whole designed to benefit the students over which they had control. Principals were urged to build on and integrate their ongoing work in diversity, their state-mandated Performance Based Accreditation plans and programs funded by other grants into an overall plan. Teachers were often under pressure to do additional planning and strategizing in addition to classroom time. For both administrators and teachers, the idea of extending meetings beyond the work day was counter to the prevailing culture and often created time pressure to do things within the "normal" 8 to 3 day. For individuals in schools this was sometimes a painful, sometimes frustrating, and sometimes exhilarating process, especially when schools perceived all kinds of fragmented demands being placed on them. Slowly the schools began to deliberately use their integrated plans as working documents to assist them to staying focused, identify gaps and areas of weakness, monitor progress and make decisions. For example, one middle school principal's reaction to an offer to add yet another innovative program to his school was "I didn't have time to discuss this with my staff, didn't have time to see how it would fit with what we were doing. So it might be a good program, but without seeing how it would fit with what we're trying to do, I had to say 'no thanks'."

Our national culture displays a propensity toward "facts and figures" and analysis. However, when it comes to the education system we are often horribly uninformed about the perceptions, procedures, implications, and actual outcomes for different groups. Often school restructuring is like being in the middle of an Escher drawing. The beginning is clear, the end will be when we get there, but the middle is murky and there is no sense of what is what. Using traditional standardized tests or graduation statistics does not offer an honest assessment of a situation. They are often used to point fingers of blame at students, their families, and their deficiencies rather than to explore what about the teaching/learning enterprise needs to be changed.

Since perception reinforces reality, school staff needed to understand the multiple perceptions that guided their and others behaviors. As part of the framework-setting conferences, we developed and instituted a climate audit and a chart for disaggregating data to help schools make informed decisions. The climate audit established a school profile on such dimensions as collegiality, governance, parent/community involvement, student issues, and curriculum and instruction materials/methods, and generated important discussions on the range of perceptions represented among respondents. This first step was to help schools and the district both determine how different groups saw issues – at that moment – and to highlight those areas where no one had information. This would help to get issues into the open and encourage the groups to find out more information, to ask deeper questions. For example, in one school, while the principal responded that there was no significant "sexual harassment in the school" the parents felt otherwise. By probing this, they learned that while the principal was thinking in terms of adult–student harassment, the parents were responding from experiences with student–student sexual harassment. The principal, until then unaware of this as a problem in his school, discovered the need to work with teachers and students to eliminate peer sexual harassment.

We recognized the climate audit was perceptual and subjective and wanted more objective data to identify systemic patterns of success and failure by race, class, and gender across subject areas and grades. Our original data disaggregation charts were too cumbersome for individual schools, especially because schools had little access to the data and none had experience in analyzing data. Working with the director of evaluation and testing, we determined what data was available, what needed to be done to disaggregate it, and how to make the data accessible to school building personnel. With the strong support of the superintendent we began to fashion a system that would provide relevant information to the schools. Like many others, this district had difficulty in developing such a system for a number of reasons. Some of this was the form in which current data was presented, the software available to cross-tabulate data, cumbersome computer systems and territorial conflicts among personnel, and a lack of consistent data collection across schools and years. It was impossible to develop a comprehensive baseline but rather we chose to begin with the newest information and begin to build a system from that.

In the meantime, several events occurred, each pointing to the urgency of developing a data system in disaggregated form, including:

- building on its commitment to valuing diversity, the school board eliminated the lower track in mathematics systemwide;
- state student achievement tests indicated a decrease in the district's scores, with possible financial implications;
- the district/community strategic planning task force (composed primarily of non-school people) identified as a system goal a 97 per cent

graduate rate by June 2000. The plan also indicated that by 2000 the academic levels and graduation rates would be equal for all groups within the district's diverse student body;

- The superintendent directed the department of curriculum and instruction to develop a database establishing a baseline and creating an information retrieval system capable of monitoring student achievement in a timely, continual, and disaggregated manner;
- The 1995 annual Day of Discussion on Diversity, which for the first time, included groups of students from most schools, indicated a growing sense of urgency about eliminating the hidden behavioral, attitudinal, and structural barriers to success for those students who have historically been at risk for failure simply because of who they are.

It was clear that the next step was to connect heightened awareness and acceptance of diversity as an asset with the day-to-day business of teaching and learning that supported high achievement for all students. The district began to identify strategies to address this next step: analysis of student data within and by each school, research on what was happening in the schools and with students, development of principals as leaders committed to diversity, continued support for the individual schools, and public acknowledgment of and support for teachers in their work of affirming diversity. Key to all this was the analysis of student data.

Introducing administrators and teachers to using data can be tricky; as with most students, their experiences with data were more in the blame category than in the decision-making reflection category. Working with the central office who developed the data software systems, we trained teams from each school on the use of data, presenting the use of data as a tool for reflection, fact-finding, and decision-making. This reinforced the understanding that data disaggregation was not intended to make comparisons between schools and was not meant to evaluate schools on their performance. Instead, the framework presented data disaggregation as a tool to help gain a clear picture of how an individual school looked on a number of dimensions such as attendance, student performance on reading, language arts, and math, and disciplinary actions, to suggest areas where additional information was needed to increase understanding of what was happening in a school, and to identify

strengths and weaknesses. Schools received information only on their own schools; district-wide comparisons were not included. Finally, the group focused on how data could be presented in constructive ways, what were key underlying questions that might be asked, and how to involve the school community in the process. They were encouraged to ask for additional data, presented in ways that they might need. These were available upon request, and included cross-tabulations by race, gender, ethnicity, and income.

Principals worked with their staff, examining who was served, how the school was or was not meeting the goals and expectations in their Performance Based Accreditation plan, and other school plans. Since this was not for external accountability, schools felt safe exploring issues they might otherwise have been defensive about. For example, when one school reviewed student achievement data, it discovered that the lowest quartile in performance measures was predominantly African-American boys. However, the analysis did not stop there. The principal asked for more data to answer her question "Who are these boys?" Cross-tabulation of data revealed that the largest percentage of young males in this quartile were special needs students. The school then asked, why was there such a large number of special needs students in this school? Who was responsible for their classification? Why was such a large group of special needs students African-American boys? Was there a pattern here? Were they all truly disabled or were they there because of some other reason? Should they be in special education at all? How did the school address the learning needs of these students – in special education or otherwise?

Another school discovered that, while attendance across race, gender, and ethnicity, was exceptional, student achievement overall was significantly under the norm. Children were coming to school – they liked being there – but the question was what, if anything were they learning? Serious discussions of teaching practices and student interactions began. Another school noted that students of color were not doing as well as the white students. This led to discussions on unconscious racism and their need to address it within the school. The challenge for this school was to move from the recognition and discussion stage of the problem – which they identified for themselves – to taking appropriate action to change old patterns. The probability of change is increased when the group has determined for itself that this is something they want to change. Such a possibility may not have happened if the same information or analysis was presented by the central office or external consultants.

Broadening the base of support

Within the Valuing Diversity framework, the educational system is seen both as a reflection of and a powerful institution within the life of the community. Schools are not seen as separate or isolated from the other segments and institutions of a community in which they exist. Boundaries between school and community are permeable, with relationships based on mutuality. Both need to recognize that they have resources to offer each other. While the community has expertise that the school system needs, the school system also has expertise it can share. In addition, schools – as micro communities – need to recognize that they are composed not only of the "formal educators" and their students. All the adults in the building have a responsibility to each other and to the students. Many schools we observed referred to the proverb "It takes a village to raise a child" as a rallying point, but did little to treat non-certified staff as full members of the school community.

We encouraged schools and the district team to extend involvement in the initiative to a widening circle of people. Constant reminders to involve parents, community agencies, teachers, administrators, and non-certified staff in meetings resulted in a new "habit of mind" so that the automatic question now has become "Who needs to be here?" and they are then included.

One major shift in attitude and behavior toward non-certified staff began with the initial in-service for all 3,500 employees in the district. For the first time, non-certified staff, teachers, and administrators moved through experiential activities and discussions in which no one could rely on their status or traditional role for answers. This shift was further supported by the superintendent who encouraged principals and school facilitators to involve non-certified staff in their buildings in professional development workshops, planning meetings, or school activities. Non-certified staff from the central office were also assigned to specific schools and encouraged to attend staff development meetings as part of a school community. In

many schools, this has become a way of doing business and is noticeable when it does not happen. For example, one school's non-certified staff complained when, at a professional development day, they went to a different session from the teachers. Pointing out this was not the case in other schools, they affirmed that they were as much a part of the school as were teachers. At other times, non-certified staff questioned the appropriateness of their involvement in workshops such as curriculum development, and as a result a special diversity training strand was developed to respond to their needs. This inclusion of non-certified staff is often supported by teachers as well, as one explains:

> What happens for kids isn't just math or science, but how they're seen by all adults and how we treat one another. If we leave custodians out of our community, what are we saying to the kids about our real values?

At the same time, a new partnership between the school district and the community institutions is emerging. In this partnership of mutuality, the school district, as a *community institution*, has reached out to other community *institutions* to consider "How do we together make sure that all our young people are given the chance and support to succeed?" This invitation to be a partner in the process from the very beginning, rather than to respond to a crisis, forged strong collaborations including:

*   increasing involvement in the annual community day of discussion on diversity, which pushes the boundaries of stereotypes about diversity in a highly conservative state, as it presents the perspectives of race, class, gender, and of people with disabilities, homosexuals, people with AIDS, homeless families, and older citizens.
*   reciprocal programs and services in which community agencies collaborate with the district to provide specific programs for students during all-day in-services, and work to parallel the work on diversity within their organizations. At the same time, teachers and students with training in conflict resolution and peer mediation offer their expertise to community agencies and groups.
*   increasing involvement with local colleges, state agencies, and regional supports, including the provision of additional training, acting as

facilitators, and undertaking research at the request of the district. Through these links the district has also increased its interactions with some of the less visible groups in the community, such as the Asian community, which sees the university's immigrant office as its advocate.

This is an ongoing process, and as change agents/researchers, we are still in the middle of trying to determine the lessons of such a vast undertaking. We entered this project, not to observe, but to work with the individuals and groups in one community as they themselves determined the breadth and depth of their efforts. While they continue to push their curriculum, policies, and practices in ways that work for them, we see the district – as a community of people working across difference – trying honestly to look at themselves and to make a real difference for all the children of the community. It appears in such major shifts as no longer holding important exams on Jewish high holidays and beginning to detrack their courses to the less visible changes such as eliminating counting teepees in elementary mathematics or meetings between bus drivers and school counselors to share information on what happens to children before and after school. This community, located not too far from the historic seat of the Ku Klux Klan, offers hope for us all. They have only just begun – change takes time – but as an African-American food services administrator hinted, the school district understands the direction and implications of its work:

I have to admit, when I first heard about this, I thought, "Oh sure, here we go again." But we've really stuck with it. Now everyone talks about diversity. People are now interested in what my

experiences are. I'm doing training with the food services staff and we're concerned about being part of this. And my son reports that things are changing for him in school. Now we have to start working on the community. If the schools are changing to value our kids, it won't help if the community remains stuck.

Note

1 "Technical" refers to a sense of teaching as a precise and scientific undertaking, with teachers as technicians responsible to implementing instructional programs and strategies.

References

Anderson, J. (1988) *The Education of Blacks in the South 1800–1935.* Chapel Hill, NC: University of North Carolina Press.

Bartolome, L. I. (1994) Beyond the methods fetish: toward a humanizing pedagogy. *Harvard Educational Review* **64** (2): 173–94.

Freire, P. (1985) *The Politics of Education: Culture Power and Liberation.* New York: Bergin & Garvey.

Freire, P. (1995) Conversation with staff from Education Development Center, Inc., Newton, MA.

Giroux, H. (1992) *Border Crossing: Cultural Workers and the Politics of Education.* New York: Routledge.

Murrell, P. C. Jr. (1997) Digging again the family wells. In P. Freire, J. W. Fraser, D. Macedo, T. McKinnon and W. T. Stokes (eds) *Mentoring the Mentor: A Critical Dialogue with Paulo Freire.* New York: Peter Lang Publishing.

Prager, K. (1992) Estimating the extent of school restructuring. *Brief to Policymakers.* Madison, Wi: University of Wisconsin, Center on Organization and Restructuring of Schools, Fall.

Rose, M. (1995). *Possible Lives: The Promise of Public Education in America.* Boston: Houghton Mifflin Company.

14 Values, Beliefs and Attitudes in Education: The Nature of Values and their Place and Promotion in Schools

DAVID N. ASPIN

In present times there is enormous interest in values issues and in the question of how we may attempt to resolve our differences over them. What Thomas Nagel (1979) calls the great 'mortal questions', such as the rights and wrongs of euthanasia, genetic cloning, and reconciliation between a nation's ethnic groups, appear on the front pages of our newspapers and on the television almost daily. It is inevitable that students in our schools will want help in coming to decide what they ought to think, how they ought to judge, which way they ought to behave in respect of these and those other values issues 'of great pith and moment', with which their lives, and that of our community, are increasingly beset.

Learning what to believe and how to behave is no less easy for those of our students who belong to a particular community of faith. For it is in such communities that these questions assume greatest importance; when confronted with issues that go to the very heart of their existence, each one of our students will know what it is like to pose the question of the rich young ruler: 'What shall I do to be saved?' This *cri de coeur* demands to be answered. And it is perhaps nowhere more appropriate to be answered than in the context of the commitments, undertakings and educational endeavours of the social, moral and religious communities that constitute the foundations, infrastructure and operating framework of schools in our plural and multicultural societies.

The nature of values, beliefs and attitudes

It is clearly important that, if we are going to express an overt concern in our community schools for values and an education in values, we should be able to articulate a view as to what we take the nature of values and their relationship to the beliefs we hold and the attitudes we adopt to be. But the question of what values might be, what a belief is or how an attitude might be defined, and how we would know one if we saw one, is not easy to answer and very difficult to grapple with. And yet attempting to come to some clarity and to reach even a provisional set of agreements about such matters is clearly a vital part of such an undertaking and an indispensable precursor to considering values education in our schools.

With respect to 'values', perhaps I should begin by making it clear that I belong to neither of two camps that one finds active in discussions about values these days – those on the one hand that I will call 'absolutists', and those on the other that we may call 'subjectivists' of various kinds.

There are some people, political and religious fundamentalists particularly, who hold that values are objective facts or features of the natural world: values are part of creation, and, like thunderstorms, the sun and the mountains, right and wrong are just features of the world; others hold that values are just there in existence and open to our intuition. The nature of values, according to such views, is such that, once one has been trained to direct one's eyes or intuitions upon them, one cannot be mistaken about their existence. This approach often leads to the kind of absolutism in matters of value that is, I am afraid, all too apparent in the actions of some fundamentalists who have recently been pronouncing the *fatwa* upon authors accused of writing blasphemous literature, murdering priests and prime ministers, and blowing up government buildings in America. These actions often are expressions of people who believe that there are absolutes in the realm of values, that brook no refusal and admit no mistake. As regards the nature of values, I do not belong to that camp.

Equally, many are the people in these post-modernist, poststructuralist days who believe that values are simply what reduces to the subjective reactions that we all experience individually to things of which we approve or disapprove. A quotation from David Hume may serve as best representing this point of view about the nature of values:

> Take any action allow'd to be vicious: Wilful murder, for instance. Examine it in all lights, and see if you can find in it that matter of fact, or real existence, which you call vice. In whichever way you take it, you find only certain passions, motives, volitions, thoughts. . . . The vice entirely escapes you, as long as you consider the object. You can never find it, 'til you turn your reflexion into your own breast, and find a sentiment of disapprobation, which arises in you, towards this action. . . . when you pronounce any action or character to be vicious, you mean nothing but that, from the constitution of your nature, you have a feeling or sentiment of blame from the contemplation of it . . . 'Tis not contrary to reason to prefer the destruction of the whole world to the scratching of my finger. (Hume 1965)

The position being articulated here is that a value judgement is the logical equivalent to some kind of statement of taste. It amounts to this: my saying that 'I like jam on my kippers for breakfast' is exactly the same, logically speaking, as saying that I regard it as a bad thing to rob elderly ladies and steal their pensions.

That kind of ethical subjectivism, and the moral relativism that goes with it, seems to me to be equally reprehensible, and on good logical grounds (cf. Gellner 1983, Lukes 1970). It is simply not the case that statements of our own subjective preferences belong in the same category of utterance as our judgements that people ought always to tell the truth, keep their promises and avoid causing unnecessary pain to others. The point of such judgements, as both Kant and Hare showed (Kant 1966, Hare 1963, 1973), is seen in the way in which the word 'ought' is used in them – in its action-guiding and generalizable force. That is a position not only above and beyond ethical subjectivism and relativism, but it is one quite different from it.

Thus, I do not regard values as natural entities, or as objects open to direct moral intuition, having some kind of absolute, uncontestable status, but

neither do I reduce them to the status of mere feelings or emotional reactions. It seems to me, rather, that values have much more status in our public, interpersonal world than people who hold these kinds of positions recognize or are prepared to admit. For me, it does make the most profound sense to ask of another person in that world: 'Ought that politician to have behaved like that? Isn't it worthwhile to give money to charity and feed the starving poor? Should we agree to the proposition that on occasion a war can be just?' – and expect to get a serious answer.

As I see it, the intelligibility and implicit normative force of questions such as these allow us to conclude that values are to do with things that take place in the public realm. We make intelligible judgements, that commend or condemn, criticize or condone acts and other important matters that take place in the world we share with others of our kind: they relate to our praise or blame of styles of behaviour, the productions and performances of artists, particular verdicts brought in by judges, particular kinds of conduct observed in the lives of politicians, the activities of schools, the policies of economic think-tanks, interpersonal difficulties that arise in the bus or on the street, occurrences that come to us as a result of the forces of nature and that have to be responded to by state emergency services, states of affairs in the community or in our churches, questions as to whether we can be happy about the present burden of foreign debt under which some countries in Southern America are struggling – all these are grist to the mill of our valuing, value discourse, value judgements, and decisions as to our own and others' conduct in the future.

Thus all these things – conduct, performances, situations, occurrences, states of affairs, productions – are associated with the ways in which we perceive them, appraise them and judge them, and the ways in which we are inclined towards or away from, attracted to or repelled by, such objects, productions, states of affairs, performances, manifestations of conduct. We choose them. We prefer them over other things in the same class of comparison. We want to follow their model or to replicate them. We want to emulate them. But much more than this (because this would simply make our reactions to them feelings), we are willing to endorse and commend those objects, performances etc., to other people. We are willing to propose to other people that such objects or states of affairs, styles of behaviour, are objects or targets, that provide us with standards of excellence that we can aim at, that are models that can function as guides for our conduct or for our judgement, in a way that each and any one of us could make our own, and commend to other people.

On this basis, it makes no sense at all to act as if my preference for jam on my kippers for breakfast is the logical equivalent of my disapproval for acts of dishonesty, violence against persons or animals, or the taking of life in any circumstances. Rather, it makes the greatest sense to discuss the question of whether an act of theft against an old age pensioner, for example, is something that we would wish to enjoin as a course of behaviour for all people indifferently.

My suggestion is that such situations, states of affairs, objects, performances, and the like – that we are inclined towards and commend to other people as worthy of emulation – set up norms and standards of excellence that in some way guide our thoughts and actions, our believing and behaving, and not just mine or yours, but those of all people. Such norms and standards are interpersonal; they are normative on the generality of the population who can experience similar regard for, give similar approval and commendation to, the objects, conduct, performances etc., to which they are applied. They give us principles to guide our conduct and by which we can all regulate our lives and strongly commend to other people to follow us in that.

This means that values are not private; they are not subjective. Values are public: they are such as we can discuss, decide upon, reject or approve. And values are public in the sense that they are interpersonal, and the subjects of notice, discussion, debate and decision that are regarded as being prescriptive – if not indeed actually coercive – for all people. Value judgements constitute bridges between us as to the ways in which we ought to believe, to conduct ourselves, or the things that we ought to admire.

More than that, values are objective. They are in quite a decided sense 'hard'. This might surprise some people but it would only surprise those people who still hold to the old outmoded conception that there are two distinct worlds – one of 'facts' and one of 'values', and that values do not belong in the world of facts. These are the people who hold that it is possible to be neutral in the curriculum with respect to the presence of values; that some school subjects are only concerned with facts, while others are only concerned with values. Some of us are familiar with the kind of thing that goes on in some of our schools, where the view held by some people is that it is only those colleagues who teach science and mathematics that are concerned with 'hard' reality, while people who teach English, history, art and religion are dealing with 'soft' subjects. Such subjects are regarded as 'soft' because they deal with beliefs, values and attitudes – with things that such people regard as fundamentally private, subjective, not amenable to objective enquiry.

Unfortunately for such people, the view that there is a realm of facts on the one hand and a realm of values on the other, and that never the twain shall meet, is certainly long outmoded, if not finally put to rest (cf. Aspin 1997). That kind of empiricist view of the nature of knowledge has now been laid to rest by a range of arguments from the philosophy of science and of language and by developments in recent thinking about human actions and interactivity. Such thinking holds that 'objective' does not mean 'hard' or 'factual' or that 'subjective' has to do with softness and the world of values. On this view, objectivity means a different kind of thing entirely.

It is not 'facts' that are objective but our intersubjective agreements as to what things shall count as 'facts' – and such agreements are constituted in the institutions that make up our social and communal life (cf. Anscombe 1958, Searle 1969). For example, without the institution of banking, monetary exchange and fiduciary trust, a dollar coin is just a brute piece of metal. Without the institution of marriage, all one has is two people of opposite sexes standing in front of a creature dressed in white. Without the institution of medicine I offer my naked abdomen to a person with a murderous weapon. It is institutions – the chief of which is the institution of human communication (Wittgenstein 1968) – that give our values their intelligibility and their objectivity. The act of writing a cheque – an enterprise full of meanings and values of the most sophisticated but coercive kind – is quite as objective as the action of looking down an electron microscope. Such transactions have the importance and normative power in the interpersonal realm that they do, because they have meanings, intelligibility and force that we not only value: they are things to which we willingly subscribe and accept as institutional agreements upon which we base our subsequent actions.

For example, suppose one is in the process of working out a contract with a builder to erect a new science or sports block in our school. That is a pretty objective undertaking, that takes place within a particular set of conventions and norms dictating what we may do, and what we actually have to do, if we are to succeed in completing the transaction. We have to sign a cheque; at the level of brute fact, all that is, of course, is just some writing on paper, yet there are certain consequent actions that follow upon that which are normative for both us and for the builder, which alter the lives of both of us. And this point remains true when we commit ourselves to giving money to charity, to travelling across distant parts of our countries in pursuit of racial reconciliation, to attending the festivals of religious and cultural communities whose languages and preferred activities we do not understand. All these involve judgements as to what is important, what is of value, how we must act in pursuit of our decisions on such matters and commit us – and commit anyone also valuing, deciding and acting in the same way – to consequent actions. Values have that 'hardness' about them in that they are fundamental parts of the fabric of our social relationships. And it is in the warp and weft of those social relationships that our movement towards the acceptance of values is articulated, is developed, is agreed, is settled, and is acted upon.

Part of coming to such decisions and translating them into action is the necessity to engage in some prior discussion and debate – things that are also part of the public realm. For instance, it is clear that in the state of Victoria in Australia, the general populace is not ready yet for the legalization of marijuana. However, Victorians will go on talking about this issue and maybe in 5, 10 or 15 years' time the discussion will come around again. Similarly, the UK Parliament is not yet ready for the reintroduction of capital punishment, even though over 80 per cent of the targeted population submitted to questionnaires recently said they wanted it. But such a view is not going yet to be translated into action because of the way in which the UK government believes it should act in such a vitally important matter, where its moral leadership must be exercised. And the same is true of such contentious matters as euthanasia, racial reconciliation and genetic cloning.

That these matters can be discussed and translated into legislative reality is a function of the overall political and social institutions and the network of interpersonal agreements in each place. Many such innovations are not going to come to fruition yet because of the normative force of the principal institutions of our societies – one example of which is the institution of political democracy – in which our values, beliefs and attitudes are shaped and find expression.

How are such disputes settled, then? How are those objectivities of value arrived at? They are reached at the level of the culture of a community; and this term connotes those absolutely fundamental matters of belief, value and attitude, in which the culture of a community is embodied and identified. Human beings have been characterized by Aristotle as 'naturally social animals'. This feature of human being predisposes us to establish conventions, norms and institutions in and by which our common purposes may be pursued, promoted and realized. And it is in such institutions that our differences of attitude, belief and value can be addressed and resolved, without the social discord or individual damage that might otherwise result when opinions differ and values clash. It is here where the bedrock nature of the beliefs that frame and shape our individual and community identities, and underlie and constitute our thinking and acting in the public and private realms we inhabit in consequence of those beliefs, becomes clear as a matter of primary importance.

The nature of belief

At this point, then, it might be helpful to say something about 'belief'. A **belief** is both a proposition or a statement of an idea or contention as true or existing, **and** – crucially – our psychological assent to it and holding of it as true. The important point here is twofold: one is the *content* of the proposition, the other is the *emotional commitment* we have to that proposition.

We make a commitment to a proposition or statement as true on various grounds – that of some external authority, that of evidence, that of the force of our own perceptions, memories, intuitions, and so on; here, too, for some people revelation and prayer have a part to play. But there is always an affective element involved in our assenting to or holding a belief: some proposition, statement or idea is put forward to us (often with some persuasive force) or something occurs to us (often with considerable resonance) and we see it as a notion or claim that can be entertained, assented to, accepted, and espoused. Sometimes we espouse such claims or notions with a very firm opinion; this can extend to a state of intense psychological conviction (often someone accepts that something is true almost in spite of the evidence, and this comes close to prejudice). Or it can go the other way and involve the stance of doubt, in which one is extremely hesitant about the strength that one can give to one's claims that something is to be taken as true; in such a case one may be prepared to do no more than merely suspend disbelief.

Beliefs relate to the psychological and subjective elements in our grasp of reality and the ways in which we interpret what we take to be our world. We can share them with other people but not in such a way that we thereby give people our warrant for acting as though what we claim is actually true (that condition is typical of our claims to 'know' something to be the case). Often, reference to our 'beliefs' implies our acceptance, tenure and emotional commitment to some particular set of beliefs. These may be political, social or theological. In this case what is referred to is a set of strongly-held commitments that are functions of our most profound and fundamental preconceptions about the nature of human beings, or society, or the divine, and/or the relationships subsisting between them, and the ways in which these commitments define and structure our thoughts, arguments, decisions and actions as a consequence. It is here where we begin to speak of 'faith', 'creed', 'credo', and 'ideology'. All these relate to people's most deeply-held convictions about the nature of human beings and the best form of society.

Perhaps an example will best make the absolutely fundamental importance of these matters of belief clear. In their book *Moral Notions* (1969) Phillips and Mounce present us with the awful situation of a pregnancy interrupted by German Measles. In the example related, the medical adviser says to the mother-to-be: 'There is only one course of action you can take and that is to terminate the pregnancy'; for her part, the mother-to-be looks at the doctor and says, 'I am sorry, I have no authority to permit murder.' The doctor is a liberal, rational scientific humanist atheist; the mother is a devoutly committed practising Roman Catholic. It is the cultures of the communities involved that settle the accepted ethical ways of dealing with the problem and determine the consequences. The doctor looks at the mother and advises her that there is over 60 per cent chance of the foetus emerging damaged in some way: is she ready for that? She responds that she is. She accepts the necessity of following the leadership of Pope John XXIII, who put the agony of such dilemmas very well when he was offered the papacy: he said '*Accipio in crucem*' (I accept it as a cross). That is part of the values determined at the level of the constitutive beliefs of the culture of that woman's community: such beliefs carry normative consequences in the ethics of the social world, and it is these ethics and these consequences that we have to accept, if we are part of such a community. Such acceptance in such cases is incumbent from time to time upon all of us (cf. Beardsmore 1969).

This, then, is to talk about the ethics of belief, and I have spoken so far only of ethical values, of the interpersonal values of behaviour. But of course there are other kinds of value too. What happens for instance when you and I go into an art gallery and look at a painting? I ask you if this is not the most stimulating view of urban decay that you have ever seen; you reply that it is absolutely awful, that it is in your eyes banal, superficial, simplistic. Or when we stand in front of the Arnolfini Wedding and I recommend you to look at the artistry of the way in which the mirror reflects back and the way in which the candelabrum is constructed and ask you whether you don't agree with my judgement that the picture is now consummate in its presentation of form. You, for your part, deny that the picture has anything to do with form, maintaining that it is a subtle exercise in illustrating bourgeois hypocrisy. What do we do or say in such cases? We start to have a discussion about the values and virtues of this particular artistic presentation. And all of that discussion will centre around the particular values we give to particular criteria of artistic intelligibility, to particular canons of meaning, to particular traditions of communication, and to particular ways in which we as audience respond to their emotive power.

We might also mention the values of sheer technical efficiency. If I want to learn to speak Mandarin, for example, might I not make progress more quickly by subjecting myself to another regime other than the one practised by teachers of Chinese language and culture in schools, by paying for a Berlitz rapid language immersion course? Or if I want to prevent thieves from re-offending, might I not more efficiently secure that by cutting off their hands? Or if I want to extract vital information from a resistance fighter in some country, I can these days apply very effective techniques of behaviour manipulation, that will extract the information with a great degree of efficiency and very rapidly. Torture is something that has its own values: speed, efficiency and completeness. This is merely to point out that there are very many human activities in which the main virtues are those merely of an instrumental kind relating to efficiency and effectiveness without regard to other considerations.

All this is to raise the question: are there different kinds of value? Perhaps we might make a list of them: there are realms of value that are moral, political, legal, aesthetic, technical, social, economic, educational, religious. The question is, are they all distinct and different from each other, or do they in the end all come down to one? There are some people – some teachers of English literature, for instance – who would say the importance of a novel is judged only by aesthetic criteria, such as style, pace, complexity of plot, development of character, balance, the architectonic character of the novel – all the criteria that are clearly 'aesthetic'. Other teachers of English might deny the sole determinacy of such criteria and argue that people's evaluation of the worth of a novel depends much more on the moral criteria of honesty, authenticity, and sincerity of purpose. I take it that such people – the Leavisites of this world – would claim that the categories of moral discourse and aesthetic discourse can be collapsed into each other. I take it too that the other people believe that there is a clear distinction between the values of aesthetics and those of ethics.

It seems clear to me that there are different criteria in the various ways in which we talk about actions, performances, objects, situations and so on, that suggest that there are indeed different realms of value. Certainly, for example, it is possible to speak of somebody as a highly efficient torturer, whose actions, when considered under moral rubrics, would be regarded as behaviour of a most opprobrious and vicious kind. Now the question is: are such different realms of value absolutely distinct from each other; and, if they are, shall we exclude some of them from the work of our educating institutions? Or is it not rather the case, as Aristotle contended, that all forms of value are sub-classes of the one overarching value, the moral (cf. Kenny 1978); that what judges do in our courts of law, that what ministers do in government and politicians in parliamentary institutions, that what

doctors do in research laboratories and operating theatres, that what sports people do on fields of play, all come under the major determining rubric of what people ought to do in order to promote human welfare and to diminish human harm? And if we agree that to be the case, then should we not feel justified in introducing and engaging in discussion of any and every issue of value into our curriculum and programmes of teaching?

That is a question I will leave with you but it is certainly one that ought to be addressed, because if it is the case that all our values and value judgements are, at rock bottom, moral judgements, then that will certainly alter substantially the regimes of teaching that we put forward in our schools for teaching values. If values are separable into distinct domains, then perhaps there are some values, maybe those of economic speculation or behaviour manipulation or genetic engineering, that we might care to exclude from the work of our educating institutions, because of the pernicious – life-threatening, not life-enhancing – effects that we believe they might well create about them and carry with them into the public forum. This is a question that I do believe we need to address as a matter of urgency in our discussions about the ways in which we regard the activities and goals of values education in our schools. And I say this because, bound up with our notions of values and the ethics of belief, are the questions of the attitudes we adopt or come to hold, and the way in which our attitudes often confirm or run counter to the ways in which we rationally consider and come to conclusions about matters of belief and of value.

The nature of attitudes

When one speaks of someone's 'attitude' to a thing, one generally refers to strong feelings, deeply rooted emotions or convictions, and psycho-physical orientations towards or away from something that they either like or dislike. Reference to an 'attitude' held or taken up by someone implies a fixed disposition, settled behaviour, or manner of acting on their part, indicative or representative of a particular feeling or opinion about or towards something. Reference to their attitude of mind connotes a settled mode of thinking on their part, an habitual mode of regarding something, a fixed disposition of feeling, liking, approving, desiring; or dislike, aversion, disapproval, revulsion away from something.

In ethics some people speak of 'pro' or 'con' attitudes; this indicates clearly that attitudes are affective in character, that they are generally positive or negative. As a school principal, for example, I might be inclined, at the rational level, to accept your arguments to establish the case for the reintroduction of Classics into the curriculum, but my negative attitude towards anything rooted in the past might militate against my doing something about it. The example helps us appreciate that, in matters of beliefs and attitudes, there is often some associated notion that attitudes are to some extent irrational and that this makes them unamenable to rational argument or persuasion. They are the psychological equivalent of an *idée fixe*.

However we may decide on these matters, there is widespread agreement among educators and others that attitudes are notoriously difficult to change and the problem of attitude change is generally regarded as one of the most difficult in any undertaking of education in general and moral education in particular. And this is why reference to attitudes and whether or how they might be changed is one of the most urgent and pressing precursors to or parts of any undertaking in the field of Values Education.

Values in school

So much about the nature of what I take values to be. I argue that they are not absolute, because they are not fixed features of the universe. Neither are they completely relative, because it does make sense to say that value words and expressions, such as 'ought', 'good' and 'wrong', do have a force and a meaning far and away beyond the subjective reactions of our own biological constitutions – as though a value judgement is some kind of moral burp. I do not hold this view either. For me values and value judgements function as bridges between us; they act as targets for emulation and as guides to conduct. They are objective: we agree upon them interpersonally, even though different people place weight upon different ones.

This position enables me to refute those people who come to us in university seminars or school staff rooms when discussion of values or values education is taking place, and dismiss our talk by voicing what they take to be the irrefutable rebuttal: 'Whose values?' By this question, as I take it, such people are endeavouring to demonstrate that values are individual, subjective, irreconcilably different, and in no way congruent, such that, on any matter of policy or practice, absolute differences of view are the norm and that therefore the only way of resolving differences in such matters is to have recourse to power of some kind. On my argument, by contrast, values are intersubjective and our awareness of difference is the start, not the end, of all discussion and attempted resolution between us. It is our institutions in which such differences and disagreements can be articulated, developed and, we hope, resolved. The values embodied and at work in such institutions are, as I say, agreed upon at the level of the culture of a community and they determine beliefs, actions and behaviours on a normative basis for a good deal longer than the mere utterance of the relativistic moment.

So much for the nature of values and what I believe them to be. This enables me to go on to the next, and for us, more important question: 'Why do we need values in education?' In a sense this is a silly question. Values are already there in education, in everything that schools do, and in all the decisions our community makes about the best ways in which we can institutionalize our child-rearing practices and purposes. When we begin to examine the work of those institutions from this perspective we begin to see values embedded and embodied in everything we do, as part of the warp and weft of our and our community's whole form of life. Values are instantiated in every word we select and speak, every piece of clothing we wear, the ways in which we present ourselves to each other, our reading of others' reactions to what we are saying, the cues we pick up, and the actions we take as a result (and sometimes get wrong, too!).

These are all parts of the value elements that underlie, structure and define our social interactions and community relationships. Words are like tokens that bear their value die-cast on their faces. The very word 'murder', for example, is not merely a description of an event: it is a very heavy negative evaluation of that event. Similarly the very word 'ship's captain' is not only a description of a job: it is an appraisal of somebody's being able to come up to the standards of competence that are constitutive of performing that role, in exercising critically important functions to do with effective transport and the safety of passengers (MacIntyre 1971). Every word we utter is like a coin, bearing description on the one hand and evaluation on the other, such that one cannot imagine the two being separated (Kovesi 1967). Values of all kinds have this status with respect to our lives and all our educational concerns.

So values are always already there in what we do in schools. They are certainly there in the issues with which education at the present time is preoccupied. These may be illustrated as follows:

The knowledge issue

What knowledge is of most worth and what shall we teach in our schools these days? Shall we be still teaching a 'saber-toothed curriculum' (Benjamin 1939) or shall we be dealing with the information technology revolution and how to 'surf the Internet'?

The economic issue

How are we to prepare our children for the future of competing in the world's market place by providing goods and services that people will want to buy from us and therefore enable us to lower our public sector borrowing requirement?

The environmental issue

The way in which we realize that we live upon a planet of finite resources and how we can deal with the ways in which we are going to construct our future after they run out.

The excellence issue

School management is deeply concerned about ways in which we are going to make our schools effective, with the ways in which the local management and evolution of powers to schools is going to place greater demands of accountability on us, with the ways in which the demands of parents and employers and the community are going to make us look to questions of performance and assessment: what kind of quality are we going to look for, what are the criteria and markers that are going to enable us to say that ours is a quality school? The excellence issue is full of these kinds of concerns.

The exceptionality issue

On average about one-sixth of our school population is affected by challenge or handicap of some kind. How are we going to integrate their special needs and concerns into the mainstream of school development and school running? How are we going to deal with people who seem to be able to master a great deal very quickly and run on well beyond the competence of their teachers? How are

we going to deal with the consideration that very shortly people will be asking to come into our schools and take lessons with us long after they have passed the age of statutory obligatory attendance at school?

The social justice issue

The OECD and UNESCO, among many other educational institutions and agencies, are deeply anxious as to whether the issue of access to computers and information technology communication is going to widen the gap in the world and in our societies between the haves and the have nots, between the class of those people who have access to educational opportunity and to employment, and the under-class of those who have not. We know already, for example, that, students who are Anglo-Saxon, male and live in the south-eastern suburbs of Melbourne have a 95 per cent chance of ensuring access to the opportunities open to them in higher education, whereas the daughters of immigrants living in the western suburbs only have chances in the order of 46 per cent. This is a 'description' of an existing state of affairs but it is a statement that also carries normative overtones, implying that there is something unbalanced about that in-balance that ought to be redressed.

Or – another social justice issue in education – we may ask how many women are, as a matter of fact, principals of schools in particular education systems, state, Catholic or other independent schools? Or again, how shall we ensure that girls can look forward to successful careers in science and engineering and technology? To these questions of gender and social class, we can add the question of reconciliation in Australia – a clear moral value, to which the last government and the High Court of Australia have formally committed us. But how, at the present time, is the policy succeeding? These are questions of social justice that are besetting us now and that demand educational consideration and social action.

The interpersonal issues

We may well be disturbed by some statistics made available by reviews of dysfunctional interpersonal phenomena in OECD member countries. The evidence suggests that, among such countries, in the workplace for which we are preparing our young people, Australia stands high in the list for workplace disaffection and disagreement; one particular state in Australia stands very high in the list for domestic violence; another state stands high in the list for child abuse; and, the worst statistic of all, Australia has now become one of the most deeply disfigured of all countries in the world for teenage suicide. These are deeply shaming statistics. They refer to existing patterns of behaviour, that we realize our educational institutions, amongst many other community institutions and agencies, ought to try and help to change.

The Australian identity issue

Here we can consider the question of what it means to be Australian, as well as the vitally important need to develop multi-cultural understanding, sympathy and regional awareness. Even in the most liberal circles there can still be awareness of, and the possibility of some dissonance and difficulty about, the different standards of behaviour, values and achievements of people who are part of a recognizably different minority group in Australia's multi-cultural society. To adopt an understanding and sympathetic approach to such matters is a difficult but important question to address in our schools.

The constitutional issue

The momentum for constitutional change may have slowed somewhat now that we have had a change of government, but within the next few years we shall be asked questions concerning our preferred form of government, what kind of person we want to be head of our state, and how that person is going to be selected. These will be questions to which answers will have to be given in the time of the adulthood of the people we are teaching now. And this is a very, very important consideration that will structure the content and mode of teaching in many of their lessons in social sciences, in history, in politics and democracy.

The health and quality of life issue

This is a matter of what counts as the concern schools have for endeavouring to get students committed to health-prolonging behaviour: healthy lifestyle and the avoidance of risk-taking behaviour. One of my former academic colleagues is deeply concerned about how to get the message of the avoidance of sexually transmitted diseases across to teenagers who know what they ought to do, but have difficulty in actually doing it. There is still a gap between the realization of what we ought to do and actually taking the action (Straughan 1982a and b).

Then there is another quality of life issue, arising from the possibility that, by the middle of the next century, a reasonable life expectancy for a number of people could be as high as 100 years. Reasonable life expectancy is already around the 80s and moving upwards all the time. We might ask how are our social resources going to deal with that, especially in view of the possibility that at the same time there may well be full-time paid employment for only 15 per cent of the population up to the age of 40.

These are among the list of vital issues with which teachers are increasingly having to concern themselves as they go about their work in our schools. And these are not matters of the future: they are matters with which we are dealing now. It is a sobering realization that it is already possible for young people to discuss these issues on a very serious basis amongst themselves: on sexual matters, for instance, it is now necessary for our children whose ages are in single figures to have the kind of information and knowledge of sex and modes of interpersonal behaviour that even at my age I find startling. And they have to have the kind of imagination and understanding now, on both a self-protective and an other-regarding basis, that even ten years ago their parents might have found unimaginable.

These are the changes that are with us now – at the same time as children and young people can 'surf the Internet' and are indeed expert at it. Many of them, and at much younger ages, are much more expert than you or I. Their expertise allows them to access all kinds of images and messages: among them, pornographic material of all kinds, or recipes for promoting civil unrest or urban violence, or lists of instructions on how to make a bomb. It is reasonable to ask, what are they to do and what are we to do when they find them? We might hope that schools will give our young people the moral awareness and strength of character to deal with such images, as we hope that we ourselves would do, and that we would commend to all people impartially – but we cannot, as my colleagues' research has shown (Moore et al. 1992) rely on it. We have to hope – and we have to work to ends that are going to conduce to the welfare of all members of our society, individually and collectively.

This is a way of underlining the contention that educational issues are shot through with value considerations at every level. Values are already present in everything a school does. It is not a case of being able to decide whether we shall import them or not: we can't not. The question is how we actually deal with such issues – and here we have to remind ourselves of and be thankful for the expertise, the professionalism, the moral judgement, and the sheer educational commitment of so many people who are on the staffs of our schools.

Let me illustrate. Three years ago, while doing a review of the Faculty of Education at the University of Sains Malaysia, I observed a lesson conducted by a Chinese student. The lesson was conducted in Malaysian – a good deal of which I could understand because of the excellence of the student's practice of teaching. She was a biology teacher giving a lesson on gene transmission. She happened to have in her book two examples of how faulty genes can affect human beings. One of her examples was the faulty gene that leads to haemophilia. Here she had a wonderful illustration on the OHP of the family trees of Queen Victoria and all of the Royal Families of Europe who were afflicted by haemophilia. She asked the questions: what were the consequences and history of this particular faulty gene? Might the Russian Revolution not have taken place had the Tsarevitch been able to be cured? A long discussion followed, in which value considerations were uppermost.

The second example was to show how a faulty gene affects the emergence of Down's syndrome and the way in which that particular transmission replicates itself from generation to generation. The teacher said, 'You know it is quite easy to stop this. We now have the techniques of bio-engineering to prevent this phenomenon before birth. In fact, we now have the techniques available to us to clone animals, to produce chickens with four legs or even to have foetuses implanted into masculine abdominal walls. The techniques are there. Shall we do these things? Does bio-engineering permit us to do anything we like? If not, why not?' And there they were: a class of 14–15-year-old Malaysian girls with a young student teacher who was taking them through these 'mortal questions' (see Nagel 1979), these profound issues of life and death, and behaviour and conduct for the future, all in association with a simple biology lesson on gene transmission and replication.

We cannot deny that we do values education in our schools already. They are part of the nature, purposes and aims of education.

The aims of education: values embodied

When we talk about 'aims of education', we might find some help in the recent document of UNESCO entitled *Learning: The Treasure Within* (Delors 1996). This report argues that education in the twenty-first century should stand upon four major pillars. These concern the need to **know**, the ability to **do**, the power to **live with** other people, the development of ourselves as persons – the power to **be**. Each of these concerns, and the undertakings that flow from them in our educating institutions, is shot through with values of particular kinds. Let us examine the values embodied and exemplified in these four concerns.

To **know** means to recognize, to remember, to understand. But there are questions of truth and proof also associated with such cognitive operations. If, for example, we hear that somebody is a member of a political party, we may reasonably ask: 'How do we know that? Is it true? Can you prove it for us?' Or – we might say to some politician – 'Are you just saying what you say about the behaviour and values of Aboriginal people or immigrants groups from knowledge, ignorance or prejudice? Isn't it important to look at the kind of stereotypes we have of different political, racial or religious groups before we can claim a public warrant to make statements about them? Shouldn't we have some regard for truth, for evidence?' It is a value that imbues our whole approach to knowledge that we have to have evidential support for what we say to warrant our right to assert our claim to know – this is a very strong, a very powerful value consideration. Truth is perhaps even more important.

To **do** – Much of our talk these days in educating institutions dwells upon the importance of our students' achieving mastery of certain key competencies – those of interpersonal communication, of the ability to build a team, of the power to learn to learn, to do research, to solve problems, to think creatively, to operate machines with efficiency and effectiveness, and so on. These are very strong competencies which permit us to ask questions of an evaluative kind about our students' grasp of them. Can you achieve the result you set out for? Can you do it with minimum possible cost and greatest possible efficiency of the machinery you are working with? Can you make as few mistakes as possible? Can you achieve greatest coverage as possible? When you talk to people, do people clearly understand what you are saying because of the range of your vocabulary and the sophisticated character of the ways in which you articulate the problem? These are among the values that we look for in people's ability to do.

To **live with other people** – In her book *Schools of Thought* (1978) Mary Warnock drew attention to the necessary preparation of students in our schools for what she called 'the life of virtue'. There is nothing grandiloquent about virtue. It means tolerating other people's right to be, respecting their own particular interests, considering those interests and allowing for their development, respecting them as ends in themselves equal with ourselves, seeing them as free agents, being able to put ourselves in their shoes when they are suffering, in pain or distress (as in the case that happened to me recently, when the daughter of a colleague committed suicide). To put oneself in other people's shoes in such a case calls upon sympathy, loving-kindness, interpersonal understanding of a rich kind so as to give support to other people in pain and distress: all these virtues were called upon in great measure in our particular community at that particular time.

The value questions here are: how we are going to help our young students in our schools to learn those vital skills of sympathy, understanding, respect for other people, consideration and concern for their interests? All these are key values in learning to live with others. Our students will soon experience the need for these themselves, in the experiences they have already had or that still await them, when they get married, have children, go to work, relate to parents, relatives and friends. All these are important value life concerns.

To **be** – while all this is going on we hope and work and try to ensure that our students are learning how to develop a sense of themselves as independent entities, having their own dignity, worth and rights – in a word, how to be themselves. Such learning involves learning how to take charge of our own needs, to look after our own interests. In all this we are learning what it is to be yourself, learning the lesson Polonius urged upon his son in *Hamlet*: 'This above all, to thine own self to be true'. The road to maturity and autonomy carries many lessons about the need to learn to be authentic, sincere, honest, to tell the truth, to act in accordance with the obligations placed upon us or that we willingly accept for ourselves – and then to take the consequences for our actions. We have to learn what it is to take responsibility for our actions and respond to other people's rightful demands that we give them the answers that they need.

These are among the concerns and values that are central to the activities of many of our schools right now. When Professor Chapman and I did our research on Quality Schooling (Aspin and Chapman 1994) we didn't ask principals in schools whether values were at work in their schools already; all agreed that they were. We were concerned to find out what were the values that people could clearly identify and were proud of and wanted to promote in their schools. We found that, while of course people in schools were concerned that their students should get to know things and become good at doing things – knowledge and excellence, to know and to do – they are as concerned about democracy, equity and justice.

On our findings, our colleagues in schools and the parents of their students are very concerned about the development and protraction of their students' careers in the workplace; but they are even more powerfully concerned about the humane values of tolerance and respect for persons, sensitivity, concern for other people, compassion, loving-kindness and sympathy. They are powerfully concerned for the development of students' independence and autonomous powers to shape their future for themselves.

They are also concerned about the health and welfare of the community in which they lived. They are concerned for the expansion of learning opportunities throughout people's life span, and they are deeply committed to community harmony and reconciliation. They want to involve themselves in the community. They want to see their schools as centres of leadership for the extension of learning in the community.

Those were amongst the core values that the schools that we investigated believed that they should embody, insist upon and actively promote in their work. As important as anything else, however, is the notion of schools committing themselves to the value of leading the community as a centre of learning for all. In this lies firmly embedded the idea that schools have a moral responsibility to see themselves as providers of access to a range of good things, to which all their students are entitled and by preserving and promoting which the health and welfare of the wider community might be assured.

In these days, in these interesting political times, there are some people who don't hold this point of view. Surely, someone once said to Margaret

Thatcher, the parable of the Good Samaritan will tell you about the virtues of compassion and loving kindness, and altruism, and going the second mile with people and giving up all you have for another person? And surely these are virtues and values of a non-economic and non-instrumental kind? Mrs Thatcher is supposed to have responded that the only thing making the parable memorable for her is the point that the Good Samaritan had the economic wherewithal that enabled him to do good.

From such a point of view, doing good belongs in the same class of entity as any other similar commodity – something that requires finance to make it work. And some people bring this kind of mentality to education as well, seeing education and knowledge as some kind of commodity, as some kind of 'thing', that one can buy and sell in the marketplace, that is dispensable and disposable; it was also reported that the same politician was inclined to see 'liberty' as just such another commodity. Indeed there are some people these days who say that the only kinds of values in education are those of the market place and competition (on this see Bridges and McLaughlin 1994, especially papers by Tooley, McLaughlin, and Grace).

For my part I repudiate the notion that education is simply something that one can enjoy or not, depending upon whether or not one has the means to access it. For me education is a public good (cf. Grace 1989, Aspin and Chapman 1994); education is like social welfare, health, justice, law and order – all goods and conditions without which our future citizens could not even get very far down the road to being able to **know**, to **do**, to **live with others** and to **be**. And, it seems to me, these values are quintessentially present in those values that we associate with notions of the 'common good', the pursuit of which is, along with the promotion of the values and welfare of particular cultural constituencies, properly regarded as one of the chief virtues and principal aims of the education offered in community schools in modern plural societies (cf. Bryk et al. 1992).

These are all the qualities and characteristics that we desire to see among the things that are added to our young people by their experiences and activities in educating institutions of all kinds, and nowhere more than in public schools. For unless young people are provided with access to the social and educational goods that enable them to develop those bodies of knowledge and understanding, competencies and skills, attitudes and dispositions,

inclination and tendencies, then they are not going even to be able to get a purchase on the first rung of the ladder that will enable them to have some prospect of 'getting it right' (Ball 1993: 2) for the rest of their lives.

Rather, if the notion of education as a commodity, that can be purchased in the market place of all such 'goods', is secured and perpetuated, then we shall be moving towards a society in which there will be a permanent divide between the rich south-eastern suburbs and the those in the outer West – a society of employed class and under-class, that will not in all essentials differ from the classes of the Elites and the Proles, that were part of the awful vision that Aldous Huxley put forward in *Brave New World* and which some people of that particular persuasion see tacitly in operation when talking about education for excellence, rather than education for virtue. After all, as recent events have forcefully reminded us, the technology to bring something like about, will all too soon be with us . . .

Instead of such a philosophy, I want to commit myself to the idea of education as a public good, towards which it is part of the moral responsibilities of teachers and educators to lead their students. I believe that, from their very foundation and in the continuing ethos of all their activities and undertakings, this is the philosophy and these are the values that are still firmly believed in, accepted and espoused by those community schools in Australia that have particular cultural or religious affiliations.

I want to end with an expression of encouragement, therefore, not merely to identify the values that we have in the curriculum, that are already at work in education, and the ways in which institutions work to realize them. Certainly it is important to pay overt attention to the place of values in the fabric of our schools' being and work, and that will involve being ready to get down to the hard work of identifying and clarifying them. Now, the skill of learning how to clarify values, to analyse policies and issues like haemophilia or Down's syndrome, to see what the value considerations are at work in our handling of them, and to judge whether the behavioural reality matches the moral rhetoric, is a key feature of our moral life and it is important that all our colleagues in education – teachers and learners – should acquire it.

For me, however, the emphasis upon values clarification only takes us part of the way. It misses out on the crucial second part of what I said at the beginning of my remarks: for values education to do its real work, it is not sufficient for people merely to desire these things, to accept them, to prefer them, to incline towards them, to seek to emulate them. People have also to accept them as binding upon themselves, as committing them to particular modes of conduct, and also to commending them to other people. One has to show that these values are generalizable and action-guiding.

For me it is not enough merely to analyse, to identify or to clarify values. There has to be an action consequence arising from such an enterprise that makes a difference to us and to everyone else. It is not enough to tell people about the avoidance of risk-taking behaviours; we have also got to try to alter the behaviour itself. That is the moral point of this whole approach to such matters. School leaders, teachers, educators in our community of schools have the responsibility and task, not only to get their students to become a part of a particular community, to hold to certain beliefs, to adopt certain attitudes, to commit themselves to certain values: they have to secure that commitment in their actions and conduct as well. Students have to belong, believe, belove and behave. And this means that as educators we must all act as models and exemplars of those dispositions, beliefs, values and attitudes that we wish our students to come to take up for themselves.

Concluding note

Perhaps one final note of caution might be in order. In the enterprise of Values Education and of educating our young people for understanding and commitment to a set of values, there are some important caveats that it is important to remember. We shall do well to remind ourselves of some important limiting considerations arising from an awareness of our own imperfections and the difficulty of the task, and attempt in a serious way to communicate to our students.

To begin with, we need to remember that making our judgements about matters of value and deciding how we should act is terribly hard. It is difficult. We need a great deal of information. We need the skills of weighing one consideration against another. We need practice in the competence of making decisions and then hooking our actions on to them. And that is not a skill that develops overnight or comes easily.

Second, we need to remember all the time that one value clashes with another. My commitment to one value – it might be telling the truth, for instance – could often clash with another – say, my commitment not to cause people unnecessary pain. An example is provided in the play *The Witness* by Rolf Hochhuth: what should the Pope in the last war have done? Should he have come out unequivocally '*mit Brennender Sorge*', as his predecessor wrote, and condemned Hitler for his treatment of the Jews and other people in the concentration camps, with all the risks to the Catholic church in Germany that that would have entailed? Or should he have tried by quiet diplomacy to struggle to keep the flame of the Catholic church and its witness alight and still flickering for the illumination of the people of God in the hostile environment of Germany in those times? The play is about a moral dilemma of agonizing proportions. We, as well as our students have to realize that in such clashes of value there is no easy way out. The only way of resolving that kind of clash is at great cost and with considerable pain. Such costs and such pains live with us for ever in the agonies that come out of trying to resolve clashes of that kind. Our students have to realize that in such matters there is no easy recipe.

The third most humbling realization is this. We need to realize that, in making moral decisions, trying to resolve clashes of that kind, trying to balance competing questions of value, not only are we never going to be right but that we shall very often prove to be only too fallible. Our students have to realize that, in deciding what we ought to do in our interpersonal relations, in the home, in the work place, in political life, in professional organizations, in church and parish work, in the community generally, we risk getting it wrong much of the time. In trying to resolve our moral dilemmas our human fallibility and frailty should be a constant reminder of the difficulties of this kind of values education. Moral education is not a recipe for moral infallibility.

In sum, we have to get over to our young people that identifying and analysing the values that are at work in the understandings that we achieve about controversial matters are things we have to act out in our lives. But producing the arguments that will help us decide to take one course of action rather than another is always going to be a difficult, painful and all too fallible a process.

Perhaps one dictum might help us to realize that

we should still carry on trying to achieve what sounds like the impossible dream. It is the very last sentence that Spinoza wrote in his *Ethics* (1677/ 1949): 'Everything excellent is as difficult as it is rare.' Maybe if we commit ourselves to understanding the nature of values and the aims of Values Education in our schools, thinking about and engaging in the kind of undertaking as that with which this publication is concerned, we might help our future citizens and our present students to make achieving that excellence in our interpersonal behaviour and our judgements of values just a little less difficult and a little less rare.

References

Anscombe, G. E. M. (1958) On brute facts. *Analysis* **18**. See further on this J. R. Searle 'How to derive 'ought' from 'is'' and G. E. M. Anscombe 'Modern moral philosophy' in W. D. Hudson (ed.) (1969) *The Is/Ought Question*. London Macmillan.

Aspin, D. N. (ed.) (1997) *Logical Empiricism and Post-Empiricism in Educational Discourse*. London, Durban and Sydney: Heinemann.

Aspin, D. N. and Chapman, J. D., with Wilkinson, V. R. (1994) *Quality Schooling: a Pragmatic Approach to Some Current Problems, Topics and Issues*. London: Cassell.

Ball, C. (1993) *Lifelong Learning and the School Curriculum*. Paris: OECD/CERI.

Beardsmore, R. W. (1969) *Moral Reasoning*. London: Routledge and Kegan Paul.

Benjamin, H. (1939) The saber-tooth curriculum. Foreword to J. A. Peddiwell *The Saber-tooth Curriculum*. New York: McGraw-Hill. Reprinted in R. Hooper (ed.) (1971) *The Curriculum: Context, Design and Development*. Edinburgh: Oliver & Boyd, in association with The Open University Press: 7–15.

Bridges, D. H. and McLaughlin, T. H. (eds) (1994) *Education and the Market Place*. London: Falmer Press.

Bryk, A. S., Lee, Valerie E. and Holland, Peter B. (1993) *Catholic Schools and the Common Good*. Cambridge, Mass: Harvard University Press.

Delors, J. (ed.) (1996) *Learning: The Treasure Within*. Paris: UNESCO.

Gellner, E. (1983) The overcoming of relativism. Unpublished lecture at the Royal Institute of Philosophy, 25 February.

Grace, G. R. (1989) Education: Commodity or Public Good? *British Journal of Educational Studies* **37** (3): 207–21.

Hare, R. M. (1963) *Freedom and Reason*. Oxford: Clarendon Press: chapter 2. See also his 'Language and moral education' in Langford, G. and O'Connor, D. J. (eds) (1973) *New Essays in Philosophy of Education* Pt. 3. London: Routledge and Kegan Paul: chapter 9.

Hume, D. (1965) A treatise of human nature. In A. MacIntyre (ed.) *Hume's Ethical Writings*. London and New York: Collier Books. The Macmillan Press: 195–6, 180.

Kant, I. (1966 edn) *Groundwork of the Metaphysics of Morals* (ed. by H. J. Paton). London: Hutchinson.

Kenny, A. (1978) *The Aristotelian Ethics*. Oxford: Oxford University Press.

Kovesi, J. (1967) *Moral Notions*. London: Routledge and Kegan Paul.

Lukes, S. (1970) Some problems about rationality. In B. R. Wilson (ed.) *Rationality*. Oxford: Blackwell. See also his Relativism in its place. In M. Hollis and S. Lukes (eds) (1982) *Rationality and Relativism*. Oxford: Blackwell.

MacIntyre A. (1971) *Against the Self-Images of the Age*. London: Duckworth: 109–72.

Moore, S. M. (1992) in J. Boldero, S. M. Moore and D. Rosenthal 'Intentions, context and safe sex: Australian adolescents' responses to AIDS'. *Journal of Applied Social Psychology* **22**: 1375–97.

Nagel, T. (1979) *Mortal Questions*. Cambridge: Cambridge University Press.

Phillips, D. Z. and Mounce, H. O. (1969) *Moral Practices*. London: Routledge and Kegan Paul. See also Beardsmore, R. W. (1969) *Moral Reasoning*. London: Routledge and Kegan Paul.

Spinoza, B. (1677/1949) *Ethics* (trans. by W. H. White 1883, revised by A. H. Sterling 1899 and J. Gutman 1949). New York: Hafner Publishing Company.

Straughan, R. R. (1982a) *Can We Teach Children To Be Good?* London: Allen and Unwin.

Straughan, R. R. (1982b) *I Ought To But . . .* Windsor, Berks: NFER-NELSON.

UNESCO (1996) (Edited by J. Delors) *Learning: The Treasure Within*. Paris: UNESCO.

Warnock, M. (1978) *Schools of Thought*. London: Faber.

Wittgenstein, L. (1968) *Philosophical Investigations* 3rd edition. Edited by G. E. M. Anscombe and R. Rhees (trans. G. E. M. Anscombe). Oxford: Basil Blackwell.

15 Ethics and Values in Secondary School Planning and Delivery

MICHAEL MARLAND

Introduction

Ethical and value issues lie at the heart of school, or would the metaphor more appropriately be 'weave through all aspects' of schooling? Aristotle declared: 'The object of education is to cause us to like what we ought to.' More recently the Education Reform Act 1988 lays down in its first section that the curriculum of a maintained school satisfies its requirements only if it: 'promotes the spiritual, moral, cultural, mental and physical development of pupils at the school and of society; and prepares such pupils for the opportunities, responsibilities and experiences of adult life' (Section 1, para. 2). The first clause is a repeat of the 1994 legislation with the very important addition of the significant 'cultural'. The second is a key extension, of very great importance for a school's central aims, but a legal demand on school planning that has been inadequately debated, explored, and implemented. Both are logically prior and hierarchically superior to the National Curriculum requirements in Sections 2 and 3. Both involve values.

However, there has been surprisingly little analysis and debate on how ethical principles are articulated, taught, and practised in schools. Indeed, it appears that in recent decades in the UK the properly perceived need to develop the school's work in sympathy with the mores of a pluralistic, multicultural society has sometimes led to a nervousness about being 'over-prescriptive'. Thus school discipline has been based on what could be regarded as 'house rules'. Even in the vigorous anti-racism work of many schools, the presentation to pupils of the anti-racist analysis has been justified and argued in self-contained terms, sometimes with little or no reference to wider ethical principles. The National Curriculum Council papers on what became called 'cross-curriculum themes' suggest some ways of approaching the required 'moral' aspects of the curriculum. More recently, OFSTED has issued some advice. The Schools Curriculum and Assessment Authority (SCAA) valuably established a committee to consider how schools might approach moral values in the curriculum, and published a useful discussion paper: *Education for adult life: the spiritual and moral development of young people* (SCAA 1996). Its successor, the Qualifications and Curriculum Authority (QCA) developed the work of earlier committees into schemes for volunteer pilot schools. The SCAA–QCA development work has been very thoughtful and practical, and we have to hope will act as antidote to the spread of 'National-Curriculumitis', which has as an unintended side-effect suppressed so much of values education.

In most of this work, the word 'ethics' is rarely used, and there is little attempt to map the relationship between the requirement for 'moral' development, the compulsory 'religious education' component of the curriculum, and the insistence on school behaviour with ethical principles. There has been surprisingly little analysis of how school students could consider ethics. The twenty-five years of the publication of the *Journal of Moral Education* is a splendid exception to this deficiency. Similarly, the MOSAIC organization, founded in 1977, continues to sharpen analysis and develop practice.

In this chapter I draw on my experiences as headteacher, my explorations of curriculum planning, and my work in pastoral care to explore some of the ways in which schools can promote an ethical education. Curriculum planning currently is too mechanical or subservient to Section 2 of the 1988 legislation, and we lack sufficient overarching curriculum-planning theory.

Positive approaches

Curriculum planning

Whole-school curriculum planning is required, not merely the legislative divisions of the National Curriculum content lists put into 'subject' courses. This requires overarching content plans, the divisions of which will vary from school to school, but which derive from the preparation of pupils 'for the opportunities, responsibilities and experiences of adult life'. These curricular plans should be logically prior to the 'course' planning, and the contents can be 'delivered' through four routes: (a) specific courses, (b) other courses, (c) the tutorial programme, and, not to be forgotten, (d) the communal life of the school.

Ethics should feature in one of those overarching plans, and not be left to chance in the individual course planning. In considering the positive ways of making and delivering the ethics curriculum policy there are two standard (but not often analysed) tensions, which I call 'contextual or specific?' and 'proactive or reactive?'

Contextual or specific

Every few years in education, we veer from one end of the corridor to the other. We move from what I call 'specific' teaching to 'contextual' teaching and back again. For example, we have a decade of saying that we will teach about sex education followed by a decade of insisting that it is something you can pick up from your environment. But both are necessary; to reckon you teach language only in context without looking at words and word patterns on their own is unrealistic. Perhaps the polarity was most clearly summed up in the title of a famous book: *Spelling: Caught or Taught?* Clearly, you cannot teach language only in a decontextualized, specific way, but equally, you cannot learn all you need in the context of use. I suggest that the same is true of thinking, considering, understanding, judging, and behaviour.

However, it is not good enough always to hope that children will learn by the context. Parents, usually the mothers, are always teaching their young toddlers. They may not call it 'teaching' but that is what it is – and sometimes it is very specific. In the same way, thinking can be taught. Perhaps you would not say to a 10-year-old: 'I want to teach you

the difference between causation and correlation', or 'I am now teaching you what a syllogism is'; but there is no reason why you cannot step outside the science or history context and teach some thinking processes: What is evidence? How do you judge? For instance, you can specifically teach the consideration of the tension between ends and means; whether there is ever justification in not being honest; or clashes in conflicting loyalties.

The same is true of ethics: we need a complementary balance of the specific and the contextual. We do not always have to wait for things to happen, but we can lead a class to speculate: 'What would you do if . . . ?' There must be times when we are explaining and discussing concepts, terms, and dilemmas. For instance, it is helpful to thinking and judging, not abstract and remote for pupils, to introduce and consider terms such as 'ethics', 'paradigm', 'objective', 'value', 'relativism'. Famous moral dilemmas of public life can be analysed. Statements by famous pundits can be considered, such as:

Muhammad: 'Hurt no-one so that no-one may hurt you.'

Aristotle: 'Man is by nature a political animal.'

Proactive and reactive

Most school activity that could be thought of as concerned with ethics is mopping up after 'trouble'. The conscientious teacher will often work very hard to make a lesson out of a reprimand, but there is usually insufficient time and an awkwardness of placing when broader ethical questions are introduced into bad-behaviour post-mortems.

In the investigation and follow-up to trouble in all walks of life from families to employment, public order to professional disputes, recourse has to be made to principles. 'That is wrong!' usually needs justifying against a code. In schools of a religious foundation this can be, and often is, done by using the behavioural precepts of that religion. All schools refer to 'the school rules', or, as more recently formulated, 'the Behaviour Code'. Secular schools sometimes refer beyond the internal rules or code to widely held expectations of decency or morality: 'Everyone knows it is wrong to . . . ' Too often, though, we rely on 'rules' or even mere exhortation, without relating our criticism to principles. Michael Young, in his account of what led to the ideals of Dartington Hall, describes his own pre-Dartington schooling in an illuminating way: 'These schools were not so categorical about their philosophies as they were about the multitudinous rules which they superimposed upon us with varying degrees of savagery' (Young 1982: 156).

Although we should like to think we are better than that, it is less common for there to be an explicit ethical code back to which exhortations or criticisms refer. Still less often is there a *specific* teaching of the building, consideration, and use of an ethical code. Partly this is because of the immense pressure on a school's curriculum from the demands of breadth: we are teaching more concepts, facts, and skills than ever before. Partly it comes from the conviction that children learn best in context. The argument goes that children cannot analyse and discuss right and wrong out of the context of an actual situation. This argument judges as ineffective the 'What if ... ?' hypothetical discussions.

I judge that for many years there has been a fear of the theoretical. Forty years or so of the development of trying to involve pupils in heuristic practical work in Science, talking and writing in English, and designing and making in Design Technology may have left too few opportunities for pupils to consider the range of principles that lie behind such activities. There is an imbalance in favour of 'doing'. David Hargreaves said in his studies of the secondary teaching of Art that there was so much doing 'there was no time for looking'. A similar problem of balance can be found in many subject courses.

This imbalance not only weakens by too drastically thinning 'theory', it also severely restricts the *range* of examples that the pupil can meet. The curriculum restriction in Design Technology is curiously analogous to that in moral considerations: because of the insistence of considering what can be directly experienced, the range of artefacts is limited by the tyranny of the work bench: only small-scale and cheap, readily available materials. Thus there is a very limited range of cultural traditions or periods; only the small scale; and only cheap woods or plastic. In religious education the historical often dominates the ethical aspects. Assemblies pretending to be 'acts of worship' are very common, and try to give life by the focus on real life rather than analytic consideration. In ethical considerations there is little opportunity to consider dilemmas of the wider, adult world, or even prepare the pupils for some of the less common but nevertheless possible older teenage ethical tensions. It also reduces the likelihood of the young person sensing in her or his current predicaments the same ethical elements as lie at the heart of major adult decisions.

Our well-meaning response to the cultural pluralism of today's global culture and local mixed society has sometimes inhibited our analysis of religious ethics. For instance the ethical implications of the second 'pillar of Islam', Sawm – the self-assurance and self-control of the month of Ramadan, is wider and ethically deeper than mere fasting from food.

There can be a specific consideration and comparison of codes drawn from a range of organizations from businesses to schools, newspapers to film companies. Martin Le Jeune (1996) rightly concludes that specifying ethical values in specific public sector posts is insufficient: 'Getting the core ethical values identified and promoted throughout society is the essential pre-condition for making public sector ethics work in the long term.' Part of this would be to compare and contrast behaviour codes. A class could be given the key requirements in three or four codes, and asked to consider the requirements: Why this? Why different? Pupils would better understand the code of the school and codes that they would come to in later employment if they had the opportunity to compare and contrast codes from different walks of life.

Such specific teaching complements the contextual. There have been some studies that really demonstrate the efficacy of specific teaching. For instance, Geoffrey Short tried 'an initiative to promote social justice' with classes of junior school children. What could be properly called an 'ethical code' on aspects of unfair discrimination on issues of gender, race, and social class was taught.

> The study provides evidence consistent with the claim that children between the ages of seven and eleven can learn to recognise certain manifestations of unfair discrimination against oppressed groups. The data further suggests that children in this age group can learn to recognise such discrimination on the basis of principles acquired in contexts that make no reference to oppressed groups. (Short and Carrington 1991: 157)

Such learning should not be left to the contextual, still less to the actual occurrence of poor behaviour.

A similar balanced approach is recommended by Roger Straughan in *Beliefs, Behaviour and Education* (1989). He points out the limitations of using the mere discussion of moral dilemmas as an educational tool: 'Judgements made about the hypothetical situation outlined in the dilemma may not be reflected in judgements that would be made in "real-life" situations.' Even if they were, the children might not act on them. Straughan recommends an interaction, so that much 'teaching' is derived from rewarding and punishing good and bad behaviour.

Therefore I argue for an ethical component to the school curriculum. There has been much excellent guidance and counselling for individual pupils in recent years. However, this requires a curriculum for the pupil behind it. I have argued:

> *The most effective individual guidance and counselling depends on the background of concepts, facts, and skills which the individual client brings to the counselling session.* I would therefore suggest that individual counselling has to depend on whole-group exploration of this necessary background. Drawing up the list of what should go into that background is essentially a curriculum matter. The curriculum components which relate especially to individual and personal growth I would call the 'pastoral curriculum'. (Marland 1989: 154)

Do not let us build our ethical education *only* into the analysis following an individual or a group's bad behaviour. Let us be not merely reactive but also proactive. This is the core of the secondary tutor's role.

Teaching behaviour

I am convinced we can specifically teach behaviour and that many tutors are doing so. Here is an example from a Year 7 tutorial period. The tutor is speaking:

> Right, we have talked about how to react when something goes wrong. I want you, you, and you to stand up in a line in that corner and pretend you're in the queue for your lunch. Leroy, you push Josey, and Josey, you fall over. The Deputy Headmistress has just come round the corner, and you have fallen against her legs.
> Good. Thank you! Now return to your seats, please. All of you read the worksheets on your desks. There is a list of eight ways in which Josey could react:
>
> Lie on her back and scream;
> Run away;
> Shout: 'It's all his fault, Miss!'

And the list also contains sensible suggestions. The tutees are pleased to react critically to the silly ones, saying: 'Oh, we wouldn't do that, Miss!' Then they discuss the most reasonable reactions in their groups. The whole tutor group then agrees the best reaction.

I think behaviour can be taught and the Americans are better at it than we English are. We sometimes regard some aspects of good behaviour as 'middle class' and feel it should not be taught to working-class children. We regard it as somehow improper to teach the courtesies because it is seen as not genuine. However, we can do our five-finger exercises on the piano but that does not stop our creativity when we become pianists. Similarly, we can teach the modes of courtesy in our society and be personal as well.

Take language. We tell young people not to speak so foully. But do we ever teach them about the offensive aspects of language itself? One summer I gave an assembly on 'foul language' to my 16-year-olds. Afterwards I had a deputation from them to say: 'Thank you very much, that was very helpful, but may we say that the other year needs it more!'

In this assembly I explained that there is no such thing as 'bad language' but only language badly used. I did not say the words because it would be embarrassing for the head to use such words. I therefore used OHP transparencies. I started with the word 'genital' and took 'gen', which means birth. I explained that all the words I was going to talk about are words that can be used unpleasantly about the most important thing to everyone in the room, which is their birth. They are either words which refer to the process that leads to birth or to the parts of the body concerned with birth. Even the racist words are about someone's birth. I said that there is usually nothing wrong with a word as a word. However, if you use it in the wrong context, you are not only being offensive to the other person and to those listening, but you are also doing dirt on the word itself and on the cherishing of that act for the future. I believe we should be positive and clear in our teaching of the use of language.

We should also teach about what Alec Dickinson, the founder of Community Service Volunteers, called the 'prison of the peer group'. We take children from the same street and put them around the same table in primary school, because we believe in the friendship group. When they go on to secondary school they all choose the same group. They make a hydra-headed group to whose members you cannot speak individually but only to the group. The art of being a student is the art of being alone without being lonely. That can be taught, but I believe we 'unteach' it by insisting on pupils working for too much of their time in groups.

I recently agreed to take in a $14\frac{1}{2}$-year-old boy who had been expelled from another school for carrying an imitation gun. He explained to me – in language which the peer group insists on, on pain of rejection – that: 'Well, sir, it's like, see, I've got to make sure the others think I'm good, see, so I had to do something, didn't I?' Child psychoanalyst D.W. Winnicott (1958) explained that the young child who is going to be independent is the one who is most closely bonded with her or his parent. But the paradox is that in schools if you build up the peer group too much, children become victims or prisoners of that peer group and cannot develop independence. This reduces their ability to inform their conduct by ethical codes. We need to teach these aspects of peer-group influence in the pastoral curriculum.

The wider behaviour curriculum

If the abstract consideration of ethics is to be *usable* by the child, she or he must have human qualities of self-understanding, appropriate self-esteem, and sensitive perception of others.

The possibility of making real use of ethical teaching in his or her actions derives from and depends on what has been developed in early childhood of the capacity to relate behaviour to belief. D.W. Winnicott said in a talk in 1968:

> In education you can hand on to the child the beliefs that have meaning for yourself and that belong to the small cultural or religious area that you happen to be born into or to choose as an alternative to the one you were born into. But you will have success only in so far as the child has a capacity to believe in anything at all. The development of this capacity is not a matter of education, unless you extend the word to mean something that is not usually meant by it. It is a matter of the experience of the person as a developing baby and child in the matter of care. The mother comes into this, and perhaps the father and others who are in the immediate environment of the baby – but initially the mother.   (Winnicott 1986: 143)

It is our task to make 'the development of this

capacity . . . a matter of education', and this is therefore a 'pastoral curriculum' component.

An international range of psychological studies has shown an amazing correlation between the security of attachment of infant and mother and that child's later behaviour: those with weaker attachment are less well behaved in their early school years and much more likely to impugn poor motives in others and to be aggressive and mistrusting. Young children who had had poor security of attachment are much more likely to see hostile intent in ambiguous situations and 'may come to expect hostility in a wide range of circumstances and to perceive even accidental trespasses as being intentional' (Suess et al. 1992: 46). This usually leads to far more aggression and poor behaviour.

A study of security of attachment of six-year-olds demonstrates that the support from their mothers is still significantly important in affecting boys' approaches to others: 'Insecurely attached boys were seen by their peers as more aggressive and by teachers as having more behaviour problems' (Cohn 1990: 159). This demonstrates that their mothers are not merely giving the young boy a feeling of security, but in so doing are conveying what schools would call a 'curriculum' of self-understanding and interpersonal skills.

The studies have shown that the mother is achieving the security of attachment with the child by in effect *teaching* the infant self-reflectiveness and the understanding of others. Behavioural issues are going to be much harder for the growing children missing this early 'teaching' and in fact 'curriculum'. They are, as D. W. Winnicott perceived, the children who will have most difficulty relating ethical principles to actual behaviour. Therefore the school curriculum has to have these elements of personal and social development in it. We are familiar with the concept of 'reading recovery', that is a curriculum for those for whom the ordinary early stages of reading have not been available or taken up successfully by the child. Some children similarly need a 'behaviour recovery' programme, for what I should call 'ethical preparedness'.

The USA High/Scope scheme, while heavily using 'active learning', is also a scheme for 'cognitive restructuring'. In two groups of disadvantaged children those who attended the High/Scope programme not only had later better reading and maths scores but higher self-esteem, lower rates of delinquency, less teenage parenthood, and better earning prospects (Berrueta-Clement et al.: 1984).

In the secondary years an analogous programme can be devised: a programme for all and a special programme of behavioural recovery for those still bringing difficulties with them. For instance, in the two campuses at North Westminster for pupils from 12–14 there are voluntary (*sic*) after-hours behaviour lessons.

There are also, I should suggest, intellectual problems in relating ethical principles to behaviour. There has not in my view been sufficient acceptance of intellectual difficulties that make it harder for some young people to 'make the connections'. For instance, a typical intellectual problem that is offered a young person by ethical questions is one of the meta-cognitive skills at which so many are weak. Jerome Bruner defined this problem well:

> To understand something as a specific instance of a more general case – which is what understanding a more fundamental principle or structure means – is to have learned not only a specific thing but also a model for understanding other things like it that one may encounter . . . A carefully wrought understanding should also permit (a child) to recognise the limits of the generalisation as well. (Bruner 1960: 25)

Much of the content of school subjects requires this ability: science, geography, history. Many very young children bring this conceptual skill to school from their experience of home. This comes from the mother's form and style of questioning the child and answering the child's questions. There is a class difference in some, but not all, aspects of this early training of thought: 'Middle-class mothers tended to make more frequent use of language for complex purposes, and used a wider vocabulary in talking to their children . . . They also took their children's "why" questions more seriously than working-class mothers' (Tizard and Hughes 1984: 158).

Those who have these verbal-conceptual interchanges at home are better placed to develop generalizing skills for school use. Development in understanding ethical principles depends heavily on this skill. It is, though, one rarely specifically taught in schools. For effective education in ethics the relationship between example and generalization must be consciously taught. One 13-year-old boy said to me recently: 'I wasn't being aggressive: I just called Miss a liar.' The conceptual gap needs teaching.

Values in the whole school curriculum

As well as the specific ethical consideration and behavioural curriculum, an ethical focus should be placed on many topics in the school's courses. In fact, a number of topics in curriculum courses provide opportunities. In May 1996 I gave an assembly both to my Lower Houses of 500 12–14-year-olds and to a Year-10 of 300 16-year-olds on the bicentenary of the first use of vaccination by Edward Jenner. The ethical issue needed highlighting and a specific focus: after inventing vaccination, as he called it, by putting cowpox pus into the young John Phipps, he risked the boy's life by injecting actual smallpox. He then did the same to a group of other boys who had suffered from and survived cowpox. He thus virtually proved that cowpox produced immunity to smallpox, and this led to the saving of millions of lives. But was his action ethically acceptable?

It is said that in Japan 'school education must open the eyes of the young towards global issues' (Luhmer 1990). We could increase the number and heighten the occasions when we relate a topic to global ethical issues.

There is also a need to ensure the school curriculum in its widest sense is delivered through the full range of school activities, from displays to classes, assemblies to tutorial work. The arts, for instance, should be used to cherish the values of the human character. There should also be many occasions in which the achievements of outstanding goodness are celebrated. 'Generosity of the human spirit' may seem a romantically vague phrase to be part of a school's ambitions, but exploring it and admiring it can be structured into curriculum content. As Aristotle said: 'a knowledge of good is a great advantage to us in the conduct of our lives' (Thompson 1953: 14). Technology, history, science, literature, languages, physical education, for instance, should all have an ethical dimension.

The working methods of a school also educate through demonstration and even the vocabulary used. How are pupils spoken to? How are visitors greeted? Are minority groups really treated with equity? The staff of a school faces a series of interlocking ethical decisions, and middle and senior managers especially so. The old joke 'Do as I say not as I do' was not devised especially with schools in mind! However, a school must ensure that its management, human relationships, work with families, care of pupils, and equity are all ethically strong. This includes the complex issues of confidentiality about pupils, families, and staff. The use of punishments, especially including exclusions, should conform to a firm and clear code. Every aspect of staffing from recruitment to promotion, from leave to references should be transparently ethical. Further, all staff (including those who are not specifically-termed teachers) teach through example. The behaviour of all a school's adults is one strand of the delivery of the values curriculum.

Conclusion

In the UK we are redesigning our schools' curricula against the 'building regulations' of Sections 1, 2, and 3 of The Education Reform Act, 1988. In doing so, let us not forget the overarching requirements of Section 1 (which I quoted at the start of this chapter) and the ethical component of those two clauses. QCA is currently facilitating this consideration with its work on moral values.

In a lecture on 22 June 1996, the Director of SCAA (as it was then called), Dr Nicholas Tate, spelt this out. He declared that there are for schools key 'values and attitudes': 'Concern for others, compassion, self-discipline, restraint, respect for the truth, enterprise – essential to the idea of the "common good"' (Tate 1996: 8).

Let us endeavour to build into each school a curriculum that gives a complementary balance between a specific study of ethical principles and values and a contextual consideration of key topics from an ethical perspective; let us *face* the emotional, experiential, and intellectual difficulties that some children bring with them by 'remedial tuition'; and let us cherish and celebrate human ethical achievement in the past and the present, across the world and in the school community. Let that community be one which potentially values values.

Acknowledgements

This paper is derived from 'Ethics, behaviour and the work of schools' published by The Institute for Global Ethics (1996) in *Britain's Agenda for the 21ˢᵗ Century: An Ethical Horizon*.

References

Berrueta-Clement, J. R., Schweinhart, L. J., Barnett, W. S., Epstein, A. S. and Weikart, D.P. (1984) *Changed Lives: The Effects of the Perry Pre-school Program on Youths Through Age 19*. Monographs of the High/Scope Press. Michigan, USA.: Ypsilanti, No.8.

Bruner, Jerome (1960) *The Process of Education*. New York: Vintage Books.

Cohn, D.A (1990) Child–mother attachment of six-year-olds and social competence at school. *Child Development* **61**: 152–62.

Education Act, 1944.

Education Reform Act, 1988.

Le Jeune, M. (1996) Government ethics and the Nolan Committee. In *Britain's Agenda for the 21ˢᵗ Century: An Ethical Horizon*. London: The Institute for Global Ethics.

Luhmer, K. (1990) Moral education in Japan. *Journal of Moral Education* **19** (I, October).

Marland, M. (1980) The pastoral curriculum. In R. Best, C. Jarvis, and P. Ribbins *Perspectives on Pastoral Care*. London: Heinemann.

Marland, M. (1989) *The Tutor and the Tutor Group*. Harlow: Longman.

Marland, M. (ed.) (1989–92) *Longman Tutorial Resources*. Harlow: Longman.

Marland, M. and Rogers, R. (1997) *The Art of the Tutor*, London: David Fulton.

Schools Curriculum and Assessment Authority (1986) *Education for Adult Life: The Spiritual and Moral Development of Young People*. London: SCAA.

Short, G. and Carrington, B. (1991) Unfair discrimination: teaching the principles to children of primary school age. *Journal of Moral Education* **20** (2).

Straughan, R. (1989) *Beliefs, Behaviour and Education*, London: Cassell Educational.

Suess, G. J., Grossmann, K. E. and Sroufe, L. A. (1992) Effects of infant attachment to mother and father on quality of adaptation in pre-school. *International Journal of Behavioural Development* **15** (1): 43–65.

Tate, N. (1996) *Why Learn?* London: SCAA, p. 8.

Thompson, J. A. K. (1953) *The Ethics of Aristotle*. London: George Allen and Unwin.

Tizard, B. and Hughes, M. (1984) *Young Children Learning*. London: Fontana.

Tizard, B. (1988) *Young Children at School in the Inner City*. Hove: Lawrence Erlbaum.

Winnicott, D.W. (1958) The capacity to be alone. In *Maturational Processes and the Facilitating Environment*. London: Hogarth.

Winnicott, D.W. (1986) Children learning. In *Home is Where We Start From*. London: Penguin.

Young, M. (1982) *The Elmhirsts of Dartington*. London: Routledge and Kegan Paul.

16 Values Education: Issues and Challenges in Policy and School Practice

MONICA J. TAYLOR

Values in educational politics and society

In Britain, values have recently become more prominent in political and educational discourse – in government statements and in the policy and endeavours of the educational agencies of government, especially the Office for Standards in Education (OFSTED) and The School Curriculum and Assessment Authority (SCAA)/Qualifications and Assessment Authority (QCA). On taking up office in May 1997 the new Prime Minister, Tony Blair, spoke of a commitment to 'decent values'. During his speech to the Labour party conference in the autumn of 1997 he set out 'Labour Values'. He said: 'They are what makes us the party of compassion; of social justice; of the struggle against poverty and inequality; of liberty; of basic human solidarity . . .' (Runnymede Bulletin 1997). Translated into educational terms, the White Paper, *Excellence in Schools* (GB Parliament HoC 1997) speaks of 'equality of opportunity', 'high standards for all', 'valuing our teachers' and 'self-esteem'. Notably, it states 'We are committed to ensuring that teaching is seen as a valued and worthwhile career for our best young people; a profession that is recognised and valued by the wider community' (p. 46). These challenges are at the heart of values education in a culturally plural society.

The fact that these statements of values and valuing have been made might be a reflection of changing times in the politics of education. But alongside such rhetoric is another language of economic values in educational policy-making and school practice – such as that of league tables, value added, accountability, target setting, performance indicators and the new concept of 'zero tolerance'. Not tolerance, but zero tolerance. It is these different kinds of values discourse that schools have to balance, if not reconcile, when they attend to their traditional interest in the personal and social education of the individual alongside their academic remit. Moreover, values education at school level takes place in an increasingly culturally diverse and pluralistic society. Traditional cultural assumptions and ethical issues are beginning to be questioned in social structures, institutions, practices, ways of life, events and experiences. Many affect young people and require an educational response.

Contemporary English society may be perceived as characterized by:

- rapidly changing social structures in patterns of work, unemployment and leisure, families and family life, geographical mobility, global communication, by which individuals, ethnic groups and institutions are differentially affected and to which they are constantly adapting;
- social, cultural, regional, local, community and family diversity, which can mask economic, gender, ethnic and racial inequalities, sometimes leading to alienation, lack of hope and aimlessness in individuals, groups and communities;
- the emergence of an entrepreneurial, cost-effective society where individual success is prized, sometimes at the expense of cooperation and 'the common good', and achievement is measured in material terms so that individual intellectual and spiritual development and the social and moral development of communities are relatively neglected;
- awareness of low standards of ethics in some areas of public life and of the questionable example set by some leading figures in politics, business, sport and the entertainment industry;

- a powerful and pervasive media which, in providing information and entertainment, shapes 'facts' and feelings and influences views and actions;
- indiscipline in some schools, with verbal and physical harassment as well as racist violence between some pupils, and sometimes assaults on teachers, affecting the learning environment and educational experience and leading to a rise in exclusions from school, disproportionately experienced by black boys;
- various horrific events involving children and young people (for example, the murders of Ahmed Ullah, Jamie Bulger, Stephen Lawrence and of headteacher Philip Lawrence) which have led some to talk of 'moral panics' and a 'crisis of values';
- the tendency for educational policy and schools to prioritize the qualities pupils need for employment rather than character development or skills for lifelong learning.

Such trends, whilst only a partial characterization, form the background to growing uncertainties and unease about public and individual values, attitudes and behaviour. These then focus on concerns about the personal and social education of the young and the respective roles and responsibilities of school, home and other influences, in a liberal pluralist democracy. Thus educators and schools are challenged to consider the nature of society in which we wish to live and how young people can be prepared to participate in its evolution and to engage with their own lifelong development.

Values in educational policy

If values in society are controversial, then values in education are even more so. But values education in schools is not an option. Values education is defined to include as key strands Spiritual, Moral, Social and Cultural Education (SMSC), Multi-cultural Anti-racist Education (MC/ARE) and Religious Education (RE). (See Figure 16.1 for a definition of values, values education and values in education.) Values – in the sense of principles, ideals or standards – underlie and permeate the school's life and work. It may sometimes appear to teachers as if schools are being asked to compensate for the social and moral ills of society. Schools, due to their contact with families and local communities, are in a special

position to address values concerns in education and, to some extent, to give a lead in the local community around the school. But it is not the role of schools to take the place of social work. Nor is a dose of values education just instrumental to being able to get on with the academic curriculum – what some might see as the *real* purpose of education. Values education itself is intrinsic to learning and being human, not just an emergency measure.

In national educational policy-making the issue is not just to *describe* schools' practices and provision, but to *prescribe* what schools' aims, objectives and outcomes for developing young people's values and their own as institutions should be. In this respect it is important to briefly highlight some national educational policy statements on values over the last decade in order to see the onus placed on schools and the guidance they have received, against which to consider their practices.

The 1988 Education Reform Act (ERA) explicitly required schools to provide a broad and balanced curriculum, paying attention to 'the spiritual, moral and cultural . . . development of pupils at the school and of society' in order to prepare young people for 'the opportunities, responsibilities and experiences of adult life' (GB Statutes 1988 Section 1 (2)). Subsequently, non-statutory guidance seemed to suggest schools should aim at limited personal autonomy set in a social framework 'The educational system . . . has a duty to educate [the] individuals to think and act for themselves, with an acceptable set of personal qualities and values which also meet the wider social demands of adult life' (NCC 1990a: 7). 'Acceptable' qualities and values were left undefined, though in everyday life what is acceptable or not is precisely what is at issue.

The five cross-curricular themes – citizenship, environment, health, economic awareness and careers – made clear reference to values. *Education For Citizenship*, for example, stated:

> Pupils should be helped to develop a personal moral code and to explore values and beliefs. Shared values, such as concern for others, industry and effort, self-respect and self-discipline, as well as moral qualities such as honesty and truthfulness, should be promoted . . . . (NCC 1990b: 4)

Despite the inherently social nature of citizenship, the emphasis here is on personal morality not social justice.

A discussion document on *Spiritual and Moral*

What Are 'Values'?

As a working definition by 'values' we mean:

principles, fundamental convictions, ideals, standards or life stances which act as general guides to behaviour or as reference points in decision-making or the evaluation of beliefs or action. (Halstead 1996: 5)

For individuals, including teachers, values are '*closely connected to personal identity and integrity*' (p. 5). In a school context we are also concerned with the values which the school promotes as a learning community.

What is 'Values Education'?

This is a relatively new umbrella term for a range of common curriculum experiences:

- spiritual, moral, social and cultural education;
- personal and social education;
- religious education;
- multi-cultural/anti-racist education;
- cross-curricular themes, especially citizenship, environment and health;
- pastoral care;
- school ethos;
- extra-curricular activities;
- wider community links;
- collective worship/assembly;
- the life of the school as a learning community.

What are 'Values in Education'?

These are the values which a school or educational institution adopts.
Values are conveyed in teaching and learning processes.
Values are embedded in school structures, management, policies, language and relationships.
Values can be both explicit and implicit.
They can be 'substantive values' (such as honesty, respect) and 'process values' (such as reflection, caring).
Values in school reflect the values and structure of society, of the education system, the National Curriculum, inspection and assessment.

Figure 16.1   Values, values education and values in education: some definitions

Source: Adapted from Taylor 1998.

Development (first issued by NCC in 1993, reissued by SCAA in 1995) was explicit about the moral values schools should promote: 'telling the truth; keeping promises; respecting the rights and property of others; acting considerately towards others; helping those less fortunate and weaker than ourselves; taking personal responsibility for one's actions; self-discipline'. SCAA also recommended that schools should reject 'bullying; cheating; deceit; cruelty; irresponsibility; dishonesty' (p. 4). Moreover, morally educated school leavers should be able to 'articulate their own attitudes and values; . . . develop for themselves a set of socially acceptable values and principles, and set guidelines to cover their own behaviour' (p. 5). Schools received these exhortations to set up their own values statements with little guidance and no resources for delivery. Ideologically these values are essentially those of an individualistic society with strong Christian underpinning. Ethnic minority communities with a more communal sense of responsibility and property might find such values problematic; emphasis on individual morality might be seen as antipathetic to the authority of religious and community leaders.

The catalyst for schools' reappraisal of their values education was the statutory requirement that OFSTED inspections report on the spiritual, moral, social and cultural (SMSC) development of pupils (GB Statutes 1992). Problems about what was distinctive about SMSC and how 'development' could be evaluated (OFSTED 1994a) led to a revised focus on school 'opportunities' for SMSC and 'how the pupils respond to that provision' including 'whether pupils are developing their own values' (OFSTED 1994b). For example,

> Cultural development refers to pupils' increasing understanding and command of those beliefs, values, attitudes, customs, knowledge and skills which, taken together, form the basis of identity and cohesion in societies and groups. It also involves: a variety of aesthetic appreciation; opportunities for pupils to develop and strengthen their existing cultural interests; and having access to a breadth of stimuli which might develop new insights and interests. (OFSTED 1994b, Part 4: 86)

In the *Framework for the Inspection of Schools* (OFSTED 1995) pupils' SMSC development is evaluated as part of the Quality of Education Provided, 'through the curriculum and life of the school; the example set for pupils by adults in the school; and the quality of collective worship' (p. 19). Inspectors' judgements should be based on the extent to which the school:

- 'provides its pupils with knowledge and insight into values and beliefs and enables them to reflect on their experiences in a way which develops their spiritual awareness and self-knowledge;
- teaches the principles which distinguish right from wrong;
- encourages pupils to relate positively to others, take responsibility, participate fully in the community, and develop an understanding of citizenship; and
- teaches pupils to appreciate their own cultural traditions and the diversity and richness of other cultures' (p. 19).

OFSTED inspections also evaluate pupils' 'Attitudes, Behaviour and Personal Development' (including the quality of relationships, the degree of racial harmony and pupils' contributions to the life of the school) on the extent to which pupils:

- 'behave well in and around the school, are courteous and trustworthy and show respect for property;
- form constructive relationships with one another, with teachers and other adults, and work collaboratively when required;
- show respect for other people's feelings, values and beliefs; and show initiative and are willing to take responsibility' (p. 17).

OFSTED inspections have consistently found that schools are better at making provision for pupils' social and moral development than their spiritual and cultural development. According to the Annual Report of Her Majesty's Chief Inspector of Schools for 1995–6, provision for cultural development, for example, is 'problematic'. At primary level 'too little is done, outside of religious education and assembly, to prepare pupils for life in a multi-cultural society' (OFSTED 1997: 17), and at secondary level, 'in many schools awareness of the contribution made by other cultures to British multi-cultural society is too low' (p. 25).

Values have also been given a higher profile through the National Forum on Values in Education and the Community, initiated by SCAA (1996a). The Forum, comprising 150 members – many nominated by national organizations with concerns for young people or education – was set up to make recommendations on:

- 'ways in which schools might be supported in making their contribution to pupils' spiritual, moral, social and cultural development;
- to what extent there is any agreement on the values, attitudes and behaviour that schools should promote on society's behalf' (SCAA 1996b: 1).

The Forum agreed that there are some shared values, but that there is no consensus on the source of these values or how they are applied. Those claiming a religious source for their values would see this as infusing their attitudes and behaviour. The Forum identified a statement of 'values' on society, relationships, self and the environment (see Figure 16.2), with implications for attitudes and action. This was more widely endorsed by a

The Self We value each person as a unique being of intrinsic worth, with potential for spiritual, moral, intellectual and physical development and change.

Relationships We value others for themselves, not for what they have or what they can do for us, and we value these relationships as fundamental to our development and the good of the community.

Society We value truth, human rights, the law, justice and collective endeavour for the common good of society. In particular we value families as sources of love and support for all their members, and as the basis of a society in which people care for others.

The Environment We value the natural world as a source of wonder and inspiration, and accept our duty to maintain a sustainable environment for the future.

(SCAA 1996: 3–4)

Figure 16.2 Statement of Values from the National Forum for Values in Education and the Community

Mori poll, and has formed the basis of guidance developed by QCA which has been piloted in fifty schools during 1997–8.

Considering these developments in policy and curriculum guidelines, questions can be raised about the extent to which SCAA's values lists and the values, attitudes, and personal qualities looked for by OFSTED correspond; and how these, in turn, relate to the list of 'values' agreed by the National Forum. How are these values articulated, perceived and interpreted in schools? And how does provision influence pupils' values and attitudes – especially given lack of research evidence on pupil outcomes (Halstead and Taylor 1998)? More fundamentally, is prescribing a list of values an appropriate activity for central government and its agencies in a liberal plural democracy? Mention of citizenship and parenting in the White Paper (GB Parliament HoC 1997: 63) as areas for development might also be noted. Much of this activity fits with possible revisions to the National Curriculum in 2000 with respect to inclusion of Personal and Social Education (PSE) and citizenship, and in line with this a government Advisory Group on

Education for Citizenship and the Teaching of Democracy was set up in November 1997 (DfEE 1997a).

Another potentially important fillip to values education may come through teacher education. The new Standards for the Award of Qualified Teacher Status (DfEE 1997b) require evidence that trainees 'plan opportunities to contribute to pupils' personal, spiritual, moral, social and cultural development'; 'set high expectations for pupils' behaviour, establishing and maintaining a good standard of discipline through well focused teaching and through positive and productive relationships'; and 'set a good example to the pupils they teach, through their presentation and their personal and professional conduct.' The new *National Standards for Headteachers* also emphasize a 'positive ethos' in school and that headteachers 'should have knowledge and understanding of . . . strategies for raising pupils' achievement and promoting their spiritual, moral, social and cultural development and their good behaviour' (TTA 1997: 3). Teachers need to be clear about their own values and attitudes in order to be aware of their practices and to reflect critically on their role as values educators. This is all the more important given the difficulties schools face, being required to pay attention to pupils' SMSC development within a minimum and imprecisely specified framework, while operating in a liberal pluralistic society, with little consensus on values issues and remaining sensitive to the values and attitudes of parents and local communities.

Values in school provision and practice – issues from research

Despite much public debate about values and educational concern about the state and status of values education in schools, little precise information exists about how schools approach values education, how their provision supports their stated values, why and how they choose certain curricular approaches and teaching strategies, and what professional support is needed. The project, Values Education in Primary and Secondary Schools (sponsored by NFER, SCAA and the Citizenship Foundation in 1997) has attempted to gather some of this missing evidence by exploring schools' perceptions of key factors in formal and informal teaching in values education and collecting examples of professional practice as a basis for policy-making and guidelines. In particular, through an evaluation of the Citizenship Foundation's '*You, Me, Us!*' materials for primary schools, it has also gathered information on the kind of materials schools take up, use and find effective, as well as their resource and support needs (Hill, Lines and Taylor 1997). Additionally, the project has surveyed secondary schools' provision for citizenship by the age of 15 to inform the International Association for the Evaluation of Educational Achievement (IEA) Civic Education Project (Kerr 1998).

In terms of methodology, the research involved a three-phased approach. First, a questionnaire survey of a nationally representative sample of 600 primary schools and 400 secondary schools was undertaken. There was a response rate of over 50 per cent. Second, from the responses (in total 337 primary and 209 secondary schools) a selection was made of around 50 schools, which appeared to have promising developments in values education according to a number of indicators (e.g. having a coordinator for the area, a good report from OFSTED, explicit reference to values in the school development plan and/or certain policies, a values statement or SMSC policy, a sense of direction in how the school was taking its values work forward and that it was linked to outcomes, whole school training and consultation with parents). Extensive telephone interviews with the member of staff with day-to-day responsibility for values education were then conducted. Third, from these schools a further selection was made of around 20 schools with interesting practices (e.g well-grounded in policy, specific curriculum or extra-curricular approaches or teaching strategies) where we undertook a programme of individually tailored day visits, observing classes and assemblies, interviewing staff, students, governors and parents and collecting documentation. A full report of the project will be available (Taylor and Lines forthcoming). This paper highlights some of the key issues and challenges which teachers and schools experience in this controversial area of education, with particular reference to cultural diversity.

Schools accept that they have a role in values education in a diverse society. As one primary school put it:

> Values education is not something new for this school. We see it as part of our natural, professional

duty to our pupils and parents . . . Our aim is to lay the foundations for every pupil to develop as a complete well-rounded individual.

But every school is faced with contestable choices about the values that it adopts as an educational institution. Some key values issues include:

- **Effective academic and values education**: how to balance the academic and the values curricula; what constitutes entitlement?; should there also be an entitlement to a values education?; the ability range of pupils, their ethnicity, social catchment, parental pressure and whether the school is genuinely comprehensive might influence this decision;

- **Response to national guidance in school values structures**: the extent to which to follow national guidance on values education or SMSC development; this has implications for the emphasis the school places on values in the foundation subjects of the curriculum, in extra-curricular activities, in the life of the school and in some form of separate provision, such as PSE;

- **Relationship between religious education and other aspects of values education**: how to make links between values education and RE and between values education and collective worship (especially in meeting statutory requirements); clearly the religious foundation of a school and the religious and cultural backgrounds of the pupils will affect decisions about policy and practice;

- **Extending cultural development**: how to take account of cultural diversity, or alternatively mono-culturalism in the school, especially in relation to equal opportunities; what attitude to take to youth cultures; how to promote an educational culture in school where being academically successful is good;

- **Whose values? What values?**: whether the school (and all schools) should subscribe to certain 'substantive values' (such as those advocated by NCC 1993/SCAA 1995) and how they should be interpreted in the school; whether it should use the framework of SCAA's National Forum on Values in Education and the Community or whether it should produce its own values statement and consider how it fits with national guidance and other related policies; how do the values in such statements fit with parents' values?; on whose authority does the school teach which values?

- **Values in the educational process**: how values education in school relates to educational and 'process values' of inquiry, critical reflection, rational discussion and the intellectual virtues of sincerity and goodwill, commitment to procedure and argument, willingness to negotiate perspectives;
- **Forming a values education partnership**: how inclusive the school can be in conducting its values education and in making and reviewing policy; how can it balance the often diverse views and values of teachers, pupils, parents, communities?; how can partnership with parents and communities contribute to pupils' personal development?

Influences

In trying to come to terms with these issues and the often conflicting pressures on them, what influences schools in their provision and practices in values education? In the survey over three-fifths of respondents in both primary and secondary schools claimed that in the last two years values education had been most influenced by staff-perceived need, a whole-school initiative and pupil-related issues (Table 16.1). Twice as many secondary as primary schools had been influenced by OFSTED inspection. In interview, for example, one head said: 'OFSTED has been the most important, because, sad as it is, it absolutely focuses your mind and they can make or break your school. It's the difference between knowing and demonstrating what you are about'. Community/parental pressure has been

Table 16.1   Main influences on values education

	Primary (%)	Secondary (%)
Staff-perceived need	74	70
Whole-school initiative	65	59
Pupil-related issues	61	61
Dearing review of National Curriculum	25	23
Revised OFSTED framework	23	18
OFSTED inspection	22	43
LEA initiative	15	10
SCAA discussion document	14	17
Other responses	29	22
No response	3	4
N =	337	209

Multiple response question, percentages do not total 100.

relatively uninfluential. And SCAA's discussion document has so far had a limited impact on most schools.

Values statement

In recent years schools have been encouraged to develop a values statement 'which sets out the values the school intends to promote and which it intends to demonstrate through all aspects of its life' (NCC 1993, reissued by SCAA 1995: 7). The survey discovered that about one-quarter of both primary and secondary schools claimed to have a values statement, which indicates the values by which the school intends its practices to be guided.

One example of a teachers' values statement in a secondary school is as follows:

> We want our school to be caring and Christian, disciplining, encouraging, happy.
> We want our pupils to achieve by being responsible, developing respect, to accept positive challenges, to commend effort and to develop spiritual understanding and moral well being.

By contrast, fewer than one-fifth of schools said that they have a policy for Spiritual, Moral, Social and Cultural Development, that is a statement about how the curriculum and other aspects of school life would promote these dimensions of experience. The issue here, of course, is whether having engaged in these developmental processes the values education experience of pupils in the school improve and whether there are SMSC outcomes. Some heads were convinced of the benefits:

> We have a values statement which underpins all actions within the school and becomes regenerated constantly through every interaction. The successful outcome is seen in everything we do   (Primary head).

> Pupils know that there is a very clear and explicit framework of values and expectations. They are able to identify the ways in which the school lives out its mission statement   (Secondary head).

Schools varied considerably – and not just by age phase – as to whether they involved pupils, parents and governors in the drawing up of values statements. The extent to which these parties are involved is not just a matter of care or ownership but also of social justice. Pupils were more likely to have a say in devising codes of conduct or class rules.

One school mentioned 'Charts for equality of opportunity are regularly devised by the children and are on display in every classroom'. Another claimed 'Children giving thought to how they would like others to behave towards them. Whole school policies written by children adopted by the school and in the school brochure'. In one multi-ethnic primary school (70 per cent Muslim, 20 per cent Sikh pupils)' the children designed posters based on the school values of respecting each other, ensuring school is a safe and happy environment, celebrating individual achievements and valuing learning at home and school, which were displayed around the school. The head believed the children learned through their own work, interpreting the values as they designed the posters. Some schools emphasised learning by doing, encouraging pupils to take responsibility with the running of the school, helping in the library, serving on the school council, staffing the reception desk (for further examples see Taylor and Lines forthcoming).

Values education in the curriculum and life of the school

Schools were also asked in which parts of the curriculum teaching and activities relating to values education take place. Table 16.2 shows their responses. Schools were almost unanimous in stating that values education takes place in collective

Table 16.2   Main areas of curriculum in which values education takes place

	Primary (%)	Secondary (%)
Collective Worship	99	98
Part of RE	93	95
Part of PSE	70	93
Permeates whole curriculum	81	68
Health	67	64
Special activities/events	63	57
Extra-curricular activities	42	52
Careers	–	56
Citizenship	34	47
Environment	60	44
Topic/project work	70	32
Economic and industrial awareness	–	34
Taught as a separate subject	–	21
Within a subject	65	19
N =	337	209

Multiple response question, percentages do not total 100.

worship and RE: 'Religious education is providing a vehicle for multi-cultural development'. Secondary schools were more likely than primary schools to see values education taking place in separately time-tabled PSE, though it appears that a growing number of primary schools now have a PSE slot. Conversely, as might be expected, primary schools were more likely to see values education as permeating the whole curriculum or in topic/project work. Notably, primary schools were much more likely to consider values issues were dealt with in subject teaching than were secondary schools. Examples of strategies used by primary schools for values education, such as Circle Time and Philosophy For Children, are to be found in the project report (Taylor and Lines forthcoming).

While these findings are not surprising, they need to be approached with some caution about the quality of provision and experience. For example, Collective Worship, whilst required by law, is problematic ideologically, in terms of provision, teacher involvement, space, frequency, and so on. Yet many schools, especially in the primary sector, value assembling together as a community to uphold the school's values, to celebrate religious festivals, as well as taking positive opportunities for spiritual reflection and for moral encouragement, as in the following example from a Church of England primary school:

> We were ushered into the school hall for assembly. The children sat on the floor and the teachers on chairs around the hall. A tape recorder was playing some music. The music was stopped and then the head lit a candle. There was silence, but a bit of fidgeting. The head referred to the candle: how a little light from the candle could be seen from a long way away, how the light seems to travel, although it is only a little flame. Then she went on to talk about hurtful words and stories about others. They operate like the light from the candle and can travel a long way. She emphasised the importance of not saying unkind things to, or about, others and how far the hurt could travel. The head then read a poem and said a prayer. The music was restarted and the children filed out and returned to their classrooms.

Assemblies can also serve the important function of bringing the academic and the SMSC aspects of educational experience together, notably through communal celebration of achievements by individuals and groups, which can also involve parents and community members (see Taylor and Lines forthcoming). 'Children strive to earn special awards and certificates and to be applauded in front of the whole school.' 'Good Citizen Awards are given out to pupils in assemblies for commendable behaviour outside school.'

Taking values education forward

The survey also asked schools how they were taking values education forward (see Table 16.3). Almost twice as many primary as secondary schools saw policy development/review as a main strategy. Secondary schools were focusing their efforts on subject content and curriculum review. Primary schools were more likely to diversify their approaches, and to include parental and community involvement. About one-quarter of both primary and secondary schools saw the informal curriculum as a way forward. Schools often work, and need to work, on several strategies simultaneously or consecutively, as in the following example:

> One school had been developing its SMSC policy for four years. Stimulated by the NCC/SCAA discussion paper, *Spiritual and Moral Development*, the school had a half-day INSET for all teachers on

moral and spiritual education as a cross-curricular theme which enabled them to see opportunities in their teaching. The senior management team then worked on a school ethos statement. This was later reduced to six core values which are reviewed in relation to PSE in half termly meetings. Tutors trialled various approaches to collective worship with a focus on 'pause for thought'. The following year staff were asked to work on draft SMSC policies in their departments. They were not asked 'What are the SMSC aspects of your subject?', but 'What attracted you to your subject? What excited you about it?'. The SMSC elements then emerged. In-service training raised awareness, but staff needed to be reminded to revisit the SMSC issues. Other developments including a Pupil Panel (like a school council), pupil counselling and a Discipline for Learning scheme, also contributed to the school's overall values education approach.

Continuing challenges

The research has provided some up-to-date baseline information and uncovered some professional challenges which include: the role of the head; professional and personal issues for teachers; training; and the role of research on values education.

Role of the head

A key finding to emerge from the research is the special role of the headteacher. Primary heads were more likely to see themselves as leading development in values education than secondary heads (over two-thirds compared with less than half). Indeed, about half primary heads in the survey saw themselves as one of the two most important people having day-to-day responsibility for values education in school. One primary head typically expressed the view that she was responsible for 'the positive ethos of the school, behaviour and quality of life for both staff and children'. Another primary head took a lead in values education in several ways: through staff meetings, assemblies, talking informally to teachers, ensuring PSE was on the timetable, involving the school in pilot projects on citizenship and effective parenting and supporting other schools with a pupil behaviour initiative.

Fieldwork in schools revealed that the headteacher needs to have a clear vision for values in the school and to be able to inspire staff to

Table 16.3 Main strategies used by schools to take forward values education

	Primary (%)	Secondary (%)
Policy development/review	70	38
Curriculum review/content	28	41
Subject content	25	49
Involvement of parents/ community	29	15
Through issues/topics (e.g. drugs, racism)	23	12
Informal curriculum	23	23
Pupil development	18	12
Staff development/INSET	16	16
Teaching strategy	14	12
Pupil involvement (e.g. school council)	18	18
Ethos	7	12
Teaching structure (e.g. specialist teams)	2	11
Other responses	24	32
No response	15	12
N =	337	209

Multiple response question, percentages do not total 100.

positively agree to share in the processes to bring this about to common purpose. '*The head is the key to trust and respect.*' The head has to be able to bolster staff morale and self-esteem in order to enable staff – teachers and non-teaching staff – to tackle controversial values issues. At the same time, adequate and well-known structures for support and development and procedures for consultation and communication should be in place. Data from across the project suggested a tentative model of the effective valuing and values learning school, with characteristics and evidence indicators which schools might care to examine in the light of their practices and the particular factors, such as cultural and ethnic diversity, which need to be explicitly taken into account (see Table 16.4).

Some heads interviewed in the project acknowledged that their school practices were less strong on cultural development. One primary head, in a largely white area of a south eastern county near to London, noted that, in addition to Christianity, pupils learnt about Islam and Judaism, but not an Islamic or Jewish way of life. On the other hand, she felt that the 'failure' to address other religions or cultures did not derive from lack of inclination, but a perceived lack of relevance to the pupils and the view that concentration on difference would be 'artificial'.

Some other heads in white areas saw it as part of their role to take a lead with pupils on cultural diversity and anti-racism. One secondary head told of his concern about a local Indian takeaway being victimized by young people, including some from the school. He decided to use assembly to speak out publicly to condemn their behaviour, to let students know the schools' position, to be positive about anti-racism, and to show that he personally felt passionately about this 'outrage'. Year 9 pupils in a group interview spontaneously remembered this assembly, 'it's a topic that sticks with you'. It had counted for them that the head had spoken out: 'He was serious about it'; 'Yeah, you knew he was serious and that he meant what he said, and that he didn't agree with it (the attack).'

Teachers: professional and personal issues

The National Foundation for Educational Research (NFER) survey showed that schools seem to accept that most teachers have a day-to-day influence and

a role to play in values education. But teachers often feel unsure or inadequate about meeting their role. Whilst this is partly due to lack of training, it is also partly due to tensions which can arise between personal and professional values which need to be more openly acknowledged and discussed. These include the following.

Explicit involvement in values education
This can manifest itself in several ways. For example, whether to attend Collective Worship (CW) can be a values conflict for teachers who wish to support and be in solidarity with their form groups but do not wish to imply a commitment to worship, or to Christianity in schools. Similarly, some teachers do not feel happy with teaching RE. While primary teachers are more likely to be expected to include RE in their curriculum coverage, secondary teachers of Humanities subjects may be called upon to deliver RE because of the shortage of qualified teachers. Even though teaching conditions permit right of withdrawal from participation in CW and teaching RE, this still causes some teachers a conflict between conscience and conscientiousness.

Revealing personal values, attitudes, behaviour
It is not possible to be a teacher without self-disclosure. Dealing explicitly with values issues in the classroom is likely to kindle pupils' interests in the teacher's own beliefs, values and life experiences. While many teachers are prepared to reveal something of themselves, they may need to set boundaries to privacy which pupils should respect. Conversely, they should be prepared to respect the privacy of the pupil, especially by not putting the pupil in a position where his or her personal life is exposed to peers.

In the 1970s concerns focused on indoctrination – the possible influence of the views of the teacher because of the teacher's authority. Sadly, due to the progressive social undermining of respect for teachers – their demoralization – which has been conveyed by parents even to primary pupils, this is less likely to be a real fear. It is more important for pupils to be aware that their teachers do have beliefs and values which they hold with conviction. But, at the same time, teachers should ask themselves how, and to what extent, their beliefs and values influence their interaction and responses to pupils, and whether it is in the intended direction. On some issues it is necessary for teachers to give an

Table 16.4 The effective valuing and values learning school

Characteristics	Evidence
Headteacher has a vision for values.	Headteacher has clear goals for values in school and the kind of ethos to be achieved by a central focus or several continuous or successive approaches.
Strong professional leadership re values.	Headteacher leads development and communication in values education, with agreement and support of senior management and with common purpose.
Values given high profile in teaching and learning and in life of school.	Academic and values development are seen as interrelated and complementary.
School promotes itself as a values learning community.	All staff agree values and SMSC development are an essential part of the school's purpose and constantly strive to improve practice.
Structures and processes to facilitate values are in place, understood and kept under continuous review.	School development plan sets out objectives, strategies and resources for values education over at least 3 years.
	Related policies (values statements, SMSC, equal opportunities, curriculum and teaching and learning) exist and are coherent.
Valuing and support for staff.	Recognition that teachers are the best resource.
	There is an SMSC/Values coordinator with SMT support, time and resources.
	Whole-school training for all staff, and curriculum training. The values dimension in teaching is on the agenda for teacher's appraisal.
	Involvement of 'experts' with school in developing professional practice.
Examining and evaluating practice.	Questioning, observing, reflecting on practices in values education.
	Examining school ethos, respect, responsibility, relationships, and celebrating achievements in SMSC development.
	Cross-curricular audits, raising awareness of values across subjects and planning inter-departmental values projects.
Empowering pupils: responsibility, self-esteem, self-discipline.	Actively involving pupils in their values learning in the curriculum and school life, with opportunities to develop responsibility.
	Having high expectations of pupils – attitudes, personal qualities and behaviour. Systems of support and sanction well known. Caring, fair and firm discipline.
Promoting and valuing home–school partnerships.	Recognition of parents' rights and responsibilities for the SMSC development of their child(ren).
	Working with parents to develop a genuine values partnership; survey parents' values expectations; discuss and generate clearer understanding of mutual expectations, boundaries and agreed practices.
Working with and valuing the community.	School sees itself as a resource for the whole community and as benefiting from the community.
	Active local involvement, e.g. in citizenship, environment, community projects.
	Being aware of clear values aims and outcomes and learning from differences and diversity.
Staff commitment and confidence about values (in) education.	Climate of openness, critical reflection and debate about values issues.
	Ethical reasoning about practices and in decision-making.
	Professional competencies, consistency and adaptability.

Source: Taylor 1998.

unequivocal lead, as in the case of the head above who delivered a clear anti-racist message. Some of the most powerful and meaningful learning experiences occur when pupils realize through the teacher's openness, confusion or emotion that the teacher is human too; for instance, when a teacher on residential was scared of abseiling but still went ahead and set an example to pupils.

Conflicts of loyalty

Teachers experience conflicts of loyalty to staff, to pupils, to school rules and practices, to educational authority procedures and the rule of law. Confidential matters, especially regarding health issues, such as pregnancy or Aids tests; or changing family circumstances, separation and divorce, new relationships within the family and economic difficulties; or conflicts with the law, can provide tests of loyalty which teachers need to reflect on in order to be clear about their ethical stance. Teachers associations, LEAs and schools have policies on confidential matters and can give advice.

Some issues represent genuine conflicts of culture or equal opportunities, which can have an impact on professional relationships, the life of the school and its standing. One headteacher reported experiencing a values dilemma at the time of the school visit. The female Muslim teacher on her staff (in a largely white school) was about to undergo an arranged marriage, despite her reluctance, as she felt obliged to respect her parents' wishes. The head said that this had 'opened her eyes' both to the fact that less traditional Muslim women still experienced arranged marriages and also to the difficulties of trying to support a stressed and, at times, distraught young woman. In this she felt that she was struggling to be both caring and fair, to balance her inclination to advise her not to go ahead with the marriage if the idea made her unhappy with the recognition that she should respect culturally different practices.

Another head who believed that there were 'fundamental truths', such as anti-racism, for which it was 'important to stand up and be counted' talked in assembly about golf, raising the question of why there were no black golfers of repute in England. He himself suggested that golf clubs might be racist. As it happened, this assembly took place during the week of the OFSTED inspection. An inspector approached him subsequently, telling

him that he was wrong: the real reason why there were no well-known black golfers was, he alleged, because they couldn't swing a golf club properly. The head felt the inspector was 'very much out of line in giving an almost eugenic point of view'. The school seriously considered making a complaint, but, on balance, decided against it.

Conflicts between the schools' values and parents' values

The meeting point for differences between school and home values is in individual pupils' behaviour. A common issue is when pupils have been fighting, when the victim cites in self-defence that he or she has been told by a parent to 'stick up for yourself'. Schools have to seek to explain to parents the behaviour codes which they operate and the reasons why, for instance, they do not condone violence. One school had taken the trouble to give a copy of its policies referring to values education (citizenship, collective worship, PSE, RE and SMSC) to every parent. But, generally, relatively few schools had surveyed parents' wishes for the values education of their children or sought to check mutual understandings of practices.

Sometimes conflicts of interest occur because of cultural differences between the school and the home; such as extended visits, arranged marriages and lack of access for girls to further or higher education. One girls' school with predominantly ethnic minority pupils (88 per cent Muslim) experienced difficulties with whether girls were allowed to participate in community projects, a paired reading scheme and industrial mentoring; but it 'was not unknown' for girls to 'disappear', sometimes to Pakistan. These are some of the most intractable issues with which the school has to deal, balancing the values of a Western society with those of communities with allegiances in their countries of origin. The short- and long-term interests of the pupils have to be balanced within the framework of law and the schools' own stated policies and common practices.

Teachers need to appreciate boundaries and to know when an issue might be controversial, misperceived or possibly detrimental to a pupil's interest. They may require the advice of a senior teacher. But they also have to be empowered to take the initiative, be creative, try new strategies and revive their own SMSC learning in the process.

Training

In the NFER survey schools were also asked what forms of further professional development in values education they had experienced and who had delivered staff development (see Table 16.5). Respondents in about four-fifths of primary and secondary schools claimed to have had informal discussion with colleagues. Almost half said they had experienced whole school training on aspects of values education in the last two years. For example, about one-third of secondary schools and up to half of primary schools claimed to have had some staff development on developing a values statement. Over half the primary schools said they had addressed Circle Time in staff development. Over four-fifths of secondary schools had considered sex education, whereas only one-quarter had given attention recently to cultural diversity. This is supported by evidence from school visits which suggests that the cultural in SMSC development may not be receiving a sufficiently high profile and that this varies from school to school and teacher to teacher.

However, in almost three-quarters of schools, staff development was carried out by a member of staff and a not insignificant minority of schools have had no staff development in values education, despite its increased national emphasis. Some schools have made some aspects of values education a priority and the extent to which they have used resources is a key indicator of commitment. For example, in one primary school where the head saw use of Philosophy for Children techniques as a possible way forward a substantial part of the training budget was used on staff training with a nationally known consultant. As a result, staff had a common focus

for their commitment, strategies and staff and pupil development, with promising outcomes.

But, looking at these findings overall, the extent and depth of staff development in such a complex, controversial and ever-changing area of education may be questioned. Formal training in aspects of values education in initial teacher training is severely limited and much of the reported training appears to rely at school level on the cascade model and the enthusiasm of an individual. Such findings raise questions of who educates the in-house trainers and are there limits to school self-renewal? Further school-based developments, which are so important given the need for consistency, coherence and progression, need the support of specific national resourcing. Resourcing for whole school staff development on aspects of values education is well spent where there is a need to transform teacher attitudes or to develop a new approach adopted by all staff. This may be especially pertinent with regard to raising awareness of cultural diversity and the ongoing need to combat racism and promote equal opportunities. Where it becomes legitimate to examine ethical dimensions of teaching teachers feel supported and nurtured by the climate of professional development and demonstrate willingness and openness to reflect on their practice.

The role of research

Compared with many other aspects of education values education is in its infancy and research into it all the more so especially in Britain. Despite the apparent value traditionally placed on pupils' personal and social development in the UK, there has been little sponsored research (Taylor 1994a), compared with the work done in North America, some European countries (Taylor 1994b), or on other aspects of teaching and learning in the curriculum. The level of understanding about SMSC development is only beginning to be examined through a critical review of research on the development of pupils' values, attitudes and personal qualities (Halstead and Taylor forthcoming), and overviews of whether moral education works (Emler 1996, Taylor 1996).

Much more research is required to indicate, for instance, how teachers can set a 'good example'; how various commonly used strategies, such as Circle Time, aid pupils' SMSC development; the

Table 16.5 Delivery of staff development

	Primary (%)	Secondary (%)
A member of staff	68	70
LEA advisor/inspector	36	30
Independent consultant	13	25
No-one	12	13
Other	7	9
None ticked	6	5
College or university tutors	4	7
N =	337	209

Multiple response question, percentages do not total 100.

relative strengths and weaknesses of different PSE structures; the values fit of the formal and informal curriculum. Clearly the teacher is the critical mediator of values, but little is known of teachers' ideologies, either in terms of their own values, their attitudes to promoting values in teaching or their values priorities. To what extent are teachers influenced by their own experiences as pupils? Do they just go along with the schools' culture on values, whether or not they affirm these values themselves? To what extent are there differences or even conflicts of values between curriculum subjects?

Above all, much remains to be done to bring about stated Labour values in educational policy and practice, especially the valuing of teachers and headteachers by enabling them to be more confident professionally about one of their most demanding but inescapable roles in promoting pupils' SMSC development. In particular, as OFSTED reports and the research reported here have demonstrated, there needs to be an increased emphasis on policies and practices to enhance cultural development, with national guidelines, if all pupils are to gain from a more coherent experience of cultural diversity. Indeed, if national educational policy is to get beyond exhortation to teach certain values there needs to be sound guidance to schools based on evaluation of what strategies and processes facilitate which objectives, in which contexts, and why. This requires giving research – preferably action research – and evaluation a higher profile. This in itself would be a statement of values in education.

Acknowledgements

This paper reports data from an NFER/SCAA sponsored project, Values Education in Primary and Secondary Schools and from an Evaluation of the Citizenship Foundation's Materials, *You, Me, Us!*. These projects have been undertaken with the assistance of my colleagues, Anne Lines, Claire Hill, Jim Jamison, Fiona Johnson, Lesley Kendall and James Badger, whose help I gratefully acknowledge. The full report of the project, provisionally entitled Values Education in Primary and Secondary Schools, by Monica Taylor and Anne Lines, is forthcoming. This paper also draws upon two other recently completed projects (Taylor 1998 and Halstead and Taylor 1998).

References

Department for Education and Employment (1997a) Blunkett announces schools' group to boost citizenship. *DfEE News*, 19.11.97. London: DfEE.

Department for Education and Employment (1997b). *Teaching: High Status, High Standards. Requirements for Courses of Initial Teacher Training.* London: DfEE.

Emler, N. (1996) How can we decide whether moral education works? *Journal of Moral Education* **25** (1): 117–26.

Great Britain: Statutes (1988) Education Reform Act 1988. Chapter 40. London: HMSO.

Great Britain: Statutes (1992) Education (Schools) Act 1992. Chapter 38. London: HMSO.

Great Britain: Parliament: House of Commons (1997) *Excellence in Schools* (cm 3681). London: The Stationery Office.

Halstead, J. M. (1996) Liberal values and liberal education. In: J. M. Halstead and M. J. Taylor (eds) *Values in Education and Education in Values*. Lewes: Falmer Press.

Halstead, J. M. and Taylor, M. J. (forthcoming). *The Development of Values, Attitudes and Personal Qualities: a Review of Recent Research.* London: OFSTED.

Hill, C., Lines, A. and Taylor, M. J. (1997). Evaluation of the Citizenship Foundation's Primary School Materials, *You, Me, Us!* Report to the sponsor. Slough: NFER.

Kerr, D. (1998) Citizenship education revisited. National case study: England. In J. Torney-Purta, J. Schwille, and J-A. Amadeo (eds) *Civic Education Across Countries: 22 Case Studies from the Civic Education Project*. Amsterdam: Eburon Publishers for the International Association for the Evaluation of Educational Achievement (IEA).

National Curriculum Council (1990a) *The Whole Curriculum* (Curriculum Guidance 3). York: NCC.

National Curriculum Council (1990b) *Education for Citizenship* (Curriculum Guidance 8). York: NCC.

National Curriculum Council (1993 Reissued by SCAA 1995). *Spiritual and Moral Development.* SCAA Discussion Papers: No. 3. London: SCAA.

Office for Standards in Education (1994a) *Spiritual, Moral, Social and Cultural Development* (OFSTED Discussion Paper). London: OFSTED.

Office for Standards in Education (1994b) *Handbook for the Inspection of Schools.* London: HMSO.

Office for Standards in Education (1995) *Framework for the Inspection of Nursery, Primary, Middle, Secondary and Special Schools.* London: HMSO.

Office for Standards in Education (1997) *The Annual Report of Her Majesty's Chief Inspector of Schools.* London: HMSO.

Runnymede Bulletin (1997) A new vision for Britain. *Runnymede Bulletin* **306**.

School Curriculum and Assessment Authority (1996a) The National Forum for Values in Education and the Community. Final Report and Recommendations (SCAA 96/43). London: SCAA.

School Curriculum and Assessment Authority (1996b)

Education for Adult Life: the Spiritual and Moral Development of Young People. (SCAA Discussion Papers No. 6). London: SCAA.

School Curriculum and Assessment Authority and National Forum for Values in Education and the Community (1996) *Consultation on Values in Education and the Community.* London: SCAA.

Taylor, M. J. (1994a) *Values Education in the UK: A Directory of Research and Resources.* Slough: NFER.

Taylor, M. J. (1994b) *Values Education in Europe: A Comparative Overview of a Survey of 26 Countries in 1993.* Dundee: CIDREE.

Taylor, M. J. (1996) Editorial: unanswered questions, unquestioned answers, *Journal of Moral Education* **25** (1): 5–20. (Also see other papers in this 25th anniversary issue, *Moral Education from the 20th into the 21st Century.*)

Taylor, M. J. (1998) *Values Education and Values in Education: A Guide to the Issues.* London: Association of Teachers and Lecturers.

Taylor, M. J. and Lines, A. (forthcoming) *Values Education in Primary and Secondary Schools.* Slough: NFER.

Teacher Training Agency (1997) *National Standards for Headteachers.* London: TTA.

Part Three

Teacher Education

17 Training Teachers for Intercultural/Anti-racist Education

FERNAND OUELLET

Introduction

This chapter argues that the challenges of religious and cultural diversity cannot be met by the educational system unless teachers are adequately trained. Many obstacles to this kind of training are identified. The most important one is probably the absence of consensus among experts on a model where the complex issues related to this sensible area would be articulated in a coherent structure defining the knowledge and skills to be mastered. After presenting an outline of such a model, the chapter discusses some other obstacles: teachers' perceptions of immigration as a threat to national identity, the perverse effects of an ideology of cultural pluralism and cultural relativism, lack of clear government policy of intercultural education and severe budgetary restrictions in education. The last section presents some suggestions on how the initial training of teachers could show more concern for the challenges of ethnocultural pluralism.

Religious and cultural diversity presents challenges for the institutions of democratic societies. More specifically, how can these institutions satisfy the aspirations of immigrants and of the members of various cultural groups while providing a space of public deliberation where divergences can be solved through democratic deliberation? How can institutions allow more space for cultural and religious diversity while promoting equality for all members of society? In other words, how can they be *at the same time* more open to diversity, more concerned with social cohesion and more dedicated to the establishment of equalitarian interactions between all citizens? These are the three major challenges to be met if institutions are to become more responsive to ethnocultural and religious pluralism. If initiatives in this direction do not put enough stress on the importance of promoting social cohesion through participation in democratic deliberation and of countering injustices and inequalities, they run the risk of provoking legitimate resistances.

Among these initiatives, the importance of preservice and in-service training of teachers has been generally recognized. In spite of this consensus, there is no consistent model of what should be the main components of programmes which prepare teachers to find adequate responses to the challenges of pluralism in education. In its recommendation on the 'formation of teachers to an education for intercultural understanding, particularly in the context of migration' (Recommendation no. R 84), the Council of Europe provided some indications for such a model. The Council, after identifying the main adjustments required of the educational systems of European countries because of the now permanent presence of populations of immigrant origin and after defining the objectives and the content of an intercultural education for all children (Perotti 1992, 1994), proposed the following techniques for the preparation of teachers to intercultural education:

- techniques to enhance observation and listening and the understanding of the situation;
- techniques to promote the establishment of relations which make it possible for the child to integrate his or her cultural experience;
- anthropological analysis which make possible an in-depth internalization of cultural relativism (that is to say that all culture is the expression of a dynamic relation of man and his spatio-temporal environment), to avoid regarding cultures as sacred and to avoid seeing intercultural education as an education aimed at identifying

the 'other' rather than knowing him in his difference and his complexity (Perotti 1992: 60–1).

These suggestions are interesting, but are not very precise and do not constitute a consistent model. It is not altogether surprising that the recommendation put forward by the Council of Europe has had little impact on teacher education. The situation appears considerably more encouraging if the many initiatives undertaken in schools to meet the challenges of cultural diversity are examined. These initiatives cannot serve, however, as the basis of a consistent model for intercultural teacher education, since they reflect a great diversity of theoretical postulates. In effect, a study sponsored by the Conseil supérieur de l'Éducation du Québec has identified seven different approaches underlying the proliferation of initiatives:

1 **Compensatory approach** which aims at providing better opportunity for success in school to minority students who are at risk for linguistic and socio-economic reasons.
2 **Knowledge of cultures** which aims at developing harmonious relations between members of distinct ethnic groups.
3 **Equalitarian heterocentrism** which tries to reconstruct the knowledge produced by science and culture and thus eliminate stereotypes of white supremacy; and which transforms the curriculum so that education conveys a truer and more just knowledge of the world than the one created within the framework of Western white man's supremacy.
4 **Isolationism** which tries to improve the standing of heritage languages and of minority cultures in schools through separate activities.
5 **Anti-racism** which educates students to be critical of discrimination in institutions and in society.
6 **Civic education** which promotes an education of human rights and democratic values.
7 **Cooperative learning** which promotes cooperative learning in heterogeneous classrooms, focusing on equalization of status (Pagé, 1993: 11–12).

None of these approaches were considered adequate in relation to three objectives that are deemed critical if school systems are to meet the challenges of ethnocultural pluralism:

1 recognize and accept cultural pluralism as a reality of society;
2 contribute to the institution of a society of rights and of equality;
3 contribute to the establishment of harmonious interethnic relations (Pagé, 1993: 101).

The study also concluded that the approach 'knowledge of cultures' is the most problematic in relation to these objectives. Unfortunately, this is the one that is the most popular among teachers (Pagé 1992: 121). Furthermore, many schools initiatives focus on the promotion and the protection of cultural particularism – a strategy that often produces unwelcome effects. In an inventory of the 'perverse effects' identified by researchers (Ouellet 1992), I have found three which have a wide social impact:

- the confinement of individuals in a permanent and immutable cultural identity which deprives them of the freedom to choose their 'cultural formula' (Camilleri, 1988/1990);
- the reinforcement of the borders between groups and the increase of the likelihood of intolerance and of rejection of the Other (Steele 1990, Pagé 1992);
- the accentuation of the difficulties of access to equality of opportunity for immigrants and members of minority groups (Steele 1990, Simard 1991, Ghosh 1991).

Too much focus on cultural particularism can produce additional negative consequences in the school context:

- the growing perplexity of the relativist teacher who has become uncertain about what he or she has the right to teach in order to respect the culture of minority students (Kleinfield 1975, Camilleri 1988/90);
- the stigmatization and the marginalization of minority students who are ascribed to a socially depreciated identity (Nicolet 1987);
- the reification and the folklorization of culture which is no more a living reality evolving with the changing conditions of society (Camilleri 1988/1990, Simard 1988/1990);
- the fragmentation of the curriculum under the impact of particularist claims[1] (Ravitch 1990).

The mere enumeration of the numerous approaches to intercultural education and of the 'perverse effects' of educational initiatives which focus on cultural particularism reveals the complexity of this field of intervention and the hazards of ill-prepared initiatives. It would appear, however, that even the teachers who are too destabilized in their professional activity by the growing cultural diversity of their classroom to get involved in a programme of intercultural formation (Charbonneau et al. 1995) are not fully aware of this complexity. When they first undertake a programme of intercultural education, they very often want to get more information about the culture of their students: 'Tell us who they are so that we might better manage them' is, according to Lorreyte (1982, 1988), the implicit demand of those who came to intercultural training sessions at the Agence des relations interculturelles in France. According to Lorreyte, it is dangerous to try to respond to this type of request, since it tends to harden identities and enclose the 'others' in a permanent and phantasmagoric identity which has nothing to do with the experience of people coming from those cultures.[2]

The components of intercultural training

What should be the main components of an intercultural education which would show an awareness of this problem and of the numerous perverse effects identified by researchers? Lorreyte proposed a double strategy: a 'pedagogy of identity deconstruction', where the homogeneity postulated for 'us' and for 'others' is systematically deconstructed, and a 'pedagogy of situation', where, in a given historic and social context, intercultural relations are analyzed in the concrete situation of contacts between individuals and groups. This approach is still very relevant and underlies the 'roundabout strategy' that I have put forward (Ouellet 1994, 1995c). Rather than trying to respond directly to the expectations of teachers, the intercultural education programme that I run takes them in a triple 'roundabout' through:

- the study of the main theoretical questions which make it possible to hold together the acceptation of cultural diversity, the search for social cohesion in a common space of deliberation and the struggle against discrimination and inequalities;
- the exploration of some aspects of the socio-economic and political situation in a foreign country and of the dynamics of the culture of its citizens and of those who have migrated in Quebec;
- the elaboration of a project of intervention which contributes to the quality of education offered to all students, in light of the new perspectives opened by the theory and of a greater sensibility to the diverse experiences of persons of minority cultural groups with whom they have had interactions during the exploration of a foreign society.[3]

Theoretical foundations

Five main axes can be distinguished in the theoretical questions that teachers must master at least minimally in order to be able to understand the challenges of ethnocultural pluralism in the wider context of the great transformations of contemporary societies and of the phenomena which provoke these changes:

1 Culture, ethnicity and identity in the context of modernity; cultural relativism and the necessity to go beyond it;
2 Obstacles to intercultural relations: prejudice, discrimination, heterophobia, racism; anti-racism and its problems;
3 Equality of opportunity, exclusion and marginalization, the vicious circle of guilt-victim, affirmative action and its perverse effects;
4 Nation, community, state; nationalism, liberalism, pluralistic democracy, citizenship; civic education, education for democracy;
5 Models for the insertion of immigrants in modern pluriethnic societies: assimilation, multi-culturalism, pluralistic integration; policies concerning immigration and integration of immigrants in some Western countries.

A brief survey of this list of theoretical questions reveals that the high level of conceptual learning proposed to teachers takes them away for a while from their practical preoccupations. The idea is not to provide them with fashionable pedagogical gadgets or didactic material already prepared which they would only have to adapt to the special conditions of their classroom. It is rather to provide them with a conceptual framework wider and more critical than the one they already possess and to bring them to redefine their perception of the challenges of pluralism thanks to the new understanding that this conceptual framework makes possible. In the process, participants in the programme are introduced to the works of scholars of many disciplines who try to understand the evolution of contemporary societies. This brings them naturally[4] to re-examine some commonly held ideas and negative prejudices towards immigrants, minority cultural groups and cultural practices, which sometimes raise problems in society. Many of these 'problems' have their roots in an inadequate understanding of democracy in contemporary pluriethnic societies. A better understanding of the concepts used by sociology, political sciences and political philosophy can help them to distinguish the false problems from those which have an objective basis (Camilleri 1992) and to accept that 'reasonable accommodations' are often the only solution to problems.

It must be recognized, however, that it takes time before teachers begin to see the importance of studying theoretical issues. In their initial teacher education, they have generally received little introduction to the approaches of the social sciences and many feel uneasy when they are confronted for the first time with the concepts of these disciplines. But those who persist in spite of this initial discomfort recognize the importance of the theoretical dimension of the programme and quickly start to enjoy it (Charbonneau et al. 449–50). The demanding strategy of 'theoretical roundabout' is more productive than a strategy based on confrontation and guilt. As well as providing teachers with the intellectual tools they need to understand what is at stake in the debates surrounding the introduction of an intercultural perspective in education and to participate in that debate, this strategy makes them more conscious of the perverse effects of initiatives based on the promotion and on the protection of particularism. Their imagination and pedagogical creativity is thus oriented towards avenues where there are less risks that their interventions will be part of the problem rather than of its solution.

The exploration of a foreign society

The importance of the second component of the 'roundabout strategy', the exploration of a foreign society, is much less evident. This component might be considered as a luxury that teachers facing urgent problems in their classrooms cannot afford. I believe, however, that teachers need an opportunity to acquire some distance from the climate of urgency and of tension which all too often is a characteristic of intercultural relations. The exploration of some aspects of the socio-economic and political situation in a foreign society, particularly if it is connected to an eventual visit to the country under study, introduces an element of pleasure to the programme. The discovery of a new cultural world can be a very pleasant and gratifying experience if it implies an initiation to a foreign literature and to the religion, the music, the art and the culinary delights of a foreign country. Some teachers might even start learning the language of that country.

Another reason to include the exploration of a foreign culture as a component of intercultural education is that it provides teachers with an opportunity to test the validity and the relevance of some of the theoretical notions that have been the object of study in the first part of the programme and gives a point of comparison that helps them to better understand their own society. When they try to analyse the cultural and religious traditions of this country in the light of these theoretical notions, they learn how to understand cultural particularities in a broader socio-political framework. In this way, they are better prepared to avoid the numerous 'perverse effects' which can be produced by activities which focus on the discovery of the culture of the Other.

Last but not least, this multi-dimensional exploration of a foreign society gives teachers the opportunity of making contacts with citizens who have recently migrated in the country and of developing with them interactions that can be lived under a mode of mutual discovery and enrichment rather than misunderstanding and confrontation.

All these reasons lead me to persist in my conviction that the exploration of a foreign culture is not a luxury for an intercultural formation in a context of global economy and of widening gap between the conditions of life in industrialized and poor countries. Far from being a luxury, this component of the 'roundabout strategy' might very well make an essential contribution to the development of a planetary vision which is required to face the new problems emerging in all countries today.

In this second component of the programme, the teachers are invited to explore some aspects of the cultural model which is dominant in the country they would like to visit and of the relations between majority and minority groups. They must write a short monograph in which they give a synthetic presentation of some of the following points:

- the religious traditions and their contemporary transformations;
- family and education of children;
- education system;
- tensions between tradition and modernity;
- relations between cultural and religious groups and state policies in this area;
- economic problems and their impact on the will to emigrate.

Teachers must consult scholars capable of advising them on relevant books and articles on the religious, cultural, social and political situation of the country they want to study. They are also invited to discuss with learned immigrants coming from that country the findings of their research, the transformation of their culture in the context of immigration, and the difficulties they have experienced in their integration to the new country.

The nature of this activity requires that teachers be free to select for themselves the country they will explore. When the teachers do not have any clear preference, they can be encouraged to select a country of origin of immigrants whose integration raises some difficulties. In the Canadian context, they should also be encouraged to explore the cultural, social and political world of Canada's First Nations. There are many obstacles to satisfying relations between these communities and the rest of Canadians and it is imperative that intercultural education includes a serious analysis of this issue.

Intervention projects

Even if there is nothing more practical than a good theory, the study of the theoretical issues we have identified and its actualization in the exploration of a foreign society are not sufficient for an intercultural teacher education programme. Teachers must also be provided with some strategies of intervention with their students and some guidelines on the way students can be prepared for ethnocultural pluralism. But the range of possible strategies and guidelines is limited by the numerous 'perverse effects' of initiatives that focus on ethnocultural particularism and reflect a non-critical adhesion to an ideology of cultural pluralism. These perverse effects represent a 'theoretical wall' which once again requires that teachers adopt a 'roundabout strategy' and approach the challenges of ethnocul-

tural pluralism in the wider context of a renewal of pedagogy.

Two areas of pedagogical experimentation seem particularly promising: the pedagogy of school exchanges and cooperative learning. The formula of school exchanges that has been developed by the Office Franco-Allemand pour la Jeunesse in the last twenty-five years (Alix and Kodron 1988, Alix 1995) presents interesting possibilities for the development of skills and attitudes which will prepare students for life in a multi-cultural society, while bringing an important contribution to the renewal of pedagogy and to the motivation of students. Its applications, however, are much more limited than cooperative learning, which can provide teachers with very powerful means to face these challenges and many others in schools today.

Cooperative learning, specially the approach designed by Elizabeth Cohen and her team at Stanford University, offers teachers very strong tools to help them overcome the feeling of powerlessness they often experience in front of the growing heterogeneity of their classroom and of the lack of motivation of many of their students. In contrast with some forms of cooperative learning where the development of social skills is given more importance than academic achievement, in Cohen's approach the development of social skills is considered a means of reinforcing the mastery of academic subjects and of high-level conceptual skills. The main particularity of her approach is the great importance it gives to the academic success of students with learning difficulties and the strategies for giving those students the help they need.

In Cohen's conception, cooperative learning is a very structured form of organization of the learning process where school work is done in small heterogeneous groups of students:

- whose members have been prepared for cooperative learning by exercises through which they can internalize new norms of behaviour in class;
- where the teacher delegates authority to the working groups who take on the responsibility of the good functioning of the group (each in turn, the members of the group carry on what Cohen calls the 'how' roles);
- where the execution of the task is preceded by a brief orientation session and followed by a retroaction session;

- where special measures are taken to equalize the status of students so that the interactions are not dominated by high status students while low status students withdraw from the task (attribution of roles, multiple skills treatment, attribution of competency). The task is designed in a way that students must rely on the diversified resources of all members of the group if they want to succeed.

Even if Cohen does not exclude the possibility that cooperative learning might be more efficient for routine learning than traditional teaching where the teacher directly supervises all that is happening in the classroom, the strategies she puts forward suppose that a priority is given to high-level conceptual learning. According to her, it is only through 'rich tasks', which require the mastery of multiple skills and aim at higher level conceptual learning, that it is possible to apply the most efficient treatment of the status problems which invariably arise in cooperative groups: the multiple skills treatment. This treatment works because it modifies the competency expectations of the students. These expectations can remain unchanged even after a successful session of cooperation where students work in collaboration to complete a task and perform the roles which have been attributed to them. What are the characteristics of a multiple skills task? They are tasks which:

- present more than one good answer or more than a way to solve a problem;
- is intrinsically interesting and gratifying for the students;
- make it possible for each student to bring a different contribution;
- use many media;
- require a variety of skills and behaviours;
- require reading and writing;
- represent a challenge.

According to Cohen, the multiple skills treatment relies on a redefinition of human intelligence: rather than asking about the level of intelligence of the students, teachers must analyse a learning situation or a given task in terms of the intellectual skills it requires. They must find ways of convincing students that the task to be accomplished in cooperation actually requires many intellectual skills. In order to reach this aim, they must identify the various skills required by the task and show that these skills are important in the daily life of adults who

often need them when they become involved with others in complex activities. Multiple skills can be identified only in tasks that aim at conceptual rather than routine learning. The students must be trained to identify these various skills in the tasks they have to complete in cooperation and they must learn to recognize them when they are performed by members of their group. This training is focused around two sentences: *nobody possesses all of these skills; each of us possess some of them*.

The multiple skills treatment constitutes the fulcrum of the second strategy put forward by Cohen to deal with status problems in cooperative groups: the attribution of competency to low status students. This attribution must be made in front of the class, it must be precise, refer to specific intellectual skills and show that these skills are relevant for the task of the group and important in real life.

Cohen's approach focuses on the dynamics of status in cooperative groups, on high-level conceptual learning and on the social skills essential for equalitarian interactions with students belonging to various social classes and cultural groups with whom they learn to perform rich and challenging tasks that even the most brilliant students would not be able to master alone. This is why her approach appears to be a particularly promising way of solving many of the difficulties teachers face as a result of the growing diversity of their classroom. This approach does not isolate cultural diversity from other forms of heterogeneity (social class, academic competence, popularity among peers) and makes it possible to 'insert the intercultural question in a global educational perspective' (Conseil Supérieur de l'Éducation, 1993: 90). It is an approach that relies on a rigorous planning, on strategies of implementation tested by many years of research and on evaluation procedures which allow for continuous adjustments.

Moreover, because it is challenging and stimulating both for students and teachers and because it puts forward strategies likely to develop in the early years of primary schooling – 'an active relation to knowledge, rather than a conformist submission to the school ritual' (Charlot et al. 1992) – this pedagogical approach has the potential to help resolve the problem of dropping out (Ouellet 1995). For these reasons, it is more likely to be integrated into the school system and to contribute to its renewal than approaches that focus on the specific problems of immigrant students or those from minority cultural groups.

Obstacles to intercultural training

The complexity and the controversial character of the issues raised by the recognition of cultural diversity in education and the risk of 'perverse effects' justify the necessity of a specific training in this area for teachers who want to be well prepared to face these new challenges. There are many obstacles that make it difficult, however, for teachers to perceive the importance of this type of training.

In a study of the motivations of teachers involved in an intercultural education programme, a team of researchers found two types of destabilizing factors which motivated teachers to participate in such a programme:

- factors related to their professional practice, in particular difficulties of communication with immigrant students and with their parents and the perception that the traditional pedagogical approaches do not contribute efficiently to the mastery of school subjects by these students;
- factors of personal destabilization provoked by the rapid evolution of Quebec society whose identity and Francophone character are perceived to be threatened by the growing presence of immigrants whose values often appear incompatible with those of the host society (Charbonneau et al. 1995).

This second factor in the destabilization of teachers might be responsible for the lack of importance accorded by teachers to intercultural education. It would not be surprising that those teachers who consider the presence of immigrants as a threat to the stability of the national culture view with suspicion any initiative aimed at making the education system more sensitive to the cultural diversity of students. For these teachers, an antinomy might appear to exist between the school's mission in the socialization of students to a specific culture (*la culture québécoise* in Quebec, the British culture in Britain) and the implicit message of an intercultural education which seems to put all cultures on the same footing (Hohl 1996).

This type of perception is not without grounds, since many initiatives in intercultural education postulate an ideology of cultural pluralism (Goulbourne 1991). Proponents of this approach seem to be unaware of the 'perverse effects' mentioned earlier and of the 'pitfalls of cultural relativism' which, in cases, can 'lead to a mystification of the right of being different which turns against those whom it was supposed to favour' (Ouellet 1994a: 154). According to Selim Abou (1992) from whom I borrowed that critique, the right to difference claimed by cultural relativism can even become a right to confinement, to oppression and to death.

It is understandable that these excesses can lead teachers to be reticent towards intercultural education which they see as an obstacle to integration of immigrants and a threat to the stability of the nation. Many of them might be tempted to retreat to an assimilationist position that hides behind the concepts of national culture and of common public culture. And so, we are caught in a sterile opposition between two extreme positions: the promotion and the protection of cultural differences or the denial of these differences and a total negation of pluralism.

There is, however, a third model, more complex and more balanced: the option of pluralistic integration or of pluralistic citizenship. Recent publications (Spinner 1994, Pagé 1996) have clarified this option to a large extent and examined its implications for education. To adopt such a model means investing less in the promotion of cultural particularism and more in the creation of multiple spaces of interaction and deliberation where each citizen will be able to participate equally, without negating who he or she is. Underlying this model is a willingness to see one's identity and relation to the group of belonging transformed in the process of interaction and democratic deliberation (Spinner 1994), but that is not incompatible with the possibility for those who so wish to give a primordial importance to their participation in this belonging group (Parekh 1989).

It must be recognized that theoretical developments in this area are still very recent and the subject of heated debate among scholars. Nevertheless, one of the major obstacles to the perception of intercultural education as an important field has been lifted as the intensification of research and the multiplication of publications has allowed for a more clear and balanced view of the challenges of ethnocultural pluralism in education and of the means to face these effectively. Fifteen years ago the lack of a substantial corpus of theoretical and applied knowledge prevented intercultural education from claiming the status of a serious university discipline, but this is no longer the case today.

However, in the context of severe budgetary restrictions in education, these theoretical developments will not be enough to modify the perceptions of teachers on the importance of a systematic training in intercultural education. Many studies in the United States, Great Britain and Canada (Sleeter 1992, Forster 1990, Ahlquist 1992, Solomon and Levine-Ratsky 1994) have revealed teachers' resistance to initiatives aimed at helping them adjust their perceptions and attitudes, their pedagogical approaches, the content of the curriculum or the organization of life in schools to promote ethnocultural equity and to prepare students to life in a pluralistic society.[5] It will be difficult to overcome this type of resistance, unless teachers receive a clear message that intercultural education is an important priority for their government. Without such orientations, it is unrealistic to expect that a substantial number of teachers will invest money, time and energy in intercultural training. The existence of a clear policy of intercultural education is especially important for teachers working in areas where the presence of cultural diversity is less substantial. In such schools, the teachers will not see the necessity of a training in this area unless the school curricula give clear indications on the knowledge and skills which must be developed by students if they are to be prepared to participate to social interaction and democratic deliberation in a pluriethnic society. An intercultural policy should then give priority to two areas of intervention:

- the enrichment of school curricula and of pedagogical approaches so that these better reflect the cultural and religious diversity of modern democratic societies and help prepare students to participate in the building of a society where religious and ethnic diversity is perceived not as a danger but as a richness which all citizens can draw on together;
- initial and in-service intercultural teacher education so that teachers can use proposed curricula with intelligence and creativity.

Furthermore, the implementation of such a policy should raise more problems in schools with little or no immigrant or cultural minority students than in multi-ethnic schools. If intercultural education is to become an important component in all schools, the school curriculum will have to provide clear indications on what students must know and on the skills they must master to participate in social interaction and in democratic deliberation in a pluriethnic society. This is a requirement if teachers are to feel personally concerned by the challenges of ethnocultural pluralism and willing to invest time and energy in acquiring the training that will help them to make an original contribution to this difficult task.[6]

An official policy of intercultural education would also make it easier to overcome another obstacle encountered by the offers of in-service intercultural teacher education. In-service sessions are often perceived by potential participants as conveying an implicit accusation of narrow mindedness and even of racism. Similarly, many policemen forced to follow intercultural training sessions perceived themselves as the object of the solicitude of 'enlightened' persons who thought they had the right to tell them what the 'correct' ideas and attitudes in matters of immigration and intercultural relations are. Not surprisingly, this type of perception did not make them very receptive toward the training offered to them (Pelletier 1990: 60). A similar perception can also be found among teachers who are offered intercultural training. An official intercultural policy could change that perception by making intercultural education an important educational challenge and by providing clear guidelines on the contribution that all schools must make to face this challenge. That type of negative perception is also less likely to arise in a training programme that does not confront directly the conceptions and the attitudes of participants towards immigration and the various cultures present in the national space and which take them on the threefold roundabout way described earlier.

Finally, if a government decides to adopt an official policy of intercultural education, it must be ready to assume the costs that inevitably will be generated by the revision of the curriculum and the training of teachers. Otherwise, such a policy would be nothing but an empty shell. Successive budgetary cuts in education have resulted in a heavier workload for teachers and in a climate of insecurity which is not favourable to in-service training. In such a context, schools cannot be given a new mandate unless support is provided to teachers willing to get the training necessary to be able to work effectively at making policy practice.

Teachers' initial training

We have seen that it is possible to distinguish three main components in intercultural teacher education: the analysis of the main **theoretical issues** related to the challenges of ethnocultural pluralism in modern democratic societies, the exploration of a **foreign cultural tradition** in its original context and in the context of immigration and the experimentation of **cooperative learning** as a means of renewing pedagogy, of favouring academic achievement for all students and of developing social skills important in a multi-ethnic society. I would like to conclude this chapter with some suggestions for making these three components an integral part of teacher education programmes.

The first idea that comes spontaneously to mind when we think of making more visible the intercultural preoccupation in teachers initial training is to add courses. But it is not the only possibility nor, according to some teacher educators (D'Anglejan et al. 1995), the most efficient. Some believe that it would be preferable to introduce explicit references to the challenges of ethnocultural pluralism and the ways to adjust to these challenges to all of the courses already in existence within teacher education programmes. It would then be possible to study the main themes identified in the first axis mentioned earlier without having to create specific courses on these themes. Cooperative learning could also be an integral part of pedagogical training. While such a strategy might appear adequate in consideration of an already overloaded teacher training programme, it presupposes that all the teacher trainers are already familiar with the intercultural issues and concerned with the challenges of intercultural pluralism, which is far from evident. It would be wiser to add at least an introductory course on these issues, while providing guidelines on the themes related to these issues which must be dealt with in other courses.

It is not only in the general pedagogical training that the preoccupation for the challenges of intercultural pluralism must be present, however. The courses preparing student teachers for various school subjects like French literature (Thérien 1991), mathematics (du Crest 1995), history (Pagé 1994, 1995), religious and moral education (Milot 1991, 1995, Ouellet 1995a, 1995b, 1996a, 1996b, 1997, Milot and Ouellet, 1997), etc., should also reflect a preoccupation with intercultural education. In some cases, such as in confessional religious and moral education, this might mean a radical reorientation of curriculum content, while in other subjects, it will simply mean a broadening of perspectives to better reflect the cultural and religious diversity of society, allowing all students to feel recognized as fully-fledged citizens. It is clear, however, that this upgrading of teacher education will only be possible if the whole school curriculum has been revised and upgraded. It is only if the school curriculum includes precise requirements in relation to the issues of cultural pluralism that it will be possible to include activities aimed at satisfying these requirements in teacher education programmes.

Practica, the supervised initiation to teaching in schools, constitute a third possible area of intervention for the development among future teachers of an awareness of intercultural issues. These practica are an important element of the new curriculum of teacher education which has been put in place recently in Quebec. Would it not be possible to strongly encourage future teachers, even those living and receiving their initial training in culturally homogeneous regions, to have at least one of their practicuum in a multi-ethnic school? This would help them to better recognize the pluralistic character of society and to be better prepared if circumstances of life or of the work market lead them to work in this type of school.

Conclusion

The issues raised by ethnocultural pluralism in education and in other institutions of society are so complex, however, that even the best programme of initial teacher education can be little more than an introduction to these issues. Initial training must be closely articulated to in-service programmes where issues can be studied in greater depth.

Many Western democratic societies have been shaken recently by debates that have made it clear that ethnocultural pluralism represents a major challenge for the future of those societies. Increasingly, schools are perceived to have a more important role to play than in the past in preparing citizens so that they are able to participate in a multi-ethnic society with openness and imagination. I have argued that schools will not be able to play that role if substantial investments are not made in the pre-service and in-service education of teachers. It is unlikely that governments will be willing to make these investments, however, unless some of the obstacles which prevent teachers and other citizens from recognizing the importance of intercultural training have at least partially been lifted. It is also difficult to imagine how such a recognition will become possible without a critical analysis of the challenges of ethnocultural pluralism and of the means to face them and without a clarification of the aims of intercultural training.

port of a policy of intercultural education and their demands of training in this field. They have all sort of good reasons not to participate to in-service training activities that are offered to them.

Notes

1　D'Souza (1993) gives a sobering account of the impact of such educational policies on the climate of racial relations on the campuses of many American Universities. He shows that affirmative action policies aiming at equality of results for black students has led to severe restriction on academic freedom. In the British context, many voices have challenged neo-Marxist anti-racist strategies which limit academic freedom and transform education into indoctrination into the politically correct leftist view (Palmer l986).

2　This type of request is also reflected in a recent survey on Ontario teachers' response to multi-cultural and anti-racist education (Solomon and Levine-Ratsky 1994: 42, 52).

3　There are interesting analogies between these three components of intercultural training and the three components that can be identified in the professional knowledge of teachers: *theories* grounded in the experience of the classroom, *images* which give life to these theories and have an impact on pedagogical interventions and *practical routines* without which teachers could not do anything in front of a classroom (Bliss 1990).

4　The partisans of anti-racist education insist on the necessity of confronting explicitly racist beliefs and attitudes (Tavares et al. 1995, Solomon and Levine-Ratsky 1994). But the strong resistance of teachers to this type of confrontation (Solomon and Levine-Ratsky 1994: 34–8) suggests that the efficacy of this strategy should be questioned. For a discussion of the excesses of anti-racist education in Great Britain, see Palmer 1986.

5　Solomon and Levine-Ratsky (1994: 7–12) give a good summary of the American, British and Canadian literature on this question. According to them, teachers' resistance has its roots in their perception of their mission as teachers: 'Resistance to equity policy can be explained when we consider that the core principles of assimilation, group discipline and physical control, meritocracy, individualism, democracy and truth are the cornerstone not only of our schools, but of a proud liberal-humanist tradition that underpin it' (p. 9).

6　Even if a policy of intercultural education is a necessary condition to the perception by teachers of the importance of intercultural training, it is not a sufficient condition. Even the best policy will have no effect if the conditions of its implementation are not clarified in such a way that the importance of intercultural training becomes evident (Lynch 1986). And this is likely not to be enough if we consider the results of the survey of Solomon and Levine-Ratsky (1994) which reveals that intercultural education and the training required to implement it is low on teachers' priorities list, in spite of their overwhelming sup-

References

Abou, S. (1992) *Cultures et droits de l'homme*. Paris: Hachette.

Ahlquist, R. (1992) Manifestations of inequality: overcoming resistance in a multicultural foundation course. In C. Grant (ed.) *Research and Multicultural Education*. London: Falmer.

Alix, C. and Kodron, C. (1988) *Coopérer et se comprendre*. Paris: Office Franco-Allemand pour la Jeunesse.

Alix, C. (1995) Échanges scolaires: exemples et réflexions autour d'une pédagogie du dialogue et de pratiques coéducatives. In F. Ouellet (ed.) *Les institutions face aux défis du pluralisme ethnoculturel*. Québec: Institut Québécois de Recherche sur la Culture: 185–206.

D'Anglejan, A., Hohl, J., McAndrew M. and Painchaud, G.(1995) L'adaptation à la nouvelle réalité pluriethnique: une priorité à la faculté des sciences de l'éducation de l'Université de Montréal. In F. Ouellet (ed.) *Les institutions face aux défis du pluralisme ethnoculturel: expériences et projets d'intervention*. Québec: IQRC: 391–417.

Bliss, I. (1990) Intercultural education and the professional knowledge of teachers. *European Journal of Teacher Education* **13** (3): 141–51.

Charbonneau, C. et al. (1995) La participation à une formation à l'éducation interculturelle: une démarche de changement. In F. Ouellet (ed.) *Les institutions face aux défis du pluralisme ethnoculturel: expériences et projets d'intervention*. Québec: IQRC: 443–55.

Camilleri, C. (1988/1990) Pertinence d'une approche scientifique de la culture pour une formation par l'éducation interculturelle. In F. Ouellet, (ed.) *Pluralisme et école*. Québec: IQRC: 565–94.

Camilleri, C. (1992) Les conditions de base de l'interculturelle. In E. Damiano, (ed.), *Verso una società inteculturale: Pour une société interculturelle*. Bergamo: ACLI-CELIM: 35–45.

Charlot, B., Bautier É. and Rochex, J.-Y. (1992) *École et savoir dans les banlieues . . . et ailleurs*. Paris: Armand Colin.

Cohen E. (1994) *Le travail de groupe. Stratégies d'enseignement pour la classe hétérogène*. Montréal: La Chenelière.

Cohen, P. (1988/1993) The perversion of inheritance: studies in the making of multi-racist Britain. In P. Cohen and H. B. Bains (eds) *Multiracist Britain*. London: Macmillan: 9–118.

Conseil Supérieur de l'Éducation (1993) *Pour un accueil et une intégration réussis des élèves des communautés culturelles*. Québec.

D'Souza, D. (1993) *L'éducation contre les libertés*.

Politique de la race et du sexe les campus américains. Paris: Gallimard.

du Crest, F. (1995) Apprendre l'arithmétique sans se renier. In F. Ouellet (ed.) *Les institutions face aux défis du pluralisme ethnoculturel: expériences et projets d'intervention.* Québec: IQRC: 285–97.

États généraux de l'Éducation (1995) *Exposé de la situation.* Québec.

Forster, P. (1990) *Policy and practice in multicultural and anti-racist education: A case study of a multi-ethnic comprehensive school.* London: Routledge.

Ghosh, R. (1991) L'éducation des maîtres pour une société multiculturelle. In F. Ouellet, and M. Pagé (eds) *Pluriethnicité, éducation et société. Construire un espace commun.* Québec, IQRC: 207–31.

Goulbourne, H. (1991) Varieties of pluralism: the notion of a pluralist post-imperial Britain. *New Community* **17** (2): 121–227.

Hohl, J. (1996) Résistance à la diversité culturelle au sein des institutions scolaire. In F. Gagnon, M. McAndrew and M. Pagé (eds) *Pluralisme, citoyenneté et éducation.* Paris/Montréal: Harmattan: 337–48.

Kautz, S. (1995) *Liberalism and Community.* Ithaca and London: Cornell University Press.

Kleinfield, J. (1975) Positive stereotyping: the cultural relativist in the classroom. *Human Organization* **34** (3): 269–74.

Lorreyte, B. (1982/1988) La fonction de l'Autre: arguments psychosociologiques d'une éducation transculturelle. *Éducation permanente* 66: *Pluralisme et école.* Québec: IQRC: 339–62.

Lynch, J. (1985) Multicultural education: supporting teacher development. *Multicultural Teaching* **3** (3): 30–1.

Lynch, J. (1986) An initial typology of perspectives on staff development for multicultural teacher education. In S. Modgil, G. K. Verma, K. Mallick and C. Modgil (eds) *Multicultural Education: The Interminable Debate.* Bristol, PA.: Falmer Press: 149–66.

McAndrew, M. (1995) La prise en compte de la diversité religieuse et culturelle en milieu scolaire: un module de formation à l'intention des gestionnaires. In F. Ouellet (ed.) *Les institutions face aux défis du pluralisme ethnoculturel: Expériences et projets d'intervention.* Québec: IQRC: 317–35.

Milot, M. (1991) *Une religion à transmettre? Le choix des parents.* Sainte-Foy: Les Presses de l'Université Laval.

Milot, M. (1995) L'école confessionnelle. *Revue Notre-Dame,* Québec: 1–13.

Milot, M. (1995a) École et religion: enjeux sociaux, culturels et éducatifs. In F. Ouellet (ed.) *Les institutions face aux défis du pluralisme ethnoculturel.* Québec: IQRC: 237–54.

Milot, M. and Ouellet, F. (1997) *Religion, éducation et démocratie. Un enseignement culturel de la religion est-il possible?* Montréal: Harmattan.

Ministère des Communautés Culturelles et de l'Immigration

(1990) *Au Québec pour bâtir ensemble. Document de réflexion.* Énoncé de politique en matière d'immigration et d'intégration.

Nicolet, M. (1987) Pédagogie interculturelle, identité des élèves et dynamique de la situation scolaire. In R. Dinello and A. N. Perret-Clermont (eds) *Psycho-pédagogie interculturelle.* Fribourg.

Noblet, P. (1993) Reconnaître ses minorités: l'expérience américaine. *Hommes et migration* 1169, Octobre: 39–44.

Ouellet, F. (1991) *L'éducation interculturelle: essai sur le contenu de la formation des maîtres.* Paris: L'Harmattan: 65–74.

Ouellet, F. (1992) L'éducation interculturelle: les risques d'effets pervers. In *L'interculturel: une question d'identité.* Québec: Musée de la civilisation: 61–108.

Ouellet, F. (1994) De la nécessité du détour en formation interculturelle. Le programme de l'Université de Sherbrooke, Communication présentée au congrès de l'ARIC, Saarebrücken, 21 p.

Ouellet, F. (1994a) Pour éviter les pièges du relativisme culturel. In F. R. Ouellette and C. Bariteau (eds) *Entre tradition et universalisme.* Québec: IQRC: 152–70.

Ouellet, F. (1995) Apprentissage en coopération et échec scolaire. In F. Ouellet (ed.) *Les institutions face aux défis du pluralisme ethnoculturel: expériences et projets d'intervention.* Québec: IQRC: 135–60.

Ouellet, F. (1995a) L'éducation religieuse à l'école: pour sortir de l'impasse. In F. Ouellet (ed.) *Les institutions face aux défis du pluralisme ethnoculturel: expériences et projets d'intervention.* Québec: IQRC: 255–71.

Ouellet, F. (1995b) L'enseignement religieux comme formation à la délibération démocratique: Communication présentée au congrès de la Société internationale de sociologie de la religion. Québec, 38 p.

Ouellet, F. (1995c) Pour développer la compétence professionnelle face aux défis de la pluriethnicité: Le diplôme et la maîtrise en formation intercultuelle de l'Université de Sherbrooke. In F. Ouellet (ed.) *Les institutions face aux défis du pluralisme ethnoculturel: expériences et projets d'intervention.* Québec: IQRC: 419–41.

Ouellet, F. (1996a) Faut-il encore enseigner la religion à l'école? *Relations,* Mars: 56–7.

Ouellet, F. (1996b) L'enseignement religieux à l'école face aux défis du pluralisme ethnoculture. In K. Fall, R. Hadj-Moussa and D. Simeoni (eds) *Les convergences culturelles dans les sociétés pluriethniques.* Ste-Foy: Presses de l'université du Québec: 219–37.

Ouellet, F. (1997) L'enseignement religieux culturel: une alternative valable à l'enseignement confessionnel? In M. Milot and F. Ouellet (eds) *Religion, éducation et démocratie. Un enseignement culturel de la religion est-il possible?* Montréal: Harmattan: 151–82.

Pagé M. (1992) Gouverner le pluralisme ethnoculturel par les institutions démocratiques. In M. Lavallée, F. Ouellet and F. Larose (eds) *Identité, culture et changement social,*

Actes du 3ᶜ congrès de l'ARIC. Paris: L'Harmattan: 113–25.

Pagé, M. (1994) Diversité culturelle et éducation au pluralisme. In K. Gürttler, M. Beer-toker and A. M. Folco (eds) *Culture ou Cultures?* Montréal: Centre d'études ethniques/Editions Images: 83–125.

Pagé, M. (1995) Un enseignement pluraliste de l'histoire aux clientèles scolaires pluriethniques. *Éducation et Francophonie* **23** (1): 35–40.

Pagé, M. (1996) Citoyenneté et pluralisme des valeurs. In F. Gagnon, M. McAndrew and M. Pagé (eds) *Pluralisme, citoyenneté et éducation*. Paris/Montréal: Harmattan: 165–88.

Pagé, M. (1993) *Courants d'idées actuels en éducation des clientèles scolaires multiethniques*. Conseil supérieur de l'éducation (Coll. Études et recherches).

Palmer, F. (ed.) (1986) *Anti-racism – An Assault on Education and Value*, London: The Sherwook Press.

Parekh, B. (1989) Britain and the social logic of pluralism. In *Britain: A Plural Society*. London: Commission for Racial Equality: 58–76.

Parekh, B. (1995) The cultural particularity of liberal democracy. In D. Held (ed.) *Prospects for Democracy*. London: Polity: 156–75.

Parekh, B. (1995) Politics of nationhood. In K. von Benda-Beckmann and M. Verkuyten (eds) *Nationalism, ethnicity and cultural identity in Europe*. Utrecht: Utrecht University: 122–43.

Pelletier, C. (1990) *L'apprentissage de la diversité au service de police de la communauté urbaine de Montréal*: Montréal: CIDIHCA.

Perotti, A. (1992) L'éducation interculturelle dans les expériences du Conseil de l'Europe. In E. Damiano (ed) *Verso una società interculturale: Pour une société interculturelle*. Bergamo: ACLI-CELIM: 54–61.

Perotti, A. (1994) The impact of the Council of Europe's recommendations on intercultural education in European school systems. *European Journal of Intercultural Studies* **5** (1).

Pourtois, H. (1993) La démocratie délibérative à l'épreuve du libéralisme politique. *Le défi du pluralisme*. *Lekton* **3** (2): 105–34.

Ravitch, D. (1990) Multiculturalism. E. Pluribus Plures. *American Scholar*: 337–54.

Simard, J.-J. (1988/1991) La révolution pluraliste. Une mutation du rapport de l'homme au monde. In F. Ouellet (ed.) *Pluralisme et l'école. Jalons pour une approche critique de la formation interculturelle des éducateurs*. Québec: IQRC: 23–55.

Simard, J.-J. (1991) Droits, minorités et identité. A l'arrière-plan de l'éducation interculturelle. In F. Ouellet and M. Pagé (eds) *Pluriethnicité, éducation, et société. Construire un espace commun*. Québec: IQRC: 155–97.

Sleeter, C. E. (1992) *Keeper of the American Dream: A Study of Staff Development and Multicultural Education*. Bristol, PA: Falmer Press.

Solomon, R. P. and Levine-Ratsky, C. (1994) *Accommodation and Resistance: Educators' Response to Multicultural and Anti-racist Education*. North York, Ont.: York University, Faculty of Education.

Spinner, J. (1994) *The Boundaries of Citizenship. Race, Ethnicity and Nationality in the Liberal State*. Baltimore and London: Johns Hopkins University Press.

Steele, S. (1990) *The Content of Our Character. A New Vision of Race in United States*. New York: St Martin's Press.

Taguieff, P. A. (1991) La lutte contre le racisme, par delà illusions et désillusions. In P. A. Taguieff (ed.) *Face au racisme I: Les moyens d'agir*, Paris: La Découverte: 11–43.

Tavares, T., Young, J. and Fitznor, L. (1995) Constructing an anti-racist professional development model: Manitoba's summer institute on education in a multicultural context. *Multicultural Teaching* **13** (2): 24–8.

Thérien, M. (1991) L'enseignement de la littérature dans un contexte pluraliste. In F. Ouellet and M. Pagé, *Pluriethnicité, éducation et société. Construire un espace commun*. Québec: IQRC: 453–67.

Wieviorka, M. (1991) *L'espace du racisme*. Paris: Le Seuil.

Wieviorka, M. (1993) *La démocratie à l'épreuve*. Paris: La Découverte.

18 A Black Hole for Values: Pupils with Problems and Teacher Education

PHILIP GARNER

Introduction

At the present time the teaching profession is under considerable attack from official government bodies, politicians and from theoreticians and pundits. The focus of this discontent has been a perceived failure, on the part of teachers, to address both the learning and the social needs of children. Criticism of the former is usually constructed as sweeping, often anecdotal, claims that 'standards' of academic attainment have fallen in schools. Those promoting such views have argued that pupils are performing less well than previously, particularly in crucial curriculum areas like English and mathematics. Levels of hysteria have been reached, particularly in the media, supported by right-of-centre political interest groups. The introduction of comparative statistics, purporting to demonstrate how English schoolchildren are falling behind their counterparts in certain parts of mainland Europe and Asia, has introduced an almost xenophobic air of concern to the matter.

At the same time, a number of recent events in or around schools, concerned or associated with problem behaviour, has served to add to the copious and ongoing level of public concern about standards of behaviour in schools. This is an issue which is 'as old as education itself and is never far from teachers' minds' (Varma 1993). In the last ten or so years, for example, there has been a huge increase in the amount of published material, both official and quasi-official, theoretical and practical, relating to how best to deal with that group of children who are now officially termed 'Pupils with Problems' (DfE 1994), and who are located, at best, 'on the margins' of formal, mainstream education (Lloyd-Smith and Davies 1996). There are calls for more Draconian punishment of even very young children, a heavier emphasis upon the exclusion from schools of children who repeatedly misbehave and the establishment of 'secure schools' for what some choose to see as 'hardened deviants'. In short, such children are no longer tolerated within the educational system, as starkly illustrated by the General Secretary of the NAS/UWT's opinion, expressed on the *News at Ten* (4 September 1996): 'I reject the notion that children have a right to an education at whatever school they choose' (*paraphrase*). This view, it should be noted, was put forward during a news item concerning a 'problem pupil' in a Nottinghamshire school.

In both cases, academic performance and unacceptable or anti-social behaviour by pupils, teachers – and frequently classroom or subject teachers and newly qualified teachers (NQTs) – take the brunt of the criticism. This is, of course, nothing new. Education has always been very much a party-political issue, upon which individual groups have sought to assume some kind of moral high ground using a supposed 'tough' stance on standards of achievement and discipline.

In the light of the foregoing I want to examine what I believe to be two axiomatic issues that are crucial to any debate on values in education and to the unenviable position that teachers are being placed in, concerning their work with 'pupils with problems'. In the next few pages, therefore, I wish to explore the relationship between the present organization and content of teacher education courses, alongside aspects of curriculum provision for one section of the special educational needs (SEN) population in schools – that group of children who are termed as having emotional and/or behavioural difficulties (EBD) and which form part of a relatively new generic category – 'pupils with problems'. I will argue, first, that teacher education courses at the present time offer nothing to their participating students in the way of opportunities or experiences relating to a 'social curriculum' for children and young people. I will then examine why such children require important curriculum adaptations and inputs, with specific reference to personal, social and life-skills, in order for them to obtain a more effective educational experience.

Underpinning this is a supporting argument that, in the present competence-driven climate of initial teaching education (ITE), insufficient numbers of NQTs are entering the profession with the requisite skills or understandings of the importance of such matters, and a commensurate ability to relate to disaffected children. Fundamentally, therefore, the debate in both spheres is about values – how we choose to construct teacher education courses, whether at ITE level or for their continuing professional development (CPD), and the nature of adapted curricula in primary, secondary and special schools for children whose behaviour is inclined to be chronically problematic.

The recent historical context: 'pupils with problems', curriculum alternatives and teacher education

In the 1980s public and professional concern regarding the unacceptable behaviour by some pupils in schools culminated in the publication of the Elton Report (DES 1989a), which examined the state of discipline in schools in England and Wales and set out a series of recommendations for action. In spite of its exhaustive treatment of the subject, the years following the Report have been evidenced both by continued, vigorous debate concerning the nature, cause and effects of problematic behaviour by some pupils in schools, the types of provision available and by various models of intervention.

Prior to Elton, both the Warnock Report (DES 1978) and the 1981 Education Act reinforced a view, and an operational reality, that little was being done to integrate EBD pupils. The period following the Act showed that, while considerable progress had been made in respect of pupils with moderate, or even severe, learning difficulties, relatively little was being done concerning those children whose learning difficulty was deemed to be associated with EBD (Swann 1991). An indication that the

education service as a whole was increasingly feeling either unwilling, or incapable, of meeting the complex needs of the EBD population during the period 1981–1988 is to be found in the continued high levels of exclusions of such children during that time (Blyth and Milner 1996).

The failure of mainstream education to deal effectively with 'pupils with problems' can be attributed to a number of factors. The perceptions and professional beliefs of teachers had been particularized by research conducted by Lowenstein (1975) which indicated that teachers were inclined to believe that incidents of severely aggressive behaviour were commonplace in schools other than their own (Armstrong and Galloway 1994). It is worth noting that Turkington (1986) argued that the 'disruptive pupil' was an invention of the media utilized by teacher unions in order to advance their claims for professional recognition. Whatever the validity of this observation, it remained apparent that, during the period leading to the Elton Report, teachers in mainstream schools were becoming more militant towards those children whose behaviour they viewed as unacceptable. One possible explanation for this state of affairs may be found in the increasing scrutiny (and frequent negative criticism) of teachers by politicians and others during this period (O'Hear 1988). Indeed, the Elton Report noted that 'the status of teachers has declined in recent years' (p. 12). Teachers became embattled and an increasing number were unable, because of their own low self-esteem, to empathize with the needs of the EBD population (Gurney 1990). Nor should it go unnoticed that a similar situation currently prevails, as witnessed by recent attacks on teacher education (Phillips 1996).

The good intentions of the Elton Report, however, were subsequently compromised by the so-called educational reforms pursuant to the 1988 Education Act. Three elements of the Act can be implicated in the failure of many schools to effectively implement Elton's recommendations relating to 'problem pupils'. First, central government's preoccupation with the establishment of a National Curriculum (NC), and the circus of assessment that accompanied it, has deflected much teacher attention away from 'social behaviour' as a central issue in learning. Indicative of this is that many teachers appear not to have heard of the Elton Report, and have been unaware of professional development initiatives resulting from funding made available to local education authorities (LEAs) for 'Elton training'. Given the pace of change and the innovation overload of the period, however, it is unsurprising that the findings of the Report were largely overlooked.

The 1988 Act also initiated both a devolution of centrally-held LEA resources to individual schools and the introduction of 'open enrolment', whereby parents (and children) were able to select the school of their choice. These developments combined to herald the arrival of overt competition between schools, both for pupils and the funds that accompanied them. In such an environment there are strong indications that many mainstream schools would be unwilling to accommodate behaviours in children that deviated from the norm, for fear of obtaining the reputation of a 'sink' school (Cooper 1993). As Armstrong and Galloway (op. cit.) put it, 'the very presence of large numbers of children with special needs, particularly where those needs arise from learning and/or behaviour difficulties, may be seen as harmful to a school's performance' (p. 186).

To these specific concerns may be added two more general factors. In terms of its demography, the SEN population in schools is spatially located in (principally) those parts of urban or metropolitan regions with high scores of indicators of disadvantage (Bash, Coulby and Jones 1985). Such schools, although they frequently have concentrations of pupils with EBD-related SENs, are often not well placed to respond to the needs of such students, whether by developing alternative curriculum provision for them or in terms of support work utilizing external agencies. Neither are they attractive to influential middle-class parents, whose children may be expected to be high-achievers in school. A second, closely related, factor is the high incidence of problematic school behaviour in children from socially and economically disadvantaged populations. Further, there is evidence that some groups, notably Afro-Caribbean children, have been disproportionately represented in recent statistics on exclusions (Parsons and Howlett 1996). Each factor implies that a 'cycle of disadvantage' (Rutter and Madge 1976) prevails, adding to the complexity of the task facing teachers in the post-Elton period.

Recommendations 4–7 of the Elton Report argued that the management of behaviour, and an awareness of issues associated with it, should become key criteria for the approval of all ITE courses. The recommendations for 'in-service training', or 'continuing professional development' (CPD) as it is now termed, were less forthright and

specific, although one of six areas for action to improve classroom management skills was identified as 'more specific in-service training' (p. 71). Recommendation 9, eschewing such a generalism, stated that 'the management of pupil behaviour should become a national priority for funding under the Local Education Authority Training Grants Scheme from 1990/91 until at least 1994/95' (p. 78). This was to ensure that the CPD needs of teachers working with 'pupils with problems' in all phases of education were met. Most recently, however, the TTA's proposals for the future of CPD funds contain scant mention of SEN, particularly, as Smith (1996) has observed, 'not even of those with "behavioural problems" about whom we hear so much'.

The Elton Report failed to emphasize the role that segregated special schools – for children who had been assessed as 'EBD' under the 1981 Act – could play in the preparation of new teachers. Few ITE courses are able to include a special school placement, because of constraints of time resulting from the move to school-based training. Nor do they appear to make good use of the wealth of expertise available in such schools, particularly in behaviour management, social skills training and adaptations of the NC to meet the needs of 'pupils with problems', the nature of which will be explored later in this chapter.

Subsequently, the recommendations for ITE contained in the Report have been acknowledged in Circulars 14/93 and 9/92, relating to primary and secondary courses respectively (DfE 1992, 1993). The Special Educational Needs Training Consortium (SENTC) has, however, noted an important discrepancy between the two. While 9/92 refers only to 'the ability to *identify* special educational needs' (my italics), 14/93 asserts the importance of 'the ability to *identify* and *provide for* [my italics] special educational needs' (SENTC 1996: 20). The ability of institutions of higher education (IHEs) to cover in detail aspects of behaviour management has, at the same time, been curtailed by the moves towards school-based training and recent research on the SEN experiences of newly qualified teachers suggesting that relatively little direct input is being obtained on matters relating to 'pupils with problems' (Garner 1996b).

The regulations concerning the approval of ITE courses do little to assuage this widespread fear. Circular 14/93, for example, makes explicit reference to the main priority of 'giving particular attention to knowledge of, and skills in teaching the core subjects of English, mathematics and science' (p. 6). The inclusion, within the Circular's main priorities, of the need for new teachers to be 'able to maintain order and discipline in their classrooms' is notable in its absence to any connecting reference to curriculum initiatives concerning social education.

It is also apparent that the current proposals for the establishment of a 'teacher education national curriculum' will be brought to fruition at a time when the tensions between what Lawton and Chitty (1988) refer to as the *bureaucratic* versus the *professional* approach to curriculum-building are all too apparent. They summarize the sharp difference between the two as follows:

> Whereas the professional approach focuses on the quality of the input and the skills, knowledge and awareness of the teacher, the bureaucratic approach concentrates on output and testing. Whereas the professional approach is based on individual differences and the learning process, the bureaucratic approach is associated with norms or bench-marks, norm-related criteria and judgements based on the expectations of how a statistically normal child should perform. Whereas the professional curriculum is concerned with areas of learning and experience, the bureaucratic curriculum is preoccupied with traditional subject boundaries. (p. 202)

Given the current orientation towards the latter, opportunities for the development of meaningful initiatives in the field of social education within reformulated ITE courses may be severely restricted.

Finally, and returning to the SENTC report, it is noteworthy that the competencies expected of teachers working with EBD pupils contain little mention of core NC subjects. Far more emphasis is placed on a pupil-centred approach, in which there is 'knowledge, skills and understanding of therapeutic strategies . . . to help pupils to develop new ways of thinking and strategies that will enable them to behave differently and develop self-esteem' (SENTC 1996: 69).

The pastoral curriculum for pupils with problems

Cooper, Smith and Upton (1994), in summarizing the post-Elton position concerning teacher educa-

tion and 'pupils with problems', state that

> Teachers in general are unprepared by their initial training, and by in-service training arrangements for dealing with emotional and behavioural difficulties . . . , and specialist teachers in the field have been shown to place their requirement for further training in the area high on their list of priorities.   (p. 3)

In a very large part this refers to both the curriculum that is offered to such children and the way in which it is delivered. A particularly important element of this is that part of the school curriculum that provides 'pupils with problems' opportunities to examine aspects of their own personal development – an area of activity which in the present section I will refer to as the 'pastoral curriculum'.

First, however, I want to make reference to the level of criticism directed at existing curricular provision offered for 'pupils with problems' by special schools and units for children with EBD. From the outset, it should be recognized that there is a view that special schools for EBD children are frequently regarded with suspicion and that their notable contribution in the field has been denigrated (Rimmer 1990), a matter not assisted by the absence of their involvement in ITE courses, as noted by Bovair (1993).

In 1989 Her Majesty's Inspectors (HMI) published a survey of provision for pupils with EBD (DES/HMI 1989b). The report summarized the findings of HMI resulting from their visits to seventy-six special schools and units in the period 1983–88. They were highly critical of the current state of provision. Their observations have been summarized by Laslett (1990) as 'a disquieting report, both in its content and its implications. It shows . . . [that] officers from local authorities, personnel from supporting services, and the staff of schools and units, are not meeting the needs of children with emotional and behavioural difficulties' (p. 108). HMI noted that

> there were examples of good practice to confirm that the educational needs of EBD children can in fact be met through good curricular planning, sound organizational arrangements and effective teaching. The evidence indicates that the difficulties in achieving this goal through the provision of small special schools and units are considerable' (HMI op. cit.: 14)

Off-site units, and the Pupil Referral Units (PRUs) established after 1994, represent a point at the middle of the provision-continuum for 'pupils with problems', located between mainstream and special schools. A major post-Elton development has been the regularization of this kind of provision. Prior to 1989 there was considerable evidence of its *ad hoc* nature, particularly in respect of referral procedures and the curriculum experienced by the young people (Blyth and Milner op. cit.). As a result, such units had 'distinct advantages over maladjusted schools . . . in that children can be placed in them without the embarrassing and delaying safeguards of special education procedures and with only minimal consultation with parents' (Bash et al. op. cit.: 116).

Circular 11/94, coyly entitled The education by LEAs of children otherwise than at school (DfE 1994), acknowledged Elton's warnings concerning the unsatisfactory nature of much off-site provision (p. 154) by placing the new PRUs on a firm statutory footing and by providing explicit guidelines concerning referral, curriculum and reintegration. This has led to some improvement in the functioning of such units (Normington and Boorman 1996), although Her Majesty's Chief Inspector (HMCI), maintains that 'Standards of attainment in the pupil referral units inspected thus far are variable, but generally too low' and that 'Overall the quality of teaching in the PRUs inspected fell below that found generally in mainstream primary and secondary schools' (HMCI 1995: 5). Although it is perhaps too early to assess the efficacy of PRUs their current situation, as outlined by HMCI, does appear depressingly reminiscent of the off-site units of the pre-Elton period (Garner 1996b).

This is not to say, however, that good work of a *pastoral* focus is not taking place in special schools and within mainstream schools. But such work has to function within a theoretical framework which makes some general, though often unspoken, assumptions about this process:

1 that education is a good thing;
2 that if it works properly, students will not only become literate and numerate, but will grow up as 'good' citizens;
3 that the inclusion of subjects such as 'civics', 'citizenship' and 'life skills' in the curriculum create good citizens in adult life.

How this is currently being done is a point at issue, and needs to be seen against a background of the prevailing belief-systems about education itself. The view of school as a place where children are

taught things within a clearly defined (usually hierarchical) social context by a group of suitably qualified adults has always been a simplistic one. Sociological analysis in education over the last twenty years has gradually revealed the interpersonal nature of school life, especially in the investigation of the 'hidden curriculum'. This has led, amongst other things, to a heightened awareness of the pupil's experience of schooling, and the role that this process plays in the development of attitudes and responses in later life. Moreover, the expansion of pastoral programmes in primary and secondary schools, as a means of generating new and positive attitudes to interpersonal relationships among pupils, is also seen as a means of promoting self esteem and the positive evaluation of others, particularly amongst disaffected pupils (Gurney op. cit.).

However, such a holistic approach to the promotion of acceptable behaviour, which relies on the pupil internalizing a particular set of values, has been seriously threatened by the demands of the National Curriculum, and its assessment. As Garner and Sandow (1993) have put it:

> PSE at any level is hardly assessable in attainment target terms: one can imagine perhaps ('Level 1: can recognise the difference between own and others' property'). Frankly, there is little time in the new framework for activities which cannot be assessed. They may feature in Records of Achievement . . . they are clearly perceived as peripheral to 'real education'. (p. 26)

Given the constraints of time in the post-1988 school curriculum, referred to earlier, it is likely that pastoral programmes are more inclined to adopt a conventional, information-giving approach, where the content, pedagogy and rules are adult determined and involve the identification of very clear instructions for daily behaviour. In addition, such an approach is often reinforced by the hidden curriculum of the school, as it is perceived by 'pupils with problems'. Often, for example, 'codes of conduct' and 'behaviour policies' are rule-governed and hierarchical, allowing no input or decision-making by pupils. Excluded from these events, the oppositional stance of some 'pupils with problems' is simply reinforced.

One example of this system of beliefs about both pedagogy and content within a pastoral curriculum is demonstrated in the *Police School Liaison Pack*. Its aims are identified as:

- To inform schools and pupils about the role of the police.
- To inform about the law and the rights and duties of citizens.
- To make young people aware of dangers.
- To help foster crime prevention.

This approach depends on the belief that instruction or information giving is conceptually linked to outcomes, as in 'If I know that I will go to jail, I will not drive away this car which does not belong to me'. Rhodes and Jason (1988) suggest that some adolescents may find that the information presented in some programmes of pastoral education contradicts their own experiences. These authors use examples of the failure of anti-drugs publicity that attempts to shock the observer into rejecting drugs. Adolescent youth are 'risk-takers', and use of illegal substances are seen by many 'pupils with problems' as an integral part of an oppositional, risk-taking subculture (Berman and Noble 1993). Top-down pedagogical approaches, often by those who the pupils most distrust, is likely to be ineffective.

What I am suggesting, therefore, is the existence of important tensions between educational programmes that enshrine the aims and expectations of society in general, and of official bodies in particular, and the needs and expectations of 'pupils with problems' themselves. This paradox can be exemplified by two excerpts from '*Police in Schools*' (1986). Here, conflicting rhetoric can be identified. On the one hand there is an emphasis upon dialogue and shared meanings: 'A main objective of the Schools Involvement Programme is to create an opportunity for dialogue between police and pupils' (p. 13), while, on the other, a more traditional view of pedagogy: 'To help with presentations general information sheets should be provided for each of the topics covered by the three main themes of the Schools Programme' (p. 13). 'Pupils with problems' could therefore perceive the process as an external rather than an internal one.

The *Education for Citizenship* guidance from the NCC (1990) provides another example, suggesting on the one hand that 'Pupils' own experiences provide the starting point in education for citizenship' (p. 15), whilst at the same time maintaining that 'The contribution of the Police Service is of the greatest importance' (p. 13). It may be that, using this kind of approach, difficulties will arise in formulating and delivering initiatives which attempt to reach 'pupils with problems', as it is this group which finds it hardest to examine their own experience productively, and because they tend to have a built in distrust of authority, and especially of the police.

Such approaches contrast sharply with the progressive concept of rooting children's education in their own emerging ideas and constructs and generates a very different view of social learning. It depends absolutely on basing the discussion in the experience of the students. Typically, such an approach may involve 'pupils with problems' originating their own rules for classroom behaviour and incorporate such approaches as esteem-building exercises, explorations of personal motives for behaving in a certain way and a wide range of pastoral care initiatives. Stevenson (1991) has argued that such approaches are especially applicable to that section of the school population that may be operating on the fringes of delinquent crime. What should be noted is that this way of working is hardly new. Tutt (1978), for example, has long advocated this kind of pastoral focus in Intermediate Treatment Units, whereby individuals are encouraged to identify the points in a sequence of events where a 'wrong' decision leads to anti-social or criminal behaviour.

Even those school-based approaches that are nominally rooted in a 'bottom-up' pedagogy may be perceived by 'pupils with problems' as implicitly supporting the *status quo*. If this is the case, it may be further argued that such programmes may be unable to reach that section of the school population which is most prone to problem behaviour. Moreover, if the content and pedagogy of social education remains fixed in the bureaucratic model explicated by Lawton and Chitty (op. cit.), the impact of even what minimal pastoral programmes remain after the onset of the NC may be severely curtailed.

A curriculum alternative: justification and rationale

Having identified both the failure of teacher education courses to provide much in the way of input regarding the 'pastoral curriculum', and the widespread failure of pastoral-based curriculum interventions in schools, I wish to conclude with a rationale for the development of alternative approaches with 'pupils with problems'. Marchant

(1995) has argued that 'the essential core curriculum for pupils experiencing emotional and behavioural difficulties is the expression of their own feelings and emotions to facilitate greater control over their own lives' (p.46) and goes on to state that 'The provision of a formal, academic, curriculum is of only secondary importance ... An official recognition of this aspect of social learning is contained in the inspection framework for schools' (OFSTED 1995), in which inspectors have to indicate the degree to which a school is promoting self-discipline and the development of self-esteem.

Over fifty years ago, the School Health regulations of 1945, in defining the term 'maladjusted pupil', stated that these were children who 'require special educational treatment in order to effect their personal, social or education readjustment'. Such 'readjustment', according to Laslett (1977) is unlikely to be achieved by 'teaching the same subjects as the ordinary school rather differently with different teachers'.

At a later date Laslett went on to argue that it is success in the 'social curriculum' that underpins any academic progression within National Curriculum subjects. He maintains that 'these other successes come about through achievements the children make in forming and sustaining successful relationships with others, and in changing unsatisfactory patterns of behaviour' (p. 111), adding the telling remark that 'I am not certain at all that this learning can be encompassed within the (*formal*) curriculum' (Laslett, 1990, op cit).

Later, Lang offered a broad validation of the importance of pastoral care programmes in the context of a whole curriculum, arguing that 'through such provision and the resulting promotion of positive school climate and ethos, not only will the healthy personal development of all pupils be encouraged but problems of pupil disaffection and disruption ameliorated' (Lang 1990: 94–5). In making this observation, Lang is presenting a challenge to traditional curriculum interpretations, and there are grounds for optimism that the official response may eventually be able to accommodate this approach. The most recent publication from the School Curriculum and Assessment Authority (SCAA), for example, has recognized the importance of an adjusted, or even alternative, version of the standard NC. Thus, it states that pupils with SEN 'may require additional, possibly specialist activities, to support their development, such as:

aspects of personal, social and health education, including independence and study skills' (SCAA 1996: 6). Whilst making no specific mention of 'pupils with problems', this can at least be used by those working with such pupils as an enabling and justifying statement for their adoption of curricular variations. Such encouragement, however, remains starkly absent in the subsequent DfEE publication concerning the education and training of 14–19 year olds (DfEE, 1996), precisely the age-range for the occurrence of most problem behaviour. While the Education Secretary, in her foreword, states that this document 'sharpens our commitment to a more coherent and effective framework for learning *in all its forms*' (my emphasis), there is a striking omission of any reference to the social needs of 'pupils with problems'.

Conclusion

In the post-1988 era of curriculum imposition, it may well be worth noting G. K. Galbraith's observation, quoted by Storm (1973), that 'Just as truth ultimately serves to create a consensus, so in the short run does acceptability. Ideas come to be organized around what the community as a whole or particular audiences find acceptable' (p. 113). We have to recognize that what occurs in schools, just as what takes place in prisons, does so with the consent of the pupils. An arbitrary, fixed curriculum is unlikely to meet real pupil need, and it is likely that those in schools who are the most disaffected – pupils with problems – will be the first to offer resistance.

References

Armstrong, D. and Galloway, D. (1994) Special educational needs and problem behaviour: making policy in the classroom. In S. Riddell and S. Brown (eds) *Special Educational Needs Policy in the 1990s.* London: Routledge.

Bash, L., Coulby, D. and Jones, C. (1985) *Urban Schooling: Theory and Practice.* Eastbourne: Holt, Rinehart and Winston.

Berman, S. and Noble, E. (1993) Childhood antecedents of substance misuse: *Current Opinion in Psychiatry,* **6**: 382–7.

Blyth, E. and Milner, J. (1996) *Exclusion from School.* London: Routledge.

Bovair, K. (1993) A Role for the Special School. In J. Visser and G. Upton (eds) *Special Education in Britain after Warnock*. London: David Fulton.

Cooper, P. (1993) *Effective Schools for Disaffected Students*. London: Routledge.

Cooper, P., Smith, C. and Upton, G. (1994) *Emotional and Behavioural Difficulties*. London: Routledge.

Department of Education and Science (1978) *Special Educational Needs. Report of the Committee of Enquiry into the Education of Handicapped Children and Young People*. London: HMSO.

Department of Education and Science (1989a) *Discipline in Schools*. London: HMSO.

Department of Education and Science (1989b) *Special Schools for Pupils with Emotional and Behavioural Difficulties* (Circular 23/89). London: HMSO.

Department for Education (1992) *The Initial Training of Secondary School Teachers: New Criteria for Courses* (Circular 9/93). London: DfE.

Department for Education (1993) *The Initial Training of Primary School Teachers: New Criteria for Courses* (Circular 14/93). London: DfE.

Department for Education (1994) *Pupils with Problems* (Circulars 8/94–13/94). London: DfE.

Department for Education and Employment (1996) *Learning to Compete: Education and Training for 14–19 Year Olds*. London: HMSO.

Garner, P. and Sandow, S. (1993) Can education prevent crime? *Pastoral Care in Education*. **11** (4): 25–9.

Garner, P. (1996a) A special education? The experiences of Newly Qualifying Teachers during training. *British Educational Research Journal* **20** (2): 155–63.

Garner, P. (1996b) A la Recherche du temps perdu: case-study evidence from off-site and Pupil Referral Units. *Children and Society* **10** (3): 187–96.

Gurney, P. (1990) The enhancement of self-esteem in junior classrooms. In J. Docking (ed.) *Education and Alienation in the Junior School*. Basingstoke: The Falmer Press.

Her Majesty's Chief Inspector (1995) *Pupil Referral Units. The First Twelve Inspections*. London: OFSTED.

Lang, P. (1990) Responding to disaffection: talking about pastoral care in the primary school. In J. Docking (ed.) *Education and Alienation in the Junior School*. Basingstoke: The Falmer Press.

Lawton, D. and Chitty, C. (eds) (1988) *The National Curriculum*. The Bedford Way Papers. London: London University, Institute of Education.

Laslett, R. (1977) *Educating Maladjusted Children*. London: Crosby, Lockwood and Staples.

Laslett, R. (1990) 'Could Do Better'. Maladjustment and Therapeutic Education **8** (2), 107–111.

Lloyd-Smith, M. and Davies, J. (1996) *On the Margins. The Educational Experience of 'Problem' Pupils*. Stoke-on-Trent: Trentham Books.

Lowenstein, L. (1975) *Violent and Disruptive Behaviour in Schools*. Hemel Hempstead: NAS/UWT.

Marchant, S. (1995) The essential curriculum for pupils exhibiting emotional and behavioural difficulties. *Therapeutic Care and Education* **4** (2): 36–47.

Metropolitan Police Schools Involvement Programme (1986) *Police in Schools*. London: Metropolitan Police.

National Curriculum Council (1990) *Education for Citizenship* (Curriculum Guidance 8). York: NCC.

Normington, J. and Boorman, B. (1996) Development, procedures and good practice at Westfields Education Provision, Kirklees. *Support for Learning* **11** (4): 170–2.

OFSTED (1995) *Handbook for the Inspection of Special Schools*. London: HMSO.

O'Hear, A. (1988) *Who Teaches the Teachers?* London: Social Affairs Unit.

Parsons, C. and Howlett, K. (1996) Permanent exclusions from school: a case where society is failing its children. *Support for Learning* **11** (3): 109–12.

Phillips, M. (1996) Back to school – To be de-educated. *Observer*, Sunday, 8 September: 14–15.

Rhodes, J. and Jason, L. (1988) *Preventing Substance Abuse Among Children and Adolescents*. Oxford: Pergamon.

Rimmer, A. (1990) Death of a school. *Therapeutic Care and Education* **1** (1): 53–9.

Rutter, M. and Madge, N. (1976) *Cycles of Disadvantage*. London: Heinemann.

School Curriculum and Assessment Authority (1996) *Supporting Pupils with Special Educational Needs*. London: SCAA.

Special Educational Needs Training Consortium (1996) *Professional Development to Meet Special Educational Needs*. Stafford: SENTC.

Smith, C. (1996) SEN – forgotten again? *British Journal of Special Education* **23** (4): 204.

Stevenson, D. (1991) Deviant students as a collective resource in classroom control. *Sociology of Education* **64**: 127–33.

Storm, M. (1973) The community and the curriculum. In I. Lister (ed.) *Deschooling*. Cambridge: Cambridge University Press.

Swann, W. (1991) Marching backwards towards selection. *British Journal of Special Education* **18** (3): 96.

Turkington, R. (1986) *In Search of the Disruptive Pupil: Problem Behaviour in Secondary Schools 1959–1982*. Unpublished PhD thesis. Department of Sociology, University of Leeds.

Tutt, N. (1978) *Alternative Strategies for Coping with Crime*. Oxford: Blackwell.

Varma, V. (ed.) (1993) *Management of Behaviour in Schools*. London: Longman.

19 Crass Materialism: A Crucial Value Education Issue
A descriptive study of pre-service teachers' values

RHETT DIESSNER

[There is a] cancerous materialism, born originally in Europe, carried to excess in the North American continent, contaminating the Asiatic peoples and nations, spreading its ominous tentacles to the borders of Africa, and [is] now invading its very heart . . .
> (Shoghi Effendi 1954/1965: 124–5)

A host of social scientists, psychologists, sociologists and economists have recognized the grave problems of crass materialism: from Erich Fromm in *To Have or to Be?* (1976); to Tibor Scitovsky in *The Joyless Economy* (1992); to Paul Wachtel in *The Poverty of Affluence* (1989); to Duane Elgin in *Voluntary Simplicity* (1993); and to David Myers in *The Pursuit of Happiness* (1992), the call has been sounded. Ronald Inglehart's (1971, 1977, 1990) research into the dangers of materialism spanned eight European nations (Germany, Belgium, Italy, France, Switzerland, Denmark, The Netherlands, and Ireland; 1977), and later included Japan (1981). It is a problem that is encountered, to varying degrees, in all nations and cultures on earth.

'Crass materialism' is defined herein as the inordinate, or excessive, valuing of material objects and activities. This includes valuing material objects and activities as an end in themselves; it also implies a hierarchical valuing of material objects and activities over the emotional, intellectual, psychological or spiritual needs of others and/or the self. Crass materialism may be seen in such behaviours and attitudes as possessiveness, covetousness, envy, non-generosity, hedonism, acquisitiveness, and greed. We will review the empirical literature that indicates crass materialism to be a serious problem, followed by a review of citations on crass materialism from the sacred literature of a variety of the world's religions. It is hoped that this will then establish the meaningfulness of the study to empiricists and rationalists, atheists, agnostics, and deists.

The problem

Review of the empirical literature regarding crass materialism

There are significant, scientifically documented relationships between a variety of personal and social ills and crass materialism. For example, the more strongly an individual endorses materialistic values, the more likely it is that he or she will express general unhappiness, racial prejudice, sexism, criminal behaviour, and drug abuse.

A variety of data-based studies have linked materialism to a deterioration of general happiness and to lessened self-fulfillment. In a summary of four studies, with a total of 834 subjects, Richins and Dawson (1992) found that people with higher levels of materialism were significantly less satisfied with their lives than those who scored lower on their materialism scale, including lower self-esteem as measured by the Rosenberg (1965) scale.

Belk (1985, 1992) has examined materialism through a questionnaire with subscales for envy, possessiveness, and non-generosity. His two studies, with samples that are multi-generational (cross-sectional) and Ns of 386 and 99, both demonstrated that the higher subjects scored on these three subscales, the less likely they were to report themselves as being happy. Additionally, Ger and Belk (1996) administered this same materialism scale to convenience samples of business majors and MBAs in twelve different countries (France,

Germany, India, Israel, New Zealand, Romania, Sweden, Thailand, Turkey, Ukraine, UK, and USA). Their study helped further establish the multi-cultural problem of materialism, by demonstrating worrisome materialism levels in samples from South East Asia, Eastern and Western Europe, North America, the Middle East, and the Pacific.

That violence and race prejudice are closely tied to economic indices and crass materialism has been described by Hovland and Sears (1940; viz. Hepworth and West 1988). It is characteristic that the very definition of 'racism' as a social phenomenon includes the systematic economic oppression of one group of people by another (cf. Rutstein 1993). As issues of ethnic strife remain problematic all around the world, teachers whose attitudes are conducive to racial harmony in the classroom become increasingly important. Additionally, Inglehart's multi-nation research (1971, 1977, 1990) has shown that those who place greater importance on post-materialist attitudes than on materialist attitudes tend to have less racial and gender prejudice and more concern with personal and societal development. As racial prejudice is one of the most central issues in the disruption of the peace of a pluralistic society, this connection between materialism and racism is highly salient.

Much sexism has been attributed to the belief that women are not as materially valuable as men (Hoffman and Hurst 1990). UNESCO estimates that women produce two-thirds of all the work hours on our planet; yet they receive only 10 per cent of the total compensation and own about 1 per cent of the planet's property. On the American scene, the roots of sexism in materialism are documented in a telling book, *Why Women Pay More* (Whittelsey 1993).

A variety of studies has linked materialism with violence, crime, delinquency, and the proliferation of illegal drugs. For instance, Greenberg (1988) found that materialist attitudes were associated with criminal behaviour among both young adult prison inmates and among teenage delinquents. Other empirical studies demonstrate the causal aspect of materialism in drug-dealers' choice of profession (Adler and Adler 1983), and the correlation of materialistic aspirations with marijuana abuse (Picou, Wells, and Miranne 1980). A clever empirical study by Summers and Morin (1995) indicates that materialism discourages the demilitarization that may help prevent war.

Review of crass materialism from the scriptures of various world religions

The following are representative samples from the sacred scriptures of world religions that indicate the problematic nature of crass materialism.

In Hinduism, it states in the *Bhagavad Gita* (Mascaro 1962), 'What power is it, Krishna, that drives man to act sinfully . . .? It is greedy desire . . . the great evil, the sum of destruction: this is the enemy of the soul' (3:36–37). 'Set thy heart upon thy work, but never on its reward. Work not for a reward' (2:47). '[G]enerosity, . . . austerity . . . renunciation, . . . peace from greedy cravings . . . – these are the treasures of the man who is born for heaven' (16:1–3).

From Judaism, the second book of Moses, *Exodus* (Bible, n.d.), it states, in the classic Ten Commandments, 'Thou shalt not covet thy neighbor's house . . . nor any thing that is thy neighbor's' (20:17). In the fifth book of Moses, *Deuteronomy*, it states, 'I command thee, saying, Thou shalt open thine hand wide unto thy brother, the poor, and to thy need, in thy land' (15:11). And in the *Psalms* of King David it is recorded, 'if riches increase, set not your heart upon them' (62:10).

In the Buddhist text, the *Dhammapada* (Raja 1956), we find, 'There one shall strive to find happiness; leaving off all pleasures, owning nothing, the learned person shall purge himself of all mental afflictions' (vi:13). 'Those who have not amassed wealth . . . whose goal is liberation from this void . . . his position is difficult to trace like that of birds in the sky' (vii:3). 'Let us live very happy, we who own nothing. Let us become enjoyers of contentment, like the luminous gods' (xv:4).

From the sixth chapter of the Christian text (Bible, n.d.), *The Gospel According to St. Luke*: 'Blessed be ye poor: for yours is the kingdom of God' (20). 'But woe unto you that are rich' (24)! 'Give to every man that asketh of thee; and of him that taketh away thy goods ask them not again' (30). And from the ninth chapter, 'For what is a man advantaged, if he gain the whole world, and lose himself, or be cast away?' (25) From the nineteenth chapter of *The Gospel According to St. Matthew*, comes the famous verses, 'Then said Jesus unto his disciples, Verily I say unto you, That a rich man shall hardly enter into the kingdom of heaven. And again I say unto you, It is easier for a camel to go through the eye of a needle, than for a rich man to enter into the kingdom of God' (23–24).

In the *Qur'an* of Islam (Muhammad 1955), from the *Surah of Repentance*, 'Those who treasure up gold and silver, and do not expend them in the way of God – give them the good tidings of a painful chastisement' (9:34). From the *Surah of Mutual Fraud*, 'And whosoever is guarded against the avarice of his own soul, those – they are the prosperers' (64:16). And from the *Surah of The Hypocrites*, 'O believers, let not your possessions . . . divert you from God's remembrance; whoso does that, they are the losers' (63:9).

From the Bahá'í Faith, Bahá'u'lláh, in his *Hidden Words* (1975) states, 'Busy not thyself with this world, for with fire we test the gold, and with gold we test our servants' (AHW: 55).

Educators and materialistic values

Of particular concern is the role of teachers in regard to the moral development of their students in the context of crass materialism. If crass materialism is the serious problem that it appears to be, then any role that teachers have in disseminating materialism is worrisome. It is well established in the empirical literature that the behaviours, attitudes, and values that are modelled before us, have a large influence upon us (Bandura 1977, 1986, Rokeach 1973, Ball-Rokeach, Rokeach and Grube 1984). Because teachers' values, in particular, are modelled in front of the 'next generation', for so many meaningful hours each day, teachers' potential to influence students' materialistic, or moral, values is enormous (Giroux and Purpel 1983, Goodlad, Soder and Sirotnik 1990).

Therefore we investigated teachers' levels of materialism. This is a report of a descriptive study; we are not formally testing any particular hypotheses nor attempting to falsify any particular null hypotheses. The meaning of our descriptive results will be discussed.

Method

Subjects

Fifty participants were selected from among the declared teacher education majors at Lewis-Clark State College in Lewiston, Idaho in the Fall of 1996. Forty-five of those fifty were randomly selected; as few males were included in the random sample, five quasi-randomly selected males were added to the sample, thus giving a sample that included thirty-eight females and twelve males. Forty-eight of the fifty selected 'European-American' as their ethnic background, one identified herself as 'Hispanic' and one identified herself as '¼ Native American and ¾ European-American'. The mean cumulative grade point average was identified as 3.5 (s.d. = 0.4), on a scale of 4; seven were sophomores, fourteen were juniors, twenty-six were seniors, and three were post-baccalaureate (seeking teaching certification); the mean age of the participants was 25.5 years (s.d. = 6.8). Twenty-eight identified themselves as followers of some Christian faith, and twenty-two indicated they did not belong to any religion.

Instruments

'The Checklist of Needs' (CN) (Diessner et al. 1996a, 1996b) lists twenty popular material objects, and requests the respondent to mark each item that they believe they *need* (cf. Ger and Belk 1996; for construct validity cf. Braybrooke 1987). A total score from 0 to 20 is possible. The CN has been shown to have moderate predictive validity for materialistic behaviour and attitudes and high test–retest reliability ($r = .92$) (Diessner et al. 1996b).

The 'Structural Level of Needs' (SLN) (Diessner et al. 1996a, 1996b) includes seven open-ended 'why' questions that the subjects responded to in writing. The first question examines the subject's own definition of what 'needs' are, and the other six questions are keyed to Maslow's Hierarchy of Needs. The responses to the questions were then analyzed using general neo-Piagetian stage-scoring technique (cf. Colby and Kohlberg 1987, Kegan 1982, Commons and Richards 1984). The SLN has been shown to have mild predictive validity for materialism and moderate inter-rater reliability (90 per cent within $\frac{1}{2}$ stage; 70 per cent within $\frac{1}{5}$ stage) (Diessner et al. 1996b).

The participants also completed a written version of the *Moral Judgement Interview* (MJI) (Colby and Kohlberg 1987). The MJI presents participants with three standardized hypothetical moral dilemmas. Responses are then stage-scored based on a neo-Piagetian theory of the development of moral reasoning structure (Kohlberg 1984; Colby and Kohlberg 1987). The MJI has established levels of inter-rater, test–retest, alternate form and internal consistency reliability; as well as construct and predictive validity (Colby and Kohlberg 1987).

The *Defining Issues Test* (DIT) is based on Kohlberg's stage theory of moral reasoning (Rest 1979, 1986, 1990). Whereas the MJI uses three dilemmas on a form and asks for the subject's spontaneous production of responses, the DIT uses six dilemmas and a multiple choice format of selecting responses. The choices following each dilemma represent the range of Kohlberg's stages and have been equalized in length and complexity of vocabulary. The most widely used and validated summary score of the DIT is the P per cent score. The P per cent score represents the relative importance that the subject imparts to morally principled responses to the six presented dilemmas, and can range from 0 to 95. In other words, if a subject has twenty opportunities to select principled responses, and does so ten times, the subject will receive a score of 50. Rest (1986, 1990) reports that junior high students' average P per cent scores are in the 20s; high school students in the 30s; college students in the 40s; graduate students in the 50s; and philosophers of ethics in the 60s. The DIT has established levels of test-retest (high .70s and .80s) and internal consistency (.70s for Cronbach's alpha) reliability; as well as construct and predictive validity (Rest 1979, 1986).

The Belk materialism scales (Belk, 1984, 1985, 1992) in their latest form (Ger and Belk, 1996) utilize a 21-item Likert scale with four subscales: a) non-generosity, b) possessiveness, c) envy, and d) preservation (collecting mementoes). The Belk (1984) scales used a variety of validation methods, including behavioural self-report that examined the number of gifts they had received versus given, and the number of items borrowed versus loaned, to validate the non-generosity subscale. Belk also calculated the number of photographs carried in their subjects' wallets to correlate with possessiveness, and the number of magazines read that concerned the lives or possessions of famous people to correlate with envy. They also obtained samples of forty photographs taken by each subject to analyze for themes of non-generosity, envy, and possessiveness. Generally their validation studies demonstrated positive and significant correlations. Additionally, Belk (1984) negatively and significantly correlated two paper and pencil measures of happiness (Gurin, Veroff and Feld 1960, Bradburn and Caplovitz 1965) with three of his materialism subscales (non-generosity, envy, possessiveness). Test–retest

reliability was reported as 0.68 and Cronbach's alpha as 0.66–0.73 (Belk 1984).

Richins and Dawson's *Consumer Values Orientation for Materialism* scale (1992) was administered to all participants. It is an 18-item Likert scale, containing three subscales, confirmed by factor analysis: a) acquisition centrality, b) acquisition as the pursuit of happiness, and c) possession-defined success. In a summary of four studies, with a total of 834 subjects, Richins and Dawson (1992) found that people with higher levels of materialism were significantly less satisfied with their lives than those who scored lower on their materialism scale. Their *Consumer Values Orientation for Materialism* scale has been validated with a variety of approaches, although they are all paper-and-pencil measures. Their validation samples included randomly chosen households who received mailings of their measure in cities of the American West and Northeast, for a total responding N of over 700. To validate their measure, they correlated its materialism score with responses to such questions as 'what level of annual income would satisfy your needs?', and 'how would you spend an unexpected $20,000?', finding that the subjects' materialism scores were positively and significantly correlated with the greater amount of income they said they needed, and amount of the $20,000 that they kept for themselves. Their materialism scale also showed significant negative correlations with a) a measure of voluntary simplicity (Leonard-Barton 1981), b) a measure of life satisfaction (Andrews and Withey 1976), and a measure of self-esteem (Rosenberg 1965). The test–retest reliability was .87 at a 3-week interval, and the coefficient alpha ranged from .80 to .88.

The *Postmaterialist Value Index* (Inglehart, 1971, 1977, 1990) differentiates material, or physical, values from non-physical, or 'post-material' values, based on Maslow's hierarchy of needs (1970). Material values are focused on our need for 'things' that maintain and keep safe our physical being. Post-material values are directed to our need for psychological and social well-being, as expressed in our valuing of belonging, esteem, self-actualization, and transcendence. Inglehart's (1971, 1977, 1990) research has shown that those who place greater importance on post-materialist attitudes than on materialist attitudes tend to have less racial and gender prejudice and more concern with personal and societal development. The survey instrument presents twelve statements that are ranked for preference by the respondent; half of which represent materialist attitudes and half post-materialist. Test–retest results between the earlier 4-item scale and the later 12-item scale show an r = .6–.7 (Inglehart 1977).

Procedures

Individual appointments were made with the subjects, during which time, in about 90 minutes, they completed the following. First they completed a demography form, and then they signed permission forms to be sent to the three informants that they had selected (close friends or family) to complete a modified Belk materialism scale about the subject. Next they wrote their definition of 'need', completed the 'Checklist of Needs', wrote their responses to questions from the 'Structural Level of Needs' interview (analysis of which included their written definition of need).

Next they completed the 'Chequebook Questionnaire'. They were given a structured guide sheet that had them look through every entry in their cheque book for the months of July, August and September 1995, and record on the sheet any expenditures that they considered generally altruistic, specifically including any 1) donations to charities, 2) donations to religious organizations, or 3) other 'do-gooder' expenditures. Following that, they were asked to record, for the same time period, their altruistic contributions in cash or in 'kind' or in 'services', and to estimate their worth in US dollars.

They then completed the *Moral Judgement Interview*, written format (Colby and Kohlberg 1987). Finally, they left the interview session with uncompleted copies of the other instruments, described in the *Instruments* section above, and a date agreed upon by which they would return them. Upon return of the completed instruments, a voucher for an honorarium of $50 US, was submitted in their name, which they received as a cheque a few weeks later.

The three informants that each subject selected from among their close friends and family, 'who knew them well', were then sent their signed permission form, a letter by the principal investigator assuring them of confidentiality, a modified copy of the Belk materialism scales (1984, 1985), and a stamped envelope addressed to the principal investigator. No more than one form was sent per household. The Belk scale was only modified to indicate that it was being completed about the subject, and not about the informant. The return rate was high: 135 of the 150 were returned, and achieving at least two returned Belk scales per subject. The two or three forms were averaged for each subject.

Results and discussion

We will briefly present the quantitative results, and put them in some context to increase their meaningfulness.

1. The checklist of needs (CN)

A total score from 0 to 20 is possible, the higher the score, the more needs were claimed. The range was 0–16, mean = 7.6, s.d. = 3.8, and the median = 8.5. It has been argued previously (Diessner et al. 1996b) that an important way to understand materialism is to investigate what people think is a 'need' versus a 'luxury'. It has been demonstrated that the greater the number of needs one claims on the CN, the more materialistic one appears on the Belk materialism scales, as completed by one's friends and family ($p = 0.57$) (ibid.).

2. The structural level of needs (SLN)

The range was stage 2/3 to stage 3/4: two participants were scored 2/3; thirty-two were scored stage 3; and nine were scored stage 3/4. See the next paragraph below.

3. Moral judgement interview (MJI)

The range in stage was 3 to 5; twelve participants were scored stage 3 Interpersonal; thirty-two at stage 3/4 Transitional; four at stage 4 Systemic; and one at stage 5 Principled. The SLN was intended to offer a neo-Piagetian stage score, similar to the MJI. As can be seen, the SLN tend to score the participants about $\frac{1}{2}$ stage lower than the MJI, but they are not statistically significantly correlated ($r = .17$, $p = .27$; Diessner et al. 1996a and b). In a review (Diessner 1994) of MJI studies it was shown that in four out of five published studies with in-service teachers as subjects, stage 3/4 transitional was most typical; and in the only MJI study with pre-service teachers indicated a mean score at stage 3. It thus seems likely that these forty-nine education majors studied in this report were typical in their moral reasoning, and perhaps advanced one $\frac{1}{2}$ stage.

4. *The defining issues test (DIT)*

The P per cent score represents the relative importance that the subject imparts to morally principled responses to the six presented dilemmas, and can range from 0 to 95. There were forty-seven usable DITs; one participant did not complete it, and two were unusable. The range of P scores was 20–78, with a mean = 40.7 (s.d. = 13.4), and a median of 41.7. In a review of thirty DIT studies with in-service and pre-service teachers (Diessner 1994), undergraduates in education showed a range of P per cent group mean scores from the 30s to the 40s. Again, the forty-nine subjects in the study reported here are in the typical range, but perhaps on the high end.

5. *The Belk materialism scales*

A subject's overall Belk materialism score could range from a low of 21 (not materialistic) to 105 (very materialistic). Of the forty-nine participants completing a Belk scale, the range of scores was from 36 to 75; the mean was 54.7 (s.d. = 8.48); and the median = 55.0. Ger and Belk (1996) gave this same scale to convenience samples of business majors and MBAs in twelve different countries: a) Romania, M = 63.13 (N = 69), b) USA, M = 61.12 (N = 228), c) New Zealand, M = 60.54 (N = 60.54), d) Ukraine, M = 59.86 (N = 81), e) Germany, M = 59.16 (N = 103), f) Turkey, M = 59.12 (N = 357), g) Israel, M = 58.88 (N = 56), h) Thailand, M = 58.25 (N = 107), i) India, M = 57.74 (N = 31), j) UK, M = 56.54 (N = 91), k) France, M = 56.47 (N = 47), and l) Sweden, M = 53.21 (N = 70). Cautiously, however, it appears that this sample of American education majors may be less materialistic than business majors in eleven of the twelve nation samples above.

The idea that education majors would be less materialistic than business majors or MBAs, fits 'common sense'. Yet, what does a raw score of 54.7 imply for our sample? On a 21-item Likert scale coded from strongly agree (5), agree (4), neutral

(3), disagree (2), strongly disagree (1), it implies that the participants disagreed (*not* strongly disagreed) with about half of the materialistic statements, and were either neutral or did not disagree with the other half of the materialistic statements. This is worrisome.

6. *Informants' Belk scales*

Two or three friends and family members confidentially completed a Belk scale concerning each of forty-nine of our participants. The two or three completed scales were averaged, thus a subject's overall Informants' Belk materialism score could range from a low of 21 (not materialistic) to 105 (very materialistic). The informants' reports showed a mean of 53.0 (s.d. = 5.97), and a median of 52.30. The subjects' self-reported scores (referred to above) demonstrated a mean of 54.7 (s.d. = 8.48), having a strong correlation with the informants' reports (r = .42, p = .003) and showing a non-significant difference between means.

7. *Richins and Dawson's consumer values orientation for materialism scale*

The possible range of scores on this scale is a low of 18 (not materialistic) to a score of 90 (very materialistic). Of the forty-seven participants with usable scales in our study, the mean score was 51.3 (s.d. = 5.2). In Richins and Dawson's validation studies (1992) they mailed the scale to large random samples in two cities in the American West and one in the American Northeast, with return rates from the low 30 per cents to the low 40 per cents. Their results: mean = 47.9 (s.d. = 10.2; N = 250); mean = 46.7 (s.d. = 8.3; N = 235); mean = 45.9 (s.d. = 9.8; N = 205). Of concern is that the education majors' mean materialism score was higher than the mean scores of these random samples.

As noted with the Belk scales above, on a 5-point Likert scale, a raw score of 51.3 is worrying; it implies that if these education majors 'disagreed' (but *not* strongly disagreed) with half the materialistic items, they were then either neutral or agreed with half the materialistic views presented. As an aside, the Belk scales and the *Consumer Values Orientation for Materialism* correlated at r = .35 (p = .015).

8. *The post-materialist value index*

This scale is based on a ranking system; if a participant chose items that represent Maslow's upper hierarchy of needs (social and self-actualizing needs) over items that represent the lower end of the hierarchy (physical and safety needs), they are coded as a 'post-materialist'. If they select the materialist needs over the post-materialist needs they are coded a 'materialist'. If they sometimes choose post-materialist needs and sometimes materialist needs, they are coded 'mixed'.

In the sample reported here, there were three materialists, twenty-six post-materialists, and twenty mixed. The fact that slightly more than half these education majors were not materialistic on this scale, is encouraging; that forty per cent of the sample were 'waffling', and are partially materialistic, and that six per cent were frankly materialistic, is worrisome.

9. *Cheque book questionnaire*

Participants perused their cheque book while in the interview session and recorded their altruistic expenditures during the 3-month period (July–September 1995). The number of cheques written range from none (twenty-seven participants) to fourteen (one participant), with a mean of 1.1 (s.d. 2.26) and median of zero. The number of *different* recipients of cheque entries, per participant, ranged from none to five (one participant), with a mean of 0.72 (s.d. 0.99) and a median of zero. In this context, 'different' refers to different organizations or persons in need, thus if someone wrote two cheques to the Foodbank and three to their church, their score would be '2'.

The gross amount of altruistic expenditures during these 3 months ranged from none to $US 397.00, with a mean of $30.90 (s.d. $70.54) and a median of zero. A weighted gross amount was also calculated. The participants had recorded their yearly income on the demography sheet in one of five categories (under 10,000 = 1; 10–20,000 = 2; 20–35,000 = 3; 35–50,000 = 4; 50,000+ = 5). The weighted amount then gave a range of 0 to $US 397.00, with a mean of $17.14 (s.d. 57.33) and a median of zero.

Besides the more objective cheque book review, the participants were also asked to record the worth of their non-cheque altruistic contributions (cash, in-kind, services). In this case the number entries

for this 3-month period ranged from none (fourteen participants) to twelve (one participant), with a mean of 1.64 (s.d. 2.09) and a median of 1.0. The number of *different* recipients of non-cheque entries, per participant, ranged from none to seven (one participant), with a mean of 1.24 (s.d. 1.22) and a median of 1.0.

The gross amount of non-cheque altruistic expenditures during these 3 months ranged from 0 to $US 360.00, with a mean of $32.98 (s.d. $66.25) and a median of $5.00. A weighted gross amount was also calculated. The participants had recorded their yearly income on the demography sheet in one of five categories (under 10,000 = 1; 10–20,000 = 2; 20–35,000 = 3; 35–50,000 = 4; 50,000+ = 5). The weighted amount than gave a range of none to $US 245.00, with a mean of $18.82 (s.d. 43.14) and a median of $2.00.

A combined cheque book plus non-cheque altruistic expenditures were combined for the following results. The number of separate donations ranged from none (eight participants) to fifteen (two participants), with a mean of 2.76 (s.d. 3.19); 'different' recipients ranged from none to fourteen, mean of 1.22 (s.d. 2.26); gross amount ranged from 0 to $US 407.00, mean $63.88 (s.d. 94.70); and gross weighted amount ranged from 0 to $407.00, mean $35.92 (s.d. 71.86).

To summarize: over a 3-month period these pre-service teachers, with an average age of 25 years, wrote one cheque, for about $30.00 to any kind of charity (charity, religious organization, or generally altruistic service). Twenty-seven of the fifty participants reported that they wrote no cheques for any altruistic reason.

It looked somewhat better in the non-cheque donation category. Fourteen participants reported that they gave no cash, or goods, or services, but that means thirty-six did. Thus the average was giving one and one half times during that 3-month period, with a mean amount valued at $32.00. These data suffer from the problems that 'self-report' data have; in particular one might worry that a 'social desirability' factor might be in play. The fact that the reported levels of giving were fairly low, however, makes this even more worrying.

Conclusion

In summary, we have reviewed the evils of materialism in a variety of cross-national, cross-cultural studies. This demonstrated that materialism is intimately involved in some of the biggest road-blocks to a peaceful, pluralistic, multi-cultural society: racism, sexism, drug abuse, violence, and nationalism. For further cross-cultural validation of the problem of materialism the sacred writings of Hinduism, Judaism, Buddhism, Christianity, Islam, and Bahá'í were briefly presented on this topic. The influence of teachers modelling materialistic or non-materialistic values was pointed out. The initial results of describing the levels of materialism of a sample of pre-service teachers was then presented, demonstrating some cause for worry. If we can believe the host of researchers and social commentators (Fromm 1976, Scitovsky 1992, Wachtel 1989, Elgin 1993, Myers 1992, Inglehart 1971, 1977, 1990), our world is dangerously materialistic, and the empirical data show teachers to be typical of the rest of society in terms of their level of materialism, we have serious cause of concern for the future.

This chapter will conclude by conceptually differentiating 'materialism' from 'moral interaction with the material world'. As stated in the outset of this chapter, 'crass materialism' is defined herein as the inordinate, or excessive, valuing of material objects and activities. This includes valuing material objects and activities as an end in themselves; it also implies a hierarchical valuing of material objects and activities over the emotional, intellectual, psychological or spiritual needs of others and/or the self. Crass materialism may be seen in such behaviours and attitudes as possessiveness, covetousness, envy, non-generosity, hedonism, acquisitiveness, and greed. In terms of moral development and moral education, materialism is an evil. Yet, it is not meant to imply that the material world is an evil, nor is interaction with the material world. In particular, interaction with the material world that is in service to the development of others, or the self, is virtuous. The just distribution of material goods is virtuous; arranging the material world to bring forth order and/or beauty is virtuous; studying the material world to produce knowledge and truth is virtuous, etc.

In particular, the focus has been upon education majors, future teachers, because it is so important that students learn to value an education for more than material reasons. So often we hear teachers urge their students to study with the rationale that studying leads to high paying employment. It is not meant to imply that economic success is bad or wrong. The concern is that a material emphasis on education lowers the moral value of the education. If we urged students to learn so that they could be more effective peacemakers, better able to enjoy and appreciate a world of beauty, and better able to love and serve others, perhaps some of the evils associated with materialism, would decline.

Acknowledgement

The author acknowledges a grant from the Higher Education Research Council of the State Board of Education, Idaho, USA, which made this research possible. This paper is based on research first presented at the Association for Moral Education conference, Ottawa, Ontario, November, 1996.

References

Adler, P. A. and Adler, P. (1983) Shifts and oscillations in deviant careers: the case of upper-level drug dealers and smugglers. *Social Problems* 31: 195–207.

Andrews, F. M. and Withey, S. B. (1976) *Social Indicators of Well-being: Americans' Perceptions of Life Quality.* New York: Plenum.

Bahá'u'lláh. (1975) *The Hidden Words of Bahá'u'lláh* (trans. Shoghi Effendi). Wilmette, IL: Bahá'í Publishing Trust.

Bandura, A. (1977) *Social Learning Theory.* Englewood Cliffs, NJ: Prentice-Hall.

Bandura, A. (1986) *Social Foundations of Thought and Action: A Social-Cognitive Theory.* Englewood Cliffs, NJ: Prentice-Hall.

Ball-Rokeach, S., Rokeach, M. and Grube, J. (1984) *The Great American Value Test.* New York: Free Press.

Belk, R. W. (1984) Three scales to measure constructs related to materialism: reliability, validity, and relationships to measures of happiness. In Thomas Kinnear (ed.) *Advances in Consumer Research*, vol. VII: 291–7. Provo, UT: Association for Consumer Research.

Belk, R. W. (1985) Materialism: trait aspects of living in the material world. *Journal of Consumer Research* 12: 265–80.

Belk, R. W. (1992) Attachment to possessions. *Human Behavior and Environment: Advances in Theory and Research* 12: 37–62.

Bible (n.d.) *The Holy Bible.* King James Version. NY: World Publishing Co.

Bradburn, N. M. and Caplovitz, D. (1965) *Report on Happiness.* Chicago: Aldine.

Braybrooke, D. (1987) *Meeting Needs.* Princeton: Princeton University Press.

Colby, A. and Kohlberg, L. (eds) (1987) The measurement of moral judgment. Volume I: *Theoretical Foundations and Research Validation.* New York: Cambridge University Press.

Commons, M. and Richards, F. A. (1984) A general model of stage theory. In Commons, M. L., Richards, F. A. and Armon, C. (eds) *Beyond Formal Operations*. New York: Praeger.

Diessner, R. (1994) *Moral Reasoning, Teacher Education and Ideological Critique*. Lewiston, ID: Lewis-Clark State College, Division of Education.

Diessner, R., Mayton, D., Washburn, K., Burklund, B., Murphy, J. and Peters, D. (1996a) *Crass Materialism: The 'root of all evil'*. A presentation at the annual meeting of the Association for Moral Education, Ottawa, Ontario.

Diessner, R., Mayton, D., Washburn, K., Burklund, B., Murphy, J. and Peters, D. (1996b) *Crass Materialism: Validation Studies of a Checklist and Stage-Structural Measure*. Manuscript submitted for publication.

Elgin, D. (1991, revised edn) *Voluntary Simplicity. Toward a Way of Life that is Outwardly Simple, Inwardly Rich*. New York: Quill (William Morrow).

Fromm, E. (1976) *To Have or to Be?* San Francisco: Harper and Row.

Ger, G. and Belk, R. W. (1996) Cross-cultural differences in materialism. *Journal of Economic Psychology*, **17**: 55–77.

Giroux, H. and Purpel, D. (1983) *The Hidden Curriculum and Moral Education*. Berkeley: McCutchan.

Goodlad, J. I., Soder, R. and Sirotnik, K. A. (eds) (1990) *The Moral Dimensions of Teaching*. San Francisco: Jossey-Bass.

Greenberg, N. (1988) Moderating the material aspirations of criminals and delinquents. *Journal of Offender Counseling, Services and Rehabilitation* **13**: 193–209.

Gurin, G., Veroff, J. and Feld, S. (1960) *Americans View their Mental Health*. New York: Basic Books.

Hepworth, J. T. and West, S. G. (1988) Lynching and the economy: a time series reanalysis of Hovland and Sears (1940) *Journal of Personality and Social Psychology* **55**: 238–47.

Hoffman, C. and Hurst, N. (1990) Gender stereotypes: perception or rationalization? *Journal of Personality and Social Psychology* **58**: 197–208.

Hovland, C. I. and Sears, R. R. (1940) Minor studies in aggression: VI. Correlation of lynching with economic indices. *The Journal of Psychology* **9**: 301–10.

Inglehart, R. (1971) The silent revolution in Europe: inter-generational change in post-industrial societies. *The American Political Science Review* **65**: 991–1017.

Inglehart, R. (1977) *The Silent Revolution. Changing Value and Political Styles Among Western Publics*. Princeton: Princeton University Press.

Inglehart, R. (1981) Post-materialism in an environment of insecurity. *The American Political Science Review* **75**: 880–900.

Inglehart, R. (1990). *Culture Shift in Advanced Industrial Society*. Princeton: Princeton University Press.

Kegan, R. (1982) *The Evolving Self: Problem and Process in Human Development*. Cambridge, MA: Harvard University Press.

Kohlberg, L. (1984) *The Psychology of Moral Development*. San Francisco: Harper and Row.

Leonard-Barton, D. (1981) Voluntary simplicity lifestyles and energy conservation. *Journal of Consumer Research* **8**: 243–52.

Mascaro, J. (1962) *The Bhagavad Gita* (trans. Juan Mascaro). Middlesex: Penguin.

Muhammad. (1955) *The Koran Interpreted* (trans. A. J. Arberry). NY: Collier.

Myers, D. (1992) *The Pursuit of Happiness. Discovering the Pathway to Fulfillment, Well-being, and Enduring Personal Joy*. New York: Avon Books.

Picou, J. S., Wells, R. H. and Miranne, A. C. (1980) Marijuana use, occupational success values and materialistic orientations of university students: A research note. *Adolescence* **15**: 529–34.

Raja, C. K. (1956) *Dhammapada* (trans. C. K. Raja). Madras: The Theosophical Publishing House.

Rest, J. R. (1979) *Development in Judging Moral Issues*. Minneapolis: University of Minnesota Press.

Rest, J. R. (1986) *Moral Development*. New York: Praeger.

Rest, J. R. (1990) *DIT Manual* (third ed.). Minneapolis: Center for the Study of Ethical Development.

Rokeach, M. (1973) *The Nature of Human Values*. New York: Free Press.

Rokeach, M. and Cochrane, R. (1972) Self-confrontation and confrontation with another as determinants of long-term value change. *Journal of Applied Social Psychology* **2**(4): 283–92.

Richins, M. L. and Dawson, S. (1992) A consumer values orientation for materialism and its measurement: scale development and validation. *Journal of Consumer Research* **19**: 303–16.

Rosenberg, M. (1965) *Society and the Adolescent Self-image*. Princeton: Princeton University Press.

Rutstein, N. (1993) *Healing Racism in America*. Springfield, MA: Whitcomb Publishing.

Scitovsky, T. (1992) *The Joyless Economy* (revised edn). NY: Oxford University Press.

Shoghi Effendi (1965) *Citadel of Faith. Messages to America 1947–1957*. Wilmette, IL: Bahá'í Publishing Trust. (From a letter originally published in 1954.)

Summers, C. and Morin, S. (1995) Politics and ethics in post-cold war demilitarization: empirical evidence for decision traps and value tradeoffs. *Peace and Conflict: Journal of Peace Psychology* **1**: 343–64.

Wachtel, P. L. (1989) *The Poverty of Affluence. A Psychological Portrait of the American Way of Life*. Philadelphia: New Society Publishers.

Whittelsey, F. D. (1993) *Why Women Pay More*. Washington, DC: Center for Study of Responsive Law.

20 Seeking a Value Consensus for Education

BRIAN V. HILL

This chapter discusses work in progress in Western Australia on developing Values Outcome Statements (VOSs) for the school curriculum. Since other chapters describe the more detailed curriculum development that has resulted, the present emphasis will be more on the social and philosophical dimensions of the project.

The immediate trigger for the project was dissatisfaction in Australia, particularly amongst non-government schools, with a 'National Curriculum' published in 1993. On the face of it, values education as such fared very badly in this curriculum, prompting a Western Australian consortium of educational leaders in the non-government sector to seek funding to review this situation. Significant grants with a potential three-year life were received from the NPDP, the federally funded National Professional Development Program.[1]

Initial research in 1994 confirmed the paucity of attention to values in the National Curriculum. In the meantime, changing balances of power at the political level led to most states objecting to what was seen as an imposition from central government, and several states developed their own statements, albeit in the first instance mostly virtual clones of the national one. By 'curriculum', I shall be referring hereafter to the State Curriculum of Western Australia, since that is the level at which the consortium developed its response, although the argument would be essentially no different for the National Curriculum.

The consortium decided it would first have to develop an 'Agreed Minimum Values Framework', on the basis of which curriculum materials could then be developed to fill the gap. These things have been done. Currently, teachers' kits are being trialled in over thirty schools; half of them, surprisingly, in the government sector. Philosophical and

classroom evaluation has been proceeding at all stages.

The project is best described as interdisciplinary action research, in that it has depended on a 'praxis' cycle of reflection and analysis followed by classroom practice, followed by further reflection intended to lead to further modifications of practice. This cycle may also serve as a model for the structure of the present chapter. That is, I will begin by summarizing the philosophical and political climate that prompted the exercise. Second, I will explain the way in which a Values Framework was developed and applied. Third, I will reflect on the issues that this process has highlighted, as a step towards doing it better in future when the consortium of stakeholders is expanded.

A climate of values in confusion

In almost every sphere of public life, modern industrialized societies are facing what Habermas has called a 'crisis of legitimation' (Habermas, 1975). Earlier societies operated within shared communities of meaning that validated a wide range of joint activities, including commerce, law, education, health care, science, and the arts. Few people were conscious of any need to make explicit the communal values on which such activities were predicated.

Indeed, they would have been as bemused then as most people still would be today to be told that their lives were largely defined by the grand narrative of the Enlightenment, albeit moderated at some points by pre-modern religious traditions. Within the academy, however, this explanation now has the status of a truism. The postmodernist critique is exposing, and contributing to, the crumbling of the foundations of modernism[2], whether of epistemology, morality or the very ontology of the self.

Which is not to say that debate on how we should live or what we should value has stalled or gone out of fashion. It is a peculiar irony of our time that while on the one hand value relativism is being zealously propagated by many academics and practised, less reflectively, by ordinary people, various absolutist value-stances are simultaneously being publicly commended, often by the same people, on behalf of such causes as nuclear disarmament, environmentalism, animal liberation, anti-racism, and radical feminism.

Meanwhile, some of the pre-modern narratives such as Christianity and some other world religions continue to enlist support amongst a surprising number of people, not only in contemporary pre-modern societies but also in modern ones. Some postmodernists are having to recycle Marx's prediction that religion would wither away, since modernity did not confirm it. Furthermore, even those who are consciously opting for a postmodern lifestyle, which forswears any ultimate concern and embraces pragmatic self-development and temporary attachments, often find themselves drawn into the quest for ultimate meanings and values by existential challenges ranging from civil war, ill-health, and retrenchment, to the collapse of close relationships or even, simply, the birth of offspring.

In fact, the discipline that, far more than religion, has been in danger of withering away under the onslaught of modernism has been philosophical ethics. In the early part of this century normative ethical approaches were being eroded by positivism, and for a time the focus of the discipline became metaethics (Frankena 1963). One attempt to restore interest in the justification of substantive ethical values appealed to the formal requirements of moral discourse (cf. Griffiths 1967, Hill 1972b), and more recent attempts have emphasized ways of life in specific communities (MacIntyre 1988, Singer 1993). Such attempts have to some degree reinstated the discipline as a quest, if not for ultimates, at least for constants.

Yet all this has happened just when modern societies, thanks to secularization (Lyon 1985) and massive cross-cultural migrations, have become profoundly pluralized. Such societies are therefore in a state of deep values confusion. What makes the situation even more serious is that the technical values central to the economic rationalism, which in many societies now occupy the middle ground by default, are proving quite inadequate to keep the peace and maintain social structures.

Are we past the eleventh hour?

One possible remedy would be to step up social regulation to minimize the incidence of deviant behaviours. But it is an illusion to suppose that every aspect of human behaviour can be brought under regulation, thereby removing the need to appeal to agreed values at a more voluntary level. It was the height of positivist arrogance, for example, for B. F. Skinner (1971) to say: 'Our job is not to make people good but to make them behave well' (see Hill 1972a).

As the postmodernist critique has shown, we do not all live in the same social reality. Rather, we bring to our interactions with other people a perception of that reality which has been constructed in our consciousness by a unique range of influences and choices. Certainly, contrary to what the social determinists maintain, we *are* capable of entering into negotiations on agreed rights and courses of action, and such negotiations do affect conduct. But we never come to the negotiating table without prior commitments.

In addition, it is always possible that the negotiators will be solely motivated to advance their own interests, even though inauthenticity of this kind fractures the bonds of community. Indeed, another commonly noted feature of postmodernizing societies is the splintering off of sub-groups and the tendency towards self-indulgent individualism (Lyon 1994). This is not all due to differences in consciously held ideologies, of course. The consumerism and niche marketing that are inherent in capitalistic forms of commerce push us in the same direction.

In reaction to such trends, a rhetoric is developing in several Western countries which calls for a revaluation of the values that underlie national life. There is renewed talk about citizenship education and the promotion of interpersonal values (e.g. Lawrence 1996, Civics Expert Group 1994). The relation between such rhetoric and the postmodernist critique, however, is ambivalent.

On the one hand, postmodernism draws attention to the rights of interest groups formerly disenfranchised by the cultural hegemony of certain privileged narratives (see the argument advanced by

Martin 1993). Now is actually a good time to renegotiate the social consensus, because it is harder for any one interest group to pull rank on the others. Postmodernism endorses pluralism.

On the other hand, however, postmodernism appears to exclude the possibility of common agreement because it also endorses relativism. It points to great divergencies between people's world-views and perceptions of reality, implying that any agreement will privilege the strong against the weak, or, at best, the many against the few. Classic democratic theory has struggled with this paradox for years.

Perhaps we have gone beyond the eleventh hour, and all that can be salvaged is the protection of the most basic individual rights by legal provisions. But even those rights are in dispute. Does one privilege whales over fishermen, or economic deregulation over welfare provision, or freedom of the press over national security?

Is agreement possible? This is not the sort of question that can be answered empirically, at least not yet. Some consider that the twin factors of cultural relativism and pluralism doom the attempt in advance. Others say that it has not yet been tried under postmodern conditions – that is, under conditions that pose a minimal threat to personal and sub-group reality constructions while attempting to maximize agreement on principles of practical cooperation.

For the moment at least, then, we are in dialogue about basic assumptions, not disputing the facts. The present project, for example, relies on the assumption that it is possible, in the nature of things, to achieve a useful measure of agreement about values. How this might be obtained will be described in a moment.

The political climate

A word about the political climate in Australia, which provided the moment of opportunity for this project. The present author, having written philosophically about issues in values education for many years (e.g. Hill 1973, 1991), has often wondered why he bothered, given the incoherent and apparently immovable attachment of Australian state schools to the policy of alleged value neutrality. But this cornerstone, always unstable, began to crumble in the early 1990s as a result of increasing concern about the direction of public education.

Australia is arguably at one and the same time one of the most secular *and* one of the most multicultural societies on the face of the earth. Distrust of authority, both political and religious, has been ingrained since the era of convict transportation. Meanwhile, migration since the Second World War has brought in a large number of non-British communities from Europe, and more recently from Asia. And with the emergence of the European Union and the industrial giants of Asia, Australia has also had to restructure its economy to relate more effectively to its neighbours around the Pacific Rim.

The 1980s were a time of loosening moral consensus, growing police corruption and greedy entrepreneurialism, leading to sobering business crashes and exposés in the 1990s. It began to become fashionable, to a degree not previously experienced in Australian history, to talk about the need for new directions.

In the first instance, as I mentioned earlier, this led State and Federal ministers of education to collaborate in the development of a 'National Curriculum' (Schools Council 1992). That this exercise was primarily driven by economic rationalist motivations was most clearly evident in its commitment to itemizing 'student outcome statements'. The focus was on cognitive content and skills, with values outcomes in short supply.

By contrast, a separate initiative from the Prime Minister's office resulted, slightly later, in a report on 'civics and citizenship education' (Civics Expert Group 1994), which bemoaned the paucity of attention to citizenship goals and values. The irony of the juxtaposition of these two government initiatives appears to have been lost on the politicians. But at least it has become fashionable to raise the question of values education in current curriculum debate.

Initiating the enquiry

Disquiet about the poverty of value outcomes in the West Australian Curriculum prompted a submission for teacher development funds to investigate the status of values education in the curriculum. The applicant consortium was convened by Dr Tom Wallace, coordinator for Anglican schools in Western Australia. The initial partners were the Anglican, Catholic, Islamic and Jewish school systems. I was approached by this group to be an academic consultant.

The first step involved a philosophical analysis of the curriculum (reported in more detail in Hill 1995). It was noted that some value statements appeared in the Curriculum Frameworks, but even these awakened few echoes in the Assessment Profiles allegedly derived from them. At the most generous estimate, out of more than 860 outcome statements spread across the eight 'Key Learning Areas' of the curriculum, only sixty referred explicitly either to processes of value analysis or to particular preferred values, and their random occurrences prevented any coherent pattern emerging.

Analysis at a deeper level revealed a preference for conformist, parochial outcomes stressing enhancement of the skills base available to the nation. The underlying view of learning was behaviouristic and atomistic, rather than holistic or personal. Some existing outcome statements were susceptible to modification to bring out more clearly their relevance to values education, but, at the least, extensive supplementation seemed to be called for.

Negotiating a framework

Before such detailed work could be done, however, it was felt that an attempt should be made to set down those values on which the consortium partners were prepared to agree. They had in common, of course, religious starting points – indeed, all were theistic in their ultimate beliefs. But historically their traditions have frequently been in bitter dispute with each other. This pilot study would be a severe test of the basic assumption that a useful level of agreement could be reached by the means adopted.

It was decided that, first, an approach loosely modelled on the 'Delphi' technique (see Linstone and Turoff 1975, O'Brien 1978) would be used. The project officer, Peter Havel, invited representatives to draft sets of model value statements, providing some examples of his own to get them started. He suggested that responses be grouped in a three-by-three matrix, distinguishing along one axis ultimate, democratic and educational values, and along the other values associated with the individual, society and the natural world. At this stage the respondents were urged to speak for their own traditions, but with a view to being comprehensible to the general public.

As might have been expected, the responses were quite disparate in content. A small working group then looked for common elements, and filled out the matrix with appropriate value statements. One modification of the taxonomy suggested by the first round of responses was to add a column for values associated with 'Life Perspectives', as shown in Figure 20.1. The integrated framework was then taken back to the respondents for further reactions. As it turned out, little further modification was required because agreement was reached gratifyingly quickly.

This was probably due in part to the fact that certain reassurances were given to participants during this phase of the exercise. It may be useful to present these as a set, though some of them actually evolved *en passant* in response to the reactions of some participants.

1 *The purpose of the exercise was not to develop a complete account to which all participants would be expected to conform, but a minimal set of agreements on which to base common action in the wider educational arena.*

Participants were initially invited to draw up submissions to the project which included their own distinctive values. Since the present exercise, however, was aimed at finding common ground for the more limited purpose of acting together in wider democratic forums, the proposed agreed statement drew from them only those elements agreeable to all. This enabled the participants both to do a service to the wider community while at the same time protecting their own commitment to values education from being devalued by that community. The State Curriculum had caused apprehension at precisely this point.

	Life perspectives	Individual	Society	Natural world
Ultimate values				
Democratic values				
Educational values				

Figure 20.1 The values matrix

2   *The category of ultimate values was included to (a) endorse the view that democratic and educational values tend to derive from people's ultimate commitments, while (b) allowing that we do not have to achieve agreement at the ultimate level before agreeing at the democratic and educational levels on the basis of proximate reasons.*

The inclusion of a band referred to as ultimate values was as much a heuristic device as a philosophical statement. It enabled participants to own and affirm their distinctive values while engaging in democratic dialogue with people of other persuasions. It reassured them that they remained free to expand the Framework categories in their own schools, consistent with continuing to honour the agreements reached in the Agreed Minimum Values Framework.

However, it was not necessary to insist on acceptance of their different world-views as justifications for whatever democratic values were agreed upon by the wider constituency. Jacques Maritain, having been involved in early discussions at the United Nations, once usefully distinguished between justifications at an ultimate level, which tend to integrate an individual's life-view, and those at a practical level, relating to what is required to enable people to work together in a democratic milieu (Maritain 1951: 112–13, 1958: 41–62). The present Framework was meant to be a contribution to defining, not the total good, but the common good.[3] In the actual words of the Preamble to the Framework (Values Review Project 1995: 7):

At a minimum, democracy consists of a society in which all people have equal rights to participate in the political process, while exercising the freedom to live as they choose, provided they do not infringe [on] the right of others to do the same. Democracy is therefore a procedural notion, not an ultimate vision for living. For this reason, people with differing ultimate values may be prepared to accept a number of values whose practical justification is the maintenance of a viable democratic state and sustainable environment, though they might have different ultimate reasons for being prepared to endorse these values.

3   *There was scope, in the listing of educational values, to go beyond the conditions required purely for the maintenance of a democratic society, and to incorporate such substantive visions of human creativity, fraternity and responsibility for the*

environment as people were prepared to agree upon.

Education would be impoverished if its *raison d'être* were confined to the criteria of rationality and democracy. The category of educational values provided scope to expand the notion of the human good on the basis of negotiation amongst people of goodwill from a variety of different ideological backgrounds. The proof of the pudding, of course, would be in the eating.

4   *Any such framework of values had to be regarded as provisional, part of its value residing in the very fact that it constituted a continuing agenda for dialogue on values in society and its schools, and provided one model for pursuing that dialogue.*

This principle again served a heuristic as well as a philosophical purpose. It enabled the project to move on to the next stage. As a consensus document, the wording of particular entries in the Framework was sometimes a compromise between philosophical consistency and a particular consortium partner's cherished wording. It may also be disputed whether some value statements were located in the parts of the matrix most appropriate to them, and there were overlaps.

At a practical level, this was all to the good. Too perfect a Framework might well discourage critical re-evaluation. Clearly, the dialogue must continue. Such dialogues need to be replayed with each new generation of staff, parents and students, for only in this way will such charters be owned by those who work under them. The most important thing was to ensure that, as far as possible, the statements included were clear enough to suggest specific curriculum outcomes to aim for. This would be 'where the rubber hit the road'. The next stage of the project was therefore crucial. Could the Framework be translated into usable guidelines for teachers?

An audit by teachers

The next stage, which went on during 1995, drew a number of classroom teachers into two kinds of audits, guided by the Values Framework. The first asked teachers to nominate which values in the framework were particularly relevant to their specialist curriculum area, and then to indicate the extent to which they felt the State Curriculum catered for these intentions.

The second invited another pilot group of teachers across the eight curriculum areas to submit samples of lessons, programmes and worksheets which illustrated ways in which the nominated values could be woven into their practice. This provided not only feedback valuable for the next phase, but materials that would serve as models and practical suggestions for teachers and for teacher development briefings, when the dissemination phase of the project came on line. Not the least exciting aspect of the audits was the growing enthusiasm of teachers to be involved in the project. They, at least, sensed that the rubber was actually hitting the road.

Developing Values Outcome Statements

A further phase involved an expert group of teachers and consultants drawing the threads together in the compilation of a bank of explicit values outcome statements in each curriculum area. After a workshop discussing the audits and procedures for drafting such statements, the participants went away to work either alone or in pairs for a short period, bringing back to a later workshop proposals which were evaluated and refined within the larger group.

In some cases, these proposals involved rewording existing outcome statements in the curriculum to make explicit the values outcomes which were implicit in them. In other cases, they constituted new additions to the set. In more than one area, the curriculum had provided no values outcome statements at all, implying that for assessment purposes the area was only concerned with knowledge and skills. Always a nonsense, such an assumption was particularly pernicious in the case of what Australians call 'LOTE', that is, learning a language other than English.

Some particular guidelines were developed to assist in the process of writing outcome statements, as illustrated in Figure 20.2. At the time of writing, this was the point the project had reached. The kits for teacher development had begun to move out into schools, the supplementary proposal on values outcome statements had become a bargaining chip in public discussion.

Whether the public sector is prepared to embrace the model of negotiation represented by the Agreed Minimum Values Framework, and the augmentation of State Curriculum requirements represented by the supplementary proposal is yet to be seen.[4] The fact remains that several possibilities have been demonstrated, and the non-government schooling sector has made a significant contribution to the public debate, apart from servicing its own schools and teachers in a new way.

Philosophical reflections

I have described the initial thinking which brought the present project into being, including problematic cultural changes and specific political initiatives. I then described the path of research and development which the project has so far followed. Two things remain to be done. One is to see if the general procedure can be broadened to a client-group wider than the original consortium, even to the extent of providing a model for action in the government sector. This will be ongoing.

The other task, in terms of our original research model, is to draw back from the action that has been initiated and to reflect as philosophically as we may on the procedures followed. There is space only to make the following four points.

1. *Presuppositional betting*

I pointed out in the beginning that no research proceeds without basic assumptions which themselves are not finally verifiable from within the model they give rise to. This has been particularly so in relation to the assumption that in our present cultural situation it is possible to achieve a sufficient consensus amongst the stakeholders to enable the compilation and educational implementation of value charters to proceed.

As is usually the case with basic assumptions underlying a general research paradigm, this one is not finally verifiable or falsifiable, because it will always be possible, in the case of a failed experiment, to say that the wrong methods were used and another approach should be devised. As to those who, more pessimistically, work from a contrary assumption that society is now too relativized for it to succeed, the burden of proof is on them to show that acting on their belief will not conduce to the very kinds of socially disabling fragmentation and segregation that such research as this is trying to avert.

1   Each VOS should imply assessment of capacity, not personal commitment.

2   Each VOS should be no more than one simple sentence, dealing with one specific area of knowledge, or specific skill or capacity.

3   Each VOS should imply what specific gains in knowledge or capacity would suitably represent achievement of the outcome in question.

4   The capacities appropriate to values education should not be confined purely to code knowledge or cognitive skills, but should include demonstrated ability to empathize with other people and take responsibility for one's free actions.

5   Having regard to the use in the State Curriculum of eight sequential levels of development covering Years 1–10, a balance should be sought between the following kinds of learning outcome relevant to values education:

- *Knowledge* about key values and value traditions which have brought society to its present point;

- The ability to *clarify* the values held by oneself and others;

- The ability to *empathize*, especially with the feelings of those who hold values different from one's own, especially in minority groups;

- The ability to understand and critically apply processes of values *justification*;

- The ability to engage in patient social *negotiation* of value agreements;

- The ability to *participate*, i.e. to make informed choices and accept responsibility for those choices.

Figure 20.2   Guidelines for writing Values Outcome Statements

Of the present project it is possible to say that this is an experiment that has not failed, though it could yet do so. Nevertheless, there have been several encouragements which have strengthened our confidence in its viability, and it has the virtue of being grounded in the belief that human beings are agents capable of rationality and regard for others. These, in short, are beliefs worth betting on.

2. *Capacity and commitment*

Second, though space does not permit detailed commentary on each of the guidelines for writing outcomes, the first is too crucial to gloss over: 'Each VOS should imply assessment of capacity, not personal commitment'. One of the things which disables much writing about values education is that no distinction is made between goals having to do with capacity and those bearing on the actual value choices that students make as a result of what they have learned.

The old view of values education, which saw it as the authoritative transmission of the cultural heritage as viewed by the ruling elite would rightly be seen today as an instance of indoctrination. Yet it is echoed in much of the current debate in the popular press. Two cautions are called for. The first relates to the propriety of trying to measure commitment as against capacity. The second relates to the limitations of current outcomes discourse, which I will deal with under the next heading.

In regard to the goal of teaching for commitment, often concealed in ambiguous references to developing 'attitudes', an important distinction needs to be made between teaching objectives and learning outcomes (see also Hill 1981). As to teaching objectives, the teacher may reasonably *hope* to influence the development of the child at all levels, including the cognitive, affective and dispositional. But ethical considerations preclude the teacher from formally grading learning outcomes which relate to personally embraced values. The enhancement of capacities – whether cognitive, affective or relational – empowers the individual, whereas the pre-emption of commitments enslaves.

It may be objected that entertaining the hope – even if we restrain ourselves from measuring it as outcome – exhibits indoctrinative intent. This could be the case, and it could embrace the whole curriculum, at least in its compulsory modes. No matter how much 'we' – i. e. the teacher or parent – think a certain value is 'good for' the learner, indoctrinating it diminishes the human agent.

The safeguard, as I have argued in many places, is to be committed, at the least, to the value of equipping children with the capacity to evaluate the claims of truth and value that are set before them, even to the point of enabling them to interrogate their own cultural conditioning. This is the primary safeguard against indoctrination, and must appear in any value charter or set of teaching objectives which purports to be educational. It refers to *capacities*, which it is perfectly legitimate for us to test. Some of them are spelled out in guideline 5 in Figure 20.2.

3. Outcomes discourse

It is not so clear that outcomes are adequately handled in discourse which focuses all the attention on specific observable learning outcomes. This is the second of the two points about values education. The discourse that has evolved around the use of performance outcomes does not enable us to say all we want to say about the curriculum process.

This kind of discourse derives from the attachment of an earlier generation to 'behavioural objectives'. The ultimate logic of this position was well represented by Mager's (1962) dictum that every valid teaching objective will imply the particular, observable behaviours which would signal that the objective had been met. This paradigm, despite having been philosophically discredited in the 1970s (e.g. Broudy 1970), has found renewed favour in the 1990s as the handmaid of managerial models that relate efficiency to outputs. Just as patients in hospitals are now often perceived as 'procedures' to be completed, so students are raw materials to be refined. Efficiency is assessed by measuring itemized learning outcomes.

This kind of discourse has at least three severe limitations. First, it does not lend itself to the consideration of such ethical issues as the one I raised a moment ago. Products do not have rights. Second,

it focuses on atomistic rather than holistic outcomes of learning. The schooled product is a repository of skills to be tapped in the national interest, rather than a human agent capable, if treated as such, not only of skilled performance, but also of integrated discernment and informed dissent. Third, the goal of reducing 'levels of attainment' to a comprehensively itemized list of outcome statements is illusory. In the Australian Assessment Profiles, mathematics consumed nearly two-fifths of the allotment. The science curriculum in England did something similar. More recently the architects of the latter have realized that, despite the number of outcomes generated, the result was nowhere near an exhaustive set, nor were many of the outcomes specific enough to dictate unambiguously what tests would prove attainment.

If, then, one were to reduce the number and make them more general, then they stand in even less direct correspondence to some particular kind of testing. But, because the number of such statements was still likely to be large, we might be misled into thinking that this was all there was to learning. Reduce the number further, and make them even more general – that is holistic – and we are back to the kinds of statement formerly associated with good educational practice. So why all the fuss?

The Western Australian Project has recognized that for the moment this kind of discourse is hegemonically dominant. The project has therefore consciously played the game, while trying in a deeper sense to subvert it. It has attempted to show that, if we are to be required to ground educational purposes in this kind of talk, then it is possible to say as much about values education as the main proponents of technical skill development want to say about that. That the National and State Curricula shirked this obligation in their Assessment Profiles was a failure of nerve.

Nevertheless, participants in the Project have felt constrained at many points by the demands of this kind of discourse, both for its blurring of the distinction between ethically allowable and non-allowable performance outcomes, and its atomistic approach to what Polanyi (1958) expounded so well so long ago as 'personal knowledge'. One may hope that as the poverty of managerialist rhetoric as applied to education becomes more manifest to the public, the opportunity will return to talk in more personal ways about aims and values, so that the wider goals of education, and values education in particular, are given their proper due.

4. The challenge of cultural pluralism

The point was made earlier that the current situation in countries like Australia is one in which it is no longer acceptable for one hegemonic narrative to override other narratives which happen to be important to minority groups present in the culture. But pluralism at the expense of the common good is no solution. The negotiation process described above has come none too soon for the Australian community.

The Project developed guidelines that have some prospect of identifying a common good which does justice to all and imparts a sense of direction to the educational process. At the same time it is only a beginning, in the sense that the consortium partners in the present instance had in common the fact that their world-views, for all their differences, were theistic. It has yet to be seen whether the process can accommodate a broadening of the negotiating fraternity to include religions with other starting points and people who hold to non-religious stances.

There are, however, grounds for hope. The distinction we drew earlier between ultimate and practical levels of justification both respects the part played in individual lives by ultimate meaning systems, while inviting people to see how far they can progress towards an identification of agreed common convictions. The strategy has been to focus on agreements, in preference to getting bogged down on particular disagreements. Where specific beliefs and values have failed to secure general agreement, they have not been treated as unimportant, but have been put on hold for further attention at a later stage, while the main process of achieving an agreed minimum proceeded. Though held over, they still earn a place as content in that part of the curriculum devoted to developing an appreciation of value-stances and honing the skills of values analysis.

The agreed values that emerge from such negotiations are, as we have already found, likely to be of two kinds: protective and purposive. Protective values concern the *rights* of individuals in a democratic society, given that they must learn to live together without exploitation of the weak, extending freedoms and opportunities to each other based on a fundamental respect for persons (see e.g. Peters 1966). Purposive values concern shared *goals and hopes*, i.e., such aspirations as enjoyment of the quest for knowledge, the creativity of each other's cultural groups, and the development of one's own particular gifts and graces. Rights discourse will tend to be more evident in the category labelled 'Democratic'; goals discourse in the one labelled 'Educational'.

It is theoretically possible that disagreement on a particular issue could be so sharp and fundamental that it overrode what had been agreed as a minimum. This would be a strong motivation for opting out of the negotiating community. A democratic society must allow that this could occur at the level, say, of choosing or founding a school. At a broader social level, however, where what was at stake were basic democratic rights and freedoms, it would represent erosion of these very principles, justifying, in the extreme case, the use of coercion to prevent such erosion.

Again, the present process offers hope of averting such a breakdown. A project originally conceived in the non-government sector now involves a considerable number of state schools in the trialling of values charters and values outcome statements. It holds out the prospect of a diversity of schools promoting particular views of life but sharing a common vision of the goods of a convivial democratic society. Requiring neither uniformity nor schism, such a prospect merits further study, particularly in the mode of action research employed in the present project.

Notes

1 In 1997 the Federal Liberal government, which had succeeded the former Labor government, in the previous year, repudiated the third year of funding on grounds of alleged financial stringency. The level of local interest has been such, however, that the consortium partners and other interested bodies have maintained the project themselves, albeit at a lower level of resourcing.

2 Usage of these terms varies widely. For consistency's sake, I apply *modernization* to a range of processes associated with the emergence of industrialized cultures, centred on economic growth, secular rationality and scientific empiricism. *Modern, -ity* then refers to the resulting state of affairs, whereas *modernist, -ism* identifies the set of normative ideas typically associated with it, without prejudging the degree to which those ideas are either causes or consequences of the state of affairs. Similarly, *Postmodern, -ity* is a state of affairs emergent in some advanced capitalist societies, whereby traditional authorities are under challenge from increasing cultural pluralism and economic instability. *Postmodernist, -ism* identifies a mind-set critical of modernism, both in its intellectual foundations and its

social consequences, which is itself heavily dependent on the presupposition that 'reality' is a social construct which differs for each individual.

3 Despite these disclaimers, this category has somewhat hindered mediations in wider circles such as the State Education Department.

4 A straw in the wind, towards the end of 1996, was the publication by a newly established State Curriculum Council of a broad rationale for schooling that at many points bears a striking resemblance to elements of the Agreed Minimum Values Framework.

References

Broudy, H. S. (1970) Can research escape the dogma of behavioral objectives? *School Review* 79 (1, Nov.): 43–56.

Civics Expert Group. (1994) *Whereas the People ...* Canberra: Australian Government Publishing Service.

Frankena, W. K. (1963) *Ethics.* Englewood Cliffs, NJ: Prentice-Hall.

Griffiths, A. P. (1967) Ultimate moral principles: their justification. *Encyclopaedia of Philosophy*, Vol. 8: 177–82. New York: Macmillan and Free Press.

Habermas, J. (1975) *Legitimation Crisis* (trans. Thomas McCarthy). Boston: Beacon Press.

Hill, B. V. (1972a) Behavior, learning and control: some philosophical difficulties in the writings of B. F. Skinner. *Educational Theory*, 22 (Spring): 230–41.

Hill, B. V. (1972b) Education for rational morality or moral rationality? *Educational Theory* 22 (Summer): 286–92.

Hill, B. V. (1973) *Education and the Endangered Individual.* New York: Teachers College Press.

Hill, B. V. (1981) 'Education for commitment': a logical contradiction? *Journal of Educational Thought* 15 (Dec.): 59–70.

Hill, B. V. (1991, reprinted 1995) *Values Education in Australian Schools.* Melbourne: Australian Council for Educational Research.

Hill, B. V. (1995) What does the national curriculum value?

In C. W. Collins (ed.), *Curriculum Stocktake: Evaluating School Curriculum Change.* Canberra: Australian College of Education: 32–45.

Lawrence, F. (1996) My manifesto for the nation. *The Times* 21 October.

Linstone, H. A. and Turoff, M. (ed.) (1975) *The Delphi Method: Techniques and Applications.* Reading, Mass: Addison-Wesley.

Lyon, D. (1985) *The Steeple's Shadow: on the Myths and Realities of Secularization.* London: SPCK.

Lyon, D. (1994) *Postmodernity.* Buckingham: Open University Press.

MacIntyre, A. (1988) *Whose Justice? Which Rationality?* London: Duckworth.

Mager, R. F. (1962) *Preparing Instructional Objectives.* Belmont, CA: Fearon.

Maritain, J. (1951) *Man and the State.* Chicago: University of Chicago Press.

Maritain, J. (1958) *The Rights of Man and Natural Law.* London: Geoffrey Bles.

Martin, J. R. (1993) Curriculum and the mirror of knowledge. In R. Barrow & P. White (eds) *Beyond Liberal Education: Essays in Honour of Paul H. Hirst*, London: Routledge: 107–128.

O'Brien, P. W. (1978) The Delphi technique: a review of research. *South Australian Journal of Education Research* 1: 57–75.

Peters, R. S. (1966) *Ethics and Education.* London: George Allen and Unwin.

Polanyi, M. (1958) *Personal Knowledge: Towards a Post-critical Philosophy.* London: Routledge and Kegan Paul.

Schools Council, Australian (1992) *National Curriculum.* Melbourne: Curriculum Corporation.

Singer, P. (ed.) (1993) *A Companion to Ethics.* Oxford: Blackwell.

Skinner, B. F. (1971) *Beyond Freedom and Dignity.* New York: Alfred A. Knopf.

Values Review Project (1995) *Agreed Minimum Values Framework.* Perth: National Professional Development Programme.

21　Values in School Planning: Can they be Explicit?

KAREN CAPLE

Introduction

The National Professional Development Program (NPDP) Values Review Project in Western Australia has been proactively investigating the extent to which values can be explicitly integrated into a school curriculum, in particular one framed within an outcomes based context. The NPDP Values Review Project was one of eighteen projects undertaken in Western Australia (WA) over a 3 year period through Commonwealth government funding, all under the coordination of the WA Cross-Sectoral Consortium (1994–96). This Consortium comprised representatives from the WA Government, Independent, Anglican and Catholic school authorities, the Government and Non-Government Teachers' Unions, representatives from Professional and Subject Associations and the WA Council of Deans of Education.

The National Professional Development Program (NPDP) was a Commonwealth initiative where funds were made available to the States and Territories over a 3 year period for teacher Professional Development (PD) activities. These funds supported national initiatives in education by recognizing the importance of ongoing teacher renewal to improve educational outcomes for students. The activities undertaken were to address the following goals:

- to facilitate the use of curriculum statements and profiles in Australian schools and to encourage key competencies and the teaching of accredited vocational education courses in schools;
- to assist the renewal of teachers' discipline knowledge and teaching skills, and help teachers to improve work organization practices and teaching competencies within schools;

- to enhance the professional culture of teachers and encourage teacher organizations to take a higher profile in promoting professional development;
- to promote partnerships between educational authorities, teacher organizations, principals' associations and universities in the provision of professional development opportunities for teachers.

Background

The perceived lack of an explicit values dimension in the National Statements and Profiles being developed for the National Curriculum framework in 1993 motivated a group of individuals from the non-government schooling sector in Western Australia to initiate the Values Project. Prior to this, the Education Department of WA had begun working on Student Outcome Statements (SOS), a set of desired outcomes in eight Learning Areas for monitoring student achievement. Both of these initiatives signalled a concern about the lack of an explicit values dimension.

At this time, the Reverend Dr Tom Wallace, Chaplain and Education Consultant for the Anglican Schools Commission in WA, convened a meeting to discuss this apparent lack of values within the proposed outcomes being developed at both national and state levels. A number of questions were raised and discussed at this meeting:

- Could SOS be modified to include a specific reference to values?
- Which values should be identified in each of the Learning Areas?
- Could values be integrated into a student

outcomes framework that was developed into eight levels?

- How could both teachers and schools integrate values more effectively and explicitly into classroom practice and school life?

Thus the NPDP Values Review Project was born, with the general aim of determining the extent to which values could be explicitly integrated into a curriculum that may be framed by Student Outcome Statements and current curriculum practices.

After funding was granted by the Commonwealth and directed to the WA Cross-Sectoral Consortium for distribution, the Project was initiated and managed by a group reflecting the partners represented in the Consortium. This management group[1] was initially termed a Reference Committee and has helped guide and advise the work and direction of the Project since 1994.

Stages in the project

- 1994 Initial planning and development of a values framework.
- 1995 Publication of the Agreed Minimum Values Framework, a framework of core shared values, established through a consensus process.
  Values Audit of Student Outcome Statement (WA version).
  School Planning Trials.
  Exploration of writing Values Outcome Statements.
- 1996 School Planning Trial in two phases.
  One day conference.
  Exploration of the placement of values explicitly into Student Outcome Statements (WA version).

This chapter documents the process and results of the 1996 School Planning Trial of the NPDP Values Review Project. However, before the trialing concepts, process and results are presented, it is critical to understand and be familiar with the Agreed Minimum Values Framework document developed by the Project.

The Agreed Minimum Values Framework

The Agreed Minimum Values Framework document, developed by the NPDP Values Review

Project and released in May 1995, is a framework of values that represents a baseline agreement of values, developed by a group of consultants who were contracted to undertake this task late in 1994.

Although this document represents a consensus position on values within the non-government schooling sector in Western Australia, it has proven to be a valuable document or tool for individual schools, systems or sectors, communities or religious groups to create or refine their own values framework to suit their own needs and purposes.

The document contains sixty values listed under three levels (ultimate, democratic and educational) and within four themes. These value words are listed in Table 21.1 under these four themes. Each value within the document is defined or expanded to give a context for its existence. For example, equality is defined as 'we affirm the equal worth and basic rights of all persons, regardless of differences in race, gender, ability, and religious belief'. Schools within the trial were encouraged to define their chosen core values in a similar manner, as part of their School Values Statement.

Overview of the 1996 school planning trial

The 1996 trial within the NPDP Values Project tested the two main areas of classroom practice and school planning.

Classroom Practice

This trial involved forty-five teachers, twenty-four government and twenty-one non-government teachers from both primary (thirty-one) and secondary (fourteen) backgrounds. The trial investigated and documented how values could be explicitly integrated into the curriculum within the context of the individual school and its community.

School Planning

This component involved twenty schools,[2] ten government and ten non-government, who developed a School Values Statement, as part of their School Ethos or Development Plan. This Values Statement clearly identified those values that were important

Table 21.1 Agreed Minimum Values Framework, NPDP Values Review Project

Life Perspectives	Individual	Society	Natural World
After-life	Access	Authority	Conservation of the environment
Family	Caring	Benefits of research	Development
Freedom of worship	Citizenship	Community	Diversity of species
God as Creator	Compassion	Conflict resolution	Domains of knowledge
God as self-revealer	Empowerment	Contribution	Environmental responsibility
Knowledge	Equality	Critical reflection	Exploitation
Personal meaning	Imperfection	Diversity	Nature is good
Religion	Individual differences	Family	Quest for truth
Religious freedom	Individual uniqueness	Morality	Rehabilitation
Religious quest	Learning climate	Multi-culturalism	Science and values
Search for knowledge	Open to learn	Participation	Stewardship
Spirituality	Opportunity	Reconciliation	Sustainable development
Study of world views	Responsibility	School as community	
Value systems	Responsibility and freedom	Social justice	
	Social nature	The common good	
	Tolerance	Value dimension	
		Welfare	

to the school, and each trial school explored ways of integrating these values into the life of the school, for instance as school policies, pastoral care or school priorities.

Aim of the school planning trial

The overall aim of the Project was to investigate the extent to which values could be explicitly integrated into the schooling curriculum, in particular one framed within an outcomes based context.

The specific aims of the school planning trial were to help each principal:

1 **explore the current situation in their school**, identifying the positive things already being done in the school in the area of values integration and listing the values currently being promoted.
2 **establish and coordinate a School Values Planning Team**, representative of a wide range of the interested parties in their school community.
3 **take part in the development of a School Values Statement** as part of the School Development Plan, where relevant.
4 help **develop strategies for integrating the identified values** within their school.
5 **foster continuing communication** between all interested parties in their school community, so that all feel part of the values integration of the school.

6 **identify directions** in which they would like the Project to proceed in future years and what they would need to do to bring this about, and what support they would need.

The school planning trial was facilitated in the trial schools by a group of specially selected and trained key facilitators,[3] all of whom worked individually within selected schools to assist principals and their School Values Planning Teams to identify and integrate core shared values into their own school and community.

Timeline for the trial

March   Expressions of interest sent to all metropolitan schools and country schools (non-government only) in Western Australia.

May   Confirmation of involvement
Facilitator training

June   Introductory meeting: the key facilitator for each school met with each principal to introduce the trial, the intended process and the expected outcomes of the trialing.

July   Facilitated workshop 1: a workshop with the School Values Planning Team at each school. Identification of core values and formation of a consultation process.

October   Facilitated workshop 2: revision of the

consultation period and draft School Values Statement (SVS). The identification of areas and strategies for future implementation.

November Reporting and evaluation of the trial and: a report on the trial (case study) and process undertaken submitted to the Project.

Stages within the school planning trial

There were nine stages within the school planning trial:

Stage 1 Awareness raising
Stage 2 Writing a draft process package
Stage 3 Training of key facilitators
Stage 4 Introductory meetings
Stage 5 Intermediary work undertaken by principals
Stage 6 Facilitated workshop 1
Stage 7 Intermediary work undertaken by School Values Planning Teams
Stage 8 Facilitated workshop 2
Stage 9 Final report

Stage 1: awareness raising

The NPDP Values Project involved some school trials during 1995 on a small scale, centred predominantly around the non-government schooling sector. A series of classroom trials were conducted by eleven teachers using a draft of the Agreed Minimum Values Framework, and these formed the foundations for the extensive trials in 1996. In addition to the trials and other associated work, an important Project milestone was the release of the Agreed Minimum Values Framework in May 1995. This document was distributed widely to individual schools and groups and was the genesis of an explicit values dimension in educational initiatives in Western Australia.

In November 1995 a series of three half-day workshops were held for principals and interested teachers to gain an insight into the work of the Project and to direct the Project into 1996. The invitation was open to all sectors, as letters were distributed to all schools, both government and non-government, in Western Australia. In total, 140 school personnel attended from ninety different schools, and the enthusiasm and interest shown

was positive for this explicit values dimension within education. The feedback gained from the workshops revolved around the following questions:

- In what ways is the current work of the NPDP Values Review Project potentially useful or of value to schools?
- Are there any important issues that need to be addressed?
- What are the needs of schools?
- What are the needs of administrators?
- Any other suggestions and ideas?

The feedback collated from this group was overwhelming. From those in attendance, thirty-one schools indicated some degree of commitment to trials in this area of values in 1996. All feedback gained from the attendees was annotated and used as a foundation for the work undertaken throughout 1996. From this gathering a network was formed and twenty-four schools subsequently engaged the Project Coordinator to give presentations to staff either in late 1995 or early 1996. It is of special note that this series of presentations was independent of the school trialing phase that occurred during 1996.

The following comments received from participants highlighted some of the important issues to be considered:

- 'The framework is a catalyst for discussion within schools which hopefully, with the use of the guidelines, will encourage individuals to contemplate the prospect of values-laden student outcomes.'
- 'My school needs to establish what are the values that it wants to impart to its students.'
- 'The extent to which parents and the external society will be influenced by these values. This impacts on the success of teaching values to the students.'
- 'Agreed values – minimum values – have to be determined by all sectors of society, not only the educationalists.'
- 'Explicit values will cohere a school emphasis on the worth of the student.'

One of the major outcomes of the workshops was for schools to indicate their level of future involvement in the project, by addressing the following questions:

- Would your school be interested in being kept informed of the NPDP Values Review initiatives?

- Are you interested in having a school visit by the Project Coordinator to give a short presentation to staff on the NPDP Values Review Project?
- Would your school be interested in the curriculum initiatives planned for 1996?
  School Planning Trial
  Classroom Practice Trial
- Would your school be able to assist in the collection of resources and examples of best practice methods that currently exist?

Early in 1996, at the beginning of the school year, a further half day workshop was held for interested school personnel. This workshop again outlined the progress of the NPDP Values Review Project and focused specifically on the trials to be undertaken during the year. Teachers involved within the initial trials during 1995 presented some of their findings and experiences to those present. The whole concept, expectations and time frame of the 1996 trials were presented and individuals and schools were asked to submit a form detailing their expression of interest in the trials, in either of the two main focus areas of school planning and classroom practice.

In February 1996, following this workshop, the Project had a major dilemma in accommodating the interest expressed, as funding for the Project was limited to only twenty schools. The level of interest expressed at the time is outlined below:

- 1995 commitment: 15 schools confirmed
                      16 schools to confirm
- 1996 commitment: 12 schools confirmed

As a result of this unexpected interest in the work of the Project, thirteen schools were not accepted, and the following criteria were used to prioritize the schools:

1 Early expression of interest and commitment from attendees at the 1995 Principals' workshops.
2 Schools committed to both components of the trial, school planning and classroom practice.
3 Order of reply.
4 Balance of school sectors and primary/secondary components.

The final group of schools selected for the School Planning Trial contained eleven primary schools, three secondary schools and six K-12 schools.[4] These schools also represented a balance within

educational sectors, as ten government schools and ten non-government[5] were involved. This selection supported the cross-sectoral nature of the Project, and covered all year groups from K to 12.

Stage 2: writing a draft process package

This stage involved researching and writing a draft process for the trial, so as all trained facilitators and schools would have a uniform approach to the trial. One of the outcomes of the trial was to test and modify this process so it could be made available to others as a model or framework. Both the process and case studies from the trial were to form the basis of a curriculum package to be developed by the NPDP Values Review Project.

The appointed writer[6] consulted widely and devised a process to undertake throughout the trial, matching the vision and guidelines provided by the Project Coordinator and the cross-sectoral management committee of the Project. An overview of the content of this draft School Planning Package is detailed in Figure 21.1. However, the content as listed does not reflect the decision to create a package that was short, precise, effective and 'user friendly' for the participants to use. Included within the draft package were a series of background readings by Professor Brian Hill (Murdoch University, Western Australia) and Dr Tim Macnaught (1995 Churchill Fellow, The Winston Churchill Memorial Trust of Australia). The work of Robert Starratt (1994) was also incorporated into the trial, with each school being given a complimentary copy of his book for optional reference. In addition to these, six appendices were attached to the package to support the work of the trial:

Appendix 1: The Agreed Minimum Values Framework
Appendix 2: A History of the NPDP Values Review Project
Appendix 3: 'A Rationale for Teaching Values' by Professor Brian Hill
Appendix 4: Advice on Creating a Vision Statement
Appendix 5: A model set of Educational Goals for Elementary and Secondary Schools
Appendix 6: 'Ethics in the Public Sector: a Discussion Paper'

At the conclusion of the Project in December 1996, the complete package with case studies was pub-

Chapter 1   *Introduction*
                    Organization of the package
                    Relevant background documents
                    Aims of the 1996 School Planning Trial
                    The trial and the Project
                    Outcomes based learning in WA schools
                    Terminology

Chapter 2   *Why values integration is important*
                    What are values?
                    Values are fundamental in schools
                    We need to reach an agreement on values in our Australian society
                    Integration of values in the school will support all members of the school community
                    A whole school aproach to values identification and integration is important

Chapter 3   *A procedure for the trial*
                    How to initiate values integration in your school
                    Identify the positive things already being done at the school
                    Identify the interested parties
                    Establish a School Values Planning Team
                    Create a draft School Values Statement
                    Set up communications within the school community
                            Communicating with staff members
                            Communicating with students
                            Communicating with parents
                            Customer focus
                            Communicating with the local community
                            A Values Questionnaire
                            A Values Newsletter
                    Revision of the draft School Values Statement
                    Create a visual School Values Statement
                    Evaluate the trial

Chapter 4   *Ongoing strategies*
                    Continue to communicate with the interested parties
                    Identify the key areas for future implementation
                    Strategies for future implementation

Figure 21.1   Contents of draft curriculum package

lished by the Project and marketed as a Curriculum Resource Package.

Stage 3: training of key facilitators

As previously indicated, four key personnel underwent facilitator training for the School Planning Trial for the NPDP Values Review Project. These four people reflected the cross-sectoral nature of the project, and came from different levels within the educational spectrum. The Project management committee envisaged that each facilitator would work with a range of schools, including those from a different background from their own in order to gain maximum benefit and effectiveness from the trials.

Stage 4: introductory meetings

Facilitators visited their allocated schools (each facilitator was allocated four to five schools) during June to brief each principal on their involvement in the NPDP School Planning Trial and to commence formally the process of the trial. This brief meeting had the following objectives in order to 'capture confidence':

1 To introduce him or herself to the principal and establish a bond for the trial.
2 To gain a brief background on the school and establish why it chose to be involved in the trial, collecting relevant documents from the school.
3 To present and discuss a brief document containing an overview of the trial, the aims of this trial, a timeline and a draft outline of the expectations of the final report required at the conclusion of the trial.
4 To present and introduce the contents of the draft School Planning Curriculum Package.
5 To confirm and arrange details for the first workshop.
6 To direct the principal to engage a team of interested people to form the School Values Planning Team in readiness for the next step.

Stage 5: intermediary work to be undertaken by principals

Before any formal trialing could commence, each school principal had to identify key people who would be interested in forming a School Values Planning Team to work within the trial. This team contained six to ten individuals representative of the whole school community. Parents, teachers, senior administrators, students, School Board or Council members and others were to be included, as the school felt appropriate.

Prior to the first workshop at each school, members of the School Values Planning Team were encouraged to read some of the background material contained within the school's copy of the draft Curriculum Package, or at least become familiar with the Project's Agreed Minimum Values Framework document.

Stage 6:   facilitated workshop 1

This half-day workshop held at each of the schools primarily involved focusing on establishing, through a consensus approach, a draft School Values Statement that would then be taken out to the wider school community for consultation. A **School Values Statement (SVS)** as defined by the NPDP Values Review Project is a simple collection

of values to affirm. It is a set of shared values for the school community and exists as a subset of a school's development plan or vision/mission statement.

The workshop was structured around Chapters 1, 2 and 3 of the draft Curriculum Package provided by the Project, and was facilitated by one of the Project's trained facilitators. The following provides an overview of the workshop, including some key definitions that were required to commence the trial.

- The aim of the Project, including the background and previous work of the NPDP Values Review Project.
- The aim of this School Planning Trial.
- What are values? A common definition is needed as a starting point. According to Lemin et al. (1994), values are determined by the beliefs we hold. They are the ideas about what someone or a group thinks is important in life, and they play a very important part in decision making. We express our values in the way we think and act.
- The distinction between values, beliefs and attitudes.[7]
  Values are one's judgement of what is important or worthwhile in life, values are articulated, developed, agreed, settled and acted upon, at the level of the culture of the community.
  Beliefs are acceptance of a thing, fact or statement as true or existing, 'beliefs' implies our acceptance, tenure and emotional commitment to a particular set of propositions about the world, a reality.
  Attitudes are settled behaviours or modes of thinking, strong feelings or convictions towards or away from something.
- Why is it important to identify and integrate values into schools?
- Examination of existing school documents, statements, plans or policies.
- Examination of other charters of values.
- Consensus activity to identify key or core values for the school using the Project's Agreed Minimum Values Framework.
- Creation of a Draft School Values Statement.
- Identification of key people or groups for consultation.
- Identification of strategies to be undertaken for consultation.
- The next step to be taken.

Stage 7: intermediary work by the School Values Planning Team

Following the development of a draft School Values Statement (SVS) at the first workshop, individual team members were encouraged to go away from this workshop to modify or 'polish up' this draft SVS. As the draft SVS represents a simple collection of school values to affirm, the facilitators introduced the notion of creating a clear, simple visual statement defining the values chosen by the team before the draft SVS was distributed for consultation.

Consultation was to occur with all key individuals or groups identified within the first workshop. In addition to identifying these people, strategies were formulated to facilitate and undertake this consultation phase. The following presents an incomplete, but extensive list of these target groups, with suggested strategies:

* Consultation Groups: Parents, teaching staff, ancillary staff, administration staff, school board or council members, students, student council, parents and citizens or parents and friends, can-teen personnel, past student body, District groups, Church groups.
* Strategies for Consultation: Questionnaire or survey, letters, newsletters, workshops for parents or students, class discussions, individual meetings or appointments, school display, assemblies, local parishes.

Following this consultation phase, which varied within individual schools depending on their specific needs and purposes, the draft School Values Statement was revised according to the feedback received by the school. In this manner, the process of consultation undertaken, should have created a sense of ownership and worth of the draft School Values Statement, within its own school community. Figures 21.2 to 21.7 show examples of draft School Values Statements.

Stage 8: facilitated workshop 2

The overall goal of this second workshop was to review, reflect on and affirm the existing draft School Values Statement, and to pursue the

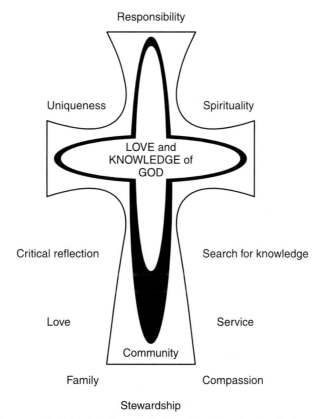

Figure 21.2   School Values Statement: St Brigid's College; Catholic College (Co-educational primary section)

Love (Corinthians 13)

We recognise that God loves us and this love is not conditioned by our weakness or lack of fidelity. His love is the dynamic force that generates life within the universe and as such in striving to be Christlike we encourage the expression of love through developing and fostering trust, openness and justice to all.

Family

We affirm the primary importance of family life and the responsibility of education of the children, in particular we believe in a stable, moral and caring home environment where the individual may grow and develop in love and safety. Such an environment encourages the interdependence of the individual and society ensuring the growth of society.

Service

We believe that just as Christ came to serve so too each person is called to find service suited to their gifts and temperament, to live the life that is within them, in responding to the needs of others, ensuring the dignity of the human person, celebrating life's achievements (of celebrating within others) and utilising our God given talents to enhance the beauty of our world, we are serving all creation.

Spirituality (God among us)

We believe that God is present in the whole universe and especially in each person. Therefore we perceive spirituality as a life long process which involves recognition and attentiveness to the presence of God within ourselves, within others and within creation. Spirituality is not merely a series of good deeds but an attitude of the heart.

Responsibility

We believe that each person has a God given freedom of will which implies that each person is responsible for his or her own actions, thoughts, and words and how these impact on themselves, each other and the world.

Search for knowledge

The desire to gain knowledge and understanding of God, and to grow in love for him is a central goal. As we grow in knowledge, our responsibilities to act in accordance with that knowledge becomes essential. A search for truth, understanding and compassion are components of our search for knowledge. Each individual should be continually open to the possibility of learning from others.

Critical reflection

We encourage critical reflection on both the cultural heritage and the attitudes and values underlying current social trends and institutions. We acknowledge the limited nature of socially constructed knowledge and the need to make students aware of this.

Stewardship

Our relationship to nature is neither that of dominators nor guardians, but rather that of stewards, charged with managing it in trust for future generations. We affirm the enjoyment of nature, and the need to preserve its diversity and balance. We are committed to developing an appreciative understanding of the natural environment, and encouraging a concern for forms of resource development which are regenerative and sustainable.

Compassion (Mark 8 : 2/1 Peter 2 : 1, 3, 8)

We seek to encourage compassion i.e. the sensitivity and concern for the well being/plight of others – as this is an essential quality for anyone who seeks to be Christlike. Compassion comes through the recognition of difficulties of others, personal experiences of receiving compassion, and the acceptance of others' efforts to develop mutual support, care and concern.

Uniqueness

Each person is different and should be encouraged to develop self-respect and realise their full God-given wholeness. Each individual should be given the opportunity to explore and develop their own unique endowments, in order that their full potential is developed. We affirm the equal worth and rights of every person, regardless of differences in race, gender, ability, and religious belief.

Figure 21.2 *continued*

> 1 To promote honesty, in words and actions.
> 2 To promote courtesy, cooperation and consideration of others so all members of the school community can work together in harmony.
> 3 To promote a sense of responsibility for the school environment, property and the needs of others.
> 4 To promote respect for ourselves through self-discipline and the development of self-esteem, in order to reach our highest potential.
> 5 To promote respect and appreciation for difference in culture, language and religion.
> 6 To promote independence, perseverance and excellence in all learning areas.
> 7 To encourage creativity, initiative and reliability.

Figure 21.3 School Values Statement: Swanbourne Primary School (Government Co-educational Primary School)

> **St Mary's AGS Junior School**
>
> We affirm:
>
> | | | |
> |---|---|---|
> | Family | Responsibility | Search for knowledge |
> | Stewardship | Empowerment | Caring |
>
> Shared School Value Statements:
> - To develop confidence through activities and challenges.
> - To develop a love of life, learning and the environment.
> - To teach and learn by love and enjoyment.
> - To develop mental, physical and spiritual wellness within our school community.
> - To demonstrate caring concern towards all people.
> - To respect and encourage family involvement for educational and social development.
> - To empower people by valuing the development of critical thinking, the creative imagination, interpersonal and vocational skills, and basic competencies in the various forms of disciplined inquiries.
> - To develop personal responsibility for conduct and impact on other people and nature.

Figure 21.4 School Values Statement: St Mary's Anglican Girls' School (Independent Primary and Secondary College)

possible implementation of such a document explicitly within the school community. The principal was asked to reflect upon both the nature and extent of the consultation period, to commence at the beginning of the workshop. In the majority of cases each school had undertaken a great deal of consultation, which demonstrated both support and enthusiasm for such an initiative and promoted the development and trialing of such a statement within the school. Each facilitator provided guidance on the format and structure of the draft School Values Statement to the group and cited examples from other schools, citing these only as an insight however, so as not to influence the group in any manner.

During this workshop, questions were asked as to if there had been any concerns or difficulties expressed during the consultation phase regarding the nature or content of the values work and trials. Two areas of concern were frequently raised:

- Why do we need this, as our school already has a philosophy/mission statement?
- Values are inherent in education anyway, why do we need to spell them out?

Both these questions highlight the fundamental goal, and subsequent need for the NPDP Values Review Project, that of investigating the extent to which **values can be identified and explicitly integrated** into school planning, policy development and curriculum initiatives.

The second phase of this workshop addressed the area of possible implementation of the draft School Values Statement within the school. It was felt that a School Values Statement, despite being a

Port Community High School strives to support a sense of genuine community, like a family. Within this school, we affirm our wish to:
- care for every member of this family;
- to be tolerant of differences;
- to respect the property, person, and wishes of each other person within the school.

In this way each member is able to contribute to the school from the richness of their uniqueness, and to receive from the school nourishment educationally, socially, spiritually and emotionally.

The staff affirm their wish to provide access for all students:
- to realize the fullness of who they can be;
- to provide the freedom for them to reach for their dreams;
- to guide them in an understanding of the responsibilities that flow from this freedom.

The school community members all affirm:
- the value of according themselves and each other the power to reach for their limits, and through this;
- to reach out into the wider world with a passion for social justice and a respect for the human and physical environment in which we live.

The core of this shared vision is hope, a confidence in the truth of what can be grasped and held and built upon throughout our lives.

Figure 21.5 School Values Statement: Port Community High School (Non-government Co-educational High School)

subset of a school's mission statement, philosophy or development plan, should be integrated actively and explicitly into all facets within the school for it to be effective and meaningful. The School Values Planning Team explored and identified key areas for implementation of the draft School Values Statement, given the framework of addressing priorities, policies and pastoral care within the school. This implementation phase was further enhanced using a list from Building an Ethical School (Starratt 1994) to facilitate discussion:

- Philosophical statement
- School Board or Council
- Senior staff/planning committee
- Student Council
- P and F
- Guidance system
- Time-tabling/scheduling
- School motto/song/emblem
- Discipline programme
- School/student handbook
- Academic programme
- Enrichment programme

Stage 9: final report

At the beginning of the trial, each school was given an outline of the final report or case study, that was

required at the conclusion of the trial. This format was developed in order to collate standard information from all schools within the trial into an easily identifiable package for publication at the conclusion of the trial. The final Curriculum Package developed by the NPDP Values Review Project will contain both aspects of the 1996 trial: school planning and classroom practice.

The following is an overview of the final requirements of the Final Report:

1 Background information:
   - Name and nature of your school
   - School Population Profile
   - Personnel involved in your School Planning Team
   - Explanation of your involvement in the trial
2 Process:
   - How did you select the members of your School Planning Team?
   - How did you identify the current situation in relation to values within your school?
   - How did you undertake the formation of your Schools Values Statement? Please provide details on the specific pathways you undertook within your school to establish the School Values Statement:

   (a) Facilitated workshops

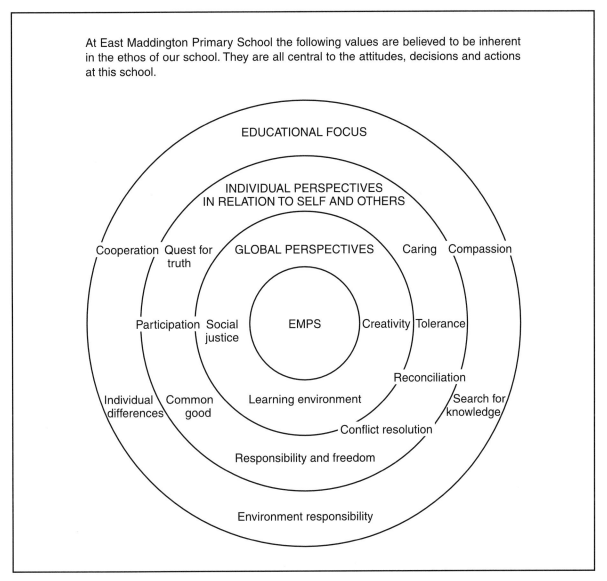

At East Maddington Primary School the following values are believed to be inherent in the ethos of our school. They are all central to the attitudes, decisions and actions at this school.

Figure 21.6   School Values Statement: East Maddington Primary School (Government Co-educational Primary School)

(b) Communication
(c) Consultation

• How did you identify the key areas and develop the strategies to implement the School Values Statement explicitly into your school planning?

(a) Priorities
(b) Policies
(c) Pastoral care

3   Reflections:

Briefly provide some of the highlights of the trial.

Did your school have any difficulty working with values? If so, what were they?

Were there any major changes that your school had to make in order to accommodate an explicit values dimension?

What effects, if any, has the trial had on the school community to date?

Do you have any feedback or suggestions on the Process section within the draft Curriculum Package, in particular Chapters 1 to 4?

4   Product:

Please provide a copy of the following samples from your trialing. These will be used to showcase the work that you have undertaken within the trial:

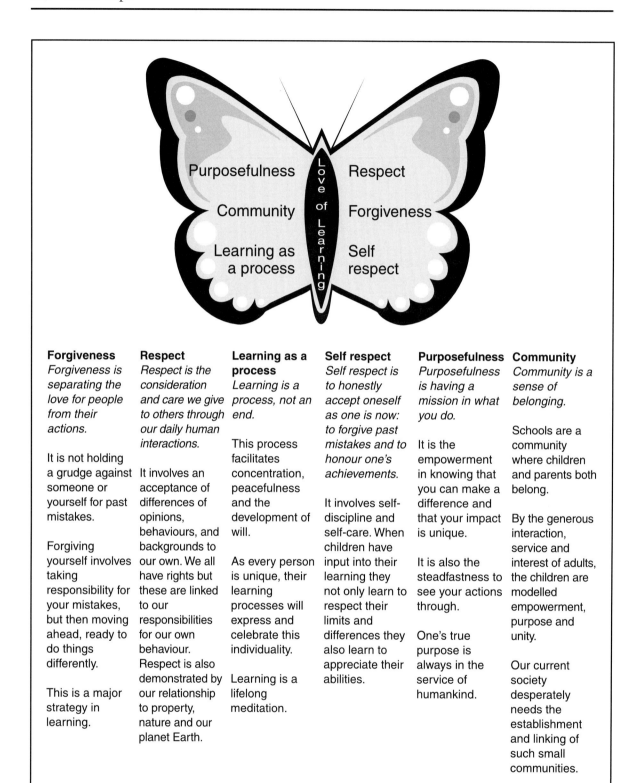

Forgiveness
Forgiveness is separating the love for people from their actions.

It is not holding a grudge against someone or yourself for past mistakes.

Forgiving yourself involves taking responsibility for your mistakes, but then moving ahead, ready to do things differently.

This is a major strategy in learning.

Respect
Respect is the consideration and care we give to others through our daily human interactions.

It involves an acceptance of differences of opinions, behaviours, and backgrounds to our own. We all have rights but these are linked to our responsibilities for our own behaviour. Respect is also demonstrated by our relationship to property, nature and our planet Earth.

Learning as a process
Learning is a process, not an end.

This process facilitates concentration, peacefulness and the development of will.

As every person is unique, their learning processes will express and celebrate this individuality.

Learning is a lifelong meditation.

Self respect
Self respect is to honestly accept oneself as one is now: to forgive past mistakes and to honour one's achievements.

It involves self-discipline and self-care. When children have input into their learning they not only learn to respect their limits and differences they also learn to appreciate their abilities.

Purposefulness
Purposefulness is having a mission in what you do.

It is the empowerment in knowing that you can make a difference and that your impact is unique.

It is also the steadfastness to see your actions through.

One's true purpose is always in the service of humankind.

Community
Community is a sense of belonging.

Schools are a community where children and parents both belong.

By the generous interaction, service and interest of adults, the children are modelled empowerment, purpose and unity.

Our current society desperately needs the establishment and linking of such small communities.

Figure 21.7   School Values Statement: Chrysalis Montesorri School (Independent Co-educational Primary School)

- A copy of your final draft School Values Statement, including 'a before and after consultation copy' if available.
- A copy of your planned implementation strategies. This section will articulate your proposed strategies for integrating your School Values Statement into the different levels within the school community. As both the trial timeline and funding do not include actual implementation, this section will consist purely of intended directions and desired outcomes for integrating an explicit values dimension into the school.

Reflections on the trial

The findings and trial data collected from the twenty individual schools involved in the 1996 trial were varied, as each undertook a unique process to suit their own school and the needs of its own school community. For ease of summary, the reflections below have been grouped by subject and not always according to the sections in which the respondents originally placed their answers. The complete Curriculum Package, containing the process, framework and case studies, is available for purchase through the Project.

Why did you choose to be involved in the NPDP Values Review School Planning Trial?

- It is very much a part of the school philosophy to guide and develop emotional and social skills in the children, so it didn't seem too big a jump to be a part of this trial. (School a)
- It was apparent that our school policy document did not clearly state the values that we as a staff were wishing to focus on in the school. We saw that value words and phrases were buried in the official Mission Statement and Performance Indicators. (School b)
- As part of a system-wide, cyclical process of school review and renewal over a period of 5 years, our school was about to review its Vision Statement and related Aims and Goals. This Values Review Trial matched closely the process of review needing to be carried out, and also supported the classroom trial being conducted within the school. (School c)

- To clarify and promote the values of Port School in a conscious manner. (School d)
- We have long sought to overtly articulate the 'hidden curriculum' of our school and this Values trial seemed to be an ideal vehicle to pursue this goal (School e)

How did you identify the current situation in relation to a values dimension within your school?

- Although we had never before had a written Values Charter or Statement, we knew that there were certain beliefs, attitudes and actions that were held and practised within the school . . . this lack of a written statement, however, made it difficult to impart specifically the values and beliefs that underlie the school's operations. (School f)
- We reviewed our school's Code of Ethics, focusing on how this actually reflects the reality of what happens at school. We also did a values audit of Montessori Philosophy and original texts to see how well these values correlated to our practices. (School e)
- The educational priorities in our school included an ongoing focus on managing student behaviour and implementation of a whole school approach for catering for children with learning difficulties. Both of these priorities affirm important values for an individual child, which if highlighted by a separate values statement would gain focus in their own right. (School b)
- We reviewed our Schools Vision Statement to assess the inherent and explicitly expressed values it contained. (School c)

How did you undertake the formation of your School Values Statement?

- Initial meetings, including our first staff meeting, were held with our key facilitator. We identified the values stated within existing documents in a whole staff workshop, e.g. performance indicators. We then brainstormed other values and the list was displayed in the staffroom for a week. During this time the staff, including support staff (e.g. library, canteen, teacher aides) and members of the P and C were able to add any values they felt were important to the school community. At the end of the week all staff and P and C were given the opportunity to vote on the six values they felt were most important for our school. The School Values Planning Team then developed six statements that would make up our School Statement. (School a)

- A facilitated workshop with the key facilitator to initiate the project and a second to work on the formulation of a possible implementation plan. The basis, process and purpose of the review were expressed to the parish through the Parish Priest; the parents through the P and F association and School Board meetings; the staff at staff meetings; the upper students, through class discussion related to the questionnaire and other related issues; and past students through a willing ex-student at the local high school. (School c)
- A draft list of values was extracted from the 'ethos' statement as per our School Development Plan, as well as our school creed. This draft list under general headings was sent to parents and staff for their consideration and feedback. (School g)
- Extraction of values from our current school brochure. Draft School Values Statement produced. Upper school Maths in Practice class constructed survey which was distributed to parents, Council and community members for consultation. Maths class collated information and School Values Statement was revised and one visual statement was chosen. (School d)
- At a session late in 1995, all teachers were introduced to the concept of values in education, the school performance indicators were examined in comparison to the values framework, and a draft statement of values for Palmyra was evolved. (School h)

How did you identify the key areas and develop the strategies to implement the School Values Statement explicitly into your school planning?

- This fits with our current school philosophy. As a priority school a large part of our emphasis in the last three years has been on self-esteem – children getting to know themselves and respect others. These programmes will continue with

perhaps more reflection on the values as stated. (School a)

- Priorities: Current issues for the school were tolerance and inclusivity. These were identified from survey responses and internal school indicators (i.e. teacher awareness).
  Policies: Review of existing school and classroom policies and practices to identify specific areas needing change will be undertaken. The School Values Statement (SVS) will form part of the School's 'Vision Statement' and will become part of the 5-yearly cyclical review process.
  Pastoral care: A review of this particular policy to identify the specific values it expresses and doesn't express will be undertaken and required changes to incorporate and express the relevant values will be included.(School c)
- For us, this Project was not to be a list of unattainable values that set about to change the children's behaviour from current practice. Rather we would identify those values seen in our everyday actions, reflected by the way we as a community interact and by the best practice of our classroom teachers. We believe we develop those values listed in our SVS by the following practice: whole school meeting, rules, cross age programmes, social skill sessions, education of the whole child, staff, community and relationships. (School f)
- We have decided to increase the teaching of philosophy and develop the concept of the Classroom as a Community of Inquiry. We will also continue with our positive affirmation and plan accordingly – award structure, affirmation days, opportunities for students to mix effectively across age groups and to work collaboratively. Values will be also public via the newsletter, assemblies, Chapel services, our school publications. Values will continue to be on every agenda for staff planning. (School i)

Briefly describe some of the highlights of the trial

- Staff receptiveness to the idea of values in education as well as the input by parents of the P and C. (School a)
- The opportunity to work very closely with parents on a project in which we all had a keen interest and from which occasions arose in which parents rather than teachers facilitated meetings for other parents. (School c)

- The most significant highlight was the chance to discuss the 'deeper' issues at length. The chance to explore this was richly rewarding and very interesting. (School k)
- The rapport and creativity that was developed and encouraged amongst group members made the process enjoyable for all those concerned. The final draft is a usable and valuable document which appears to have been well received and supported by all staff. This will have a very positive impact on the school planning process and on the perception of the school in the community.(School j)
- The initial concern about the process of priority selection being turned into a positive commitment for Values as a school priority.(school h)
- The main highlight was the opportunity to review our existing structures and processes and evaluate the extent to which the values were finding their way into everyday practice in the organization. (School n)
- The development of a School Values Statement gave us the opportunity to openly discuss values education in a government school. Many teachers believed this was outside their job description. (School b)
- The trial's highlight was the staff reflection, commitment to action and especially the staff team unification that was brought about by the trial's implementation. (School l)

Did your school have any difficulty working with values? If so, what were they?

- Our only difficulty was in keeping the focus strictly on values as distinct from attitudes and beliefs. (Catholic School c)
- Not a serious or obviously apparent difficulty, but there are a few staff members not so convinced or supportive. (School m)
- No, working with explicit values is fundamental to our everyday school life. (School n)
- Yes, some staff have philosophical issues with 'values in education': these have yet to be resolved: concern expressed with accountability in this area. (School g)
- Initially we had to overcome the concept that 'values education' meant 'religious education'. Once this idea was expanded to include democratic and educational values, most people were happy to explore further. (School b)

- We had no difficulties in recognizing the importance of values in education. The only difficult area for our community is the concept of GOD, particularly as expressed in the Ultimate section of the Agreed Minimum Values Framework. Whilst we did not wish to ignore this section, we did seek to separate spirituality from any set religion. To us, the values we uphold in daily action are indeed an expression of any meaningful definition of God. (School e)
- Our school did not have any difficulties working with values. Everyone in the school community accepts values as part of our existence. (School i)

What effects, if any, has the trial had on your school community to date?

- There appears to be a greater consciousness about the importance of bringing values more into the fore. (School a)
- Renewed and increased awareness of, and interest in, the values promoted by our school. (School c)
- There has been an enthusiasm about working on the statements, because stakeholders can see a practical and useful impact being easily obtained. (School k)
- The group are very enthusiastic and are considering values much more explicitly and implicitly in all their professional duties. Parents appear to be pleased that the school has a statement of values which they appear to endorse. (School j)
- It has brought parents and staff into a closer working relationship and a relationship that has shared values. The school is a happier environment. There have been fewer disciplinary problems. (School i)
- It has already broadened the perspective of teachers on the curriculum. 'Extra' activities have been viewed as integral and fundamental curriculum initiatives. (School e)
- The values effort has provided a unified staff focus on the one project as well as providing an opportunity for staff to review and renew their commitment to these values ideals. (School l)
- Created an excitement among students in terms of gaining fair treatment by teachers in the classroom. They saw this as a means by which relationships between students and teachers would be improved. (School n)

- Increased support, communication about, and reassurance for the areas related to moral education and behaviour. (School m)

Conclusion

The National Professional Development Program in Australia has provided a valuable pathway for the Values Review Project to undertake major developments in the field of values in education. The establishment of a framework of core shared values and the formation of a trialed process for curriculum planning has been of major significance.

The reflections provided from the 1996 trials indicate clearly that the NPDP Values Review Project's School Planning Curriculum Package, published in early 1997, provides an excellent process for identifying and integrating core shared values into educational communities. The acceptance of and respect for the diverse and independent nature of each group using the Package has demonstrated that in a multi-cultural society it is feasible to select core shared values and integrate them into educational practice.

Acknowledgements

The NPDP Values Review Management Committee wishes to acknowledge the contribution made by three key people associated with the Project's 1996 Conference held in Perth, Western Australia: Professor David Aspin, Monash University, Australia; Professor Brian Hill, Murdoch University, Australia; and Dr Mal Leicester, University of Nottingham, United Kingdom. These three people have contributed valuable support, guidance and insight into developments within the Project.

Notes

1 The Management Group of the NPDP Values Project:

Reverend Dr Tom Wallace (Chair)	Anglican Schools Commission
Mr Glenn Bennett	Education Department of WA
Ms Karen Caple	Project Coordinator
Assoc. Professor Cynthia Dixon	Edith Cowan University
Dr Ian Fraser	Association of Independent Schools (WA)
Mr Tony Giglia	Catholic Education Office of WA
Mr Peter Havel	Kingsway Christian College (Inaugural Project Coordinator)
Mr Tim McDonald	Australian Association of Religious Education
Mr Chris Reimers	Catholic Education of WA
Mrs Frances van Riessen	Secondary Education Authority

2 The total number of schools involved in both aspects of the trial was twenty-six as overlap did occur.

3 These facilitators were Reverend Dr Tom Wallace (Anglican Schools Commission), Mr Alan Atkinson (Education Department of WA), Mr Keith McNaught (Catholic Education) and Ms Karen Caple (Project Coordinator).

4 In Western Australia, 'K' as in K-12 schooling, is termed 'pre-primary', as it is the year prior to a child's first year at primary school (age 5).

5 Non-government schools refers to schools that are church based, including Catholic Schools, and other independent or private schools. i.e. not government system schools.

6 The appointed curriculum package writer was Ms Jane Grellier, from Jane Munroe and Associates.

7 The distinction between values, beliefs and attitudes is from a paper by Professor David Aspin for the NPDP Values Review Project contained within the final School Planning Curriculum Package.

References

Hill, B. V. (1985) In another world: educational responses to modern pluralism. *Journal of Christian Education* **84** (Nov.).

Hill, B. V. (1993) An education of value: towards a value-framework for the school curriculum. A monogram prepared at the request of the Committee for the Review of the Queensland School Curriculum in July 1993.

Hill B. V. (1996) Civics and citizenships and the teaching of values. *Australian College of Education Journal* March, **22** (1, March).

Lemin, M., Potts, H. and Welsford, P. (eds) (1994) *Values Strategies for Classroom Teachers*. Hawthorn Victoria: ACER

Macnaught, T. (1995) Report: 1995 Churchill Fellow. The Winston Churchill Memorial Trust of Australia.

Macnaught, T. (1995) Teach 'em values (Part 2). *Church Scene*, **5** (7, November).

National Professional Development Program (NPDP) Values Review Project (1995) *Agreed Minimum Values Framework* ISBN 0 646 24458.

Starratt, R. J. (1994) *Building an Ethical School: A Practical Response to the Moral Crisis in Schools.* London: Falmer Press.

Additional note

The NPDP Values Review Project in Western Australia has published the two Curriculum Packages developed as a result of the trials carried out throughout 1996. The project also has a series of four videos from the 1996 conference: *Students, Schools and Values: Values Outcome for Schools in the Twenty-first Century.* Contact the Project Office for details:

NPDP Values Review Project
Association of Independent Schools of WA
3/41 Walters Drive
Herdsman Business Park
Osborne Park WA 6017
Western Australia
Phone: 08 9244 2788
Fax: 08 9244 2786
E-mail: aiswa@ais.wa.edu.au

Index